# Nguyễn Cochinchina

## Southern Vietnam in the Seventeenth and Eighteenth Centuries

T0350127

Li Tana

# NGUYỄN COCHINCHINA

## SOUTHERN VIETNAM IN THE SEVENTEENTH AND EIGHTEENTH CENTURIES

SOUTHEAST ASIA PROGRAM PUBLICATIONS
Southeast Asia Program
Cornell University
Ithaca, New York
1998

Cornell Southeast Asia Program Publications
640 Stewart Avenue, Ithaca, NY 14850-3857

Studies on Southeast Asia No. 23

Printed in the United States of America

ISBN  978-0-87727-722-4

Cover art: Seventeenth-century map of a portion of Đàng Trong, reprinted with permission from Toyo Bunko.

# CONTENTS

# ACKNOWLEDGMENTS

When I first came to Australia in 1988, I was as anxious and nervous as could be: my English was limited, so was my knowledge of Vietnam. I came from China, a country that had been isolated for a long time, both from other parts of the world and, tragically, from Vietnam. Thus to me, coming to Australia was the most precious chance in my life.

My gratitude therefore first goes to David Marr, who brought me here as my supervisor, helping and guiding me in every possible way with his superb understanding of Vietnam. My profound gratitude to Anthony Reid, who is always considerate and gives as much intellectual support and encouragement as one can expect.

I was particularly fortunate to meet Keith Taylor in Hanoi, to whom I owe a debt of gratitude for his warm support ever since.

I am also grateful to Chen Yu-long, Esta Ungar, John Fincher, the late professor Chen Ching-ho, Ann Kumar, David Bulbeck, Greg Lockhart, Craig Reynolds, Terry Hull, Peter Xenos and Thiện Đỗ. Each helped me in different stages with different aspects, all are indispensable. My gratitude to Professors Alexander Woodside, O. W. Wolters, and David Chandler for their encouragement on my manuscript.

I am forever indebted to Nola Cooke, who has whole-heartedly contributed her enthusiasm and intellectual support both to my doctoral dissertation and this revised version for publication. The book would not be in its present form without her countless hours of careful reading and editing the various drafts, as well as our many long and stimulating conversations on the contents. I thank God for giving me such a genuine and generous friend.

Piere Manguin and Nguyễn Thế Anh helped me with sources when I was doing research in Paris as did Mme. Christiane Rageau. In Vietnam, Nguyễn Đức Ninh, Đỗ Văn Ninh, Nguyễn Đình Đầu, Cao Tự Thanh, Hùynh Lứa, and numerous other scholars and friends generously helped me to understand Vietnam better. I owe them all a great deal.

I would like to thank the Hán-Nôm Institute and the Institute of History in Hanoi for allowing me to read the manuscripts which made my research possible. My special thanks also go to Phan Đình Nham, Director of National Archives no. 2 in Saigon, and the Hoi An Relics Management Board, both of which open-mindedly let me read anything relevant to my work.

The Australian National University facilitated and supported my research generously. My many thanks to Dorothy McIntosh, Lesheng Tan, Julie Gordon, and Jude Shanahan for tolerating my carelessness and ignorance and providing a warm and friendly atmosphere in the department. My thanks also to Norah Foster and Kristine Alilunas-Rodgers who helped me with reading French sources. I would also like to thank Adam Orvad of Wollongong University, who kindly produced the maps found in this book.

My husband Lihong has been devoted to me selflessly. Because of visa problems, my only son, Ben, stayed in China and never saw me once for all the long four years when I was doing my PhD in Australia. I am deeply grateful for my family which has suffered for my career.

All the errors in this book are my responsibility.

# Map 1

# INTRODUCTION

I t is never easy to pinpoint exactly where, when, and how a significant historical chance takes place. But in the Vietnamese case, we can point to a year and an event which brought Vietnam almost three-fifths of its present area through a family decision to leave the capital.

When Trịnh Kiểm took over the power of the Lê dynasty in 1546, the formerly allied Trịnh and Nguyễn families were set to become enemies. Nguyễn Hoàng, foreseeing the trouble to come, is said to have asked Nguyễn Bình Khiêm, a famous seer and scholar, what to do. Nguyễn Bình Khiêm pondered for a long time and replied: "*Hoành Sơn nhất đái,vạn đại dung thân* (The Hoành Sơn mountain area would be suitable to inhabit for thousands of generations)." Nguyễn Hoàng then asked his sister, the wife of Trịnh Kiểm, to persuade her husband to send him away as military commander of the distant frontier region of Thuận Hóa. Nguyễn Hoàng's gambit was successful. The year was 1558.

Trịnh Kiểm only wanted to get rid of an enemy. He failed, and gave Nguyễn Hoàng a kingdom instead. A chain of events happened which changed the whole of Vietnamese history in particular and Southeast Asian history in general.

Although Nguyễn Hoàng started developing his political center in the south in the beginning of the seventeenth century,[1] he continued to pay taxes to the Lê-Trịnh in the north in his reign. His son Nguyễn Phúc Nguyên, however, stopped doing so beginning in 1620,[2] which became the direct cause for the Trịnh's seven campaigns against the Nguyễn between 1627 and 1672. All the Trịnh efforts failed.[3]

The Nguyễn were far weaker than the Trịnh in almost every way. The north had a well-established state system, which allowed the Trịnh to control three or four times more land than the Nguyễn and to maintain armed forces three or four times as large. What is more, the Trịnh ruled the land occupied for many centuries by Vietnamese and governed its own people, while the Nguyễn kingdom was established on the former lands of Champa, which had a brilliant culture and a remarkably different tradition from that of the Vietnamese. Yet not only did the Nguyễn survive and repel seven campaigns by the Trịnh, but they also pushed their

---

[1] See Keith Taylor's "Nguyen Hoang and the Beginning of Viet Nam's Southward Expansion," in *Southeast Asia in the Early Modern Era*, ed. Anthony Reid (Ithaca: Cornell University Press, 1993), pp. 42–65.

[2] *Đại Nam Thực Lục Tiền Biên* (Chronicle of the Nguyen Dynasty Premier Period), vol. 2 (Tokyo: Keio Institute of Linguistic Studies, 1961), p. 32. (Hereafter *Tiền Biên*.)

[3] There were certainly other factors involved besides the Nguyễn's determination to keep its independence. Since the Mạc family was not completely defeated by the Trịnh until 1677, strictly speaking, there were three political forces in Vietnam during the one hundred years between 1570 and 1670: the Mạc occupied the Sino-Vietnamese border areas, the Trịnh were centered in the Red River delta, and the Nguyễn developed southward from the Huế area. While the Trịnh's war effort against the Nguyễn was somewhat checked by the existence of the Mạc, the pressure from the north became the real drive for the Nguyễn's southern expansion.

borders deeper south, as far as the Mekong delta. Was it by chance that forces in a new environment survived and even won victories, while those that remained in familiar surroundings lost?

I became interested in the phenomenon of new Vietnamese political forces rising in the southern direction and successfully challenging the political center in the north. This did not begin or end in the late sixteenth century. If we mark the important events that took place from the beginning of the fifteenth century to 1802 on the Vietnamese historical map, we will find that the location of each such events moves progressively southward. Lê Lợi rose in Thanh Hóa, south of the Red River delta, in the early fifteenth century; Nguyễn Kim's uprising against the Mạc, in the Thanh Hóa and Nghệ An area, occurred in 1533; Nguyễn Hoàng began to set up his power base in Quảng Trị in 1558; the Tây Sơn rose in Qui Nhơn in 1771; and Nguyễn Ánh established his base in the Gia Định area in the 1780s.[4] All these events were part of the larger process of *Nam Tiến*, the Vietnamese southward expansion.

This gradual expansion to the south kept creating a frontier where Confucian scholarship, even though it became the dominant ideology in the north from Lê Thánh Tôn's reign (1460-1497), was basically unknown and not appreciated. This seems to suggest a promising periphery where new political forces could develop themselves. The Nguyễn which we are going to explore in this study provided such a context for Vietnamese history.

From the seventeenth century onward, the Red River delta ceased to be the only center of Vietnamese civilization; a completely new picture unfolded. Another center—Huế—appeared in addition to Thăng Long; another economic area, Thuận Quảng, emerged in addition to the Red River delta. It formed no simple extension of the old economic area. Rather, we see a new region developing, with a different cultural background and people functioning in quite different circumstances. As the southern Vietnamese recognized in the new names they gave these two regions—the "inner region" (*Đàng Trong*) to their own, and the "outer region" (*Đàng Ngoài*)[5] to the north—clear differences now existed that marked two different ways of being Vietnamese. The difference between the two terms indicated clearly that while the two regions were distinct, for southerners they were also equal.

This was a dramatic and fundamental change in Vietnamese history, its significance comparable to Vietnam's securing its independence from China in the tenth century. At first sight, it may seem merely the story of the political survival and flourishing of a family which had lost power at court in Thăng Long; in its nature, however, it involved the flourishing of a new state system and a new culture.[6]

Though these changes in two centuries no doubt played a constructive role in Vietnamese culture, they also created disruptions within communal solidarity which were unacceptable to the nineteenth century Vietnamese literati who wrote the official history of those two centuries. As David Marr has pointed out, Vietnamese:

---

[4] Tạ Chí Đài Trường discusses this in his *Lịch Sử Nội Chiến ở Việt Nam* (Saigon: Văn Sử Học, 1973), p. 38.

[5] The two terms appeared in Alexandro de Rhodes's *Dictionarivm Annamiticvm, Lvsitanvm, et Latinvmope* (Rome: Typis, & Sumptibus eiusdem Sacr. Congreg, 1651), p. 201. These terms were likely coined by the southerners in the 1620s.

[6] From 1600, Nguyễn Hoàng had decided to go it alone, without reference to the court in the north; his descendants pursued this vision with remarkable consistency.

historians often are asked to balance the elements of continuity in their story against the elements of change, to delineate the persistence of traditional symbols and attitudes from the apparent acceptance or development of new concepts and values among the people being studied.[7]

Indeed. The following quote confirms his observation:

In the second year of Minh Mạng (1820) the emperor ordered the *Quốc Sử Quán* [Historical Board of the Kingdom] to compile the history of the kingdom, with all the styles, the ways of expression, and the facts to be weighed and adjusted before it is recorded.[8]

Surely many records were rejected in this process of weighing and adjusting. The unorthodox, or non-Confucian, elements of Đàng Trong society, such as slavery, or contacts—even marriage alliances—between the Nguyễn and the Cham, the Japanese, and the Khmer, were all sacrificed as part of the historiographical price rendered for achieving such balance in the nineteenth century, perhaps in the same way non-Confucian elements in the official history written in the fifteenth century had been discarded.

The Nguyễn regime has not fared much better at the hands of modern northern Vietnamese scholars writing before 1992. The reason for this is obvious to any visitor to the National History Museums in Hanoi or Ho Chi Minh City: national unity and resistance to foreign aggression are the two themes deemed central to the Vietnamese experience. The Nguyễn, of course, flouted them both. First, the Nguyễn regime destroyed national unity for two hundred years, and second, Nguyễn Ánh defeated the "heroic" Tây Sơn movement with the help of "Western colonialists," an outcome that many Marxist historians have noted with disapproval.

Possibly because of this, there has been a tendency among official Hanoi historians to downgrade the history of Đàng Trong. The Nguyễn kingdom is usually presented merely as a local variant of the Confucianized Lê/Trịnh regime and culture, exhibiting few real differences from Đàng Ngoài. Only one "Đại Việt" in the seventeenth and eighteenth centuries, with general "Vietnamese characteristics," tends to be discussed.[9] However, I want to argue quite the opposite: that not only did two Vietnamese states exist at the time, but that the southern one possessed special and distinctive characteristics which enriched Vietnamese culture in the long term. In this study, therefore, I focus on change rather than continuity, and on differences rather than similarities, in order to bring out Đàng Trong's significance to Vietnamese history.

One further point should be mentioned. For too long this region has only been known by its European name of Cochinchina which, when first recorded by Tome

---

[7] David Marr, *Vietnamese Anticolonialism, 1885-1925* (Berkeley: University of California Press, 1971), p. 4.

[8] See *Hàn Các Tạp Lục*, a manuscript kept in the Hán-Nôm Institute of Hanoi, p. 18, shelf number A.1463.

[9] See, for instance, the official history compiled by the Committee of Social Sciences of Vietnam, *Lịch Sử Việt Nam* (A history of Vietnam) (Hanoi: Khoa Học Xã Hội, 1971), chapter 7.

Pires in 1515, referred to Đại Việt generally.[10] It is likely that Pires's "Cauchy Chyna" came from the Portuguese, who had borrowed it in turn from contemporary usage in Melaka. There it was derived from a Malay corruption of the old Chinese name for Vietnam, Jiao Zhi, with the suffix "China" to distinguish it from a similarly name Indian town. As the civil wars of the sixteenth century created a separate Nguyễn state, the term "Cochinchina" came to be applied solely to this new realm, and this practice was formalized in European usage in 1679, when the Pope approved the establishment of a separate Apostolic vicariat of Cochinchina. It was only in the late eighteenth century, with the emergence of the far southern region of Gia Định/Đồng Nai as the base of Nguyễn resistance against the Tây Sơn, that this area became known in missionary accounts as Lower Cochinchina, a name it would retain for decades after its colonial conquest in the 1860s. This study uses Đàng Trong or Cochinchina interchangeably, since both refer to the same region in the seventeenth and eighteenth centuries.

What most interests me, however, is not the best name for the southern area designated by this term so much as the fact that the place itself has always meant a new land, and new possibilities, in Vietnamese history. The south had long beckoned to traditional Vietnamese. Countless folksongs describe the mixture of eagerness and of fear generated by going to the new land.

> *Làm trai cho đáng nên trai*
> *Phú Xuân cũng trải*
> *Đồng Nai cũng từng*

> (To act like a man, you have to be a man,
> You should see *Phú Xuân*, you should be in *Đồng Nai*.)

They also described its enormous potential for development:

> *Ruộng đồng mặc sức chim bay,*
> *Biển, hồ lai láng cá bầy đua bơi*

> (Birds fly to their hearts' content across the fields,
> Fish race in droves in the immense sea and lakes.)

In practical terms, too, the south was also the only place into which Vietnam could hope to expand, as the famous eighteenth-century Đàng Trong mandarin, Nguyễn Cư Trinh, explained: "There is no way to the west, and it is too hard to go the north, therefore we should do our best to advance to the south."[11]

This expansion to the south became the real motive force of Vietnamese history. Although several significant events occurred in the north, and there were important institutional changes over time, none matched the push south for long-term importance. For hundreds of years, only a few important events happened in Thăng

---

[10] Tome Pires, *The Suma Oriental of Tome Pires* (London: The Hakluyt Society, 1967), p. 114: "The kingdom is between Champa and China."

[11] Nguyễn Cư Trinh, *Sãi Vãi*(A dialogue between a monk and a nun), quoted from Nguyễn Đăng Thục, "Hai trào lưu di dân Nam tiến" (Two waves of the Vietnamese southward expansion), *Việt Nam Khảo Cổ Tập San*, 6 (1970): 170.

Long (later, Hanoi), once the political center and social model for all Vietnam. The power struggles, wars, famines, and even the glorious victory that Nguyễn Huệ won over the Qing, were nothing new. As the Tây Sơn commented, "royal khí [vital energy] is totally finished in Thăng Long."[12] By the eighteenth century, Thăng Long was a historical site, a great work completed in ancient times. Only to the south did there exist an arena for new trends and new heroes.

Vietnam was not unique in this expansion. During the same era, the Burmans also pushed from the north to the south, and the Thai from east to west. By the start of the nineteenth century, all this movement had resulted in a radical reorganization of mainland Southeast Asia and formed a fundamental pattern of historical experience that differentiated Vietnam from China, as Victor Lieberman has pointed out: [13]

> Whereas Qing-era settlement on the northern frontier had only the most marginal economic significance for the empire as a whole and left the political structure of China's heartland basically untouched, Vietnam's expansion between 1470 and 1835 all the way to the lower Mekong radically transformed that country's political dynamic, not to mention its economy, demography, and ethnic extension. So fundamental a configuration between the fifteenth and nineteenth centuries resembled Burmese and Thai patterns more closely than that of China.

Numerous Vietnamese scholars have traced the political history of the two centuries of Vietnamese division, whether in French or Vietnamese,[14] as have several non-Vietnamese historians.[15] I do not intend to replicate here what they have already done, but rather to explore thematically the economic, social, and cultural features of Đàng Trong society which I believe sustained its long political success against all the odds. Given the thematic structure of this study, however, it may be useful to touch briefly on a few important political milestones in Đàng Trong in those two centuries.

Although Nguyễn Hoàng decided to develop his own political center in the south, he continued to pay taxes to the Lê/Trịnh in the north throughout his reign. War finally broke out in 1627, following the refusal of his son, Nguyễn Phúc Nguyên, to continue sending taxes north. Despite seven campaigns against the Nguyễn between 1627 and 1672, the Trịnh forces, fighting far from home, with extended

---

[12] *"Tiểu hết vương khí"* in Vietnamese. This sentence appeared in a letter sent to Qian Long emperor of China by Nguyễn Huệ in August 1789. Quoted from Hoa Bằng, *Quang Trung Nguyễn Huệ, Anh Hùng Dân Tộc* (Saigon: Bốn Phương, 1958), p. 224.

[13] Victor Lieberman, "Local Integration and Eurasian Analogies: Structuring Southeast Asian History, c. 1350-c. 1830," *Modern Asian Studies* 27, 3 (1993): 539.

[14] For example, Lê Thành Khôi's *Le Viet Nam* (Paris: Les Editions de Minuit, 1955), and *Histoire du Vietnam des origines a 1858* (Paris: Sudestasie, 1981); Phan Khoang, *Việt Sử Xứ Đàng Trong* (Saigon: Khai Trí, 1969); and Tạ Chí Đài Trường in *Lịch Sử Nội Chiến ở Việt Nam* (Saigon: Văn Sử Học, 1973).

[15] Joseph Buttinger, *The Smaller Dragon* (New York: Praeger, 1958); Jean Chesneaux, *Contribution à l'histoire de la nation vietnamienne* (Paris: Editions Sociales, 1954). Yang Baoyun, *Contribution à l'histoire de la principaute des Nguyen au Vietnam meridional (1600-1775)* (Geneva: Editions Olizane, 1992); Keith Taylor's "Nguyen Hoang and the Beginning of Viet Nam's Southward Expansion" is the most recent important contribution to the understanding of Nguyễn history. In *Southeast Asia in the Early Modern Era*, ed. Anthony Reid (Ithaca: Cornell University Press, 1993), pp. 42-65.

supply lines and fewer cannon, failed to dislodge them. The half century of invasion from the north then gave way to a century of peace, in which northern Vietnam receded in importance in southern eyes. Whereas the earlier Nguyễn lords had perceived themselves as commanders-in-chief, and the armed forces had acted as the principal organ of government, once the wars finally ended a trend began towards asserting royal status. In 1702, the Nguyễn ruler unsuccessfully sought Chinese approval to become an independent vassal, a move that culminated in 1744, with a series of important ritual and symbolic reforms that proclaimed Nguyễn Đàng Trong was a new Vietnamese kingdom that had risen in the south.

Even in the shadow of repeated attacks from the north, the Nguyễn never lost interest in expansion to the south. Their new southern conquests came in three main stages. The first brought them the territory from Cù Mông to Phan Thiết, essentially the land of the neighboring state, *"nagara* Campa," or Champa in English scholarship. Champa counterattacked several times, but failed each time, and in 1693, the Nguyễn effectively laid claim to the whole area, giving it the Vietnamese name of Thuận Thành. Although a Cham rebellion soon after forced the Nguyễn to offer Panduranga vassal status, Vietnamese settlers continued to filter into the area. In the eighteenth century the Nguyễn court appointed its own magistrates to regulate their affairs. Nevertheless, the final vestige of Champa, Panduranga, survived as a vassal of Huế until it was obliterated in the early 1830s by the centralizing emperor, Minh Mạng.[16]

The second and third stages saw Nguyễn authority spread through an opportunistic use of Chinese immigrants and asylum seekers. The northern region of the Tiền Giang River, formerly Cambodian territory, had came under Nguyễn political influence in 1658, but was only established as an administrative region, Gia Định, in 1698, thanks to the settlement of three thousand Ming loyalist refugees there in 1679. The third stage took place in the west, at modern Hà Tiên and its eastern vicinity, when the local Chinese ruler, Mạc Cửu, became a Nguyễn tributary in the early eighteenth century. If Gia Định helped attract Vietnamese into the Mekong delta, Hà Tiên was equally significant, both as a center of foreign trade and because it attracted acquisitive Nguyễn eyes to envision further westward expansion into Cambodia. In the eighteenth century, Vietnamese chronicle sources which had previously described so many campaigns against the Cham would be filled with descriptions of campaigns against the Khmer.

The two-hundred-year history of Đàng Trong was brought to an abrupt end when the Tây Sơn rebellion broke out in 1771 in the central highlands and spread to the Quảng Nam area. The main causes of this rebellion lay in the inadequate government response to fundamental changes within the Đàng Trong economy in the previous two decades. A permanent decline in overseas trade, which had been the mainstay of government revenue and the wider economy alike, combined with a disastrous inflation that followed a well-meaning, but ineptly executed, attempt to replace dwindling imports of foreign coins with locally made ones. A palace coup in 1765 added a political dimension to the mounting economic crisis by fostering a dangerous factionalism within the ruling class, still largely composed of descent groups whose original ancestors were men who had followed Nguyễn Hoàng south in the sixteenth century and settled in the same area of Thanh Hóa. The Tây Sơn

---

[16] Po Dharma, *Le Panduranga (Campa) 1802-1835. Ses rapports avec le Vietnam* (Paris: EFEO, 1987), 2 vols.

early exploited these divisions and claimed to be leading a legitimist revolt against the usurping regent who had become particularly unpopular as the author of steep tax increases designed as a desperate measure to shore up plummeting government revenues. Those most seriously affected by the increased taxes were upland peoples, and they formed the mainstay of the rebellion at the start.

Seizing the opportunity presented by the Đàng Trong civil war, the Trịnh invaded Huế. It is thanks to this that we have today the single most important contemporary source reporting on eighteenth-century Đàng Trong, a miscellaneous account of the border region written by the high Trịnh official, Lê Quý Đôn.[17] The Trịnh attack forced the Nguyễn royal family to flee to the Mekong delta where virtually all of them, except Nguyễn Ánh, a son of the prince dislodged in Trương Phúc Loan's palace coup, were killed by the Tây Sơn in 1777. After a period of exile in Siam, Nguyễn Ánh was able to return to Gia Định when the 1789 Chinese invasion in the north distracted his Tây Sơn foes. When the great Tây Sơn general and short-lived emperor, Quang Trung, died accidentally in 1792 on his way south to fight Nguyễn Ánh, the balance of forces shifted. From his Mekong delta base, Nguyễn Ánh was finally able to fight his way north and re-enter his family's capital in 1801, after nearly thirty years absence. In 1802, he marched unopposed into Hanoi under the new reign title of Gia Long, inaugurating the last dynasty of traditional Vietnam.

This study aims to focus on the economy and society of Nguyễn Cochinchina, bringing out as fully as possible the experience of ordinary Vietnamese in the area. It begins by examining the demographics of the new land and with the ways Nguyễn rule most affected the Vietnamese settlers there. The next chapters discuss the role of foreign merchants and the trading economy of the region which made it unique in Vietnamese history. It then considers Đàng Trong society and the localization of the Vietnamese population, before moving on to discuss Vietnamese relations with the uplanders and the causes of the Tây Sơn rebellion which ended two centuries of flourishing success.

---

[17] Lê Quý Đôn, *Phủ Biên Tạp Lục* (A compilation of the miscellaneous records when the southern border was pacified) 2 vols., with Chinese version (Saigon: Phủ Quốc Vụ Khanh Đặc Trách Văn Hóa, 1973); *Lê Quý Đôn Toàn Tập* (Complete works of Lê Quý Đôn), vol. 1, *Phủ Biên Tạp Lục* (Hanoi: Khoa Học Xã Hội, 1977).

# THE NEW LAND

## THE PHYSICAL SETTING

For most of its history, much of this new land belonged to the poly-ethnic state of Champa, which embraced both mountain peoples and lowland Cham traders and agriculturalists.[1] Physically, the region had two distinguishing characteristics. First, the Trường Sơn mountains (or the Annamite Chain), with their rich forest cover, ran the whole length of the country, gradually declining in height from north to south. Second, the mountains were divided horizontally by several fast flowing rivers and numerous spurs of the Chain. The land formed a number of narrow basins with little geographical continuity. The Cham state was organized accordingly, in a series of principalities running from east to west, from the sea to the mountains, as is indicated by the way ancient groups of monuments are sited in separate valleys that lack any direct link with one another. *Zhu Fan Zhi*, a Chinese traveler's book of the thirteenth century, described this arrangement. Volume One reported Champa had eleven vassals, which current research suggests are better understood as separate (and often competing) principalities of the one "*nagara* Campa." Given these geographical difficulties, it is amazing that the Nguyễn ever managed to establish a unified state in "the world's least coherent territory," as Gourou later described it.[2]

Districts of Champa mentioned in the Cham inscriptions followed the main natural divisions of the country. They were Amravati, Vijaya, and Panduranga. The first two contained relatively large lowland areas suitable for cultivation. Amravati,[3] present day Quảng Nam, featured a rich plain of almost 1,800 square kilometers, watered by the Song Thu Bon (the 'Great River' in Cham inscriptions) and its several tributaries. Vijaya, in central Champa, corresponded to the bountiful Bình Định plain, with a total area of 1,550 square kilometers. It is bounded by two distinct mountain ranges, with two valleys watered by the rivers Sông Đa Rằng and Sông Lai Giang. The third, Panduranga, represented the southern part of the country. It consists of three valleys[4] which are easily accessible from one to another.

The Hải Vân Pass between Huế and Đà Nẵng forms a climate frontier: to the north of it, the climate type is a mixture of tropical and subtropical, with a distinct winter lasting from three to five months. To the south, the climate has a typically

---

[1] Longer discussion of Champa, drawn from recent French scholarship, can be found at pp. 31 ff. below.

[2] Pierre Gourou, *The Peasants of the Tongking Delta*, vol. 1 (New Haven: Human Relations Area Files, 1955), p. 3.

[3] *Ming Shi* (History of Ming) translated this place name as A-mu-la-bu, while *Zhu Fan Zhi* called it Wu-ma-ba.

[4] The three valleys are: Nha Trang, watered with the Sông Cái; Phanrang, watered by the Sông Dinh, running from the Lâm Viên plateau to the sea; and the Phan Rí and Phan Thiết area, watered by the Sông Lũy and Sông Cái.

inter-tropical character.[5] In contrast to the northern portion of Trường Sơn, which is narrow and rugged, the southern portion widens and forms a plateau area, known as Tây Nguyên, or the Central Highlands. It covers approximately twenty thousand square miles, is one hundred miles wide, and two hundred miles in length. These uplands, populated by numerous minority peoples, historically served as a place of refuge where defeated lowlanders could flee to regroup and retain some autonomy.

## VIETNAMESE SOUTHERN EXPANSION BEFORE NGUYEN RULE

Some Vietnamese historians have suggested that all Vietnamese history before the nineteenth century can be summed up in two phrases: *Bắc cự* (resistance to the North, meaning China) and *Nam tiến* (expansion to the South). If *Bắc cự* aimed at insuring Vietnamese survival in regard to China, then *Nam tiến* was necessary for Vietnamese development. Yet this *Nam tiến* was no simple linear progression, as it is so often presented, no essentialized preordained sequence by which the "Vietnam" of the tenth century became the "Vietnam" of today. There was no historical teleology at work here, but rather a series of different episodes responding to particular events or opportunities, and sometimes determined by little more than military accidents.[6]

Whereas the later pattern of southern expansion was shaped by the physical objective of occupying land, events which have been claimed as early episodes of *Nam Tiến*[7] were aimed instead at seizing people and treasure, a typical pattern in Southeast Asian warfare. For example, in 982, when Lê Hoàn of the Early Lê dynasty launched an attack on Champa, he seized one hundred Cham ladies of the royal harem and the Champa royal treasures.[8] On a smaller scale, such expeditions might have happened again and again. Thus, for example, the Vietnamese annals reported the release of 360 Cham prisoners detained in Thăng Long in 992[9] and noted similar Vietnamese raids on Sino-Vietnamese border areas in 995, which yielded Chinese prisoners.[10] Indeed, for several centuries after, wartime Cham captives and their descendants often made up a sizable proportion of those living near the Vietnamese capital. The Chams did not sit idle, either. Between 979 and 997 they made several raids on the newly independent Đại Việt capital and along its southern frontier. All these raids and expeditions hardly differed from the general pattern of Southeast Asia warfare, then and later, and are more appropriately understood in the context

---

[5] *Vietnam—Geographical Data* (Hanoi: n.p.,1979), p. 34.

[6] For a recent and articulated discussion on the term *"nam tiến,"* see Keith Taylor, "Regional Conflicts among the Viet Peoples between the Thirteenth and Nineteenth Centuries," at Seminar "La conduite des relations entre sociétiés et états: Guerre et paix en Asie du Sud-Est," Paris, November 1996, pp. 6–11.

[7] See Trương Bá Phát, "Lịch sử cuộc Nam tiến của dân tộc Việt Nam" (The history of southward expansion of the Vietnamese people) in *Sử Địa* (History and Geography) 19 & 20 (1970).

[8] *Đại Việt Sử Ký Toàn Thư*, ed. Chen Chingho, vol. 1 (Tokyo: Institute of Linguistic Studies, Keio University, 1984), p. 189. (Hereafter *Toàn Thư*.)

[9] Ibid., vol. 1, p. 193; see also G. Coedes, *The Indianized Sates of Southeast Asia*, ed. Walter F. Vella, trans. Susan Brown Cowing (Honolulu: East-West Center, 1968), p. 125.

[10] *Toàn Thư*, vol. 1, p. 194.

of general and frequent warfare between Southeast Asian countries than as the early stages of the Vietnamese southward movement.

Expansionary operations were certainly conducted by Vietnamese rulers in their southern border areas, but they seem driven more by strategic considerations than economic ones. For example, in 992 Lê Hoàn sent thirty thousand men to build a road from modern Cửa Sót (Thạch Hà county, Hà Tĩnh province) to the Cham-Việt border in the Hoành Sơn area.[11] No doubt this was the first official land route opened between Vietnam and Champa, and hence was used by generations of Vietnamese migrants to the south in later years. Yet Lê Hoàn's aim had only been to attack Champa more easily. For the same reason, a canal had been dug in Thanh Hóa not long before, in 983.[12] Not coincidentally, nine years later the Cham abandoned their newly vulnerable capital, Indrapura (modern Trà Kiều, in Duy Xuyên county, Quảng Nam).

Vietnamese chroniclers later claimed that three Cham prefectures located in modern Quảng Bình and Quảng Trị provinces were annexed as a result of a Vietnamese expedition of 1069,[13] and that the two prefectures of O and Lý (in modern Thừa Thiên province) were transferred to Vietnamese rule as the bride-price given by the Cham king Che Man for princess Huyền Chân, in 1306. Yet this region long remained a contested area which experienced see-sawing battles for supremacy between the two kingdoms. We see this when Trần Duệ Tôn (r. 1372-1377) was preparing to attack Champa in 1376. He ordered a road built from Cửu Chân (modern southern Thanh Hóa province) to Hà Hoa (modern Kỳ Anh county, Nghệ Tĩnh) to the north of Hoành Sơn mountain, the traditional border between Vietnam and Champa.[14] Part of this road might have been rebuilt over the old one from 992 but, interestingly, the extension was added to its northern sector, from Thanh Hóa to Nghệ Tĩnh, rather than being built in the supposedly former Cham territory. This strongly suggests that the region under firm Vietnamese control was still basically the old Vietnamese territory until as late as the end of fourteenth century.[15]

In fact, during the reign of the great Cham king called Chế Bồng Nga by the Vietnamese, or A-ta-a-zhe by the Chinese, the Chams twice raided Thăng Long, in 1371 and 1378. They forced the king of Đại Việt to move the statues at his ancestors' tombs from Thăng Long to modern Hải Dương province in 1381. Following up his victories, Chế Bồng Nga threatened not only to retake all the lost Cham territories, but the two southern Vietnamese provinces of Nghệ An and Thanh Hóa as well.[16] At the time, the Chams posed a real threat to the existence of late Trần dynasty Đại Việt: Vietnamese kings fled from them, and Vietnamese commanders, including Hồ Quý Ly himself, repeatedly retreated when facing them in battle. Among the ordinary

---

[11] *Toàn Thư*, vol. 1, p. 193. "To Địa Lý [prefecture]," according to the text. As Địa Lý prefecture was not officially ceded to Đại Việt until 1069, this road could only be built within the Vietnamese border.

[12] *Toàn Thư*, vol. 1, p. 190; Đào Duy Anh, *Đất nước Việt Nam qua các đời* (The Vietnamese territory during different dynasties) (Hanoi: Khoa Học, 1964), p. 290.

[13] *Toàn Thư*, vol. 3, p. 245.

[14] *Toàn Thư*, vol. 7, p. 446; Đào Duy Anh, *Đất nước*, p. 178.

[15] The territory of Đại Việt was invaded by the Cham several times in this period, notably in 1076 when Cham and Khmer joined forces with the Chinese to attack the Vietnamese.

[16] *Toàn Thư*, vol. 8, pp. 453-456. See also John Whitmore, *Vietnam, Ho Quy Ly, and the Ming (1371-1421)*, Lac-Viet Series no. 2 (New Haven: Yale Center for International and Area Studies, Council of Southeast Asia Studies, 1985), pp. 22-23.

people panic reigned. In 1383, the Chams even occupied the Vietnamese capital, Thăng Long, for six whole months.[17] The Việt-Cham contested area now became Thanh Hóa and Nghệ An, provinces of Đại Việt, rather than the former Cham territories of O and Lý prefectures. With hindsight, from a victorious Vietnamese point of view, these events might appear to constitute little more than a temporary setback, a brief victory staged by the ultimately doomed Chams. However, when placed in their historical context and viewed inside that context, they figure as more serious challenges, for Cham resistance efforts were potentially devastating to Đại Việt, "tearing its political system apart,"[18] and severely challenging its very existence.

Vietnamese royal power was only truly reestablished when the Cham threat disappeared, as Whitmore has rightly pointed out.[19] Perhaps it was because of the arduous experiences of the late fourteenth century that the new strongman, Hồ Quý Ly, came to view Việt-Cham relations from a new military and political perspective. Unimpressed by the old system of maintaining contested dominion over the border territories, Hồ saw the need for firm control, "since, as Chế Bồng Nga had demonstrated, the former state of loose control could be overthrown at any time."[20] He thus established an administrative system in the newly acquired areas that extended down to the district level. To this political solution he added a military dimension. Hồ sensed that the only way of saving Đại Việt from another such catastrophe was to push the Việt-Cham border as far south as possible. His own power base, located in Thanh Hóa and Nghệ An rather than around the capital area of Thăng Long, also served this purpose. From there, Hồ made military campaigns against Champa almost every year from 1400 to 1404, and not only regained the previously lost Cham territories but also pushed the Việt-Cham border to modern Quảng Ngãi province. To secure Vietnamese rule, Ho's government pressed rich but landless Vietnamese to migrate there. To make sure that they could not simply move back to the north when need arose, as must have happened in the past, Hồ even ordered these ordinary people be tattooed, something previously only done to criminals.[21] Although Hồ Quý Ly's reign was the shortest in Vietnamese history, his era (1400-07) was thus characterized by a much more determined Vietnamese push to expand south, which set the tone for the later period.

The Quảng Nam-Quảng Ngãi area gained by Hồ Quý Ly was again lost to the Chams during the Ming occupation. When a series of maps of the great territories of Đại Việt were presented to Lê Thánh Tôn in 1469, there were only two prefectures shown for Thuận Hóa province: Tân Bình and Thuận Hóa, both north of Hải Vân Pass.[22] Not long after, however, the Vietnamese side went back on the offensive, with Lê Thánh Tôn's attack on Champa mounted in 1471, an attack which enabled the Vietnamese to capture and hold the capital, Vijaya.

---

[17] *Toàn Thư*, vol. 8, p. 457.

[18] Whitmore, *Vietnam, Ho Quy Ly*, p. 21.

[19] Ibid., p. 31.

[20] Ibid., p. 75.

[21] *Toàn Thư*, vol. 8, p. 482.

[22] *Toàn Thư*, vol. 12, p. 676; Đào Duy Anh, *Đất nước*, pp. 153-154.

## THE PIONEERS

For the Vietnamese, the far southern land was originally defined as a place of banishment for criminals or a place of refuge for political dissidents or malcontents generally. Following the Trần dynasty example, the Later Lê dynasty also used the distant south as a place of exile. Phan Huy Chú's magisterial early nineteenth century survey of the institutions of former dynasties, *Lịch Triều Hiến Chương Loại Chí*, recorded that from 1474, only three years after Lê Thánh Tôn's war of conquest, the court decided to banish criminals to the former Cham region. A person was to be sent to Thăng Hoa (modern Thăng Bình, in Quảng Nam) for lesser crimes, to Tư Nghĩa (modern Quảng Ngãi) for worse crimes, while exile to Hoài Nhơn (Quy Nhơn, in modern Bình Định) served as the worst such punishment.[23]

The area was also traditionally a refuge for Vietnamese political refugees and malcontents. When Lê Thánh Tôn enumerated the crimes that the Chams had committed before he attacked Champa in 1471, one of those crimes was harboring Vietnamese criminals.[24] After the Ming invaded Đại Việt in 1407, the south became a haven for political dissent. When Trần Giản Định, the son of former king Trần Nghệ Tôn (r. 1370-72), rose against the occupiers his supporters moved actively between Thanh Hóa and Hóa Châu (in modern Quảng Điền county, Thừa Thiên). Hóa Châu was also the base for Trần Quý Khoách, king of the so-called Later Trần (*Hậu Trần*), 1407-1413. Later, too, an unknown number of loyal subjects of the Lê also sought sanctuary in the south. One family history in Quảng Nam, for example, relates that their ancestor was a high officer of Lê Duy Trị, brother of Lê Kính Tôn (1600-1619). When Lê Kính Tôn was forced by the Trịnh to hang himself in 1619, Lê Duy Trị and his followers escaped to Đông Sơn county, Thanh Hóa. From there in 1623 they moved to Thanh Châu village, Điện Bàn county, Quảng Nam.[25]

Given this background, it seems natural for Nguyễn Bỉnh Khiêm to have suggested that Nguyễn Hoàng go south. But this notable refugee did not go alone. The *Tiền Biên* records many mandarins and their families who followed Nguyễn Hoàng to the Thuận Hóa area in 1558, as well as several families from the Nguyễn home county of Tống Sơn in Thanh Hóa.[26] Many other men classified as *hương khúc* and *nghĩa dũng* (retainers of rich families, usually equipped with their own arms) came too. No doubt many of them were prompted to pull up stakes and move south by mixed motives, motives that might include not only loyalty to Nguyễn Hoàng but also self-interest, for the migrants hoped to find a brighter future in the new land. And indeed, many of those who came south with Nguyễn Hoàng or under his rule,

---

[23] *Lịch Triều Hiến Chương Loại Chí, Hình Luât Chí* (Huế: Nhà in Bảo Vĩnh, 1957), p. 531.

[24] *Toàn Thư*, vol. 12, p. 680.

[25] From a Lê family history of Thanh Châu village, Thanh Châu Tổng, Điện Bàn county, Quảng Nam province. Quoted from Nguyễn Chí Trung, "Bước đầu tìm hiểu về quá trình hình thành khối cộng đồng cư dân Hội An" (The first step in understanding the process of establishing the residential community of Hoi An) (roneo, 1988, in possession of author), p. 33.

[26] Nineteen of twenty-two first-rank officials of the Nguyễn originally came from Tống Sơn county, in Thanh Hóa. They included top generals like Nguyễn Hữu Dật, Nguyễn Cửu Kiều, and Trương Phúc Phan as well as half (five) of the Nguyễn queens before 1802. Other top officials also came from Thanh Hóa families, like General Nguyễn Hữu Tiến and the key strategist, Đào Duy Từ, both from Ngọc Sơn county. See *Liệt Truyện Tiền Biên*, vols. 3 and 4 (Collection of Biographies of the Nguyen Dynasty, Premier Period) (Tokyo: Keio Institute of Linguistic Studies, 1961).

particularly those from Tống Sơn county, did improve their families' fortunes. Most settled in the area from modern Quảng Bình to Thừa Thiên, where the ordinary followers formed "a class of privileged citizens," as Leopold Cadiere has described them.[27] Villages settled by the former Tống Sơn soldiers whom Nguyễn Hoàng brought south, perhaps originally as many as one thousand men, were exempted from taxes and corvees, and their members formed a sort of gentry group who were entitled to hold office in any village of the kingdom. The families of their original leaders enjoyed correspondingly greater advantages, in particular that of providing from among their number the most senior members of the military and political entourage that helped the Nguyễn family rule Đàng Trong.

It is hard to find firm traces of early Vietnamese migration. However, certain village names in Quảng Bình and Quảng Trị may hint at their history. According to Phan Khoang, some village names in modern Minh Linh (Quảng Bình province), written in the *Ô Châu Cận Lục* in Chinese as "xã Phan xá" and "xã Ngô xá," in Vietnamese *nôm* script actually meant *Nhà Phan* (Phan families) and *Nhà Ngô* (Ngô families). If so, these names suggest the early migrants here might have lived mainly by descent groups or possibly clans.[28] Curiously, similar village names cannot be found in the northern part of the Minh Linh region, possibly because, as Cadiere argued, when Vietnamese came down from the north in the twelfth century they went directly to the more fertile land at Lâm Bình (around Lệ Thủy in Quảng Bình), leaving the Bố Chính area untouched until the Lê Thánh Tôn reign.[29]

Some family histories from the Quảng Nam-Quảng Ngãi region also contain tantalizing references to aspects of the early southern expansion. For instance, an inscription on a tablet of the Trần family in Cẩm Thanh village in the Hội An area records the entrepreneurial efforts of one former soldier who not only brought his family to the war, no doubt hoping to settle them afterwards, but went on to organize the foundation of a whole new village:

> In the Hồng Đức period (1470-1497) our ancestor was recruited from Thanh Hóa to fight in the land of the Cham, together with his family. Because he performed well in battle, he was allowed to stay in the Quảng Nam area. Discovering a big river close to the sea [probably the Thu Bon river], he gathered people to come and set up the village here. This tablet was set up on [January 10, 1498].[30]

This inscription confirms that demobilized soldiers, as apart from those in officially organized military settlements (*đồn điền*), formed one source of pioneers; but unfortunately we cannot even guess their number as the sources wildly disagree on the size of the army.[31] Other family registers also show ordinary peasants seizing the

---

[27] Leopold Cadiere, "Le mur de Dong Hoi," *Bulletin de l'Ecole Française d'Extrême-Orient* (hereafter BEFEO) 6 (1906): 93

[28] Phan Khoang, *Việt Sử Xứ Đàng Trong* (A history of Đàng Trong) (Saigon: Khai Trí, 1970), p. 54.

[29] Leopold Cadiere, "Geographie historique du Quang-Binh d'après les annales imperials," *BEFEO* 2 (1902): 66.

[30] Nguyễn Chí Trung, "Bước đầu tìm hiểu về quá trình hình thành khối cộng đồng cư dân Hội An," p. 32.

[31] According to the *Toàn Thư*, seven hundred thousand soldiers went to fight the Chams. The *Khâm Định Việt Sử Thông Giám Cương Mục* (Text and explanation forming the complete mirror of the history of Vietnam), however, says the army only had 167,800 soldiers before 1471.

opportunities opened up by military conquest. For example, from the Hoàng family history in Cẩm Nam village, Hội An:

> Our ancestor was a northerner. Because our king captured the king of Champa, in the Hồng Đức period our ancestor took advantage of the favorable situation down here to establish himself.[32]

All these scant sources tend to confirm that although the Quảng Nam area officially fell into the hands of the Vietnamese in 1402, they did not really control it before 1471. Thus, the pattern of Vietnamese settlement between the twelfth and the fifteenth centuries was one of separate, scattered groups. The Chams never stopped trying to get their former lands back, nor did the Lê dynasty officially seek to expand further, if only because rapid dynastic decline set in two decades after the death of Lê Thánh Tôn in 1497.

However, the establishment of the breakaway Nguyễn regime from about 1600, when Nguyễn Hoàng left the north never to return, marked a watershed in the *Nam tiến* process. From then on southern expansion became a popular movement, both protected and stimulated by the new Nguyễn *chúa* (or Lords). Early manpower shortages quickly prompted generous government inducements to migrate from the jurisdiction of the Lê/Trịnh administration further north. New arrivals, for example, did not pay taxes in the first three years of residence, and fields they developed themselves were considered private land. Before 1669, too, the taxation system was poorly organized and many places may have hardly paid land tax at all.[33] Nevertheless, despite these advantages, the main cause of immigration was undoubtedly the deteriorating situation in Đàng Ngoài villages.

### LATER DEMOGRAPHIC CHANGE

Two patterns of migration existed during much of Nguyễn rule: internal and external. Internal migration could be either undertaken voluntarily by individuals or social groups like a family or even a whole village, or might be organized by the Nguyễn government. Voluntary internal migration usually occurred when the descendants of earlier immigrants pushed further south. This was a relatively common occurrence in Đàng Trong. Very few families ever went directly from the north to the deep south. A typical example is that of the 1866 rebel, Đoàn Hữu Trưng, of Phú Vang county, Thừa Thiên province. According to his family history, his ancestors originally shifted south from either Thanh Hóa or Nghệ An during the Lê dynasty, that is, some time before about 1600. They first went to Quảng Bình and set up a village called Chuồn, where they stayed for a "long time." Then they traveled further south to Thừa Thiên. The village they set up here was called Chuồn

---

Although Lê Thánh Tôn recruited more troops to fight against the Chams (260,000, according to the *Toàn Thư*), the whole army probably never numbered higher than two hundred thousand. Most would have returned north afterwards. However, even five thousand remaining behind would have had significant demographic and political consequences. See *Khâm Định Việt Sử Thông Giám Cương Mục* (Text and explanation forming the complete mirror of the history of Vietnam), 8 vols. Reprint (Taipei: The National Library of Taiwan, 1969).

[32] Nguyễn Chí Trung, "Bước đầu," p. 33.

[33] See Chapter Five of this book.

Ngọn (the branch of Chuồn), and the Chuồn village in Quảng Bình was renamed Chuồn Gốc (the root of Chuồn).[34] There are many similar cases of this gradual Vietnamese expansion from north to south, with a number of settlers finally ending in the far south of Lower Cochinchina. One such, the family of Phạm Đăng Hưng, a high official of the Gia Long reign and king Tự Đức's grandfather, is recorded in the *Đại Nam Liệt Truyện Chính Biên*. His original ancestor brought the whole family from the north after Nguyễn Hoàng set up his power in Thuận Hóa. They first stayed in Vũ Xương county (in modern Quảng Trị province), but then moved further south to Hương Trà county (in Thừa Thiên). Đăng Hưng's great-grandfather then moved the family further south to Quảng Ngãi, after which his grandfather shifted them even further, to Gia Định.[35]

Government-organized migration usually took the form of establishing military colonies at frontier areas, whose soldier-settlers fought or farmed as occasion demanded. Government-organized civilian relocation was much rarer, but at least one instance is recorded in *Tiền Biên*. It happened in 1698, after Nguyễn Phúc Chu had set up Gia Định prefecture by creating four distinct administrative units: Phuc Long and Tân Bình districts, both designated by the civil term *huyện*, and Trấn Biên (later Biên Hòa) and Phiên Trấn (later Gia Định) which became separate *dinh* (or military districts). Each was endowed with its full complement of military and civilian officials, and army and naval units. The process was said to be "opening widely this land for one thousand miles, on which more than forty thousand households were gathered, [they] then recruited wandering people (*xiểu dật*) from Bố Chính (Quảng Bình) south and let them to go and live [there] so it could be populous."[36] Unlike areas further south in the delta, land and population in Biên Hòa and Gia Định were said to have been measured and registered, and taxes set accordingly.

External immigration fell into two basic forms: deliberate and involuntary. For the first category, the Thanh Hóa-Nghệ An area, a poor sub-region in Trịnh Vietnam with an uncertain climate, prone to famine, played a crucial role. These two provinces provided many new settlers, especially in the later sixteenth century, as geographic proximity made the journey to Thuận Hóa comparatively easy. The traditional organization of extended family ties in villages here, as in those further north, may have facilitated such emigration south. The family structure, which organized settlers according to their membership in descent groups or clans and thus encouraged them to move as part of such a group, increased their security by providing the leadership, mutual assistance, and support unavailable to lone individuals or nuclear families. A Lê family tablet set up in Cẩm Phô village, Hội An recorded one such joint migration:[37]

---

[34] *Danh Nhân Bình Trị Thiên* (Famous people in Quảng Bình, Quảng Trị, and Thừa Thiên province), vol. 1 (Huế: Press of Thuận Hóa, 1986), pp. 128-129.

[35] *Đại Nam Chính Biên Liệt Truyện Sơ Tập*, vol. 5 (Tokyo: Keio Institute of Linguistic Studies, 1962), p. 1071.

[36] *Đại Nam Thực Lục Tiền Biên* (Chronicle of the Nguyen Dynasty Premier Period) (hereafter *Tiền Biên*), vol. 7 (Tokyo: Keio Institute of Linguistic Studies, 1961), p. 103. For a detailed discussion of this, see Nola Cooke, "Regionalism and the Nature of Nguyễn Rule in Seventeenth-Century Đàng Trong (Cochinchina)," *Journal of Asian Studies* (forthcoming, 1998), Part III.

[37] Nguyen Chí Trung, "Bước đầu," p. 35.

It is said that our ancestors came here shortly after the Gia Dụ emperor [Nguyễn Hoàng] opened up the Thuận-Quảng area. They came from the north, but we do not know which province precisely. They came with three other clans, the Hoàng, the Trần and the Nguyễn clans.

This is not to deny the importance of immigration by individuals or smaller family units. No doubt many poor men came to the Nguyễn area hoping to make their fortunes on the frontier, although few succeeded as spectacularly as Đào Duy Từ. Son of an entertainer, and thus barred from the examinations and official position in the Lê/Trịnh north, Duy Từ's talents won him recognition and high office in the south. In return, his strategic advice, which led to the early 1630s building of the great defensive walls in Quảng Bình, played a fundamental role in preserving Nguyễn power against the Trịnh.

One common explanation for Vietnamese expansion southward is population pressure on limited agriculture land, but closer inquiry suggests the immediate causes which drove large numbers of people to the south, especially from the Thanh-Nghệ region, were famine and war. The late sixteenth century saw one of the most disastrous periods recorded in the Vietnamese annals. From 1559 to 1597 inclusive, there were fourteen years in which refugees featured in the Lê annals, *Toàn Thư*, as they did again in 1608.[38] Here are some typical excerpts from 1572 and then 1594:

Nghệ An harvested nothing this year, what is more, pestilence broke out. Half of the people died. People fled either to the south, or to the northeast.

And:

The harvest in several counties around the Hải Dương area is very poor, people are so hungry that they eat each other. A third of the population has died of starvation.[39]

This was perhaps the longest period of disaster in Vietnamese history, with civil war raging for several decades and fourteen out of forty-nine years proving disastrous for agriculture. The northern population at this time must have been at a very low point. In addition to those who died from starvation and pestilence, the war between the Lê and the Mạc took a heavy toll, with more than forty major battles between 1539 and 1600, usually in the region from Thăng Long to Thanh Hóa. Then as the war neared its end, and fighting raged across the more populous Red River plains, *Toàn Thư* recorded the decapitation of well over twenty thousand Mạc soldiers between 1589 and 1593 alone.[40] One modern Vietnamese scholar has estimated that the Lê Restoration claimed the lives of "several hundred thousand young men,"[41] and this figure does not take into account the multitude of other victims of the fighting.

---

[38] In 1561, 1570, 1571, 1572, 1586, 1588, 1589, 1592, 1594, 1595, 1596, and 1597.

[39] *Toàn Thư*, vol. 3, pp. 867 and 902 respectively.

[40] *Toàn Thư*, vol. 17, pp. 887-899.

[41] Trương Hữu Quýnh, *Chế độ Ruộng đất ở Việt Nam* (The land system in Vietnam) (Hanoi: Khoa Học Xã Hội, 1983), vol. 2, p. 16.

In contrast to the miserable situation in the north, the Thuận Hóa area was relatively peaceful. Although the Mạc tried to attack Thuận Hóa in 1571, Nguyễn Hoàng defeated them. Both the *Toàn Thư* and the nineteenth-century Nguyễn chronicle of this period, the *Tiền Biên,* said that the area "had no thieves and people did not close their doors at night, while many foreign ships came to trade here."[42] It was a natural haven for refugees coming from the north. Although *Tiền Biên* only twice mentioned refugees flooding into Thuận Hóa, in 1559 and again in 1608, *Toàn Thư* often recorded people fleeing their homes during this period and heading either to the south or the northeast, both less populated areas.

The late sixteenth century thus saw the first big wave of Vietnamese migration to what soon became the Nguyễn principality of Đàng Trong. As a historical event, it was similar to the Chinese larger-scale emigration from the north to the Yangtze River delta in the East Jin dynasty (fourth century CE). Before this period the flow of people migrating to the south had been rather sporadic; but now their motives were much stronger and their aims more definite. The peace and security offered by strong Nguyễn rule overcame any uncertainties lingering from the past and, by seeming to reconfirm Vietnamese rights to the area, greatly encouraged migration.

In the seventeenth century, during the fifty year Trịnh/Nguyễn struggle, emigration from the north to the south still continued, as a recent study by a Vietnamese scholar Huỳnh Công Bá clearly suggests. According to this study, family genealogies of sixty-three clans in northern Quảng Nam recorded that their ancestors came to the region during the war period between the Trịnh and the Nguyễn.[43] But some migration was involuntary. The most famous example concerns the capture of thousands of Trịnh soldiers in 1648, and their eventual resettlement as pioneers in Phú Yên province. Their fate was decided by the ruling *chúa*, Nguyễn Phúc Lan (r. 1635-1648), who consulted his court about the future of the prisoners following their defeat. Some argued they should be banished to "the high mountains or the islands," for fear they would create trouble, while others advocated letting them return home, after prudently executing their officers. The *chúa* disagreed. He said:

> South of Thăng Bình and Điện Bàn lies the old territory of Champa where very few [Vietnamese] people live. If we put the captured soldiers on this land, give them oxen and farm implements, provide them with food to eat, and let them clear the land, then in several years they could produce enough for their own needs. After they marry and have children, in twenty years the children can be soldiers of the country. I foresee no trouble at all from them.[44]

The result was that:

> The soldiers were divided into villages, fifty to each village, and given half a year's supplies. Further, the *chúa* ordered better-off people to lend them food. The resettled people were allowed to seek their livelihood from the mountains

---

[42] *Toàn Thư*, vol. 3, p. 868; *Tiền Biên*, vol. 1, p. 23.

[43] Huỳnh Công Bá., "Công cuộc khai khẩn và phát triển làng xã ở bắc Quảng Nam từ giữa thế kỷ XV đến giữa thế kỷ XVIII" (The opening and development of the villages in the northern Quảng Nam region, from mid-fifteenth to mid-eighteenth centuries), abstract of PhD thesis, Hanoi Normal University, 1996, pp. 9-10.

[44] *Tiền Biên*, vol. 3, pp. 51-52.

and lakes. And so villages flourished from Thăng Hoa and Điện Bàn to Phú Yên, and the families eventually became registered households.

However, enemy soldiers were not the only source of involuntary settlers at the time, with common people forcibly removed from Lê/Trịnh territory possibly accounting for even more unwilling immigrants than the Trịnh army. Outside Đại Việt, the taking of captives was characteristic of Southeast Asian warfare, and for the same reason that motivated the Nguyễn: in regions of low population and abundant land, the control of human resources was vital for a ruling elite's chances of maintaining its power and wealth. But whereas the ethnicity of the captives was not politically significant to Thai or Burman rulers, the Nguyễn were especially concerned to increase the number of their Vietnamese subjects, who were the principal source of military conscripts. Such unorthodox behavior by the ancestral Nguyễn kings may not have come to light in nineteenth-century court sources if not for a fortuitous consequence of the forcible removal of ordinary people out of the seven Nghệ An counties in the mid-1650s: among those seized and transported was the great-grandfather of the later Tây Sơn rebel brothers. As the dynastic biography for the Gia Long reign laconically noted, commenting on Nguyễn Huệ, the most brilliant of the Tây Sơn leaders:

> His ancestor was from Hưng Nguyên county, Nghệ An. His great-great-grandfather was captured by our army during the year of Thịnh Đức (1653-1657), [when the Nguyễn attacked and occupied seven counties of Nghệ An], and was put to the Tây Sơn Nhất in Quy Ninh area.[45]

Several other sources confirm this event,[46] although none estimate the number of people involved nor record any other examples. It seems logical to assume, however, that like the rulers of other expanding Southeast Asian kingdoms at the time, the Nguyễn would have actively encouraged, if not forced, the relocation of people temporarily under their control. But the political consequences of such large-scale involuntary resettlements may have been rather different from those envisaged at the time. It is surely not entirely coincidental that the Quy Nhơn-Phú Yên area later became a Tây Sơn rebel stronghold, and one of the last anti-Nguyễn bastions to fall to Gia Long in 1801.

## THE VIETNAMESE POPULATION OF ĐÀNG TRONG: AN ESTIMATE

The region under Nguyễn control can be divided into three areas, according to the different periods in which they were secured by Vietnamese. The first is the Thuận Hóa area, which became part of Đại Việt in the fourteenth century. Next came

---

[45] *Đại Nam Thực Lục Chính Biên Liệt Truyện Sơ Tập*, vol. 30 (Tokyo: reprinted by the Oriental Institute Keio University, 1963), p. 1331.

[46] See Ngô Thời Chí, *Hoàng Lê Nhất Thống Chí* (Paris-Taipei: Collection Romans & Contes du Vietnam écrits en Han, Ecole Française d'Extrême-Orient & Student Book Co. LTD, 1986), p. 61; *Tây Sơn Thuật Lược* (Saigon: Phu Quoc-vu-khanh Dac trach Van Hoa, 1971), p. 1, although the year there is given incorrectly as Dương Đức and not Thịnh Đức. Hưng Nguyên county, however, was not among the seven counties captured by the Nguyễn in the mid-seventeenth century.

Quảng Nam, Quảng Ngãi, and Quy Nhơn, Vietnamese land in any real sense only after Lê Thánh Tôn's expedition in 1471. The remaining land of modern southern Vietnam, from Phú Yên to the Mekong delta, was taken by the Nguyễn from 1611 to 1758. We will try to estimate population growth in those three areas one after the other.

First let us glance at the data we have for the Thuận Hóa area:

**Table 1: Number of Villages and Taxpayers in Thuận Hóa, 1417-1770**

| Year | Number of Villages (*xã*) | Number of Taxpayers (*đinh*) |
|---|---|---|
| 1417 | 116 | 10,400[47] |
| 1555 | 688 | — [48] |
| 1770 | 1,436 | 126,857[49] |

I assume that the figures for 1770 are reasonably reliable because Thuận Hóa had the longest history of Vietnamese occupation in the south, contained the capital, and was under the direct control of the central government. In 1770 the government could certainly count the numbers of villages in Thuận Hóa, if not in every other region. The information above suggests the numbers of taxpayers averaged eighty-eight per village in 1770, close to the estimated 110 for the north at the same time.[50] Therefore using the formula $[LN (P1 / P0)] / t \times 100 = r$, the population growth in the Thuận Hóa area can be estimated as:

**Table 2: Estimated Population in Thuận Hóa, 1417-1770**

| Year | *xã* | Estimated Households | Estimated Population | Annual Growth Rate |
|---|---|---|---|---|
| 1417 | 116 | 12,760 | 63,800 | |
| 1555 | 688 | 75,680 | 378,400 | 0.56% |
| 1770 | 1,436 | 157,960 | 789,800 | 0.15% |

This table suggests a relatively high population growth in the late fifteenth century. The influence of migration can be seen clearly, although the number of villages in 1,417 listed above may be lower than the true figure.

The later period of the Nguyễn in Thuận Hóa saw a slower rate of increase in population. This is easy to understand, since the arable land here is poor in quality and limited in area. Lê Quý Đôn said in 1774 that in Lệ Thủy and Khang Lộc counties there were on average only five to six *sào* (about 0.2 hectare) of land per person, barely enough to survive on. Even so, the table shows the established annual growth rate here from 1417 to 1770 to be about 0.3 percent, higher than the rate calculated for the north in the same period. Perhaps the real meaning of the table is to suggest the most rapid population growth in the Thuận Hóa area took place during a period of time stretching from 1471 to the first half of the seventeenth century, that is during

---

[47] *Ngan-nan tche yuan* (Hanoi: Imprimerie d'Extrême-Orient, 1932), p. 62.

[48] Dương Văn An, *Ô Châu Cận Lục*, trans. Bui Luong (Saigon: Văn Hóa Á Châu, 1961), pp. 21-24.

[49] *Phủ Biên*, vol. 3, p. 105b.

[50] For the detailed analysis supporting these calculations, see Appendix One.

the early Nguyễn period. If so, the main reason for this growth could only be immigration. After that the growth tended to stabilize.

Although complete population data on Quảng Nam is not available, it does allow us to isolate a case study in Điện Bàn prefecture, one of the most populous regions in the Nguyễn territory. We have two sets of figures on the villages in Điện Bàn, one provided by *Ô Châu Cận Lục*, written in 1555, and the other by *Phủ Biên Tạp Lục*, written in 1776. Điện Bàn was a district under the Lê, but was upgraded into Điện Bàn prefecture by Nguyễn Hoàng in 1604.[51] While only sixty-six villages existed in Điện Bàn in the mid-sixteenth century, according to *Ô Châu Cận Lục*, by 1776 they had multiplied into 197 villages (*xã*), under which 317 settlements were attached (nineteen *thôn*, seven *giáp*, 205 *phường*, and eighty-six *châu*).[52]

Comparing the village lists from the two documents, of the five districts under Điện Bàn prefecture, only Hòa Vang, An Nông, and Diên Khánh districts contained some old village names of the former Điện Bàn district, while Tân Phúc and Phú Châu had none. This seems to suggest clearly a quite rapid, even sudden, population movement to the region, most likely in the seventeenth century. Another interesting point is that there is always a long list of the subordinate settlements under the old villages, usually much longer than the list of the original villages, which again indicates vigorous growth in the region during the two hundred years of the Nguyễn.

How would we interpret this population growth then? If there were an average of eighty-eight households per village, as we calculated in the Thuận Hóa region, and an average fifty households per settlement, assuming that the settlements subordinated to those villages had lower population, and thus fewer households, then the population growth rate would be as follows:

| Table 3: Estimated Population in Điện Bàn, 1555-1777 | | | | |
|---|---|---|---|---|
| Year | *xã* | Estimated Households | Estimated Population | Annual Growth Rate |
| 1555 | 66 | 5,808 | 29,040 | |
| 1777 | 197 | 17,336 | 86,680 | 0.78% |

This estimation certainly suggests an amazing yet reasonable rate of growth, considering the main population growth of the Nguyễn period would occur in the Quảng Nam rather than the Thuận Hóa region, as we discussed above.

As for the Mekong delta, both the data and historical records show that it did not become populous with Vietnamese before Nguyễn Ánh went there in the late eighteenth century, after the Tây Sơn had deposed his family. It is no coincidence that for the whole Nguyễn period not a single figure survives for the villages south of Quảng Nam. Far southern villages were particularly loose and unstable. Villagers kept moving; indeed whole villages might have moved. A sense of community and of belonging to one special place grew up quite late in the far south.

But the Vietnamese newcomers were hardly the only occupants of the new southern land. Throughout the whole period, Đàng Trong sustained a very large

---

[51] *Tiền Biên*, vol. 1, p. 28.

[52] Dương Văn An, *Ô Châu Cận Lục*, p. 41; *Phủ Biên* (Hanoi edition), vol. 1, pp. 83-86. Huỳnh Công Bá estimates that about six hundred units existed in this region in the period, based on some other local sources. See Huỳnh Công Bá, "Công cuộc khai khẩn," p. 15.

non-Vietnamese population, so much so that Vietnamese often formed a minority as the frontier shifted. They had to deal with a variety of indigenous peoples, often designated commonly as *mọi*, a culturally specific term meaning "savages" or people of a non-Sinic civilization. But the Chams, and then later Chinese (and some Khmer) whom Vietnamese settlers encountered as they pushed south, all came from literate, complex societies whose cultural development matched the immigrants' own. Vietnamese responses to the challenges of southern cultural plurality ultimately redefined their own sense of cultural identity over these two centuries. We will conclude here by introducing the other main non-Vietnamese groups in Đàng Trong, beginning with the people of Champa and the Chinese immigrant population, and concluding with the complex patchwork of minority peoples.

## CHAMPA AFTER 1471

Until very recently, few scholars doubted Champa was geographically limited to the plains between the mountains of the Annamite Chain and the South China Sea. Colonial era discoveries of Cham archeological sites deep in the mountains had been taken as evidence of attempted lowland domination, or at most relations of vassalage.[53] However, recent French research based on newly translated later Cham texts indicates that the kingdom of Champa traditionally incorporated both the coastal plains and their hinterlands in the Annamite Chain and the high plateau to the west.[54] In addition, the sources show that the population of the kingdom, contrary to former belief, consisted not simply of ethnic Chams, but equally included groups of Austronesian speakers, such as the Jarai, Rhade, Curu, and Roglai, as well as Austroasiatic speakers like the Mnong and Stieng. This is a most significant discovery: it revolutionizes our understanding of Champa. Previously, scholars had followed the line established in Aymonier's first study of the area, in which he had applied an inappropriately "nationalist" model that held Champa was the land of the Chams, in much the same way that France was the land of the French. Yet, as Po Dharma has recently shown, the etymology of the word *cam* has nothing to do with that of "Campa," either historically or ethnographically. While *cam* referred to the Chams, "Campa," in the context of *"nagara* Campa"—the name given to the kingdom by its own people—denoted a confederation embracing Chams and uplanders alike.[55]

Neither epigraphic evidence nor historical documents in later Cham make any distinction between the people of the plain and of the mountains, using the same

[53] Gerald Hickey, *Sons of the Mountains*, pp. 89-120, summarizes the previous scholarship on Champa.

[54] Unless otherwise indicated, this section summarizes the recent research. See in particular, Po Dharma, *Le Panduranga (Campa) 1802-1835. Ses rapports avec le Vietnam*, 2 vols. (Paris: BEFEO, 1987); *Actes du Seminaire sur le Campa organisé à l'Universitaire de Copenhague, le 23 Mai 1987* (Paris: Travaux du Centre d'Histoire et Civilisations de la Peninsule indochinoise, 1988), especially Bernard Gay, "Une nouvelle sur le composition ethnique du Campa," pp. 49-56; and Po Dharma, "Etat des derniers recherches sur la date de l'absorption du campa par le Vietnam," *Actes du Seminaire*, pp. 59–70. See also Pierre-Bernard Lafont, "Les grandes dates de l'histoire du Campa," in *Le Campa et la Monde Malais* (Paris: Centre d'Histoire et Civilisations de la Peninsule Indochinoise, 1991), pp. 6–25.

[55] See Bernard Gay, "Une nouvelle sur la composition ethnique du Campa," p. 50.

term, "*urang* Campa" for all the people of *nagara* Campa, wherever located. Indeed, many kings of Champa in this later period were uplanders by origin, something the neglect of later *cam* texts had hidden from historians until recently. Among them was the most famous post-1471 king, Po Ramo (or Po Rame) who reigned from 1627-1651. By birth he was a Curu, a member of the upland people descended from intermarriage between an earlier refugee Cham group and the local Roglai and Koho.[56] Fourteen kings who were descended from him ruled *nagara* Campa until 1786. Uplander marriages remained common in the royal family: Po Rame's most famous son, Po Saut, who took the throne in 1655, was the offspring of a Rhade (or perhaps Koho) wife. In addition, the chronicles and royal archives mention numerous high dignitaries belonging to uplander groups, both at court and in the administration. A dozen uplanders were among the people venerated as gods in the pantheon at Kate, in the premier ceremony of the year in which all the people remembered the great figures of *nagara* Campa. On this ritual occasion, the guardians of the royal treasures of Champa, all mountain people, revealed that these figures were venerated by the participants. Many of these treasures remained in the uplanders' safe-keeping until the French colonial era.[57]

All this new information suggests that, uniquely in mainland Southeast Asia, *nagara* Campa was "a poly-ethnic country where all ethnic groups had equal rights."[58] As a kingdom composed of different ethnic groups situated in the central highlands as well as the coastal plains, *nagara* Campa remained viable long after Lê Thánh Tôn's massive victory. In 1611 this kingdom attacked the Nguyễn, hoping to recover the lost territory of Quy Nhơn, but its failure allowed the Vietnamese to expand as far south as Cape Varella. After a second failed attack in 1653, Vietnamese territory reached Cam Ranh. The last such attack was mounted by Panduranga alone in 1692; the force sought to take back Kauthara, which had been annexed by the Vietnamese in 1653. After the 1692 victory, the Nguyễn lord decided to incorporate the remainder of Champa, changing its Vietnamese designation from Chiêm-thành to *trấn* Thuận Thành, and dividing it into three districts (Phan-rang, Phò-hải and Phan-rí). In late 1693, however, the people of Panduranga revolted so successfully that they caused the annexation to be reversed. Panduranga was recognized within its 1692 frontiers—though henceforth it was always called Thuận Thành in Vietnamese texts—and its ruler treated as a tributary king (*vương*), although Vietnamese magistrates remained to regulate the affairs of Vietnamese settlers in the area.

Despite the success of the revolt, Cham military power had effectively been broken, and the die was cast. Taking advantage of the protection extended by Bình Thuận prefectural magistrates, and of the possibility of buying land in Panduranga, Vietnamese immigrants flocked to the region and their numbers increased. By the end of the eighteenth century they formed numerous enclaves enjoying extra-territoriality, heedless of Cham objections. Panduranga's strategic location between the Tây Sơn base area of Quy Nhơn and the later Nguyễn stronghold in the Mekong delta meant it was inevitably drawn into the battles of the Tây Sơn era. Rival Cham princes fought for the Tây Sơn and for the Nguyễn. Gia Long rewarded his Cham lieutenant in the early nineteenth century by establishing him as the tributary ruler of

---

[56] Hickey, *Sons of the Mountains*, p. 113

[57] Ibid., pp. 106-07.

[58] Bernard Gay, "Une nouvelle sur la composition ethnique du Campa," p. 55.

Panduranga, an arrangement that lasted until the mid-1830s, when Gia Long's successor, the centralizing emperor Minh Mạng, finally extended direct Vietnamese administration to the area and tried to extinguish Cham cultural identity.

## CHINESE IMMIGRANTS

Chinese immigrants accounted for a considerable percentage of Đàng Trong's population growth in these two hundred years. Geographically they were concentrated in three regions. The first was the Huế and Hội An area, where the establishment of the Chinese communities went back to the mid-seventeenth century, and the first village for Ming loyalist immigrant Chinese [Minh Hương] was established.[59] Most Chinese here seem to have been involved in trade and commerce. By the mid-seventeenth century they formed a sizable community, according to a 1642 report by the Dutch East India Company official, Johan van Linga, who estimated that there were "at least four to five thousand lazy Chinese" in Hội An alone.[60]

Overall Chinese numbers increased greatly in 1679 when about three thousand soldiers who, with their leaders, had escaped from the Qing came to Đà Nẵng seeking asylum. While such a large, disciplined body of armed men presented a potential threat in Thuận Hóa and upper Quảng Nam, if directed to the south as pioneer settlers they represented a great opportunity. Recognizing this, the Nguyễn court shrewdly sent them as far as possible, to the thinly settled Cambodian land around modern Biên Hòa and Mỹ Thọ where some Vietnamese had already begun to farm. The move nominally extended Nguyễn authority to the Mekong delta for the first time and established a protective military presence there at no cost to the Phú Xuân government, still involved in the Trịnh wars. As a result of this large Chinese settlement, this part of the north-eastern Mekong delta became the second main area of Chinese presence in Đàng Trong. The migrants established agricultural settlements here and developed a prosperous rice trade which in turn attracted more Chinese migrants. Their numbers multiplied, and in 1698 Nguyễn authorities set up two villages, Thanh Hà and Minh Hương, as official residential locations and began to register the Chinese migrants and their local offspring.

The third region was to the south-west of Lower Cochinchina, on the modern Việt-Khmer border at Hà Tiên. Founded in 1681, this trading port and its immediate hinterland to the east were soon flourishing under the leadership of the émigré Chinese Ming loyalist and former minister at the Khmer court, Mạc Cửu.[61] Its success quickly drew the unwelcome attention of Siam, which was itself in the process of expanding, and caused Mạc Cửu to apply for Nguyễn protection in 1708, whereupon Nguyễn Phúc Chu appointed him commandant of Hà Tiên. By this act the distant Nguyễn court was drawn even further into the politics of the far south and into inevitable conflict with the region's traditional Khmer rulers.

---

[59] Chen Chingho, *Historical Notes on Hoi-An (Faifo)* (Carbondale: Center for Vietnamese Studies, Southern Illinois University, Monograph Series IV, 1973).

[60] W. J. M. Buch, *De Oost-Indische Compagnie en Quinam* (Amsterdam: H. J. Paris, 1929), p. 122.

[61] Chen Chingho, "He xian zhen ye zhen mo shi jia pu zhu shi" (Notes on the genealogy of the Mac family in Hatien) *Quo le taiwan xue wen shi xue bao* (Bulletin of the College of Arts of Taiwan National University) 7 (1956): 89-90.

Although some Chinese migrants arrived in large groups as political refugees, more common were the people who came of their own accord from Fu Jian and Guang Dong provinces. Although data on them is very scanty, the registration records of the Minh Hương village in Hội An, for example, show that in three years during the 1740s thirty-five to forty people came each year, mainly from Fu Jian and most were unmarried young men of about twenty years of age.[62] At about the same time, the French missionary Jean Koffler estimated that there were at minimum thirty thousand Chinese dispersed throughout Cochinchina, engaged largely in trade.[63] This dominant demographic pattern of immigration by young unmarried males naturally led to marriages between Chinese and Vietnamese, the offspring of whom became known generally as "Minh Hương." Such intermediate communities, once firmly established, tend to duplicate themselves readily over time, making them "capable of quite rapid population growth," as William Skinner has noted.[64] That this occurred in Nguyễn Cochinchina is suggested by the 20,241 Minh Hương we noted were officially registered in Quảng Nam alone in 1805, a number almost equal to the registered Vietnamese taxpayers there.

What was most distinctive about Chinese migration to southern Vietnam under the Nguyễn was its steady and continuous flow, and its non-elite nature. In the past, Sinic elements in Vietnamese elite culture had always made Đại Việt a congenial place for individual Chinese immigrants, perhaps seeking to flee political changes further north. Migration had existed for centuries before the Nguyễn, but always at a trickle. Earlier migrants had assimilated individually and disappeared into the Vietnamese elite, leaving only Sinic family names as evidence of their ancestor's presence. Before the Nguyễn period, the conditions never existed for such people to established permanent "Chinese" communities. But now comparatively large-scale immigration of traders and laborers into a region of historically low Vietnamese settlement combined to form a critical mass that resulted in a distinct and permanent Chinese segment within Đàng Trong society.

## THE NON-VIETNAMESE POPULATION

As the Vietnamese moved south into what became Đàng Trong, the physical configuration of the land, with the coast to the east and often abruptly rising high mountains to the west, determined their basic settlement pattern in the more fertile coastal lowlands and river valleys. None of this land was empty: not only Chams but other indigenous peoples also lived on the choice coastal strip, and some remained after the Vietnamese arrived. With the exception of the Chams, however, few of these peoples stayed very long in those areas marked by Vietnamese incursion (though a few did persist in areas of poor soil or where Vietnamese penetration occurred later, for instance, the minority people Bernard Bourotte reported still farming delta lands in Quảng Ngãi well into the twentieth century[65]). When confronted with organized

---

[62] Manuscript kept in The Hoi An Relics Management Board, Hội An.

[63] Jean Koffler, "Description historique de la Cochinchine," *Revue Indochinoise* 15 (1911): 460.

[64] William Skinner, "Creolized Chinese Societies in Southeast Asia," in A. Reid, ed., *Sojourners and Settlers: Histories of Southeast Asia and the Chinese* (Sydney: Allen & Unwin, 1996), p. 53

[65] Bernard Bourotte, "Essai d'histoire des populations montagnardes du sud-indochinois jusqu'à 1945," *Bulletin de la Société des Etudes indochinoises* (ns), XXX (1955): 18. I wish to thank

Vietnamese power, most apparently retreated into the hinterlands of the Central Highlands, a traditional haven for refugees, where they joined an array of minority peoples already living there.

Even these minority peoples in the mountains formed no homogenous group. Linguistically, they belonged to two major language stocks: Austronesian languages predominated among the Jarai, Rhade, Roglai and Chru of the Cham-influenced Bình Thuận, Nha Trang and Phan-Rang areas, while Mon-Khmer language patterns predominated among ethnolinguistic groups like the Bahnar, Sedang, Hre, and Katu to their north, and the Mnong, Maa, Stieng and Sre down to Đồng Nai to their south. Within these broad groups there further existed an evolving pattern of dialects, only some of which reflect particular ethnic and cultural identities.[66] The Central Highlands, which appeared from the coast as a forbidding mountain range, was in fact an immense limestone tableland with comparatively easy access from the west and the south, and from the north via river valleys. Because of this, its various peoples had long come under the influence of surrounding Khmer or Cham civilizations, as well as that of northern newcomers like the Lao, who were establishing principalities along the north-western border at the same time that the Nguyễn were extending their rule down the southern coast.[67]

The incorporation of Austronesian speakers into *nagara* Campa was substantial, but it did not produce a hegemonic political entity, for in general minority peoples resisted any attempts to establish or impose a hierarchy or authority that took precedence over the village. Even the charismatic Jarai shamans, the Potao Ea, Potao Apui, and Potao Angin, or Masters of Water, Fire, and Wind, whose prestige extended north to the Bahnar and sometimes the Sedang, enjoyed a mystical authority derived from spiritually powerful objects in their possession and not temporal power. They never met, and rarely showed themselves, for fear of supernatural consequences. From the fifteenth century to 1860, the two more potent shamans (Water Master and Fire Master) participated in a ritual exchange of precious objects with Khmer kings, as they did also with the Nguyễn from 1751, with interruptions due to war and rebellion. While written Khmer and Vietnamese sources have caused scholars to see these exchanges as "tribute," it is unlikely that either the shamans or their people understood them that way.[68] As late as 1851, when the French missionary Bouillevaux entered the Central Highlands from the Cambodian side, local informants said the Kings of Cambodia and Cochinchina sent these mystical figures presents every three years.[69]

Although relatively small in number and scattered throughout Đàng Trong, all these peoples would play an important role in the history of the Nguyễn. They were the main sources of slaves to open up Đồng Nai; they supported the Tây Sơn; and many of the products which made Cochinchina famous to the outside world originated with them. Including the minority peoples makes the complex picture of

Nola Cooke for this information. "*Mọi biển*," a term from the Quảng Bình area, designating people who lived by fishing on the sea. The word *Mọi* here may be regarded as an indication that either the Cham or other fishing peoples resided in the region for some time after the arrival of Vietnamese.

[66] Hickey, *Sons of the Mountains*, pp. 4-19

[67] Bourotte, "Histoire des montagnardes," pp. 27-29, 33-38, 52-55.

[68] Ibid., pp. 24, 29-32. Hickey, *Sons of the Mountains*, pp. 157-160.

[69] Hickey, *Sons of the Mountains*, p. 66.

Nguyễn history all the more intricate, even though our sources about them are much more limited.

# NGUYỄN RULE

## INTRODUCTION

Nguyễn rule exerted an impact most directly on the Vietnamese in the new land in two main ways. The first, in the desperate mid-seventeenth century decades of war with the Trịnh, was through the armed forces. The second, prevalent during the comparatively calmer eighteenth century, was through the evolution of the Nguyễn fiscal system. Together they represented a basic shift in emphasis in the Nguyễn style of rule from the unabashed military regime of early Đàng Trong, which symbolically organized the whole country into fighting units, to the mid-eighteenth century independent kingdom with its own approach to the problems of civil government. The self-perceptions of Nguyễn rulers reflected the change: in the seventeenth century, the Nguyễn Lord (*chúa*) was general-in-chief of the armed forces, and only such a person could become paramount ruler; but from the start of the eighteenth century, Nguyễn rulers saw themselves as royalty, with all that such an elevation in status and prestige implied. However, rather than consider the ruling elite and court politics, which feature in most histories of this period, this chapter tries instead to consider the ways Nguyễn rule most affected the lives of their Vietnamese subjects. We begin with the seventeenth century military regime, which made it possible for Nguyễn rule to survive in the first place.

## THE MILITARIZATION OF EARLY ĐÀNG TRONG

When Nguyễn Hoàng came to Thuận Hóa in 1558, the Lê Restoration war against the Mạc usurpers had another generation left to continue. The frontier protectorate soon passed under military rule as the existing Lê civil officials recognized Nguyễn Hoàng's authority. Rather than reorganize this administration after 1600, Nguyễn Hoàng and his successors continued essentially to rule through a military structure whose senior levels were almost always filled by an entourage of men originating from families of the Thanh Hóa retainers who came south with Nguyễn Hoàng or shortly thereafter. A network of personal relations based on birth, marriage, and patronage knit this ruling group together, while its inherited privileges tended to create an elite social stratum that surrounded, and intermarried with, the Nguyễn ruling family.[1] Military officers largely drawn from this elite class of Thanh Hóa descendants controlled the country, which was organized into twelve units called *Dinh* (literally "army headquarters"), each controlled by soldiers called "protectors" (*trấn thủ*). These administrative terms remained in use throughout the

---

[1] See Nola Cooke, "Some aspects of Nguyễn Rule in Đàng Trong (Cochinchina)," unpublished manuscript, 1997.

Nguyễn period, and were only finally replaced in the early 1830s when Minh Mạng established a system of provinces (*tỉnh*) and governors (*tổng đốc* or *tuần phủ*). Until the 1830s, too, military officers remained hierarchically superior to civil officials, and always held the most important provincial posts. There was no southern equivalent in these three hundred years to the northern proverb: *Quan văn thất phẩm đã sang, quan võ tứ phẩm còn mang gươm hầu* (a seventh grade civil official is glorious, but a fourth grade military officer is still nothing).

For the early Nguyễn, military rule was the only practical option. There was no established literati elite in the Thuận Hóa-Quảng Nam area to staff an elaborate civil administration. When the court established a small administrative apparatus in 1614, it seemed to have had difficulty staffing the three offices (*ty*) that administered law and personnel (*Xá-sai*), finance (*Tướng-lại*), and rites (*Lệnh-sử*). Basically they serviced the army, administered the area around the capital, and gathered the taxes owed on court lands. Their functions were poorly defined and articulated, with their organization outside the capital an ad hoc affair where different combinations of the three offices were more likely than representation by them all.[2] These loose arrangements, reflecting convenience and changing circumstances were typical of Đàng Trong at the time. Everything seemed in a state of flux: individuals, families, villages, and even the capital itself, were all liable to move from one location to another. The only well-articulated organ of power was the army. As a result, one of the first and basic Nguyễn policies concerned with the local Vietnamese population mandated conscripting as many men as possible and training them to meet all requirements. In 1632, *Tiền Biên* reported the establishment of a triennial recruiting system based on a full-scale recruitment every six years, and a lesser levy every three years. As a significant indicator of priorities at the time, a clerical examination was tacked onto the six yearly cycle. The graduates of this "spring examination," called "exempted students" (*nhiêu học*), had their tax waived for five years and could work in the three *ty*.

The Nguyễn armed forces not only contained soldiers but also a company of craftsmen able to satisfy whatever needs might arise for the state, the ruling family, and its retainer elite, even its guests. For instance, when the visiting Chinese monk, Da Shan, needed accommodation in 1694, the *chúa* ordered the army to build it. After three days and nights, a five-room house stood ready for him. Only then was the amazed monk informed that "the craftsmen in the country were all soldiers."[3] No doubt the royal palace and many temples were also constructed by the military. Nor were only craftsmen whose skills had a direct military application involved: a 1741 list of soldiers in Hội An included dye-workers and shoe-makers.[4] From this it might seem that the armed forces were a separate world within Đàng Trong society, except that, as *Tiền Biên* repeatedly stated, the army and the people were regarded as one, as *quân dân* compared to the more usual *dân* or *bách tính* of the north.[5] This alone

---

[2] *Liệt Truyện Tiền Biên*, vol. 2 (Collection of Biographies of Nguyen Dynasty, Premier Period) (Tokyo: Keio Institute of Linguistic Studies, 1961), p. 31.

[3] Da Shan, "Hai Wai Ji Shi," (Overseas Journal) in *Shi qi shi ji Guang Nan Xin Shi Liao* (A new source about Quảng Nam in the seventeenth century), ed. Chen Ching-ho, vol.. 1 (Taipei: Committee of Series of Books of China, 1960), p. 22.

[4] *Bạ Phú Ngô*, 1741, manuscript, kept in The Hội An Relics Management Board, Hội An.

[5] When northerners used the term *binh dân* (soldiers and people), it always referred to financial affairs rather than to the people generally. See *Đại Việt Sử Ký Toàn Thư*, ed. Chen

suggests how great an impact the war and military priorities must have had at the local level, among ordinary Vietnamese.

The Nguyễn recruiting law was very strict. In approximately 1671 Vachet reported that "a man will lose his head if he is found trying to avoid being a soldier." He also added that if a recruiting officer accepted a sub-standard conscript, he too would lose his head.[6] Judging from Da Shan's 1690s account, the process of military recruitment manifested itself in each village as little less than a disaster:

> Every third and fourth month army officers went to the villages to round up soldiers. They captured all the fit men over sixteen years old, tied them to bamboo yokes and took them to the army . . . They could not go home to live with their families until they were sixty years old. Their families were only allowed to visit them and bring some clothes. This situation meant that all the men left in the villages were either old or disabled. It also encouraged parents to send their sons to become Buddhist monks when they were still teenagers, out of fear that they would otherwise be captured by the army.[7]

Da Shan was describing the situation after the Trịnh wars had finished, when the state was no longer threatened and people were undoubtedly less inclined to comply with its conscription demands. Nevertheless, the report certainly suggests the evasions and resistance the Nguyễn would have faced in the seventeenth century if they had made a concerted effort to enforce unpopular policies among their Vietnamese subjects.

In this respect it is significant that earlier observers did not perceive military life as the bleak prospect Da Shan describes. From their accounts, it seemed an acceptable way of life. Vachet, for example, said soldiers cohabited with their wives in small separate dwellings, each with its own kitchen and personal garden. These dwelling units were joined by palings into barrack rows, with identical barracks structures sited fifteen meters opposite each other. More spacious accommodations for officers stood at the end of each row.[8] Abbé de Choisy's account also confirms that "almost all the soldiers in Cochinchina were married," although he added "they could hardly support their own wives."[9] This arrangement is not surprising: in an area where manpower was short and population growth politically vital, keeping large numbers of men unmarried until they were sixty would have been folly indeed. Nor were the armed forces a drain on resources since, as Da Shan explained, "when they [the conscripts] were not needed as soldiers they worked for the state."[10] Furthermore, and in contrast to Pierre Poivre's mid-eighteenth century observation

---

Chingho (Tokyo: Institute of Linguistic Studies, Keio University, 1984), vol. 3, p. 952 and p. 958. (Hereafter *Toàn Thư.*)

[6] Quote from Georges Taboulet, *La geste française en Indochine, Histoire par les textes de la France en Indochine des origines à 1914*, vol. 1 (Paris: Maisonneuve, 1955), p. 67. See also Phan Du, *Quảng Nam qua các Thời đại* (A history of Quảng Nam) (Saigon: Cổ học Tùng Thư, 1974), p. 97.

[7] Da Shan, "Hai Wai Ji Shi," vol. 1, p. 23.

[8] Taboulet, *La geste française en Indochine*, pp. 66–67.

[9] Abbé de Choisy, *Journal du voyage de Siam fait en 1685 et 1686*, ed. Maurice Garçon (Paris: Editions Duchartre et Van Buggenhoult, 1930), p. 257.

[10] Da Shan, "Hai Wai Ji Shi," p. 23.

that Đàng Trong soldiers "were poorly fed and even more poorly paid,"[11] seventeenth-century sources agreed that Nguyễn regular soldiers were comparatively well off. A Dutch report of 1642, for example, noted soldiers received the equivalent of ten to twelve Spanish *reals* (about 8.5 *quan*), 360 pounds of rice and two bolts of coarse cotton cloth each year.[12] To put this into perspective, the same source claimed that married registered taxpayers (aged eighteen to sixty) paid eleven *reals* tax per year, meaning, if it is correct, that one taxpayer supported one soldier at the time. Thus if soldiers actually got 8.5 *quan* per year, it represented quite a lot of money.[13]

In addition to the regular soldiery, each region raised its own local troops (*thổ binh*) and subordinate troops (*thuộc binh*). Unpaid except through indirect compensation gained from tax exemptions, they probably doubled as the reserves and the local militia, perhaps even working as laborers or porters when required. These units, reportedly many times larger than the regular soldiery, may have tripled or quadrupled the number of men for whom military service was the defining experience of Nguyễn rule in the seventeenth century. This militarization of society was unlike anything known in the Lê/Trịnh north, where long-settled, internally cohesive corporate villages were the social norm and bedrock of society. It may be that from the late 1620s to the 1670s, up to half—or more—of the adult male Vietnamese population (with rare exceptions the only ones conscripted for military service[14]) were involved with the armed forces in one way or another. As far as the state's organization of labor was concerned, this must have shaped Đàng Trong society more along Southeast Asian lines, where interlinking sets of personal relations from the ruler down organized the control of manpower and distanced it from the northern Vietnamese model, where internally self-governing villages acted as quasi-autonomous intermediaries in the allocation of manpower to meet the royal government's demands. No such villages existed in seventeenth century Cochinchina, where wartime exigencies ruled the lives of the people. In such a situation it is easy to understand why *Tiền Biên*'s standard formula describing the common people would be *quân dân* (soldiers and civilians), particularly in its early years, instead of the term used in the north: *bách tính* (literally one hundred family names, i.e. the civilians).

In seventeenth-century Cochinchina, the regular army was the main organ of Nguyễn power and the organizing principle of the state. It owed this status and role directly to its continued success in the war against the Lê/Trịnh north. Nguyễn military victories in turn were critically dependent on their organization and their modernization—of the artillery in particular—to counter the great numerical

---

[11] "Description of Cochinchina, 1749-50," in Li Tana and Anthony Reid, *Southern Vietnam under the Nguyễn, Documents on the Economic History of Cochinchina (Đàng Trong), 1602–1777* (Singapore: Institute of Southeast Asian Studies/Economic History of Southeast Asia Project, Anstralian National University, 1993), p. 70.

[12] Cited in W. J. M. Buch, *De Oost-Indische Compagnie en Quinam* (Amsterdam: H. J. Paris, 1929), p. 121.

[13] Choisy said the soldiers were paid monthly five *livres* (five francs) in money, one box of rice, and some fish sauce. See Choisy, *Journal du voyage*, p. 257.

[14] Only one source refers to non-ethnic Vietnamese conscripts, saying there were "some soldiers rounded up from the mountains." However, they may have been used in non-military support roles like porters or laborers. Lê Đản, *Nam Hà Tiệp Lục*, manuscript kept in École Française d'Extrême-Orient, Paris, shelf number I481.

superiority of the Trịnh. Because the artillery was so important to the survival of seventeenth-century Đàng Trong, we will consider it separately after briefly surveying the other crucial components of the Nguyễn armed forces, the navy and the elephant troops.

## THE NAVY AND THE ELEPHANT TROOP

The eleventh-century Vietnamese navy had been sufficiently formidable to take on Sung China and the sea-going Chams, but by the fourteenth century we hear little of it. In the fifteenth century, however, the new Lê dynasty began to develop its galleys into a potent force by equipping them with a number of wooden-barreled cannons in 1428.[15] In 1465, Lê Thánh Tôn approved a collection of tactics and discipline for naval use[16]; a century later, the Nguyễn inherited this naval tradition and further extended it.

Đàng Trong's difficult terrain meant that the navy was a vital component of the Nguyễn armed forces, used regularly as coastal transport to move supplies and troops quickly and efficiently. It also patrolled or guarded the entrances of strategic rivers and canals, as well as taking part in battles at sea against the Trịnh and, in the 1640s, against the Dutch.[17] So central was the navy to Nguyễn military organization that its basic fighting unit was actually called a "boat" (or galley, *Thuyền*), according to *Tiền Biên* usage of 1653.[18] Naval service was part of the common experience of most Cochinchinese conscripts. Da Shan reported they were adept both at land and sea, for "after men were trained as soldiers the court sent each of them to learn a skill. After that, they were sent to different galleys (*Thuyền*) to be drilled."[19]

This fact may help explain the implied confusion between Vietnamese and western sources about the number of Nguyễn galleys in the seventeenth century. In 1618 Borri said the Nguyễn ruler "had always more than a hundred galleys well furnished in good readiness."[20] By 1642, the Dutch reported the number was between 230 and 240, adding that each galley was manned by sixty-four men and equipped with various firing pieces.[21] No doubt this figure reflected a wartime naval expansion, and certainly something of this order would be required for us to accept Alexandre de Rhode's guess that Đàng Trong had "at least two hundred galleys."[22]

---

[15] *Toàn Thư*, vol. 2, p. 555.

[16] *Toàn Thư*, vol. 2, p. 654.

[17] Some Vietnamese historians think that, during this period, northern galleys were more like river craft (*giang thuyền*), while southern galleys were more suitable for the sea (*hải thuyền*). The idea is interesting but needs further substantiation. Nguyễn Việt, Vũ Minh Giang, and Nguyễn Mạnh Hùng, *Quân Thủy trong Lịch Sử Chống Ngoại Xâm* (The navy in the history of opposing foreign invaders) (Hanoi: Quân Đội Nhân Dân, 1983), p. 295.

[18] *Đại Nam Thực Lục Tiền Biên* (Chronicle of the Nguyen Dynasty Premier Period) (hereafter *Tiền Biên*), vol. 4 (Tokyo: Keio Institute of Linguistic Studies, 1961), p. 55.

[19] Da Shan, "Hai Wai Ji Shi," vol. 1, p. 23.

[20] Christoforo Borri, *Cochinchina* (London, 1633. New York: Da Capo Press, facsimile republished, 1970), p. H5.

[21] Buch, *De Oost-Indische Companie en Quinam*, p. 122.

[22] Alexandre de Rhodes, *Histoire du royaume de Tunquin*, Vietnamese edition (Ho Chi Minh City: Ủy ban Đoàn kết Công Giáo, 1994), p. 33.

This was confirmed by the Abbe de Choisy's figure of two hundred, in 1686.[23] Whatever the case, it is worth noting that military service in seventeenth century Đàng Trong exposed a historically huge proportion of ordinary Vietnamese men to the sea and to seafaring, to an extent unknown in the north. This familiarity with the sea may in turn have helped bring about a small but significant direct Vietnamese involvement in overseas trade, a radical departure from previous Vietnamese tradition which we will consider in the next chapters.

To support the navy, the Nguyễn established a special coast-watching group, the *tuần hải* (sea patrol), who reported regularly and were backed up by a series of watchtowers along the coastline.[24] They also organized military re-supply stations along the coast, though our only information about them is indirect, taken from Da Shan's experience in 1695. Traveling in a galley with sixty-four soldiers, the monk was disturbed to find no cooking utensils on board until he learned there were supply points established along the coast where food was prepared for travelers like himself and his military companions.[25] Unfortunately, *Tiền Biên* usually only mentions such important but commonplace strategic activities if the ruler himself was involved in some way as, for example, in a 1667 entry which noted the *chúa Hiền* (Nguyễn Phúc Tần, r. 1648-1687) supervised in person the dredging of Ho Xa port (Quảng Trị) to allow rice to be transported there.[26]

When we turn to the elephant troops, where Tongking is concerned, European estimates of the number of elephants commanded by the Trịnh tend to be higher than the Lê chronicle's modest estimate of one hundred in 1610.[27] Alexander de Rhodes thought the Trịnh had three hundred elephants in the 1650s,[28] while Samuel Baron's figure was slightly higher: he calculated there were between three to four hundred elephants in the 1680s.[29] Wild elephants were quite rare in the north, so the only means of tripling the Trịnh elephant troop in forty years would have been by war, tribute, or trade, and none of these means apparently produced more than a scant supply of elephants in the seventeenth century.[30] Cochinchina, on the other hand, enjoyed the great advantage of being able to breed elephants virtually

---

[23] Choisy, *Joural du voyage*, p. 253.

[24] *Tiền Biên*, vol. 3, p. 48. The towers are pictured in an early seventeenth-century Japanese painting called "Scroll of the Chaya's ship trade to Cochinchina," now kept in the Jomyo temple in Nagoya; also in a drawing of ships on the Faifo River (Thu Bồn river), in John Barrow, *A Voyage to Cochinchina, in the years 1792 and 1793* (Kuala Lumpur: Oxford University Press, 1975).

[25] Da Shan, "Hai Wai Ji Shi," vol. 4, p. 2.

[26] *Tiền Biên*, vol. 5, p. 73.

[27] *Toàn Thư*, vol. 3, p. 928.

[28] Alexandre de Rhodes, *Histoire du royaume de Tunquin*, p. 33.

[29] Samuel Baron, "A Description of the Kingdom of Tonqueen," in A. W. Churchill, ed., *A Collection of Voyages and Travels*, vol. VI ( London: 1732), p. 7.

[30] Today only three provinces from the Trịnh area—Lai Châu and Sơn La in the northwest, Nghệ Tĩnh in the center—have elephants. Although some may have been procured from Thai or Mường peoples in the northwest, in the seventeenth and eighteenth centuries Vietnamese relations with these peoples seem no closer than their relations with the Lao on the western border. According to *Toàn Thư*, Lao from modern Xieng Khoang province only began sending elephants as tribute to the Trịnh at about 1700, after the Nguyễn war had finished; before that, they would probably have had to trade for them.

everywhere but in Quảng Nam, making credible a 1642 Dutch estimate that the king owned six hundred war elephants.[31]

In the seventeenth century, the Nguyễn rulers took a close personal interest in drilling their elephants troops, as they took an interest in naval and army training in general. Even in the 1690s, the *chúa* still perceived himself as military commander-in-chief and acted accordingly. During Da Shan's stay, the ruler spent a fortnight personally supervising elephant troop training. The visiting monk was invited to accompany him and left a vivid account of the proceedings:

> The king was sitting on an elephant which was taller and larger than any other, with his guards around him. In the western part of the arena stood ten elephants with red lacquer saddles [. . . each of which] could hold three soldiers.[32] . . . The *xiang nu*[33] held hooks and stood by the elephants.
>
> In the east part of the ground [about one thousand meters away] stood five hundred soldiers with knives, spears and guns in their hands. . . . As soon as the signal was given the soldiers ran firing towards the elephants, but the beasts stood still. Then the bronze drums began beating, the *xiang nu* poked the elephants' flanks and they furiously charged the soldiers, who all started running to escape them. The elephants bowled over some soldiers, and the soldiers riding the elephants then jabbed those poor soldiers [underfoot] with hooks and spears, causing them to bleed. . . . This battle allowed the court to distinguish the best and the worst elephants. Promotions and punishments for officers and soldiers were also based on its results. . . . The king then told me that each elephant was surrounded by fifty soldiers during battle. . . .[34]

These elephants, Da Shan was told, had "greatly benefited the country" in the war against Tongking.

But if Nguyễn Cochinchina owed its survival to any one military unit, it was surely to its artillery.

## THE NGUYỄN ARTILLERY

Artillery was known in Vietnam from at least the fourteenth century. Chế Bồng Nga, the great Cham king, had been killed by Vietnamese cannon fire in an abortive Cham invasion of 1390. The *Ming Shi* (History of Ming) even claimed the Chinese learned how to build cannons from the Vietnamese after they invaded Đại Việt in 1407,[35] although this probably refers to a particular type of weapon, since Kublai Khan had used artillery in his 1281 attempted invasion of Japan, and cannons built in

---

[31] "A Japanese Resident's Account," in Li and Reid, *Southern Vietnam under the Nguyen*, p. 31.

[32] A Dutch account described it as "a small house in which can sit four men and their drivers with firearms." See Buch, *De Oost-Indische Compagnie en Quinam*, p. 122.

[33] Slaves who led the elephants, whom Borri called *Nayre*, or possibly "*nài rồ*" meaning savage elephant-keeper.

[34] Da Shan, "Hai Wai Ji Shi," vol. 2, p. 26.

[35] *Ming Shi*, vol. 92 (Beijing: reprinted by Zhong Hua Shu Ju, 1974), pp. 2263–2264.

1372 and 1378 have been unearthed in northern China.[36] More to the point here, cannons were no novelty to the Nguyễn. In 1593, a long campaign by Lê Restoration forces against the Mạc ended almost immediately when Nguyễn Hoàng brought "large cannon of all types" to the battle. It caused a sensation. As Keith Taylor put it, "there is an air of the exotic and the marvelous in the northern annal's perception of Nguyễn Hoàng's arrival. He bursts with amazing wealth and a wonderful engine of war into a scene straitened by poverty and powerful enemies."[37]

We do not know when the Nguyễn got their first cannon nor its provenance; but as Japanese merchants were usually forbidden to export firearms[38] and Chinese traders had difficulty accessing artillery, it seems most likely the guns came mainly from Macao.[39] Cristoforo Borri, a Vietnamese speaking Jesuit resident in Vietnam during the 1620s, asserted the rather curious view that the first European artillery had arrived fortuitously, via shipwrecks. According to him, the decision of Nguyễn Phúc Nguyên (r. 1613–1635) to rebel was prompted by finding himself "suddenly furnished with divers pieces of artillery recovered and gotten out of the ship-wreck of sundry ships of the Portugals and Hollanders. . . ." More relevant here, Borri went on to observe that, by constant practice, the Cochinchinese army had become "so expert in the managing of them, that they surpass our Europeans."[40] At last, regardless of the artillery's original source, its value and significance were immediately understood by the early seventeenth-century Nguyễn.

Artillery was critical to Nguyễn defense right from the start. According to the *Tiền Biên*, when in 1631 the Nguyễn built the first of the two great defensive walls in Quảng Bình, the Lũy Nhật Lệ, cannon were set every four meters along the twelve thousand meter wall, with a large battery at every twelve to twenty meters. "Ammunition," it added, "was so abundant that the depots were like mountains."[41] Given that in 1642 Johan van Linga had estimated the Nguyễn's cannon numbered only two hundred,[42] quite such a wealth of cannonry seems unlikely at the start of the 1630s. But even allowing for an element of boastful exaggeration in the nineteenth-century Nguyễn source, there can be no doubt of the vital role artillery played in ensuring Đàng Trong's survival. As Boxer recognized, no mainland Southeast Asian state except "Annam, or Cochinchina" ever developed its artillery

---

[36] Liu Xu, *Zhong Guo Gu Dai Huo Pao Shi* (A history of cannon in ancient China) (Shanghai: Shanghai Ren Min Press, 1989), p. 53.

[37] Keith Taylor, "Nguyễn Hoàng and Vietnam's Southward Expansion," in Anthony Reid, ed. *Southeast Asia in the Early Modern Era: Trade, Power, and Belief* (Ithaca: Cornell University Press, 1993), p. 53.

[38] Geoffrey Parker correctly noted this in *The Military Revolution: Military Innovation and the Rise of the West, 1500-1800* (Cambridge: Cambridge Univrsity Press, 1988), yet his claim that "they carried no guns at all" was not correct. In 1628 a Red-seal ship, which took several cannons and 200 muskets to Taiwan, was arrested on this account by the Dutch Governor-General in Taiwan. See Qi Jia Lin, *Tai Wan Shi* (History of Taiwan) (Taipei: Zili Wanbao Press, 1985), p. 17. The original source it used is *Beziehungen der niederlandischen Ostindischen Kompanie zu Japan in siebzehnten Jahrhundert*, p. CXXII.

[39] Before 1660, Dutch-controlled Taiwan might have provided another source of firearms for the Nguyễn except that Nguyễn relations with the Dutch were generally poor, so it seems unlikely.

[40] Borri, *Cochinchina*, p. H3.

[41] *Tiền Biên*, vol. 2, p. 20.

[42] Li and Reid, *Southern Vietnam under the Nguyễn*, p. 30.

into a really effective arm,[43] and historians have long credited the superior Nguyễn ordnance as one of the main reasons they were able to defeat a determined army many times larger than their own.[44] Arguing more generally, Victor Lieberman has recently suggested how significant for state formation in seventeenth- and eighteenth-century mainland Southeast Asia was the presence or absence of a decisive element like access to advanced weaponry. Partly on this basis, Siam developed into a strong state while neighboring Cambodia and Laos were correspondingly weakened.[45] The same logic surely applies to seventeenth-century Đàng Trong.

The reason why the Nguyễn were able to maintain access to, and superiority in, artillery may lie in the fact that they cast their own cannon locally. Exactly when this started remains a question. Earlier scholars thought that a Portuguese, Joao da Cruz, had set up this foundry as early as 1615[46] but, as Pierre-Yves Manguin has recently argued, it then made no sense for the Nguyễn to have sent three thousand kilograms of copper to Macao in 1651 so that cannons could be made for them there. Instead, Manguin believes da Cruz arrived in 1658.[47] Yet *Tiền Biên* recorded the existence of a cannon foundry with eighty workmen in 1631, located in a Huế quarter called Phường Đức (casting quarter)[48] where da Cruz later worked.[49] Technical differences between Vietnamese and Portuguese methods of cannon casting may account for this confusion, with the more advanced European techniques for casting larger ordnance displacing local methods once da Cruz arrived. Certainly, by the time da Cruz died in 1682 the Nguyễn were producing most of their cannons locally, following Portuguese methods. Only this can account for the reported six-fold increase in their number from two hundred in 1642, to 1,200 in Poivre's 1750 narrative.[50]

Exactly how useful those cannon were by the 1750s is moot, however. During the seventeenth century, no traveler to the region had failed to mention the impressiveness of the Nguyễn army.[51] But nearly three generations after the Trịnh-Nguyễn wars had ended, Poivre roundly criticized the Đàng Trong military, and the artillery in particular: "The Cochinchinese take no notice, or are unaware, of what could make this artillery useful. None of the cannons has got six shots to fire and

[43] C. R. Boxer, *Portuguese Conquest and Commerce in Southern Asia 1500-1750*, (London: Variorum Reprints, 1985), pp. VII 165–166. By using the term "Annam," he may also have included Tongking in his assessment.

[44] For instance, see Lê Thanh Khôi, *Le Viet Nam* (Paris: Les Editions de Minuit, 1955), p. 251; D. G. Hall, *A History of South-east Asia* (London: Macmillan & Co Ltd., 1968), p. 415.

[45] Victor Lieberman, "Local Integration and Eurasian Analogies: Structuring Southeast Asian History, c. 1350-c. 1830," *Modern Asian Studies* 27, 3 (1993): 493.

[46] See Leopold Cadiere, "Le Mur de Đồng hới," *Bulletin de l'Ecole Française d'Extrême-Orient* (hereafter BEFEO) VI: 125 n; Charles Maybon, *Histoire moderne du pays d'Annam, 1592-1820* (Paris: Librarie Plon, 1920), pp. 97-99; Lê Thanh Khôi, *Le Viet Nam*, p. 246.

[47] Pierre-Yves Manguin, *Les Portugais sur les côtes du Vietnam et du Campa* (Paris: Ecole Française d'Extrême-Orient, 1972), pp. 202-206.

[48] *Tiền Biên*, vol. 2, p. 41.

[49] For da Cruz see Louis Chevruils's account in Adrien Launay, *Histoire de la mission de Cochinchine 1658-1823, Documents historiques*, vol. 1 (Paris, 1923), p. 16.

[50] Li and Reid, *Southern Vietnam under the Nguyễn*, p. 70.

[51] They were so impressive that even Navarette, who never saw them, wrote of them in glowing terms. See Domingo Navarette, *The Travels and Controversies of Friar Domingo Navarrete, 1618-1686*, ed. J. S. Cummins, vol. 2 (London: The Hakluyt Society, 1962), p. 381.

most of the cannonballs are not of the right caliber."[52] This scathing assessment seems to have been confirmed when the Tây Sơn first rebelled, when none of these hundreds of artillery pieces were reportedly used in battle.[53] By then Nguyễn rulers may have begun to perceive their cannon in the same way as elsewhere in Southeast Asia, as "more a means of boosting morale and expressing the supernatural power of the state than of destroying the enemy," to borrow Anthony Reid's words.[54] By then, too, Nguyễn rule had moved away from a military-style regime towards an eclectic administration which erected a facade of normative Chinese state institutions (including examinations and civil bureaucracy) over a system of local usages. None of the changes impacted more on local Vietnamese than eighteenth century developments in the fiscal system. The remainder of the chapter focuses on this topic, after surveying the shift towards a less military-based government.

## AN EIGHTEENTH-CENTURY SHIFT TOWARDS CIVIL GOVERNMENT

From the late seventeenth century on, the Nguyễn having effectively won the war against the Trịnh, the sources show a shift in the forms of Nguyễn rule towards a more civil style of government. We see it in the slow rise in political importance of the two main civil officials in the countryside, the *ký lục* (personnel) and the *cai bạ* (revenue), and in particular in the expansion of the examination system. In 1646, a nine year examination cycle (the "autumn examinations") had been added to the "spring" exam attached to the six year recruiting cycle. Essentially, the new cycle consisted of two examinations: a principal examination (*chính hộ*), whose few graduates could become officials or teachers; and a test of poetic composition (*hoa văn*) whose graduates won tax exemption and the chance to work in the three government offices. The greatest change occurred under Nguyễn Phúc Chu, who reformed the system in 1695 by introducing a palace examination and a special contest for recruits to the three government offices that included practical questions on taxes and financial arrangements, the latter an entirely new innovation in the Vietnamese examination system.[55]

One also finds evidence of the move towards a more regular administrative system in the Nguyễn rulers' assumption of royalty. The trend began in 1687, at the accession of Nguyễn Phúc Trăn whose first recorded act was to confer titles and royal diplomas on the spirits of the realm.[56] Nguyễn Phúc Chu followed his example in 1691. Two years later he gave the royal title of "national lord" (*quốc chúa*) to his father and himself.[57] In 1702 he formalized the situation by applying, albeit without success, for Beijing's recognition as a separate tributary ruler.[58] Undeterred by this setback, in 1709 Nguyễn Phúc Chu cast a national seal that became an heirloom

---

[52] "Description of Cochinchina," in Li and Reid, *Southern Vietnam under the Nguyễn*, p. 71.

[53] There is no record of artillery being used in Nguyễn conflicts with the Khmer in the late seventeenth century, perhaps because they lacked mobile field pieces.

[54] Anthony Reid, "Europe and Southeast Asia: The military balance," Occasional Paper No. 16, James Cook University of North Queensland, 1982, p. 4.

[55] *Tiền Biên*, vol. 7, pp. 99-101.

[56] Ibid., vol. 6, p. 88.

[57] Ibid., vol. 7, p. 97.

[58] Ibid., vol. 7, p. 106.

passed down to Nguyễn Phúc Ánh, the future Gia Long emperor.[59] It appears in a 1715 inscription at the Thiên Mụ temple near Huế. A 1729 inscription at Hà Trung temple shows a different but still royal seal, that of his successor, Nguyễn Phúc Trú (r. 1725-38) containing the words "seal of the king of Đại Việt" (*Đại Việt Quốc Vương Tri Ấn*).[60] Finally in 1744 Nguyễn Phúc Khoát completed the transformation from warlord to monarch by "mounting the kingly throne" in Phú-Xuân, one of several ritual and symbolic changes that categorically established the Nguyễn *chúa* as a king in his own kingdom.[61]

As the monarchy was established, a related transformation took place in the government: the development of a more civil, less military, administration. The concept of *dinh*, a term designating territorial divisions rather than military groups, began to emerge when the territories were subdivided into *phủ* (or prefectures), a purely civil term of Chinese origin long used in the north. While military officers remained in charge of the *dinh*, civil officials administered the *phủ*; some of these officials were appointed directly after having passed the examinations with high marks. At court, too, civil mandarins who had been recruited via the examination process, whose families lacked any connection with Nguyễn Hoàng or Tống Sơn county, began to filter into senior positions. The great exemplar is the Nguyễn Đăng family, including the illustrious Nguyễn Cư Trinh, whose four generations of civil officials vied for importance in the Official Biographies of the period with the other great eighteenth-century civil lineage, the Nguyễn Khoa family, whose original ancestor had followed Nguyễn Hoàng south but had lacked the necessary Thanh Hóa and military credentials to flourish in the seventeenth century.[62]

The process of incorporating these rising local men into the court and the ruler's entourage was not always easy or comfortable. The sources preserve several traces of discord between the old military retainer elite and the new civil officials. For example, in 1689, Nguyễn Hữu Hào, son of the famous general Nguyễn Hữu Đật of Tống Sơn county origin, led an army against the Khmer, with the civil official Hòa Tín as an assistant. Hòa Tín later accused the general of corruption, saying he had failed to push forward his military advantage after accepting gifts from the Khmer, an accusation that later caused Nguyễn Hữu Hào to be stripped of all his posts.[63] A similar situation occurred in 1755, when Nguyễn Cư Trinh accused a less well-connected general of the same offense in a campaign against the Khmer, with the same result.[64] At least one civil mandarin, Nguyễn Khoa Đăng, even dared confront the *chúa*'s own relatives, who habitually took large sums of money from the treasury without repaying them. He stopped the palanquin of the *chúa*'s own sister in the street and shamed her by publicly demanding she repay her debts. When she

---

[59] Ibid., vol. 8, p. 113.

[60] For the 1715 one, see the inscription "Ngự kiến Thiên Mụ từ chung," kept in Hán-Nôm Institute, Hanoi, shelf number 5683. The 1729 inscription's shelf number is 5703, kept in the same institute.

[61] They included the use of royal terminology, including redesignating Phú Xuân as "the capital" (đô thành) rather than "principal [army] headquarters" (chính dinh), and the construction of a royal ancestral temple, a *tôn miếu*. For the full list, see *Tiền Biên*, vol. 10, p. 139.

[62] For Nguyễn Đăng family, see *Liệt Truyện Tiền Biên*, vol. 5, pp. 251-257. For Nguyễn Khoa family, see *Liệt Truyện Tiền Biên*, pp. 258-261.

[63] *Liệt Truyện Tiền Biên*, vol. 6, pp. 93-95.

[64] Ibid., vol. 10, p. 146.

complained to her brother, Nguyễn Phúc Chu refused to reprimand Đăng, and gave her the funds to repay the treasury instead. Other defaulters soon followed suit.[65] But although Đăng rose to unprecedented heights for a civil official, his influence was essentially personal, not institutional, and his power depended directly on royal protection. Consequently, as soon as the *chúa* died in 1725, Đăng was murdered by a general of Tống Sơn county origin, Nguyễn Cửu Thế.

On the surface, it would appear that the reforms of 1744 which reorganized the bureaucracy into the six Boards traditional in China and Tongking should have tipped the balance of power towards civil officials. Yet it is unlikely that they did so. As Cadiere noted long ago when discussing the alteration in costume that accompanied these reforms, the changes of the 1740s were highly symbolic in nature. They responded partly, at least, to the threat to Nguyễn rule implicit in the widespread prophecy that predicted the Nguyễn would "return to the capital" in the eighth generation. Nguyễn Phúc Khoát's 1744 reforms fulfilled the prophecy by transforming Phú-Xuân into the capital, and the Nguyễn into royalty, with the appropriate paraphernalia, including a Chinese-style administrative structure. But it is doubtful that the practices and processes of government changed significantly. The creation of six Boards, for example, did not double the number of top-ranked civil officials, as in practice two of these posts were usually held concurrently by the same man. Nor did the reforms displace the central organ of government, the supreme council presided over by the *chúa* and containing the five senior military and four senior civil officials.[66] When a northern-style Sinic examination system was introduced in 1740, it was suspended for twenty-eight years after its first trial, thus severing graduate recruitment to the budding civil bureaucracy at its source.[67]

That the 1744 changes to government were largely symbolic and ritual is also evidenced in the fiscal system, where their passage has left no obvious trace. In the eighteenth century, as the northern threat receded into memory, local Vietnamese experienced Nguyễn rule increasingly through the taxation system, and especially through the distortions created in it by Nguyễn innovations in revenue raising and official payment. The rest of the chapter considers these issues.

## THE NGUYỄN TAXATION SYSTEM: AN OVERVIEW

Traditionally in Đại Việt, the state raised most of its revenue from head taxes and land taxes, although a range of secondary taxes existed along with the liability of adult male taxpayers to conscription and labor service in proportion to the number of taxpayers registered in their village. The system depended fundamentally on effective and consistently revised censuses of the adult male population, and on accurate and appropriately updated surveys of village land holding. To achieve both results, the royal government needed an efficient civil bureaucracy and the cooperation of local village authorities. At the advent of a new dynasty or during the reign of a particularly strong and popular king, enough of these prerequisites might combine to produce a relatively accurate snap-shot of the adult male population and

---

[65] Ibid., vol. 5, pp. 259-260.

[66] Phan Khoang, *Việt Sử Xứ Đàng Trong* (A Vietnamese history of Đàng Trong) (Saigon: Khai Trí, 1969), pp. 509-510.

[67] *Liệt Truyện Tiền Biên*, vol.s 10 to 11, pp. 135 and 154.

the landholding pattern in the villages at the time. But more often, and especially where registered males were concerned, the results obtained derived from an often corrupt collusion between royal officials and local authorities, who agreed and recorded a notional number of taxpayers that in no way reflected actual numbers in the villages. The lower the figure, the greater the local advantage, since the tax burden was then shared out among all the adult males within the village according to communal custom and the wishes of village authorities. In times of disaster, however, when village numbers fluctuated wildly as peasant refugees fled to other areas, state demands based on these agreed notional figures bore down heavily on reduced local populations. The increased burdens in turn often drove even more adult men from declining villages to places whose rising population was not reflected in their tax registers. Such an influx increased population pressure on land in some areas, while it left fields deserted, and hence untaxed, in others. Population mobility was thus a constant threat to the state's revenue base in the traditional system.

Such a system was doomed to function poorly in seventeenth-century Đàng Trong, where not just individuals but whole villages were liable to move from one place to another, where an open southern frontier always beckoned, and where the organs of civil government were primitive. Yet, despite this, the seventeenth-century Nguyễn taxation system seems to have rested principally on the head tax, with foreign sources agreeing that its rate was very high. The Japanese Fransisco, for example, said in 1642 that a married man paid eleven *reals* per year (about 8.5 *quan*).[68] Vachet, who lived there for fourteen years from 1671, gave a similar figure of five thousand cashes (8.3 *quan*) a year,[69] while Choisy in 1687 gave a lower rate of five to six *ecus* (or 4.5 to 5.4 *quan*) a year.[70] It is impossible to verify these claims against Vietnamese sources. Textual analysis shows the 1632 *Tiền Biên* assertion that head tax was set at the level of Lê Thánh Tôn (approximately 0.8 *quan*) was copied directly from the late-eighteenth-century *Phủ Biên*, and most probably derived from the 1760s, or even the early 1770s.

As no other Vietnamese source discusses seventeenth-century taxes, and foreign observers generally agree with each other, we accept their evidence that the head tax was the main tax, as it was the only one ever mentioned, and it was much heavier in the seventeenth century than in the eighteenth.[71] The reason for this may lie in the absence of an effective land tax at the time, which itself reflected the technical difficulties in levying such a complicated tax without an adequate administrative mechanism. If, as late as 1695, Da Shan described the process of conscription as little more than kidnapping raids on the villages, it may be that for much of the seventeenth century the head tax was administered in a similarly random fashion, with the rate set high to compensate for the low number of actual payers. The high head tax rate also no doubt reflected the fact that, until the 1670s at least, a very large

---

[68] Buch, *De Oost-Indische Compagnie en Quinam*, p. 121.

[69] Taboulet, *La geste française en Indochine*, vol. 1, p. 63.

[70] Choisy, *Journal du voyage*, p. 254. He mentioned on p. 253 that 600 cashes = one *ecu* and ten *sols*, therefore one *quan* = 0.9 ecu at the time.

[71] Koffler said that in the 1740s and 1750s a man aged between eighteen and seventy paid five florins (4.25 to 5 *quan*) per year. Koffler, "Description historique de la Cochinchine," *Revue Indochinoise* 15 (1911): 570.

proportion of adult males were exempted from paying taxes as members of the army, the local militias, or as the descendants of Tống Sơn county immigrants.

It was not until 1669, more than a century after Nguyễn Hoàng's arrival in Thuận Hóa, that *Tiền Biên* recorded an attempt to formalize a systematic land tax: "Measure the cultivated land and set the land taxation rule."[72] While we can assume from other hints that land tax had existed before 1669, especially in the Nguyễn base area of Thuận Hóa, it was probably low yielding and irregular.[73] Unfortunately, we do not know the level at which the reformed land tax was originally set because the *Tiền Biên* entry of 1669 simply copied a *Phủ Biên* figure from the later eighteenth century, when land taxes were relatively high and had displaced the head tax as the most important component of state revenue. What does seem likely, however, is that right from the start the Nguyễn broke with previous Vietnamese practice, which had always taxed communal land at a higher rate, and applied a single rate to private and communal land alike. Table One, which compares land tax rates in Tongking and Cochinchina in the eighteenth century, shows how different the two regimes were in this respect. The unitary rate in Đàng Trong reflected the preponderance of private land ownership, especially from Quảng Nam south. The single rate may have also reflected the sheer administrative difficulty of gathering enough detailed information to set differential rates, especially in newly developing southern areas with high proportions of private land but low official penetration. In the late-eighteenth-century Mekong delta, for example, Lê Quý Đôn quoted Nguyễn tax records to show that fields here were not recorded in terms of their size or fertility, but as simple plots of earth: "In Tân Bình there are three thousand taxpayers and more than five thousand plots of rice land. . . . In Định Viễn there are more than seven thousand taxpayers and seven thousand plots of rice land,"[74] and so forth. In this newly opened area, the Nguyễn government was more concerned to enumerate taxpayers than to measure or categorize land. This was no doubt the case for areas further north at earlier stages of development and may well have reflected the situation in Thuận Hóa and Quảng Nam before the 1669 reforms.

---

[72] *Tiền Biên*, vol. 5, p. 73.

[73] For example, *Liệt Truyện Tiền Biên* for 1687 recorded that the government "excused people from paying the land tax which [had] increased in 1669," clearly indicating land tax had existed before the reform. *Liệt Truyện Tiền Biên*, vol. 6, p. 88.

[74] Lê Quý Đôn, *Phủ Biên Tạp Lục* (hereafter *Phủ Biên*), vol. 3 (Hanoi: Khoa Học Xã Hội, 1977), p. 112a.

| Table 1: Land Taxes, North and South*[75] | | |
|---|---|---|
| •For Communal Land per mẫu | | |
| North 1728 | North 1740[a] | South (?–1774) |
| first grade | 116.6 thăng | 60 thăng | 40 thăng |
| second grade | 93.3 thăng | 48 thăng | 30 thăng |
| third grade | 70.0 thăng | 36 thăng | 20 thăng |
| •For Private Land per mẫu | | |
| North 1728 | North 1740 | South (?–1774) |
| first grade | 35.0 | 18 | 40 |
| second grade | 23.3 | 12 | 30 |
| third grade | 11.6 | 6 | 20 |

* Amount of land measured in *mẫu*.[76] Amount of taxes measured in *thăng*.[77]
a. The 1740 reduction seems a special case, perhaps prompted by the natural disasters of the time.

Unfortunately, we have little hard information about the eighteenth-century taxation system before that preserved in *Phủ Biên* for the late 1760s and early 1770s. This means that we cannot describe how the fiscal system reacted to the slowly worsening monetary crisis from about the 1720s, when changes in external markets choked off the import of copper coins. Lack of specie ultimately prompted a disastrous attempt by Nguyễn Phúc Khoát in the late 1740s to increase the money supply by casting poor quality zinc coins locally. The result was an inflationary spiral that must have put great pressure on government finances, but about which we know little before the late 1760s. By then, as discussed in Chapter Four below, overseas trade had declined drastically and with it one of the principal sources of state revenue.

*Phủ Biên* did record one tantalizing detail from 1741, however. That year, Nguyễn Phúc Khoát ordered a list made of all the taxes that had been collected between 1738 and 1740, including those which had been officially levied but not paid.[78] We might assume this was a prelude to a tightening of the tax system, and perhaps it occurred when the money supply first began noticeably to affect government revenue. Revenue from the uplanders seems to have been the object of particular attention. In 1758 special arrangement was made to collect the unpaid taxes from the Phú Yên region.[79] Taken together, these two fragments suggest the

---

[75] Northern figures here are from Nguyễn Đức Nghinh, "Góp phần nghiên cứu triều đại Tây Sơn: Từ mấy văn bản thuế dưới Triều Quang Trung và Cảnh Thịnh" (A contribution to research on the Tây Sơn dynasty: On some tax records of the Quang Trung and Cảnh Thịnh periods), *Nghiên Cứu Lịch Sử*, no. 5 (1982), p. 38. The measure used in the north was *bát*. According to Lê Quý Đôn, one *bát* in the north equals one *thăng* in the south. See *Phủ Biên*, vol. 3, p. 92b.

[76] One *mẫu* = 3,600 square metres in the north, and 5,000 square metres in the central Vietnam south. See "Glossary of Vietnamese Terms," in Li and Reid, *Southern Vietnam under the Nguyễn*, p. 146.

[77] One *thăng* = 0.5 litres of rice. Ibid., p. 147.

[78] *Liệt Truyện Tiền Biên*, vol. 10, p. 135.

[79] Ibid., vol. 10, p. 148.

same conclusion: even by the 1760s, the organs of Nguyễn rule lacked the ability fully to enforce the state's fiscal demands. If too much pressure was applied, people often responded evasively. In a quintessentially Southeast Asian manner, some even moved beyond Nguyễn power entirely, according to Poivre's mid-century account:

> The prince overburdens them with taxes beyond their means, and the mandarins with extortion and corvée duties. Consequently it is observed that the kingdom loses people every day. Many Cochinchinese leave their native land to go to live on neighboring islands; others escape to the mountains of Cambodia and go as far away as the Kingdom of Siam.[80]

We should not press the point too far: not everyone could leave, nor would everyone wish to. Yet the threat of large-scale migration away from highly taxed areas must have been real enough to cause local officials to bend the rules and either fail to collect an undetermined proportion of taxes or collect only a lesser amount which they kept themselves.

The lack of earlier comparative data and the need for caution in the face of our ignorance means we cannot assume the rapacious taxation system revealed in *Phủ Biên* from 1769 was the norm for late Đàng Trong. Some aspects do seem typical, however, especially the large proportion of tax-exempt individuals recorded for Quảng Nam protectorate in 1769. Despite the development of the land tax, it seems from these records that the real burden of the head tax may have remained comparatively high here, and perhaps elsewhere, because a considerable proportion of registered taxpayers were exempted. If we calculate average taxes from *Tiền Biên* alone, we get a low eighteenth century head tax rate per registered taxpayer in Thuận Hóa of 1.21 *quan*, with 1.47 *quan* for Quảng Nam and further south.[81] But cross-checking with the *Phủ Biên*—the main source of the *Tiền Biên*—reveals an important discrepancy between the number of registered men (*đinh*), and of those who actually paid taxes in Quảng Nam. In Điện Bàn county, for instance, there were 29,705 registered males in 1769, but only 16,995 of them paid tax. To come closer to a genuine average, we must use the number of actual taxpayers in the calculation, as in Table Two. This process reveals that about 40 percent of men here paid no taxes to the state, although 85 percent of state revenue at the time came from this area.[82]

---

[80] "Description of Cochinchina," in Li and Reid, *Southern Vietnam under the Nguyễn*, p. 7

[81] *Tiền Biên*, vol. 11, pp. 154-155.

[82] My calculations from data in the *Phủ Biên* (Hanoi edition), pp. 178-183. These figures should only be treated as indicative, as there are no other sources that can be cross checked.

| Table 2: Average Tax Paid per Taxpayer in Quảng Nam Protectorate, 1769 | | | |
|---|---|---|---|
| Area | Taxpayers Registered | Actual Taxpayers [%] | Average per Taxpayer* |
| Điện Bàn | 29,705 | 16,995 [57%] | 4.07 |
| Thăng Hoa | 19,980 | 12,696 [63%] | 4.15 |
| Quảng Ngãi | 22,246 | 8,711 [39%] | 3.78 |
| Quy Nhơn | 24,227 | 10,815 [45%] | 8.62 (4.46 or 3.49)[83] |
| Phú Yên | 6,804 | 4,439 [65%] | 4.25 |
| Bình Khang | 5,102 | 3,414 [66%] | 2.69 |
| Diên Khánh | 3,057 | 1,806 [59%] | 3.25 |
| Bình Thuận | 13,995 | 13,129 [93%] | 1.67 |

* Amount of taxes measured in *quan*.

Head tax still made up more than half of a taxpayer's dues. Table Three below shows its dominant position for the Thuận Hóa and Quảng Nam areas.[84] The head tax also included several minor imposts, which can be summarized as money for corvée and gifts (*điều*). Table Four records these in Thuận Hóa and Quảng Nam. It seems likely that these elements of the head tax might not have increased much over the years.

The 1769 figures also suggest that people in Quảng Nam paid more land tax as well. According to the Saigon edition of *Phủ Biên*, for every one thousand *thăng* of rice produced, a Thuận Hóa peasant paid 2 percent in kind and sixty *đồng* (or cents, one string of coins contained six hundred *đồng*) in money. But from Quảng Nam south, every one thousand *thăng* of rice harvested attracted 120 *đồng*, or twice the cash tax of Thuận Hóa.[85] Lê Quý Đôn reported that people claimed that these taxes only appeared after 1765,[86] when the Regent Trương Phúc Loan manipulated the succession in order to place a malleable child on the throne instead of an older candidate (the father of Gia Long, who would later become emperor). The Hanoi

---

[83] According to Lê Quý Đôn, *Phủ Biên*, in 1774 the secondary taxes from Thuận Hóa and Quảng Nam totaled 76,467 *quan*, with 62,545 *quan* from Quảng Nam areas. The main taxes collected from Quảng Nam in 1769 were 241,995 *quan*, plus 56.68 bars of gold (101,164 *quan*). From Thuận Hóa in 1773 they were 153,600 *quan*. The *Tiền Biên* put the figures for two different years into the entry of 1769. See *Tiền Biên*, vol. 11, pp. 154-155.
  Regarding the 3.49 estimate in parentheses: *Phủ Biên* (Hanoi edition) gives 61,685 *quan* and 20 cashes for Tân Lập Thuộc, and 4,210 taxpayers. Having checked the taxes paid according to different categories in this area from the same source on pp. 169-170, I thought that it might be wrong either in 16,685 *quan* and 20 cashes (which would be 3.96 *quan* per person, closer to the description of the text) or 6168 *quan* 5 *tien* and 20 cashes (giving 1.46 *quan* per person rather than 14.6 *quan* per person, as the first figure suggests). The problem arises because *Phủ Biên* was first printed this century and hand copying allows easy mistakes. Yet, the text may be correct, if one considers that uplander families in Thuận Hóa could be taxed from fifteen to seventy *quan* each.

[84] When analyzing the Tây Sơn's taxes in the north, Nguyễn Đức Nghinh includes the taxes on new rice and transportation into *tien dung* (head tax). See Nguyễn Đức Nghinh, "Góp phần nghiên cứu triều đại Tây Sơn," *NCLS* 5 (1982), pp. 36-42. I therefore include these two taxes in this section, and compare them with those of the north. On head tax, see also Nguyễn Thanh Nhã, *Tableau economique de Viet Nam aux XVII et XVIII siècles* (Paris: Editions Cujas, 1970), pp. 36-38.

[85] *Phủ Biên*, vol. 3, pp. 100a-101b, 109a-111b.

[86] *Phủ Biên*, vol. 4, p. 2a.

edition of *Phủ Biên*, taken from a different manuscript source, suggests these steep tax increases did not occur until after 1769. This edition records that every one thousand *thăng* of rice attracted a tax of 2 percent in kind and a cash tax of 180 *đồng* in Quảng Nam,[87] or three times the rate in Thuận Hóa. This gives a ratio of one *thăng* of rice for every nine *đồng* paid in tax. But if we examine the proportions of paddy rice and *đồng* paid in 1769 in Quảng Nam, we find quite a different ratio, as Table 3 shows. If the figures are accurate, these results imply that the "triple regulation" happened after 1769.

| Area | Rice Paid (in *thăng*) | Cash Paid (in *đồng* ) | Proportion |
|---|---|---|---|
| Điện Bàn | 25,805 | 164,145 | 1:6.36 |
| Thăng Hoa | 53,689 | 383,508 | 1:7.14 |
| Quảng Ngãi | 22,382 | 100,740 | 1:4.5 |
| Quy Nhơn | 41,125 | 317,228 | 1:7.71 |
| Phú Yên | 8,285 | 49,059 | 1:5.92 |
| Bình Khang | 5,628 | 35,572 | 1:6.32 |
| Diên Khánh | 5,616 | 26,324 | 1:4.68 |
| Gia Định (Tân Bình) | 12,154 | 11,636 | 1:0.96 [88] |

**Table 3: Paddy Rice Paid in Quảng Nam, 1769**

Beside noting the additional land taxes of nine *đồng* per *thăng* of rice, the Hanoi edition of *Phủ Biên* specified other charges that were said to form part of the land tax regime. They were:[89]

• Four *thăng* of rice and 120 *đồng* per one thousand *thăng* of rice taxed as officials' salaries, plus sixty *đồng* for them to buy betel;

• Two *thăng* of rice and 150 *đồng* per one thousand *thăng* of rice paid, as gifts to the officials;

• Three hundred *đồng* for carrying each one thousand *thăng* of paddy into the granaries;

• Thirty-five *đồng* for every *mẫu* of land to maintain the granaries;

• Five *đồng* for every 0.1 *mẫu* (0.66 ha) of land for miscellaneous expenses;[90]

• Sixty *đồng* per sack for sewing rice sacks;

• Eighteen *đồng* for each *quan* paid in tax, to keep oil lamps lit in granaries.

At the absolute minimum, this would have meant that the tax on every 1,000 *thăng* of harvested rice had leapt from 2 percent to 8 percent in kind, and from 180 *đồng* to well over five hundred *đồng* in cash. This list of supplementary imposts argues either for a grasping regime in which peasant producers even had to pay for oil to illuminate the state granary, or, as seems more likely, for a more or less

---

[87] *Phủ Biên* (Hanoi edition), p. 164.

[88] The low proportion of Gia Định area might be due to the commutation of some taxes levied in cash into payment in rice. At the same time, it showed that the tax collection in the remote areas was not yet formalized.

[89] *Phủ Biên* (Hanoi edition), pp. 164-165.

[90] The Nguyễn dynasty kept this levy, but only at three cashes per *mẫu*, which was 6 percent of the levy in the early 1770s. See *Nông Thôn và Nông Dân Việt Nam Thời Cận Đại* (Countryside and Peasants of Vietnam in the modern Period) (Hanoi: Social Sciences Press, 1990), p. 99.

desperate attempt to raise revenue and salaries from new sources. In this respect it is interesting that *Phủ Biên* did not give the amounts of money collected per area under these regulations, as it usually did. This suggests that the supplementary taxes, like the rule designating a ratio of nine *đồng* per one *thăng* of rice, came out after 1769[91] and, like many taxes before them, were never successfully implemented. They exceeded both the taxpayers' willingness to pay and tax officials' ability to collect.

That these increases mostly affected the land tax system may reflect Nguyễn recognition of the growth of large land ownership from Quảng Nam south and the Nguyễn desire to shore up revenue by collecting taxes according to property size there. We know that large estates existed from early in the development of the Mekong delta. As the Vietnamese historian of the southern land system, Huỳnh Lứa, has indicated, among the many poor peasants who went south to become small landowners were also rich families who relocated with their servants, animals and other belongings.[92] Such households were well placed to survive and rapidly prosper in the new land, as we see from Lê Quý Đôn's observation that a single family there might own fifty to sixty slaves and three hundred to four hundred oxen.[93] This certainly represents a large economic unit in terms of traditional Vietnamese agriculture.

*Phủ Biên* records showed that Quảng Nam Protectorate had three categories of farmhands compared to only one in Thuận Hóa. However, it added, not all were real farmhands, at least not in Điện Bàn county. Here, ten in every hundred taxpayers could be assessed as farmhands and thus pay a lower head tax even though they were actually owner-peasants.[94] Nevertheless, it still seems likely that a large number of peasants in Quảng Nam were hired hands and that there was a significant difference in the size of properties throughout the area. But why would people prefer to be hired hands in an area where land was still relatively abundant? The most likely answer lies in the way taxes were levied from Quảng Nam south. Lê Quý Đôn claimed taxes here were generally heavier than those in Thuận Hóa; yet the three head taxes levied on a main taxpayer (*trạng*) in Quảng Nam were actually lower than those in Thuận Hóa. It was heavier land taxes that accounted for the extra revenue collected here compared to Thuận Hóa. In Quảng Nam a farmhand paid between 35 to 75 percent of the taxes levied on a *trạng* taxpayer, so that the taxation system itself encouraged smallholders, who could supplement their income from their own few fields, to become farmhands. In turn, the process stimulated the growth of large land ownership, one of the characteristic features of the Đàng Trong agricultural economy

---

[91] A regulation concerning woven mats paid with rice in Quảng Nam would seem to confirm this. In the earlier report, Lê Quý Đôn said that with every one thousand *thăng* of rice, five mats were to be paid, together worth 0.2 *quan*. However, later he said that in Quảng Nam, four mats were collected with each one thousand *thăng* of rice, each mat worth 0.2 *quan*. In other words, for every one thousand *thăng* of rice, the equivalent of 0.8 *quan* of money was paid, rather than 0.2 *quan* as he stated before. However, if we look at the list of money that Quảng Nam paid for mats in 1769, it is clear that it paid according to the 0.2 *quan* rule, not the 0.8 *quan* one. It seems therefore that this rule, as well as the additional land taxes we referred to above, most likely appeared after 1769.

[92] Discussion with Prof. Huỳnh Lứa in Saigon, August 2, 1990.

[93] *Phủ Biên*, vol. 6, p. 243b. For an English translation, see Li and Reid, *Southern Vietnam under the Nguyen*, p. 126.

[94] *Phủ Biên* (Hanoi edition), vol. 3, p. 162. No reason is given for this arrangement, which may represent a compromise between the state and village administrations.

from Quảng Nam south. To allow such wealthy people to pay only several *quan* per head, and to let registered males reduce their taxes by becoming farmhands, meant a real loss of funds to the government. When shoring up state revenue became vital, lifting land tax returns became correspondingly more important here.

Whatever the reason behind the sudden sharp tax increases after 1769, their results were catastrophic for the Nguyễn government. They generated popular discontent in the Quảng Nam protectorate and, as we will see later, helped to ensure the early rapid spread of the Tây Sơn rebellion there. But even without the tax issue, the cost of the Nguyễn administrative system by the 1770s would have undoubtedly sparked a similar response. We conclude with an examination of this Nguyễn initiative.

## THE NGUYỄN ADMINISTRATIVE SYSTEM

In Đàng Trong, unlike in the Lê north, the administrative system formed part of a complex web of fiscal relations. In 1695, Da Shan noted that to become a supervisor of overseas trade (*cai phủ*) cost ten thousand *taels* of silver (or about twenty thousand *quan*) payable within ten days of application.[95] As with their Cham neighbors, official salaries were directly funded by the taxation system. This represented a real departure from the situation that had existed since the thirteenth century in Đại Việt, where officials were remunerated in cash and kind (often in land),[96] and a shift towards the far more usual mainland Southeast Asian practice of paying officials by allocating to them the labor and taxes of a number of royal subjects. In Đàng Trong these designated taxpayers were called "fertile men" (*nhiêu phu*); the number of "fertile men" assigned to each official increased relative to the importance of the post.

In the eighteenth century the Nguyễn added further complications to the basic system. Perhaps building on the notion of payment by officials, in 1707 it was decided that every official had to purchase a certificate of office, ranging in price from 1.5 to 13 *quan*, or be regarded as an ordinary taxpayer.[97] Some time later the *chúa* further ruled that his officials ought to compensate him for the taxes foregone when he assigned *nhiêu phu* directly to them. Thus, separate from the taxes of ordinary people collected as state revenue, Nguyễn kings also took money from their officials under various pretexts as private revenue. By mid-century, an official had to repay the king for his certificate and seal, offer monetary gifts on the ruler's birthday and New Year's Day, pay for his superiors' betel, present gifts to their children, and even recompense palace women. In addition, officials seeking promotion had to outlay huge sums.

Let us consider a *Phủ Biên* example from 1766. When four positions were filled that year at the prefectural level or below, the successful applicant for the highest post, that of prefectural secretary (*ký phủ*), had to pay 540 *quan* and 372 *đồng* to the king and then pay an additional 117 *quan* and 181 *đồng* to superior officials, plus 360

---

[95] It should read *cai phủ tàu*, the officer who supervised overseas trade. Da Shan, "Hai Wai Ji Shi," vol. 5, p. 27.

[96] The amount of cash given varied, while salary land was tied to specific positions. See Phan Huy Chú, *Lịch Triều Hiến Chương Loại Chí* (Saigon: Nhà In Bao-Vinh, 1957), pp. 224-232.

[97] *Tiền Biên*, vol. 8, p. 110.

*đồng* more for them to buy betel. When the money was presented he also had to give a further eight *quan* and 180 *đồng* for the officials' children. In all, this position cost 664 *quan* and 186 *đồng*, proceeds shared between the king and the applicant's hierarchical superiors. The next most expensive post, county secretary (*ký huyện*), required 223 *quan* and 80 *đồng* to the king and then 48 *quan* and 155 *đồng* to superior officials, plus another 360 *đồng* for their betel and another five *quan* and 120 *đồng* for their children, totaling 277 *quan* and 105 *đồng*. To become canton head (*cai tổng*) required 165 *quan* and 135 *đồng*, while a lowly clerkship in a county office (*duyên lại*) cost 82 *quan* and 270 *đồng*.[98] On top of these outlays came the ordinary expenses of office: the initial costs of certificates (1.5 to four *quan* for these posts),[99] and seals (1.3 to 1.9 *quan*),[100] and then the recurrent annual expense of monetary gifts to the kings and to their superiors. The prefectural secretary, for example, had to contribute over fourteen *quan* per annum in gifts at the king's birthday and at New Year, while the county secretary and canton head each had to find more than seven *quan* for the same reasons.

The same system applied at the village level. Village headmen[101] under the Nguyễn also had to pay head tax, unlike their counterparts in the older, more cohesive and better organized villages of the Lê north. Thus while Nguyễn headmen received 1.8 to 2.7 *quan* from their *nhiêu phu* each year, they were liable for a head tax of 2.35 to 3.45 *quan* per year, as well as having to pay for their certificates and outlay other money as gifts at the king's birthday and New Year's Day. All this came in addition to a 47 *quan* payment necessary to secure the post in the first place. Nevertheless, the position was amazingly attractive at the time. So many people paid for these posts that, in the 1770s, a single village might contain up to seventeen *tướng thần* and twenty *xã trưởng*.[102]

The practice of selling positions created a disastrous excess of officials. In 1769, 278 officials crowded Thăng Hoa prefecture alone. Taxpayers recorded here only totaled 14,349, giving an incredible ratio of one official to every fifty-two recorded taxpayers.[103] This extraordinary burden was triple that of Qing dynasty taxpayers in China, where the bureaucratic machine reached the most elaborate level in Chinese history.[104] If we add the offices of Quảng Nam and the central government in Huế to the nine Nguyễn prefectures, we arrive at minimum three thousand high and low officials in eighteenth-century Đàng Trong. The office of overseas trade (*tàu vụ*) alone contained 175 officials. It was said that Nguyễn Phúc Tru (r. 1725-1738) intended to reduce official numbers in 1725 when he succeeded to the throne,[105] but nothing seems to have happened. To do so was hardly in the ruler's own interest: it meant

---

[98] *Phủ Biên*, vol. 3, pp. 125a-126b.

[99] *Phủ Biên*, vol. 3, pp. 124-135.

[100] Ibid., p. 124b. Proceeds from the sale of official seals went to palace women and lower functionaries.

[101] This includes both *tướng thần* and *xã trưởng*. These positions were similar, with both acting as village heads and mainly collecting village taxes.

[102] *Phủ Biên*, vol. 3, p. 122a.

[103] Ibid., pp. 123a-123b.

[104] In the early Ming dynasty the proportion of officials to registered people was 1:2299, in the early Qing dynasty it was 1:911. See He Bo Chuan, "Guan duo zhi huan" (A disaster of redundant officials), *Guang Jiao Jing Yue Kan*, Hong Kong (December 1988): 47.

[105] *Tiền Biên*, vol. 9, p. 126.

fewer officials to collect taxes and less personal revenue from officials for the king. The amounts must have been very substantial. If each officer paid only nine *quan* on average each year to the king, quite a conservative estimate given the examples cited above, it would yield him at least twenty-seven thousand *quan*, or one-third of the secondary taxes of the whole country in 1769. This source of revenue might have increased in importance as overseas trade declined in the 1760s.

In an administrative system where low official salaries bore no relationship to the high, recurrent costs of office, officials at all levels could only recoup their expenses by squeezing those below them in the hierarchy in a repeating process that finally ended with the common people. Even before the disastrous inflation of the 1750s and 1760s exacerbated both needs and demands, Poivre described the results of the existing system:

> a man who according to the law and his condition need pay the King only three *quan* a year will pay six by dint of harassment from the mandarins. It is their income and that of their officers.[106]

By the 1770s, as inflation and dwindling foreign trade put mounting pressure on state revenues and sources of official salaries, Poivre's exemplary taxpayer was even more heavily burdened, if we accept Lê Quý Đôn's report that, "while the government got one-third [of the money collected] the other two-thirds went into the officials' pockets."[107] When the government attempted to raise taxes in the early 1770s, and to press its claims more rigorously, to protect their own income and interests its officials had little alternative but to wring as much as they could from the people. As we noted, there was a limit to what they could extract from Đàng Trong Vietnamese without causing them to flee elsewhere. As we will see in Chapter Six, by the 1770s uplanders were less able to evade Nguyễn tax collectors and attracted an increasingly disproportionate share of the tax burden. But what must have seemed an expedient opportunity to tap a flourishing revenue source to the struggling government in Phú Xuân very soon proved to have been a potentially explosive gamble: uplander taxes might have been one of the primary triggers of the Tây Sơn rebellion that brought down the Nguyễn state.

---

[106] "Description of Cochinchina," in Li and Reid, *Southern Vietnam under the Nguyễn*, pp. 74-75.
[107] *Phủ Biên*, vol. 4, p. 1b.

# THE FOREIGN MERCHANTS

## INTRODUCTION

Traditionally, Vietnamese authorities did not seek to encourage trade, overseas trade in particular. The thirteenth-century Chinese traveler's book, *Zhu Fan Zhi*, summed up Đại Việt's usual attitude towards trade in a single sentence: "This country does not trade [with foreigners]."[1] Little had changed by the fifteenth century. Documents from Okinawa (or Ryukyu), one of Asia's great trading hubs at the time, recorded only one contact with Đại Việt, and that was the result of an Okinawan initiative.[2] With Luzon, this made Vietnam unique in Southeast Asia as standing outside Ryukyu's trading circle. Siam and Malacca, on the other hand, appear repeatedly in these documents, revealing the strong trade connections with the outside world that Tome Pires's account confirms. But two centuries later the situation had been transformed. Comparing the fifteenth and sixteenth century Okinawan documents with the seventeenth- and eighteenth-century Japanese trading records, the *Kai-hentai*, a striking change is immediately obvious: in the early seventeenth century, the emerging Nguyễn state headed the list of Japanese trading contacts in mainland Southeast Asia. More ships (and junks) now traded with Đàng Trong than with Siam and Cambodia.

Fortuitously, Cochinchina had been born at exactly the right time, into an "age of commerce," as Anthony Reid has put it.[3] It was this lucky conjunction between internal political change and external economic development that enabled the new southern Vietnamese state to become rich enough and strong enough in a few short decades to be able to secure its independence from the north and to fund its expansion to the south. Without trade and commerce, it is doubtful whether Đàng Trong could even have survived. Despite its abundant natural resources, the fledgling state lacked too many essentials like manpower and money, and it was confronted by the difficulties inherent in establishing itself in a new land wrested from another people and culture. Overseas trade was the engine driving Đàng Trong's spectacular development. It is the crucial factor explaining how this thinly populated land was able to resist an enemy which had access to double or triple Cochinchina's resources in almost every way. For other Southeast Asian countries

---

[1] Zhao Ru Shi, *Zhu Fan Zhi*, vol. 1 (Beijing: Zhong Hua Shu Ju, 1956), p. 1.

[2] Recorded in *Rekidai Hoan* (Precious Documents of Successive Generations), a collection of documents and letters exchanged between Ryukyu and other Asian countries. The only entry concerning Vietnam was an official letter sent there in 1509, very different in style and with much richer gifts than normal to other Southeast Asian countries, and thus more like inter-government contacts than a trade relationship. See Atsushi Kobata and Mitsugu Matsuda, *Ryukyuan Relations with Korea and South Sea Countries* (Kyoto: Atsushi Kobata, 1969), p. 185.

[3] For the term, see Anthony Reid, *Southeast Asia in the Age of Commerce 1450-1680*, 2 vols. (New Haven: Yale University Press, 1988).

the question of overseas trade may only have been a matter determining whether they were rich or poor. For early Cochinchina, it was a question of life or death.

The year 1600 formed a watershed for overseas trade in Cochinchina. Before then, trade had occurred without government attention or interference. Portuguese traders had arrived from Macao in the 1550s, but the most important impetus to local trade came in 1567 when the Ming emperor reversed the dynasty's traditional policy banning South Sea trade and decided to allow trade and navigation with Southeast Asian countries, although continuing to ban direct trade with Japan. A decade later, one Chinese source reported fourteen junks were coming from Fujian to Thuận Hóa bearing copper, iron, and porcelain to trade.[4] But in the 1590s, the Japanese government began to authorize foreign trade by issuing Red Seals to certain legitimate traders (*shuin-sen*) who circumvented the Ming prohibition by visiting entrepôt ports where they bought Chinese goods. Cochinchina benefited particularly from this traffic. Of the ten authorized Japanese trading ships listed in an official report written by the governor of Fu Jian in the 1590s, three went to Cochinchina, mostly in search of lead and saltpeter.[5]

In 1600, however, local political considerations intruded on this more or less free trade. When Nguyễn Hoàng finally gave up hope of winning power in the north, he returned determined to set up the best possible relations with overseas trading countries.[6] Concerned to protect his Thuận Hóa-Quảng Nam power base against future northern hostility, he turned to foreign trade to provide the needed resources to meet the coming dangers. If encouraging foreign trade was a solution to Nguyễn Hoàng's predicament, in the Red Seal ships he found a means already at hand. The Japanese trade gave Đàng Trong, and its Nguyễn rulers, hope for the future. This chapter introduces the foreign merchants—principally Japanese, Chinese, and European—whose trade and commerce was to prove so vital for the survival of the new state. We will consider them in turn, beginning with the Japanese.

## THE JAPANESE

The Red Seal ships did not occasion the first official contact between Japan and Cochinchina. That honor fell to a Japanese pirate, Shirahama Kenki. The first Japanese to be mentioned in the *Tiền Biên*, Kenki, was ironically mistaken for a Westerner when, in 1585, he "came to Cửa Việt with five large ships and plundered the coast."[7] Nguyễn Hoàng's sixth son led a squadron of more than ten galleys to the port where he destroyed two of the pirates' ships, causing Kenki to flee. The same Kenki featured sixteen years later in a letter from Nguyễn Hoàng to Ieyasu, the first

---

[4] *Quan Zhe Bing Zhi Kao*, cited by Chen Chingho, "The Chinese street in Hoi An and its trade in the seventeenth to eighteenth centuries," *Xin Ya Xue Bao* (New Asia Journal) 3, 1, (1960): 279

[5] Though the report noted that lead and saltpetre were produced in Cambodia and Siam, only one Red Seal Ship went to each of these destinations. Instead, the Japanese bought these commodities from Luzon, Macao, and Cochinchina where they had been traded by the Portuguese. *Ming Jing Shi Wen Bian* (A Collection of reports to the emperors in the Ming Dynasty) vol. 400 (Hong Kong: Photomechanical printed by Zhu Li Press, n.p. ), p. 4334.

[6] See Keith Taylor, "Nguyen Hoang and Vietnam's Southward Expansion," in *Southeast Asia in the Early Modern Era*, ed. Anthony Reid (Ithaca: Cornell University Press, 1993), pp. 42–65.

[7] *Đại Nam Thực Lực Tiền Biên* (Chronicle of the Nguyen Dynasty Premier Period) (hereafter *Tiền Biên*), vol. 1 (Tokyo: Keio Institute of Linguistic Studies, 1961), p. 24.

Tokugawa shogun, in 1601. In 1599 Kenki's ship had been wrecked in the Thuận An seaport, and "not knowing that Kenki was a lawful merchant," as the letter tactfully explained, a Thuận Hóa magistrate had attacked him and was killed in the fighting. Although the generals had wanted to execute Kenki in revenge, he was still alive in prison when Nguyễn Hoàng returned from the north in 1600.

Nguyễn Hoàng immediately grasped the convenient pretext of Kenki's case to make an overture of good will to Japan, under the guise of wanting "to continue [our good] relations according to previous examples," as his letter discreetly phrased it. The Tokogawa reply praised the Vietnamese actions in the case, and added that in future only certified Red Seal ships, those carrying the same seal as shown on the shogun's letter,[8] should be deemed lawful Japanese traders.[9] Regular trade between the two countries then began. Between 1601 and 1606 Nguyễn Hoàng exchanged correspondence annually with Tokugawa Ieyasu, with all the initiative on the Vietnamese side.[10] His eagerness surely encouraged Japanese to come to Đàng Trong, and the results contrasted with the situation further north where the Trịnh only made official contact with the Japanese government in 1624, and then in a half-hearted way that ended in 1628 with a Japanese government ban on trade with Đại Việt.[11]

The Red Seal trade became very significant with Nguyễn Cochinchina, as Table 1 reveals.

---

[8] Hayashi Akira et al. compilers, *Tsuko ichiran*, vol. 171 (Tokyo: Kokusho Kankokai, 1912-13, Tokyo), p. 483; for the English translation of this letter, see Kawamoto Kuniye, "The international outlook of the Quảng Nam (Nguyễn) regime as revealed in *Gainan Tsuusho*," in *Ancient Town of Hoi An*, ed. The National Committee for the International Symposium on the ancient town of Hoi An (Hanoi: Foreign Languages Publishing House, 1991), pp. 111-112.

[9] This situation pertained generally to overseas Japanese shipping from 1603, as government control of trade tightened there. For details see R. Innes, "The Door Ajar: Japan's Foreign Trade in the Seventeenth Century" (PhD dissertation, University of Michigan, 1980).

[10] There were eight letters from Nguyễn Hoàng, and two gifts sent separately to the Tokugawa government by him in these six years. Six letters were sent from Tokugawa's side. See *Tsuko ichiran*, pp. 481-487. According to the same source, amazingly, there was a large black Cochinchinese ship with 1200 people on board, bringing with them gifts to Tokugawa, including a tiger, an elephant, and two peacocks, arriving at Nagasaki in 1602. See *Tsuko ichiran*, p. 483.

[11] The first letter sent by Trịnh Tráng (r. 1624-57) to the Japanese king in 1624 placed inter-governmental contacts ahead of trade (" . . . we are interested in getting on good terms with your government rather than [with] those small traders"), and ended cordially. But a second Trịnh letter sent in 1627 betrayed a condescending attitude towards the Japanese king: "Ten bolts of silk granted to the Japanese king." It is perhaps not surprising that the Japanese banned trade with Tongking in the next year. See *Tsuko ichiran*, vol. 172, pp. 493–496.

**Table 1: Number Of Japanese Shuin-Sen To Southeast Asian Destinations (1604-1635)\***

|       | Annam | Tongking | Cochin China | Champa | Cambodia | Siam | Luzon |
|-------|-------|----------|--------------|--------|----------|------|-------|
| 1604  | 4     | 3        |              | 1      | 5        | 4    | 4     |
| 1605  | 3     | 2        |              | 1      | 5        |      | 4     |
| 1606  | 2     | 1        |              | 1      | 3        | 4    | 3     |
| 1607  | 1     |          |              | 1      | 4        | 4    | 4     |
| 1608  | 1     |          |              | 1      | 1        | 1    |       |
| 1609  |       | 1        | 1            |        | 1        | 6    | 3     |
| 1610  | 1     |          | 3            |        | 1        | 3    | 2     |
| 1611  | 2     |          | 3            |        |          | 1    | 2     |
| 1612  |       | 1        | 3            |        |          | 2    | 1     |
| 1613  |       | 1        | 6            |        | 1        | 3    | 1     |
| 1614  |       | 1        | 7            |        | 2        | 3    | 4     |
| 1615  |       |          | 5            |        | 1        | 5    | 5     |
| 1616  |       | 1        | 4            |        |          |      | 1     |
| 1617  |       | 2        | 5            |        |          | 1    | 1     |
| 1618  |       | 3        | 7            |        | 2        | 1    | 3     |
| 1619  |       | 3        | 1            |        |          |      | 1     |
| 1620  |       |          | 5            |        | 1        |      | 2     |
| 1621  |       | 1        | 2            |        | 1        |      | 4     |
| 1622  |       |          | 1            |        |          | 2    | 2     |
| 1623  |       | 2        | 2            | 1      | 2        | 3    | 1     |
| 1624  |       | 2        | 2            |        |          | 1    | 2     |
| 1625  |       | 1        |              |        | 1        | 2    |       |
| 1626  |       |          |              |        |          | 1    |       |
| 1627  |       |          | 1            |        | 1        | 2    |       |
| 1628  |       | 2        | 2            |        | 2        | 3    |       |
| 1629  |       |          | 1            |        | 1        | 1    |       |
| 1630  |       |          |              |        |          | 1    | 2     |
| 1631  |       | 1        | 1            |        | 1        | 1    |       |
| 1632  |       | 2        | 3            |        | 4        |      | 2     |
| 1633  |       | 3        | 2            |        | 1        | 1    |       |
| 1634  |       | 3        | 2            |        | 2        |      |       |
| 1635  |       |          | 1            |        | 1        |      |       |
| Total | 14    | 36       | 70           | 5      | 44       | 56   | 53    |

Sources: Iwao Seiichi, *Shuin-sen Boeki-shi no Kenkyu*, Ko Bun Do, Tokyo, 1958, p. 107.

\* Only one shuin-sen visited Thuận Hóa in 1604 and one visited Cajian (Quảng Nam) in 1604; from the record, it appears that no other Red Seal ships visited these two places after 1604.

Interestingly, this table also reveals considerable Japanese confusion before 1611 about what to call the region under Nguyễn control. *"Cajian"* is *Cacciam* (Cham province), or in Vietnamese, *Kẻ Chiêm* (the Cham place), both referring to Quảng Nam. "Annam" mainly refers to Hưng Nguyên county, Nghệ An, although in a 1605 letter from Nguyễn Hoàng to the Tokugawa government there is mention of one ship, supposedly heading to "Annam," which went to Cochinchina rather than Nghệ An. The fact that Nguyễn Hoàng styled himself "Lord Thụy Quốc, supreme military commander of Annam" may have been the source of this Japanese confusion over the term "Annam." As late as 1611, "Annam" and "Cochinchina" both still appear on the list, though from 1612 on "Annam" disappears completely; either Hưng Nguyên county could no longer compete with Hội An, or the Japanese adopted the name "Cochinchina" from the Portuguese, (or perhaps both).

It should be noted, too, that the name "Champa" also disappeared from the list after 1609, the year that "Cochinchina" made its first appearance. In the next twenty-seven years, Champa appeared only once more, in 1623. Champa's trading decline seems to have been a direct result of the rise of Hội An in the first decade of the seventeenth century.[12] But Cochinchinese competition did not only affect the Chams; Red Seal trade with Cambodia, Siam, and Luzon all diminished, especially in the ten years after 1611.

What initially drew the Japanese to Đàng Trong was silk. They could get silk more easily here because Japanese residents in the main port, Hội An, could collect raw silk in advance of their ships' arrival. This activity became so important that the price of silk in the local market came to reflect the movement of the Red Seal Ships.[13] The Japanese, like the Chinese later, used the north monsoon in January and February to sail to the South China Sea region, and then returned home when the wind swung to the south in July. Aware of this, Cochinchinese silk producers divided their crop into two classes, according to the expected time of Japanese arrival: "new silk" was that harvested from April to June, in time for the Japanese to buy; while "old silk" was that harvested from October to December. Because the junks usually had to leave Cochinchina before July 20,[14] this silk crop had to await their return in the following April. "Old silk" therefore only fetched about 100-110 *taels* per *picul* (or about sixty kilograms), while the "new silk" brought 140-160 *taels* per *picul*. Prices could go even higher. For example, the VOC (Verenigde Oost-Indische Compagnie) records noted that silk cost a high 180-200 tael per *picul* in 1633 when two of its ships arrived in Cochinchina that year, because two Japanese junks had just bought four hundred thousand *reals* worth.[15]

---

[12] Scholars agree that the revenue of Champa mainly came from trading the produce of the mountains and the sea. Growing Vietnamese trade in these commodities so seriously undermined Cham trade that in the later seventeenth century the Chams sent only one ship to Batavia in 1680, and two ships to Malacca in 1682.

[13] Iwao Seiichi, *Shuin-sen to Nihon-machi* (Red Seal Ships and the Japanese Street) (Tokyo: Kei Bun Do, 1966), p. 117.

[14] Thành Thế Vỹ, *Ngoài thương Việt Nam hồi thế kỷ XVII, XVIII và đầu XIX* (Foreign trade in Vietnam in the seventeenth, eighteenth, and nineteenth centuries) (Hanoi: Sử Học, 1961), p. 165.

[15] W. J. M. Buch, *De Oost-Indische Compagnie en Quinam* (Amsterdam: H. J. Paris, 1929), p. 24. I am very grateful to Professor Anthony Reid, who kindly translated and summarized Chapter Two and Chapter Three of this book for me. My information about relations between the Nguyễn and the VOC mostly come from him and from Ms. Ruurdie Laarhaven.

There were various reasons for Cochinchina's popularity with Japanese merchants. Paramount among them was no doubt the chance to trade with China, though this opportunity alone hardly explains why the Japanese would sail to distant Vietnam rather than Manila or Macao.[16] Tokugawa suspicion of foreigners probably played a part in directing Japanese Red Seal trade away from these European enclaves, with their potentially subversive return traffic in missionaries. But what may have ultimately tipped the scale towards Đàng Trong was the personal interest its rulers took in facilitating overseas trade, even at the expense of its neighbors, as an incident in 1611 shows. When a ship bound for Siam was carried to Cochinchina by a storm, Nguyễn Hoàng quickly informed them that "Siam was in chaos and I could not bear to let the ship get into trouble, so I invited them to stay here to trade and treated them with sincerity." When the ship departed, he dispatched some gifts back to Japan with the request that "if you feel well inclined towards us, please send the ship back to our country next year."[17]

The involvement of Nguyễn rulers was important in keeping favorable relations with Japan. Nguyễn Hoàng himself took the initiative with an extraordinary gesture in 1604, when he adopted as his son Hunamoto Yabeiji, a merchant and the first envoy of the Tokugawa government to Cochinchina. He followed up with two letters to the Japanese government, the first announcing he had adopted Hunamoto, and the second asking the Japanese authorities to send Hunamoto back to Cochinchina again with his ship.[18] Nguyễn Hoàng's son, Nguyễn Phúc Nguyên (r. 1613-1635), tried to improve relations even further. In 1619, he married one of his own daughters to Araki Sotaao, another Japanese merchant. Given a Vietnamese name, the new son-in-law became a noble in Cochinchina.[19] These personal contacts did help to bring ships to Cochinchina: of eighty-four Red Seal Ships sent to Annam[20] and Cochinchina from 1604 to 1635, Hunamoto and Araki commanded seventeen between them.[21]

In this period the Nguyễn rulers also actively involved themselves in trading. In a 1634 letter from Nguyễn Phúc Nguyên to the Japanese merchant Toba, another adopted son, the king asked Toba to take one thousand *taels* of silver to buy goods (mainly luxury items, such as "fifty bowls made of half gold and half silver, fifty plates, the same quality," etc.). Then again in 1635, he sent Toba three hundred *lang* (or 11,340 grams) of raw silk and asked that he buy goods for him in Japan to the value of the silk.[22] In November 1633, we find a report to the Governor General of the Netherlands East Indies that three Japanese junks had come to trade in

---

[16] Innes, "The Door Ajar," pp. 59–62.

[17] *Minh Đô Sử*, MS, kept in the Institute of History, Hanoi.

[18] *Minh Đô Sử*; see also Kamashima Mocojiao, *Shuin-sen Boeki-shi* (A history of trade carried on by the Red Seal Ships) (Tokyo: Kojin Sha, 1942), p. 579.

[19] The *Nagasaki Shi*, a book edited in Japan in the eighteenth century, says there was a marriage contract made with a piece of beautiful paper. See *Nagasaki Shi* (A history of Nagasaki) (Tokyo: Nagasaki Bunko Kanko Kai, 1928), p. 427. No Vietnamese source at the time seems to mention such a marriage at all.

[20] Since we cannot identify which went to Nghệ An and which to Cochinchina, we have to include all of them.

[21] Iwao Seiichi, *Shuin-sen boeki-shi no kenkyu* (A study on the Red Seal Ships) (Tokyo: Ko Bun Do, 1958), p. 185 (hereafter *Shuin-sen*).

[22] Kamashima, *Shuin-sen Boeki-shi*, pp. 506-507.

Ayutthaya from Cochinchina, one of them being "sent by the king and some high officials of Cochinchina, intending to invest in the deerskin business."[23] The *Dagh Register gehouden int Casteel Batavia Vant* also says that in 1634 three Japanese junks came to Siam from Cochinchina, one of them sent by the king, hoping to sell their cargoes to either "Moors" or Chinese.[24]

Once war started with the Lê/Trịnh north in 1627, Nguyễn cultivation of the Japanese government bore other fruit. In 1628, four rather anxious letters were sent to the Japanese government, from correspondents including the Nguyễn king and a number of powerful merchants, each asking the Japanese not to trade with Tongking. The response was an immediate ban on Japanese merchant dealings with the Trịnh. The Nguyễn kept the pressure on, constantly reiterating the request until 1635, the year the Japanese quit overseas trading. This stream of letters reveals the extent to which commerce involved much more than making money for the Nguyễn—it had become a matter of their survival.

There are two other reasons that Japanese merchants might have been attracted to Đàng Trong, apart from the access it provided to Chinese goods and the personal interest taken in them by its rulers. The first was commercial: Hội An, the major port of Cochinchina, was a well-regulated entrepôt without very high duties that allowed Red Seal merchants to buy Southeast Asian goods conveniently. The second was cultural. The Japanese seem to have felt at ease with the local people. Certainly, they perceived similarities between Vietnamese, Korean, and Mongolian peoples, all of whom shared with the Japanese in the great cultural inheritance of Han civilization. Thus these peoples alone were classified in *Wakan Sanzai Zue*, a Japanese-Chinese dictionary published in 1713 in Tokyo, as *ikoku* (different countries) compared to the rest of Southeast Asia, which was lumped with the Dutch, Indian, and Arabic peoples as *gaii* (remote barbarian countries).[25] And as the ready intermarriage between Japanese traders and Vietnamese women suggest, not to mention the adoptions of Japanese merchants into the ruling family, the Vietnamese reciprocated this comfortable feeling of similarity.

All these factors helped to make Cochinchina Japan's most important trading partner in the early seventeenth century. So desirable was the Cochinchinese trade in the early seventeenth century that some Japanese merchants apparently forged Red Seal licenses in order to trade with Đàng Trong in the 1620s,[26] while others presented gifts in the hope of obtaining the coveted Red Seal licenses to go there.[27] Although trading in the licenses did occur, it was not legal, as an incident recounted by the English merchant Richard Cocks reveals. In 1617, on behalf of William Adams, Cocks sold a Red Seal license issued for Cochinchina, and a junk, to a Chinese for 1,200 *taels* of silver.[28] The Chinese sold the license to a Japanese, who then sold it to his captain

---

[23] Iwao Seiichi, *Shuin-sen*, p. 264.

[24] *Dagh Register gehouden int Casteel Batavia Vant*, Chinese translation by Guo Hui and Cheng Da Xue, vol. 1; 2nd. edition (Taipei: Taiwan Sheng Wen Xian Wei Yuan Hui, 1989), p. 117 (hereafter *Dagh Register*).

[25] *Wakan Sanzai Zue* (A large Japanese-Chinese dictionary) (1713. Reprint, Tokyo: Nihon zuihitsu taisei kanko kai, 1929), p. 10.

[26] Iwao Seiichi, *Shuin-sen*, p. 87.

[27] Entry of November 3, 1618, *Diary of Richard Cocks*, vol. 2 (London: White & Co., 1883), p. 92.

[28] Ibid., vol. 1, p. 333.

for three hundred silver *taels*. When the Tokugawa government found out, it took Adams to court for it.[29]

During this period, one-quarter of all Japanese Red Seal ships traded with Nguyễn Cochinchina. Although we know that silk was the most prized commodity they imported from Southeast Asia, several other luxury items were also keenly sought, as the following list shows:[30]

> Tongking: Yellow silk, spun silk fabric, damask silk, thin damask silk,[31] *ba xi* silk,[32] cardamom, cinnamon,[33] turmeric[34]
>
> Champa: Calambac, sharkskins, cotton (made of kapok)
>
> Cambodia: Deerskins, lacquer, ivory, wax, honey, black sugar, buffalo horns, rhinoceros horns, betel, *shaulmoogra* seeds, pepper, sharkskins, peacocks' tails, cotton, *yukin*
>
> Siam: Brazilwood for dyeing, deerskins, sharkskins, buffalo horn, lead, tin, Indian cinnabar, camphor, kapok, elephant tusks, rattan, coral, aloeswood
>
> Patani: Pepper, sharkskin, elephant tusks
>
> Cochinchina: Yellow silk, spun silk fabric, damask silk, longzhao, aloeswood, calambac, *ba*, sharkskins, black sugar, honey, pepper, gold, rattan

The table suggests that products from Cambodia and Siam were generally worth more than those from Cochinchina. Deerskin, mainly from Siam, probably made an important difference here. We know that, apart from silk, deerskin formed a staple item purchased by the Japanese Red Seal Ships. Originally this trade did not benefit Cochinchina. But after some Japanese came to live in Hội An, the situation improved. Thus we find in a letter to the VOC from the head of the Dutch factory in Ayuthia that in November 1633 a Japanese junk had arrived from Cochinchina, loaded with about one hundred tons of goods to trade for deerskins.[35] This was not the only junk reported sailing from Cochinchina to buy deerskins here. A few months before, in May 1633, a Japanese junk from Cochinchina had also bought ten thousand deerskins in Siam, though many had been subsequently burnt in a fire in the Japanese street in Ayuthia.[36] This seems to have begun a trend towards Japanese junks out of Đàng Trong buying deerskins in Siam for transshipment to Red Seal ships trading with

---

[29] Ibid., vol. 2, p. 94.

[30] Iwao Seiichi, *Shuin-sen*, pp. 241-242.

[31] There were two kinds of this product: the one produced in Tongking called "Tongking *linzi*" was smoother and thicker than that of Japan. See *Wakan Sanzai Zue*, vol. 1, p. 355.

[32] A kind of thin, hard wearing woven silk, used for making trousers. Iwao wrote it as *ba xi*, but I suspect there are two kinds of woven silk here: *ba* and *you*, *xi* was mistaken as *you*. According to *Wakan Sanzai Zue* , the *you* produced in Tongking was the best. See *Wakan Sanzai Zue*, pp. 357 and 358.

[33] *Wakan Sanzai Zue*, vol. 1, p. 216: "There were many cinnamon trees in these mountains, and the cinnamon of this country [Tongking] enjoyed the reputation of being of the first quality; but since the two countries [Tongking and Cochinchina] have been at war, a large number of trees have been burned and destroyed, so that there is at present quite a limited supply of cinnamon."

[34] A kind of grass used to dye cloth.

[35] Quoted from Iwao Seiichi, *Shuin-sen*, p. 119.

[36] Iwao Seiichi, *Shuin-sen*, p. 264.

Cochinchina. This shift may well account for the decline in the number of Red Seal ships going to Siam (as shown in Table 2), and certainly explains why deerskin became a Cochinchinese export to Japan in the 1640s. According to the *Daghregister des Comptoirs Nangasaque,* almost every ship from Quảng Nam took deerskins to Japan from 1641 to 1648, sometimes up to 8,800 skins in one junk.[37] So heavy was the Japanese demand that when the VOC in Batavia sought fifty thousand skins from Siam in 1641, they could not fill the order because the Japanese and Chinese from Cochinchina had bought up much beforehand.[38]

Specie and silver were also a significant part of the Japanese trade, though we will defer discussing the lucrative coin trade until the next chapter. The value was enormous: for instance, the early Jesuit missionary Cristoforo Borri reported that Japanese junks often brought silver to the value of "four or five million" to Cochinchina,[39] while the Japanese scholar Iwao Seiichi has concluded from certain Dutch sources that each Red Seal ship carried Japanese *kan* ranging in value from a minimum of four hundred thousand copper coins in the early period to 1,620,000 copper coins in later times.[40] From this it seems undeniable that the Red Seal trade with Japan stimulated a real economic boom in early seventeenth-century Cochinchina and made it possible for the Nguyễn to afford the expensive modern arms that enabled them to fight off the north. The evidence is clear: Đàng Trong's existence as a separate Vietnamese state rested directly on its successful commercial and economic development in these crucial decades.

---

[37] *Daghregister des Comptois Nangasaque,* Japanese translation with title *Nagasaki Oranda shokan no nikki,* by Murakami Naojiro (Tokyo: Iwanami Shoten, 1938).

[38] *Dagh Register,* vol. 2, p. 318.

[39] Christoforo Borri, *Cochinchina* (1633. New York: Da Capo Press, facsimile republished, 1970), p. 12. Unfortunately, Borri did not stipulate in what currency he valued this silver: it is too large an amount for silver taels, or even Japanese copper coins. He may have had a European currency in mind.

[40] The Japanese *kan* was worth one hundred *taels* of silver or one thousand copper coins.

**Table 2: Number Of Chinese Junks To Japan From Southeast Asian Countries**

**(1647-1720)**

|           | Tongking | Quảng Nam | Cambodia | Siam | Patani | Malacca | Jakarta | Bantam |
|-----------|----------|-----------|----------|------|--------|---------|---------|--------|
| 1647-1650 | 7        | 11        | 4        |      | 1      |         | 4       |        |
| 1651-1660 | 15       | 40        | 37       | 28   | 20     |         | 2       | 1      |
| 1661-1670 | 6        | 43        | 24       | 26   | 9      | 2       | 12      |        |
| 1671-1680 | 12       | 40        | 10       | 23   | 2      |         | 31      | 1      |
| 1681-1690 | 12       | 29        | 9        | 25   | 8      | 4       | 18      |        |
| 1691-1700 | 6        | 30        | 22       | 20   | 7      | 2       | 16      | 1      |
| 1701-1710 | 3        | 12        | 1        | 11   | 2      | 2       |         |        |
| 1711-1720 | 2        | 8         | 1        | 5    |        |         | 5       |        |
| Total     | 63       | 203       | 109      | 138  | 49     | 8       | 90      | 3      |

Sources: For the period 1647-1674, see Iwao Seiichi, "Kinsei Nitshi-boeki ni kansuru Suryoteki kenkyu," *Shigaku-zatshi*, vol. 62, no. 11, p. 19; for the year 1647, I also used *Daghregister des Comptois Nangasaque*, Japanese translation by Murakami Masajiro, Iwanami Shoten, Tokyo, 1938 for reference.

For the period 1674-1720, my main source is *Kai-hentai*, ed. Hayashi Shunsai (Tokyo: Toyo Bunko, 1958-59). However, I added some figures missed in *Kai-hentai* from *Tosen Shinko Kaitoroku Toijin Fusetu Gaki Wappu Tomecho* (Material for a study of Chinese merchants sailing to and from Japan in the Edo period), ed. Osamu Oba, the Institute of Oriental and Occidental Studies, Kansai University, Kyoto, 1974.

Though the Japanese were important they were not Đàng Trong's only trading partners at the time. The next sections consider the others, beginning with the Chinese.

## THE CHINESE

Chinese trade with Cochinchina only really became possible on a regular basis when Ming Mu-zung lifted the ban on overseas trade to Southeast Asia in 1567. Information for the late sixteenth and early seventeenth centuries is patchy, but one 1631 entry in the *Daghregister* for 1631-1634 suggests Cochinchina may have already been a relatively popular destination: of the twenty junks leaving China for Southeast Asia noted there, five went to Batavia, five to Cochinchina, five to Cambodia, two to Patani, two to Siam, and one to Singgora (Songkhla).[41] But as Hội An's role as an entrepôt grew, so did its attractiveness to Chinese merchant shipping. Table Two gives the number of Chinese junks from Southeast Asian countries to

[41] *Dagh Register*, vol. 1, 1631-1634, p. 66.

Japan between 1647 and 1720,[42] revealing that a large proportion (about 30 percent) of them departed from Quảng Nam. Taken together with Table One, which showed that one-quarter of all Red Seal ships traded with Cochinchina, these figures reinforce our picture of the importance of Cochinchina to China-Japan trade in the seventeenth century.

Yet Table Two does not give the whole story of Chinese trade with Cochinchina. Scattered references suggest Taiwan might also have played a significant role in the seventeenth century. One Dutch source of 1661 referred to Taiwanese junks trading for goods, like rice, saltpeter, sulfur, tin and lead, with Southeast Asian countries including Cochinchina.[43] More specifically, another Dutch source recorded that in 1665 the ruler of Taiwan, Coxinga (Zheng Cheng Gong), sent twenty-two trading junks to Southeast Asia, four of which went to Quảng Nam.[44] In addition, the Japanese record of overseas traders to Japan from 1644-1724, *Kai-hentai*, also noted three Taiwanese junks bought Cochinchinese rice to Taiwan in 1683.[45]

Both geography and climate made Cochinchina an attractive destination for Chinese merchants. Junks could make the round trip from Quảng Nam easily, profiting from changing monsoon winds. Those trading with Japan could profit equally from wind conditions to sail from Hội An to Cambodia before going to Japan, although most of the junks that sailed from China to Hội An only traded there before heading directly to Japan, according to *Kai-hentai*.[46] As Buch commented, the reason so many Chinese came each year to Quảng Nam was its convenient access to a wealth of Southeast Asian products:

> that they found here a center for trade with various nearby countries and places. Pepper was brought here from Palembang, Pahang, and neighboring areas, camphor from Borneo, sapanwood, ivory, *serong bourang*, gumlac, and their *lankiens* [cloth?], coarse porcelain, and other wares. With what remained, they bought further [local] pepper, ivory, cardamom etc., so that their junks mostly returned full to China.[47]

An eighteenth-century Cantonese trader named Chen was even more lyrical in his praise of Quảng Nam as a perfect trading destination:

> It is only six days and nights from Guangzhou to Thuận Hóa and Quảng Nam by sea. . . . It only takes four days and nights and one *geng* [twenty-four hours is ten *geng*] to Sơn Nam [the main port of Tongking], but the goods that can be carried back are nothing but rice and from Thuận Hóa only pepper. Whereas the goods that can be brought from Quảng Nam are so abundant that it seems nothing cannot be obtained from there, it is superior to all other ports of Southeast Asia.

---

[42] Despite the general impression that most Chinese junks were from Canton and Fujian, at least ninety percent of Chinese junks in the Japan-Cochinchina trade were from Ning Po. See Hayashi Shunsai, comp., *Kai-hentai*, 3 vols. (Tokyo: Toyo Bunko, 1958-49),

[43] Cao Yong He, *Taiwan Zao Qi Li Su Yan Jiu* (A study of early history of Taiwan) (Taipei: n.p., 1979) p. 378.

[44] Quoted from Cao Yong He, *Taiwan Zao Qi*, p. 377.

[45] Hayashi Shunsai, comp., *Kai-hentai*, vol.1, p. 392.

[46] Ibid., vol. 16, p. 1154-1155 and vol. 33, p. 2579.

[47] Buch, *De Oost-Indische Compagnie en Quinam*, p. 68.

The goods come from Thăng Hoa, Điện Bàn, Quy Nhơn, Quảng Ngãi, Bình Khang, and Nha Trang, being carried by ships, boats, and horses, by land and by sea, gathered in Hội An. That is why Chinese like to come to buy goods and carry them back. The goods here are so abundant that even a hundred big ships cannot carry them out of here.[48]

Indeed, so lucrative was the Cochinchina trade that, according to some Dutch sources, high Japanese officials still tried to invest in it, through Chinese merchant middlemen, after the official "closed-door" policy was implemented. These sources claim that in 1637 these Japanese received a profit of no less than fifteen thousand *taels* of silver from the Chinese merchants involved, making them very enthusiastic about this sort of dealing. Thus when three junks came to Firando in that year, Nicolaes Couckebacker, the VOC director there, was stopped from hindering their trade by high officials, both in Firando and Nagasaki, with personal interests at stake.[49] But the situation did not last indefinitely. In 1689 the Japanese government moved to reduce trade links by limiting the number of permitted Chinese junks to seventy per year. Cochinchina did relatively well in the quota set for junks from Southeast Asian countries; it got three, compared to two for Batavia, Cambodia, and Siam, and one for Tongking.[50] A few decades later, in 1715, the Japanese government cut trade links even further, limiting Chinese junks to a mere thirty per annum, and allowing only one junk from each Southeast Asian country; only shipments from Quảng Nam, Siam, and Batavia were allowed to reach the maximum value of three hundred thousand copper coins.[51]

However, Đàng Trong's trading economy did not suffer from the Japanese withdrawal because the Chinese rapidly replaced the Japanese. The late seventeenth and early eighteenth centuries brought even better conditions for Chinese traders and laid the foundation for Chinese domination of southern Vietnam's trade for the next two centuries. Chen Chingho noted three main reasons for this. First, the ceasefire between the Trịnh and the Nguyễn in 1672 brought a century of peace for both sides, until the Tây Sơn rebellion broke out. When no longer at war, and thus no longer in desperate need of imported weaponry, both regimes became less tolerant towards European merchants. This created opportunities for Chinese to play an intermediary role between the two sides. Second, at this time the Chinese commercial companies of Canton, represented by the *shi san hang* (the thirteen lines of business) co-operated actively and effectively, especially the *Cong Hang*, so that their junks "began to provide European ships with Vietnamese products, and at the same time, to provide Vietnam with the Chinese goods and European products which she needed." Third, the 1715 Japanese reduction of overseas trade which cut the number of permitted Chinese junks and limited the value of their trade to six hundred thousand *taels* of silver caused many junks which had previously frequented Japan to

---

[48] Lê Quý Đôn, *Phủ Biên Tạp Lục* (hereafter *Phủ Biên* ), vol. 4 (Hanoi: Khoa học xã hội, 1977), p. 34b.

[49] *Dagh Register*, vol. 1, p. 214.

[50] Iwao Seiichi, "Kinsei nisshi boeki ni kansuru suryoteki kosatsu" (A study of the Chinese and Japanese trades), *Shigaku-zatshi* (Journal of History) 61, 11: 107.

[51] Tongking and Cambodia were allowed two hundred thousand worth. Ibid., p. 108–109.

head for Southeast Asian ports.[52] In 1695 Bowyear had estimated there were about ten to twelve Chinese junks trading in Hội An each year, coming from Japan, Canton, Siam, Cambodia, Manila and Batavia.[53] After 1715, their number had so increased that by the 1740–1750s there were eighty each year, excluding ones from Macao, Batavia, and France.[54] From these figures it seems that half or more of the Chinese junks barred from Japan turned to Hội An instead.

Chinese merchants did good business in Đàng Trong. Unlike western traders, their cargoes were not too expensive for the common people, and thus Chinese goods "sold out very quickly, [with] nothing left," as merchant Chen expressed it.[55] Whereas the main profit of western merchants lay in buying rather than selling, Chinese traders profited both ways. This must surely have encouraged more of them into the Đàng Trong market.

But perhaps a greater local reason for Chinese trading success here can be traced to the Nguyễn's openness regarding trade with China. Traditionally, Vietnamese rulers in the north had tried to keep Chinese merchants at a distance from the Vietnamese, especially from its capital. In 1149, Lý Anh Tôn had opened Vân Đồn (Vân Hải island) as the port of trade, and for several hundred years it was the main place of Chinese trade, until Phố Hiến was set up on the same basis in the seventeenth century. The Nguyễn behaved quite differently once they realized that Đàng Trong needed trade if it was to survive. They decided to use Japanese and Chinese merchants to their own advantage. Not only did they let them live and trade in Cochinchina, but they also employed them as government officers. Both Japanese and Chinese ships carried cargoes and letters from the Nguyễn rulers to Japan or Batavia, as for example in 1688 when a Chinese junk transported a cargo for the ruler of Quảng Nam,[56] while another Chinese junk took a letter from *chúa* Nghĩa (Nguyễn Phúc Trăn, 1687–1691) asking the Japanese government to cast coins for Cochinchina.[57] In 1673, prince Diễn even tried to borrow five thousand *taels* of silver from Wei Jiu Shi, a Chinese merchant who had lived in Cochinchina before moving to Japan.[58] This favorable Nguyễn attitude to the Chinese and Japanese repaid them handsomely. As Borri commented: "The king receives a great revenue out of [attracting Chinese and Japanese merchants], by his duties and imposts, and the country an unspeakable gaine."[59] Indeed, the Đàng Trong economy prospered for over one hundred and fifty years, until the mid-eighteenth century, thanks to its fundamental basis in foreign trade.

---

[52] Chen Chingho, *Historical Notes on Hoi-An* (Carbondale: Center for Vietnamese Studies, Southern Illinois University, 1973), Monograph Series IV, pp. 25-26, quote p. 26.

[53] Alastair Lamb, *The Mandarin Road to Old Hue* (Toronto: Clarke, Irwin & Co. LTD, 1970), p. 52.

[54] Jean Koffler, "Description historique de la Cochinchine," *Revue Indochinoise* 16 (1911): 585.

[55] *Phủ Biên*, vol. 4, p. 35b

[56] Hayashi Shunsai, comp., *Kai-hentai*, vol. 1, p. 854.

[57] Ibid., vol. 2, p. 1034.

[58] Quoted from Chen Ching-ho, "Shi qi ba shi ji hui an zhi tang ren jie ji qi shang ye" (The China town of Hoi An and its trade during the seventeenth and eighteenth centuries), *Xin Ya Xue Bao*, 1, 3 (1960): 298.

[59] Borri, *Cochinchina*, p. 12.

## THE WESTERNERS

According to Manguin, Portuguese first contacted Vietnamese in 1516, with the first official contact with Champa coast following in 1523.[60] Relations were often irregular. While Lamb claimed that the Portuguese began to visit "Fai-fo" (the European name for Hội An) regularly from about 1540,[61] it seems unlikely that regular trade would have begun before the 1550s, when the Portuguese took Macao. Even so, they were surely the earliest Westerners to come to Cochinchina.

By 1584 there were already some Portuguese living in Cochinchina.[62] Even so, Portuguese trade with Cochinchina was definitely secondary to the Macao-Japan trade in the early seventeenth century. Two events changed that situation for both sides. When the Portuguese lost the Japanese trade they turned seriously to mainland Southeast Asia, Macassar, and Larantuka-Solor-Timor as alternate trading partners; this pattern prevailed from 1640 onward. Trade with Cochinchina was mainly in local products—yellow silk, eaglewood, calambac, and some benzoin—and copper brought there by the Japanese.[63] The Nguyễn change of heart had come earlier, in 1627. When the Trịnh-Nguyễn war broke out, cannons became vital to their survival. As Boxer noted, the Nguyễn rulers were "very anxious to secure [guns] from the Bocarro's celebrated gun foundry at Macao, which functioned between 1627 and 1680 and produced what were acknowledged to be the finest bronze guns in the East."[64] It is perhaps no accident that the existence of this Macao foundry coincided closely with the years of Trịnh-Nguyễn war (1627-1672). Although its bronze and iron cannon sold readily throughout Asia, the Nguyễn and the Trịnh were undoubtedly two of the Macao foundry's biggest customers.

Boxer also believed that "though fundamentally hostile to the propagation of the Christian faith in their territory, the Nguyễn more or less connived at the presence of Roman Catholic missionaries largely with the object of obtaining guns and gunners from Macao."[65] While some relationship may have existed between guns and the presence of Jesuit missionaries, the Nguyễn had other, more official uses for them in Đàng Trong, as we see from Nguyễn Thanh Nhã's list of Jesuits employed at court by the Nguyễn rulers generation after generation. In 1686 Chúa Hiền forced his doctor, Bartholomeu da Costa, who was traveling back to Europe, to return from Macao to resume his post. Nguyễn Phúc Chu employed Antonio de Arnedo in 1704 and De Lima in 1724 to teach him mathematics and astronomy. Võ Vương (Nguyễn Phúc Khoát, r. 1738-1765) similarly employed Neugebauer and Siebert, who died in 1745, and then Slamenski and Koffler in their place. In 1752 he appointed Xavier de

---

[60] Pierre-Yves Manguin, *Les Portuguese sur les côtes du Viet-Nam et du Campa* (Paris: Ecole Française d'Extrême-Orient, 1972), p. 3.

[61] Lamb, *The Mandarin Road to Old Hue*, p. 19; George Birdwood, *Report on the Old Records of the India Office*, (London: W. H. Allen & Co., Limited, 1891), p. 175.

[62] Manguin, *Les Portuguese*, p. 186.

[63] C. R. Boxer, ed. and trans., *Seventeenth Century Macau* (Hong Kong: Heinemann Educational Books Ltd., 1984), p. 37, citing a list drawn up by the Portuguese Chronicler-in-Chief of India.

[64] C. R. Boxer, *Portuguese Conquest and Commerce in Southern Asia, 1500-1750* (London: Variorum Reprints, 1985), p. VII 167.

[65] Boxer, *Portuguese Conquest*, p. VII 167.

Moteiro as a geometrician and Jean de Loureiro as a doctor.[66] That Europeans worked officially in the court, even if only as doctors, was something quite new in Vietnam. In China only the Mongols (Yuan dynasty) and Manchus (Qing dynasty) ever employed Westerners at court, while in Vietnam the Nguyễn rulers continued to do so until the 1820s.

In the early seventeenth century, the Dutch also sought trade opportunities in Cochinchina, or "Quinam," as they called it at the time. The first attempt probably occurred in 1601, when Jeronimus Wonderaer and Albert Cornelis Ruyll, two merchants employed by the VOC, spent at least two months vainly trying to establish trade relations and to buy pepper in Cochinchina. Although they were given an audience by the *chúa*, they seem not to have enjoyed their time there.[67] In 1609, the VOC established a factory at Firando in Japan, hoping to enter the lucrative Japanese silk market. As they could not trade directly with China, their attention turned to Tongking and Cochinchina as silk producers. From 1613 to 1617 the VOC sent four ships from Firando to Đàng Trong, but with little or no success. Even worse, the 1614 journey cost a Dutchman his life when he was implicated with an English merchant, Peacock, who had offended the Nguyễn ruler; both were executed.

Dutch interest persisted, however. In 1622, the value of the annual Japanese silk market was estimated at over one million *reals* by a Dutch agent in Firando, and the chance of sharing such huge profits kept Cochinchina in their minds.[68] In 1633, they finally established a lodge in Faifo; but their venture capital was too small to compete with the Japanese—625 *reals* and 150 *picul* of lead,[69] compared to the four hundred thousand *reals* that two Japanese Red Seal ships brought to Cochinchina that same year. In 1634 they brought 57,287 *gulden*, only to find Japanese so dominant in the local economy that they could only invest 37,403 *gulden*.[70] From 1633 to 1637 two Dutch ships a year visited Đàng Trong, usually sailing from Firando via Taiwan before heading to Batavia.[71] But none could make headway against the Japanese in their principal interest, the purchase of silk. This was largely because the silk market was controlled by Japanese living in Hội An, who often went to silk growing areas (mainly Thăng Hoa and Điện Bàn counties in Quảng Nam) to buy up a whole crop in advance.

Dutch failure to penetrate the Cochinchinese silk market led them to turn to Tongking, as we see from the *Daghregister*. In February 1636, they began investigating trade with Tongking, where it was said that 1500 to 1600 *picul*s of raw

---

[66] Nguyễn Thanh Nhã, *Tableau économique du Viet Nam aux XVII et XVIII siècles* (Paris: Editions Cujas, 1970),p. 203; see also C. B. Maybon, *Histoire moderne du pays d'Annam* (Paris: Plon, 1920), pp. 140-141; Phan Phát Huồn. *Việt Nam Giáo Sử*, vol. 1 (A history of Catholicism in Vietnam) (Saigon: Khai Trí, 1965), p. 166.

[67] "The trials of foreign merchant. Jeronimus Wonderaer's letter from Vietnam," translated by Ruurdje Laarhoven, in Li Tana and Anthony Reid, *Southern Vietnam under the Nguyễn, Documents on the Economic History of Cochinchina (Đàng Trong), 1602-1777* (Singapore: Institute of Southeast Asian Studies, Singapore/ECHOSEA, Australian National University, 1993), pp. 6-26.

[68] Buch, *De Oost-Indische Compagnie en Quinam*, p. 18.

[69] Ibid., p. 26.

[70] Buch, "La Compagnie des Indes Nederlandaises et l'Indochine," *Bulletin de l'Ecole Française d'Extrême-Orient* (hereafter BEFEO) XXXVI (1936):133.

[71] See *Dagh Register*, vol. 1, pp. 126, 137, 190, and 202.

silk and five thousand to six thousand bolts of silk fabric were produced each year, at reasonable prices.[72] After the first successful voyage there in early 1637,[73] Dutch attention began to turn to Tongking. Their persistence paid off, and Tongking silk quickly established itself as a major part of the VOC trade with Japan between 1635 and 1655, as Table Three shows:

| Table 3: Distribution of the VOC Transport of Silk to Japan 1635-1668 (1,000 Gld.) | | | | | | | |
|---|---|---|---|---|---|---|---|
| From | Taiwan | % | Batavia | % | Tongking | % | Total |
| 1635-1640 | 9,228 | 87% | 399 | 4% | 966 | 9% | 10,630 |
| 1641-1654 | 1,611 | 23% | 1,827 | 26% | 3,538 | 51% | 6,981 |
| 1655-1668 | 64 | 1% | 5,920 | 77% | 1,687 | 22% | 7,671 |

Source: P. W. Klein, "De Tonkinees-Japanese zijdehandel van de Verenigde Oost-indische Conpagnie en het inter-aziatische verkeer in de 17e eeuw."[74]

For the VOC, the period 1641-1654 was a golden time of buying silk cheaply in Tongking and selling it at profits of up to 250 percent in Japan. Indeed, Tongking's low price made its silk the most profitable of all silk carried by the VOC between 1636 to 1668, with an average annual profit of 186 percent, compared to 119 percent on Chinese silk.[75]

From 1638,[76] when the Dutch shifted their interest to the north, until the death of Nguyễn Phúc Lan (*chúa* Thượng, r. 1635-1648), Dutch relations with Cochinchina remained bad, with Portuguese-Dutch rivalry heightening the tension. Several armed conflicts between Nguyễn and Dutch forces resulted in the 1640s, which are considered separately in Appendix 2. Around 1650, however, the new ruler *chúa* Hiền (Nguyễn Phúc Tần, r. 1648-1687) sued for peace in a message to the VOC through Binggam, the head of the Chinese in Batavia.[77] The VOC responded by sending Willem Verstegen to Cochinchina and a generous treaty was agreed upon in December, 1651, which allowed the Dutch "free and frank" trade, "not to be inspected, [and to be] free from the payment of the import and export duties which the Chinese, Portuguese and other peoples must pay."[78] Perhaps not surprisingly the treaty never worked, and the Dutch closed their factory in Fai-fo in 1654.

---

[72] *Dagh Register*, vol. 1, p. 153, 160-161.

[73] For this voyage, see J. M. Dixon, trans. from French, "Voyage of the Dutch ship 'Grol,'" *Transactions of the Asiatic Society of Japan* (Tokyo: reprinted by Yushodo Booksellers Ltd., 1964), pp. 180–215.

[74] In W. Frijhoff and M. Hiemstra, eds., *Bewogen en bewegen* (Tilburg: Gianotten, 1986), p. 171. I am grateful to Professor Reid for translating it for me.

[75] Ibid., p. 170. My calculation from figures in the article. Another source says that Tongking silk sold for the same price in Japan as in Holland during this period. See C. R. Boxer, *Dutch Merchants and Mariners in Asia, 1602-1795* (London: Variorum Reprints, 1988), p. 151.

[76] Some scholars have argued that the Nguyễn confiscation of two Dutch ships in 1633 began the conflict, but the matter had been settled at the time and commerce continued, as Daghregister entries showed. *Dagh Register*, vol. 1, pp. 100, 101-102, 130, 138, 158, 173, 181-182.

[77] According to the Vietnamese, it was the Dutch who took the first action. See *Biên Niên Lịch Sử Cổ Trung đại Việt Nam* (Annals of Vietnam, the Ancient and Middle Ages) (Hanoi: Social Sciences Publishing House, 1987), p. 314.

[78] Anthony Reid, "The end of Dutch relations with Quinam, 1651-2," in Li Tana and Anthony Reid, *Southern Vietnam under the Nguyễn*, p. 34.

It was silk that also attracted the English to early Cochinchina. As Richard Cocks wrote: "It is certain there cometh twice as much silk yearly to Cochinchina [from China] as there doth to all three places of Bantam, Pattania, and Syam, and wants not other good pieces of stuffs."[79] Yet there was hardly anything between England and Cochinchina that could be called trade in the two hundred year history of the Nguyễn, only tragic stories one after the other.

The first English effort at commercial relations with Cochinchina occurred in 1613. Tempest Peacock and Walter Cawarden, two merchants sent by Richard Cocks, chief of the newly established English East India Company factory at Firando, ventured to Faifo on a Japanese junk.[80] They carried with them a letter written by King James I to the ruler of Cochinchina, plus 720 pounds sterling, and "a thousand *pesos* in *rials* of eight" (perhaps about eight hundred sterling). They never returned. At first everything seemed to be going well, the king bought some of their goods and treated them kindly. Then suddenly Peacock was dead, and Cawarden's fate remained a mystery—at least it was a mystery according to the earlier sources, such as Cocks's diary and Adams's report. Later writers like Maybon and Hall[81] amended these earlier reports, saying Cawarden was killed and Peacock's fate remains a mystery. Either way, it was a fateful beginning.

At first, Dutch and English both blamed each other. The Dutch charged that an English man had caused a Dutchman be executed by the "Quinamers," because "the king of Quinam failed to realize how offensive to each other Dutch and English were."[82] The English, however, held that "the king of Cochinchina [had acted] in revenge for some injuries offered him by the Dutch certain years past."[83] Seeking to be reimbursed from Cochinchina, Cocks then sent Edmond Sayer and William Adams to Faifo in 1617, but they seemed to have failed in claiming goods from or reimbursement for the earlier cargo and failed also in profiting from the cargo they carried themselves.[84] According to Adams the voyage to Cochinchina had cost him at least eight hundred *taels*.[85]

Another English attempt to create a base of operations for the China trade on Pulo Condore also ended in death. English and Vietnamese accounts disagreed on the cause and even the date of the event. The English version claimed that Allan Catchpole, president of the English East India Company factory, "got some Maccassers to serve for soldiers, and help build a fortification, and made a firm contract with them to discharge them at the end of three years." For some reason he reneged on the contract, so the "revengeful and cruel" Maccassers killed almost all of

---

[79] F. C. Danvers and William Foster, eds., *Letters Received by the East India Company from Its Servants in the East*, vol. 4 (London: Sampson, Low, Marton & Co., 1896), p. 17.

[80] Cocks, *Diary*, vol. 2, p. 264, Cocks to Wickham, April 1, 1614.

[81] See C. B. Maybon, *Histoire Moderne du pays d'Annam*, p. 65; D. G. Hall, *A History of South-East Asia* (London: Macmillan, 1961), p. 358. It may be that a Japanese who had been their host and the "young king of Cochinchina" were responsible for the murder, according to a footnote in *The Log-Book of William Adams, 1614-19*, ed. C. J. Purnell (London: Eastern Press, 1916), pp. 291-92, n. 2.

[82] Buch, *De Oost-Indische Compagnie en Quinam*, p. 12.

[83] Richard Cocks, *The Diary of Richard Cocks*, vol. 2, p. 268, "Cocks to Richard Wickham," July 25, 1614.

[84] Lamb, *The Mandarin Road*, p. 15.

[85] Cocks, *Diary*, vol. 1, p. 293.

the English in 1705.[86] However, the *Tiền Biên* placed the killings in 1703, well before the expiration of the contract. It claimed a Nguyễn general, Trương Phúc Phan, had recruited fifteen Javanese (or Malays) and had ordered them to pretend to serve the English in order to find a chance to kill them. And, it adds, the Nguyễn rewarded the Javanese for their deed.[87] However, while the *Tiền Biên* account of their deaths might be accurate, its dating cannot be, as numerous English ships reported dealing with a "President"—who could only be Catchpole—on Pulo Condore in 1704.[88]

## THE SOUTHEAST ASIANS

The trade links that existed between Đàng Trong and other Southeast Asian countries should not be neglected in this discussion. Though not well documented, these links seem to have played a small but significant role in Cochinchina's trade. Historically, however, their most important feature was probably that they were reciprocal relations. For the first time since the Lý dynasty, numbers of Vietnamese set out on trading voyages, while neighboring kingdoms were able to trade with a Vietnamese state without having to disguise their commercial relations as "tribute" to the emperor.

Trade with Manila began in 1620 and reached its peak at the end of the 1660s when four Đàng Trong junks per year sailed there.[89] During this period, Đàng Trong junks also voyaged regularly to Batavia. In 1637, for instance, the *Daghregister* recorded one junk, loaded with Cambodian rice, had arrived in Batavia. It also noted that the junk, owned by the king and high officials (presumably of Đàng Trong), would ship the equivalent of three hundred tons of rice from Cambodia to Cochinchina.[90] This particular trade was not unusual at the time; in 1636, sources repeatedly mention rice exported from Cambodia and Siam to Cochinchina.[91] The Nguyễn rulers also traded directly with Siam. In 1632, for example, we hear of a junk they dispatched to Siam that carried ten thousand *taels* of silver as capital.[92] Trade was not restricted to royal families and high officials. The *Kai-hentai* gives us a glimpse of much wider participation when reporting the comment of some Chinese merchants in Siam: "We are familiar with Guang Nan people who from time to time visit Siam, where we have seen them."[93] However, Cochinchinese did not only visit Siam. By the 1660s, according to French missionary accounts, a sizable Cochinchinese community existed in the Siamese capital at Ayuthia. Christopher Goscha argues

---

[86] Alexander Hamilton, *A new account of the East Indies*, ed. William Foster (London: The Argonaut Press, 1930), p. 110.

[87] *Liệt Truyện Tiền Biên*, vol. 7, pp. 106-107.

[88] H. B. Morse, *The Chronicles of the East India Company Trading to China, 1635-1834*, vol. 1 (Clarendon: Oxford University Press, 1926), pp. 130, 137.

[89] P. Chaunu, *Les Philippines et le Pacifique des Ibriques* (Paris: SEVPEN, 1960), pp. 60-62.

[90] *Dagh-Register gehouden int Casteel Batavia Vant*, Chinese translation, vol. 1, p. 198.

[91] Jan Dircsz Gaelen, "Journal ofte voornaemste geschiedenisse in Cambodia," in Hendrik Muller, *De Oost-Indische Compagnie in Cambodia en Laos: Verzameching van bescheiden van 1636 tot 1670* (The Hague: Nijhoff for Linschoten-Vereeniging, 1917), pp. 61-124.

[92] "Journal of Brownuershaven and Sloterdyck in 1633," quoted from Iwao Seiichi, *Shuin-sen*, pp. 263-264.

[93] Hayashi Shunsai, comp., *Kai-hentai*, vol. 20, p. 1589.

that some at least were sailors or small merchants involved in wider Southeast Asian commercial networks since missionary reports mentioned they spoke Portuguese, the lingua franca of regional commerce at the time.[94]

Nevertheless, a larger number of ships originating in neighboring states no doubt came to trade in Hội An, then departed from Cochinchina to foreign markets. Bowyear provided a list of countries and the products they brought to Cochinchina:

From Siam, petre, sapan, lac, necarie, elephant's teeth, tin, lead, rice.
From Camboja, camboia, bejamin, carldamons, wax, *lac*, necarie, coyalaca, and sapanwood, dammar, buffalo's hides, deer skins and nerves, elephant's teeth, rhinoceros's horns, etc.
From Batavia, silver, brimstone, petre, coase bastaes, red and white, vermilion.
From Manila, silver, brimstone, sapan, cowries, tobacco, wax, deer nerves, etc.[95]

The presence of Vietnamese traders in the Southeast Asian commercial world has tended to be overwhelmed by the dominant role of merchants and middlemen from other parts of Asia, especially Japan and China. Yet, the fragmentary sources do indicate an attempt by seventeenth-century Đàng Trong, encouraged by its Nguyễn rulers, to develop its own trade with its neighbors. As with Siam so with China, we find hints of ordinary Vietnamese participating in overseas commerce, probably for the first time in their history. Thus the *Hai Fang Cuan Yao* recorded that in 1611, seventy-three people who had set out to trade with China were captured at sea near Wenzhou. Later they were joined by another twenty-five people. All claimed to be from Hà Đông county, Thăng Hoa prefecture (Quảng Nam) of "*A Nam*," which can only be "Annam."[96] This valuable piece of information is the only direct confirmation we have that ordinary Vietnamese sometimes became privately involved in overseas trade with China. However, the existence of seaworthy sampans from at least the early seventeenth century[97] combined with official encouragement for trade makes it likely that many more Vietnamese people were engaged in overseas trade than we can currently verify, certainly many more than at any time before—or possibly after.

It seems a long way from Nguyễn Hoàng's calculating self-exile to Thuận Hóa in 1558 to the flourishing of the Đàng Trong ruled by his successors, for Đàng Trong was one of the most competitive states in mainland Southeast Asia in the late seventeenth century. Yet it took only a century, indeed a few decades, if we count from 1600 when Nguyễn Hoàng began seriously to build the country. Trade was the basis of this development, and the engine which drove it; without overseas trade even the existence of the state must have been in doubt. The next chapter continues our study of this key factor.

---

[94] Christopher E. Goscha, "La presence vietnamienne au royaume du Siam du XVIIe au XIXe siècle: Vers une perspective peninsulaire." Paper presented at the Seminar "La conduite des relations entre sociétés et Etats: Guerre et paix en Asie du Sud-Est," Paris, November 1996, pp. 3–6.

[95] Lamb, *The Mandarin Road*, p. 53.

[96] Wang Zai Jin, *Hai Fang Cuan Yao*, vol. 10.

[97] Goscha cites Nicholas Gervaise's 1680s comment that for a long time southern Vietnamese had used a certain type of bamboo to build craft "in which they sail the high seas with as much assurance as if they were in the largest Vessels." See Goscha, "La presence vietnamienne au royaume du Siam," p. 4.

# MONEY AND TRADE

Official encouragement of foreign merchants rapidly created a situation in the Nguyễn state that was unique in Vietnamese history: Đàng Trong developed a money economy in which most normal transactions were carried out in currency, rather than in cash and kind. Money and trade were the foundations on which the state rested and the pillars of its prosperity, yet the Nguyễn government adequately controlled neither of these key factors. In the long term this situation was fraught with dangers for an economy and society that had become so reliant upon them. In this chapter we will examine the economics of Cochinchina's foreign trade in more detail, considering the import-export economy, the volume of shipping, and the problems that arose from a money-based economy in the eighteenth century.

## AN IMPORT-EXPORT ECONOMY

As mentioned in the last chapter, in the early period Cochinchina exported many goods previously imported. The manifest of a junk coming from Cochinchina to Japan in 1641 typifies the range of goods available in Cochinchina:

> satin, roothout, black sugar, sharkskin, sittouw, Quảng Nam raw silk, poris cocos, deerskin, pepper, nutmeg, buffaloes' horn, wax, sitcleed, white panghsij, peling,[1] camphor, red gielem, *ruzhen*, calambac, rhinoceros horn, aguila wood, quicksilver, Cambodian lacquer, *conincx hockin*, gold brocade, velvet, tin.[2]

Of these commodities, the deerskin probably came from Siam, the lacquer from Cambodia, the camphor from Brunei, the nutmeg from Banda Island in eastern Indonesia and the *conincx hockin* (most probably a kind of silk fabric) from Fujian. Neither gold brocade nor velvet were locally produced, although *Wakan Sanzai Zue*, a seventeenth-century Japanese dictionary, did list Tongking, along with the Netherlands, Canton and Fujian, as a source of velvet. While the silk fabric, such as white panghsij, pelingh, red gielem, and *ruzhen*, might have been produced in Cochinchina, the quantity recorded (4,800 rolls) seems far too much for local production alone. In any case, the sources agree that most woven silks came from China and Tongking.

At least one-third of the goods in this manifest were not produced in Cochinchina. This was to be expected at a time when Đàng Trong actively exploited

---

[1] "Peling" here is most probably *peh ling* in the dialect of Chang Zhou and Quan Zhou areas, meaning "white ling," a kind of fine silk, most commonly in white, but sometimes red or blue. *Ruzhen* in this text might be another kind of silk fabric.

[2] *Dagh-Register des Comptoirs Nangasaque*, Japanese translation by Murakami Masajiro (Tokyo: Iwanami Shoto, 1938), vol. 1, pp. 32–34.

its favorable geographical position to channel trade between China and Japan through its principal port. Although the sources are scanty, it seems possible that to encourage this trade the Nguyễn levied few, if any, customs duties in the early seventeenth century. In the 1610s, Edward Saris and William Adams found that a gift of European ordnance dispensed with the need for any further customs duties[3]; while in the 1620s Borri insisted that "the king of Cochinchina does refuse no nation to enter," leaving his port "free for all sorts of strangers."[4] This fortunate situation helped make Hội An so prosperous that its people lived almost entirely from commerce. As the Cantonese trader, Chen, noted with approval: "There [was] nothing that cannot be obtained there."[5] This characteristic abundance helps explain why Hội An was regarded as "superior to all other ports of Southeast Asia." As the *Phủ Biên* boasted, "there were so many hundreds of kinds of goods displayed in the markets [there] that one could not name all of them."[6]

Like Champa before it, then, Hội An flourished as a regional entrepot. But equally like Champa, and almost from the start, it also exported certain local commodities, chief among them calambac and gold. Calambac, a precious eaglewood only found in some Southeast Asian countries, had previously been the most prized product of Champa and continued to retain its value, as a description from 1600 shows: "It is black and contains oil, and is worth fifty *cruzados* a catty among the Portuguese, while in its own kingdom it passes weight for weight with silver."[7] It was an important export item in seventeenth-century Cochinchina. Some Chinese traders even found it worthwhile to wait up to a year to buy enough calambac for a cargo to Japan, because of its inflated value there. Where calambac cost about five *taels* per pound at source in the 1620s, and about fifteen in the Hội An market, once landed in Japan it fetched forty times its original price (or about two hundred *taels* per pound).[8]

Calambac and eaglewood were derived from the same natural source, and they are often confused. As Pierre Poivre's description makes clear, there were:

> three sorts of eaglewood. The first is called *khi nam* [*kỳ nam*], the heart of the aloe tree which is so resinous that a fingernail can be inserted into it as into wax. It is very dear [. . . ]: it is calambac.
>
> The second sort is called *tlam hieong* [*trầm hương*], in French *Calembouc*. It appears almost as resinous as the other, but it has more wood and consequently is lighter and harder. However when it is thrown into water, it does not float ... It is brown in color with many small black spots due to the resin which gives that sweet and pleasant odor which makes it sought after by Orientals for

---

[3] William Adams, *The Log-Book of William Adams, 1614-19*, ed. C. J. Purnell (London: Eastern Press, 1916), p. 294. The notes in brackets are given by Purnell.

[4] Christoforo Borri, *Cochinchina* (London, 1933. New York: Da Capo Press, facsimile republished, 1970), p. I2.

[5] Lê Quý Đôn, *Phủ Biên Tạp Lục* (hereafter *Phủ Biên*), vol. 3 (Hanoi: Khoa Học Xã Hội 1977), p. 35a.

[6] Ibid.

[7] Quoted from C. R. Boxer, *The Great Ship from Amacon* (Liboa: Centro de Estudos Historicos Ultramarinos, 1963), p. 195 n 24.

[8] Borri, *Cochinchina*, p. d2. Borri valued the calambac in ducats, which were worth four to five *taels* of silver each at the time. For calambac in Japan, see Hayashi Shunsai, comp., *Kai-hentai*, vol. 3 (Tokyo: Toyo Bunko, 1958-59), p. 1804.

disinfecting their houses and making up their perfumes. [It] is worth from seven mạch [= 60 cash] to one quan, up to one quan and a half per pound.

The third sort is eaglewood proper. The country people call it thie hieong [tiên hương]. It is whiter, lighter, less resinous than the other two sorts. It sells for thirty to forty quan a pic [picul, about sixty kilograms] depending on the year. The three sorts are the same tree more or less ripe and more or less resinous.[9]

Such detailed knowledge of different kinds of eaglewood is interesting for other reasons, too. It suggests a frequent trade between lowlanders and the uplanders who harvested the eaglewood and also hints at the spread of a money economy into the mountains by the eighteenth century.

As for gold, it always topped the list of local products in both Asian and European travel accounts (as it had done with Champa). Nevertheless, the amount of gold exported was never large, as indicated by the amount raised by the gold tax which, in the mid-eighteenth century, was never more than 880 silver taels per year.[10] Gold was produced in four main areas: Phú Vang county (in modern Thừa Thiên province), Thăng Hoa prefecture (Quảng Nam), Quy Nhơn, and Phú Yên, although Thăng Hoa prefecture of Quảng Nam was the most productive. Interestingly, according to a French report of 1748, the gold price fluctuated according to the commercial season, as did the price of silk, which was cheaper in winter. If this is true, it is a striking example of how much foreign trade influenced the local economy.[11]

By the 1630s and 1640s, other local commodities began to be exported, a development that greatly strengthened the Đàng Trong economy. The first significant local product to emerge on the Cochinchinese market was sugar. In 1642, when Johan van Linga listed the merchandise that could be obtained annually in Cochinchina, among the more obvious goods like silk (one hundred piculs), eaglewood (fifty to sixty piculs), calambac (forty to fifty catties), and pepper (one hundred piculs) was a more surprising entry: three hundred to four hundred piculs of black sugar (about eighteen to twenty-four tons).[12] If this 1642 figure is correct, the production and export of black sugar must have more than doubled in the next two decades, since in 1663 Japanese figures show sixty-one tons of Quảng Nam black

---

[9] See Poivre's journal, pp. 432-433. Pierre Poivre, "Journal d'un voyage du vaisseau de la compagnie le Machault a la Cochinchine depuis le 29 août 1749, jour de notre arrivée, au 11 fevrier 1750," reproduced by H. Cordier in Revue de l'Extrême-Orient III (1885): 364-510. Here I used the translation by Kristine Alilunas-Rodgers in "Description of Cochinchina, 1749-50," in Li Tana and Anthony Reid, Southern Vietnam under the Nguyễn: Documents on the Economic History of Cochinchina (Đàng Trong), 1602–1777 (Singapore: Institute of Southeast Asian Studies, Singapore/ECHOSEA, Australian National University, 1993), p. 91, footnote 33 for "Eaglewood." According to Đại Nam Nhất Thống Chí, the best kỳ nam came from Khánh Hòa, while that found in Phú Yên and Quy Nhơn was inferior. See Đại Nam Nhất Thống Chí, Lục Tỉnh Nam Việt (Gazeteer of Greater Vietnam, the six southern provinces), vol. 2 (Saigon: Nha Văn Hóa, Phủ Quốc Vụ Khanh Đặc Trách Văn Hóa, 1973), pp. 1281-1282.

[10] Phủ Biên, vol. 4, p. 37a.

[11] Report of Adrien Dumont, cited in Georges Taboulet, La geste française en Indochine, vol. 1 (Paris: Maisonneuve, 1955), p. 121.

[12] W. J. M. Buch, De Oost-Indische Compagnie en Quinam (Amsterdam: H. J. Paris, 1929), p. 121.

sugar went there alone. Table One shows the quantity of sugar brought to Japan by Chinese traders in 1663, expressed in *jin* (two *jin* = one kilogram).[13]

| Table 1: Sugar Imported To Japan In 1663 | | | | |
|---|---|---|---|---|
| Origin | Number of Junks | White Sugar | Black Sugar | Sugar Candy |
| Siam | 3 | 142,000 | 45,400 | |
| Cambodia | 3 | 12,300 | 71,400 | 2,200 |
| Quảng Nam | 4 | 30,260 | 122,000 | 150 |
| Tongking | 1 | 42,000 | 23,000 | 900 |
| Taiwan | 3 | 50,800 | 37,000 | 1,700 |

Sugar production was obviously stimulated by overseas trade and seems to have continued to grow. Nearly a century later, in 1750, Poivre reported that China alone imported more than forty thousand barrels of white sugar each year from Hội An,[14] and about 400 percent profit could be made from it.[15] Sugar production suffered badly during the Tây Sơn period. "On account of the ruined state of the country for a long period of time, little more sugar was manufactured than answered home consumption; and the Chinese junks, disappointed in their loading, ceased to come in search of more," Ambassador Macartney noted. His embassy was able to buy sugar for under four pence a pound, with some even cheaper, at a penny a pound.[16]

Although Cochinchina produced less silk than Tongking, silk always figured on trade lists to Japan. For example, the *Daghregister* for 1637 reported that in July of that year, five junks, crewed by Japanese residents of Cochinchina, Chinese and several local Vietnamese, took five tons of inferior Chinese silk and thirteen to fifteen tons of Quảng Nam silk to Japan. It added: "Before leaving, they will be able to buy twelve thousand to thirteen thousand *can* [or six to 6.5 tons] of new silk there and bring it with them."[17] Here we might have a crude figure for new silk production in Cochinchina in the 1630s, since Japanese residents there virtually controlled the market by buying up whole crops in advance, as noted previously. While Borri said that silk was also exported to Laos from Cochinchina,[18] it may have been of a lower quality or produced in areas less accessible to the resident Japanese.

---

[13] Nishikawa Joken, *Zoho ka-i tsushoko* (Kyoto: Rakuyo Shorin, 1708). Quoted from *Zhong Guo Hai Yang Fa Zhan Shi Lun Wen Ji* (Essays on the history of China's maritime development) (Taipei: Research Institute on Three Principles, Central Research Institute, 1986), p. 148.

[14] Taboulet, *La geste française*, vol. 1, p. 138.

[15] "Memoires divers sur la Cochinchine," *Revue de l'Extrême-Orient*, II (1883): 329. But on p. 360 the author said the profit from sugar was 100 percent. In 1822, Crawfurd said that twenty thousand to sixty thousand *piculs* (one thousand to three thousand tons) of sugar were sent to China from Hội An each year, and another five thousand *piculs* (250 tons) sent to the European settlements in the straits of Malacca. See *Journal of an Embassy from the Governor-General of India to the Courts of Siam and Cochinchina* (Kuala Lumpur: Oxford University Press, 1967), p. 474.

[16] "Macartney's letter to Dundas" in Alastair Lamb, *The Mandarin Road to Old Hue* (Toronto: Clarke, Irwin and Co. Ltd., 1970), p. 176.

[17] *Dagh Register gehouden int Casteel Batavia Vant*, Chinese translation by Guo Hui and Cheng Da Xue, vol. 1, 2nd. edition (Taipei: Taiwan Sheng Wen Xian Wei Yuan Hui, 1989), p. 182 (hereafter *Dagh Register*).

[18] Borri, *Cochinchina*, p. D.

Other precious woods (apart from eaglewood), locally produced, were traded in such quantity that they made up another staple export item. In the mid-eighteenth century, Poivre listed, among others, rose wood, iron wood, sapan wood, cinnamon, and sandal wood as exports,[19] while Bowyear remarked that good wood was so abundant that the Spanish from Manila imported it to build their galleons.[20] So plentiful was the supply that, with the exception of eaglewood/calambac, virtually all other precious woods were sold relatively cheaply before the 1770s. Thus *Phủ Biên* reported that Cantonese traders could buy fifty kilograms of ebony wood for six-tenths of one *quan*, while the same amount of lacquer wood cost only one *quan*. For thirty *quan*, it added, people could buy enough of the best quality wood to build a five-room house.[21] This timber industry must have employed large numbers of people, from the wood cutters to those involved in its transport to the traders who dealt in it. Access was easy, even without the use of wheeled transport, since forest stands were not restricted to the distant mountains. Until the 1770s, "there used to be plenty of old tropical trees around the Huế area, with many tree trunks measuring ten arm spans around," according to Lê Quý Đôn's *Phủ Biên.*[22] This remained the case until 1774, when the Trịnh army descended on Huế. More than thirty thousand soldiers and servants camped there for a year, using whatever wood came to hand for their cooking, sometimes including "precious wood such as *trắc* and *giáng hương,* [enough to] fill a whole house," and thus laying waste to the timber industry around Huế.[23]

For most of the seventeenth century, as far as we can tell, all trade was comparatively free, even for a luxury item like calambac. In 1632 *chúa* Nguyễn Phúc Nguyên (r. 1613-35) had considered imposing a royal monopoly on pepper, calambac and bird nests, but had been dissuaded from it by a senior court strategist, Đào Duy Từ.[24] The end of the Trịnh-Nguyễn war, however, seems to have brought about a reassessment of this free-trade policy. In the late seventeenth century, Japanese records increasingly complained of strict government control over the calambac trade and of its diminishing supply.[25] At about the same time, customs duties seem either to have been applied or raised for European traders. In 1695, for example, Bowyear proposed the English would pay five hundred silver *taels* (about five hundred *quan* at the time) in customs duty per ship to trade with Cochinchina.[26] Fifty years later, in the 1750s, European ships were charged up to eight thousand *quan*. For instance, a Dutch ship in 1752 paid eight thousand *quan* in arrival tax,[27] while a French ship from Pondichery in 1753 was asked for eight thousand *piastres,*

[19] Pierre Poivre, "Memoires divers sur la Cochinchine, 1744," *Revue de l'Extrême-Orient* II (1884): 328.

[20] Lamb, *The Mandarin Road,* p. 55.

[21] *Phủ Biên,* vol. 6, p. 205b.

[22] *Phủ Biên,* vol. 6, p. 211b.

[23] *Phủ Biên,* vol. 6, p. 208a.

[24] *Đại Nam Thực Lục Tiền Biên* (hereafter *Tiền Biên*) (Chronicle of Greater Vietnam, Premier Period of the Nguyen) (Tokyo: Keio Institute of Linguistic Studies, Mita, Siba, Minato-ku, 1961), vol. 2, p. 41.

[25] See Hayashi Shunsai, comp., *Kai-hentai,* records from 1686 onward.

[26] Lamb, *The Mandarin Road,* p. 50.

[27] W. J. M. Buch, "La Companie des Indes neederlandaise et l'Indochine," *Bulletin de l'Ecole Française d'Extrême-Orient* (hereafter BEFEO) XXXVII (1936): 153.

twice what they had been promised by the Nguyễn in 1752.[28] In concert with this rise, it seems that other cargo taxes also increased from the end of the seventeenth century, although again the evidence is patchy. One early French source reported that the late seventeenth-century tax was "very small,"[29] no more than 3 to 4 percent, while a biography of the officer in charge of overseas trade at the time, Khổng Thiên Như, reported that ships' cargoes were weighed on arrival and charged at 5 to 10 percent.[30] These two sets of figures may have been influenced by a trend that saw cargo taxes increase from the beginning of the eighteenth century; by the 1750s, Kirsop claimed cargo tax was 12 percent.[31]

The main primary evidence for these duties and charges comes from the *Phủ Biên*, although a near identical list exists in the *Tiền Biên* where it was vaguely described as being in force from "the early days of the country." Its placement in 1755, however, suggests these charges probably came into effect about then, perhaps as a way of increasing revenue to fund Nguyễn Phúc Khoát's lavish construction program begun at the capital in 1754.[32] The regulations also mandated that traders found trying to cheat the customs would have their ships and goods confiscated; and that only legitimate commercial vessels would be allowed access to the ports. *Phủ Biên* gives the following list:

| Table 2: Duties On Arrival And Departure (In Quan) | | |
| --- | --- | --- |
| Ships From | Tax on Arrival | Tax on Departure |
| Shanghai | 3,000 | [not mentioned] |
| Canton | 3,000 | 300 |
| Fujian | 2,000 | 200 |
| Hainan Island | 500 | 50 |
| Europe[33] | 8,000 | 800 |
| Macao | 4,000 | 400 |
| Japan | 4,000 | 400 |
| Siam | 2,000 | 200 |
| Luzon | 2,000 | 200 |
| Palembang | 500 | 50 |
| Hà Tiên | 300 | 30 |
| Sơn Đô[34] | 300 | 30 |

[28] Adrien Launay, *Histoire de la mission de Cochinchine 1658-1823, Documents historiques*, vol. 2 (Paris: Archives des Missions Étrangères, 1924), p. 354.

[29] Taboulet, *La geste française en Indochine*, vol. 1, p. 86.

[30] "Tiểu truyển Khổng Thiên Như," a manuscript kept in the Hội An Relics Board, Hội An, Vietnam.

[31] Robert Kirsop, "Some account of Cochinchina," in A. Dalrymple, *Oriental Repertory* (London: East India Company, 1808), pp. 242–243.

[32] *Tiền Biên*, vol. 10 (Collection of Biographies of Nguyen Dynasty, Premier Period) (Tokyo: Keio Institute of Linguistic Studies, 1961), p. 144.

[33] Any European-rigged ships.

[34] Prof. Chen Chingho suggests that Sơn Đô was Chantaboun, a port close to the Siam-Khmer border. See "Shi qi ba shi ji zhi hui an tang ren jie ji qi shang ye" (The Chinese Town and its trade in Hội An in the seventeenth and eighteenth centuries), *Xin Ya Xue Bao*, no. 1, vol. 3, p. 310. Yet might this *Sơn Đô* instead be Phố Hiến, a city in Sơn Nam Hạ province in the lower

But what effect did this booming import-export economy and the development of commodity markets in silk, sugar and wood, among others, have on local society and on the lives of ordinary Đàng Trong Vietnamese?

First, from early in the seventeenth century, when able-bodied men became increasingly liable for military service, and women and non-conscripted men were increasingly drawn into market-based commerce or production, a situation developed here unique in mainland Southeast Asia: a large part of the population found it necessary to purchase imported rice to live. This was particularly the case for people living near the capital in Thuận Hóa. Contemporary sources frequently reported that rice was imported from Cambodia and Siam to Cochinchina throughout the seventeenth century.[35] The visiting Chinese monk, Da Shan, thought it was because agricultural land in the Thuận Hóa–Hội An area was poor and limited, but this was only one cause. As Robert Innes has shown, in the 1630s Đàng Trong Vietnamese were so enthusiastic about producing for the Japanese silk and sugar markets that they replaced rice with mulberry bushes and sugar cane in many fields.[36] For their own staple food, they relied on rice from Cambodia,[37] a dependence that occasionally led to serious crises. For example, when a poor harvest prompted the Cambodian king to forbid the export of rice in 1636, it resulted in a "big famine" in Thuận Hóa in 1637.[38] This lack of interest in agriculture by people in the Thuận Hóa region continued until the late eighteenth century when, as Lê Quý Đôn observed, cheap rice from the Mekong delta was so abundant that people in the capital area did not need to "work hard on the land."[39]

The export market and overseas demand also stimulated trade specialization within Đàng Trong.[40] In the sugar industry, for example, a system of specialized household production developed, with different groups involved in growing the cane, in initially processing it into a sugar juice, and then in refining the juice into white sugar. As the sugar juice was kept in urns while awaiting further processing, increasing sugar production in turn stimulated a small new local industry devoted to supplying the growing number of urns and jars required.[41]

---

Red River delta, and the most important port of Tongking in the seventeenth and eighteenth centuries?

[35] *Dagh Register*, vol. 1, p. 198; "Bowyear's Narrative," in Lamb, *The Mandarin Road*, p. 53.

[36] Mulberry trees were already remarkably numerous in the 1620s. Borri: "These high Mulberry trees, by whose leaves the silk-worms are nourished, are as plentiful here in these large plains, as hempe is with us." See Borri, *Cochinchina*, p. D.

[37] Robert Innes, "Trade with Japan: A Catalyst Encouraging Vietnamese Migration to the South in the seventeenth century," unpublished source, n.p. p. 6. My gratitude to Keith Taylor for providing me this valuable paper.

[38] *Tiền Biên*, vol. 3, p. 46; see also R. Innes, "Trade between Japan and Central Vietnam in the Seventeenth Century: The Domestic Market," unpublished paper, n.p., p. 6.

[39] *Phủ Biên*, vol. 3. Here I used the translation from Li Tana and Anthony Reid, *Southern Vietnam under the Nguyen*, p. 105.

[40] Victor Lieberman, "Local Integration and Eurasian Analogies: Structuring Southeast Asian History, c.1350-c.1830," *Modern Asian Studies* 3, 27 (1993): 498.

[41] I am grateful to Prof. Phan Đài Doãn, who pointed out this to me in 1990. Also see Thành Thế Vỹ, *Ngoài thương Việt Nam hồi thế kỷ XVII, XVIII và đầu XIX* (Foreign trade in Vietnam in the seventeenth, eighteenth, and nineteenth centuries) (Hanoi: Sử Học, 1961), p. 239.

These observations illuminate the nature of the Nguyễn economy. It was not the characteristic "subsistence economy" supposedly typical of traditional Southeast Asia. Rather, it was commercially driven to a remarkable extent, but driven more by foreign than indigenous interests, as Alexander Woodside has pointed out.[42] So crucial was overseas trade that it was not harvests which set the standard for a good or bad economic year, but instead the number of ships or junks that arrived in Cochinchina determined the health of the economy, as an anecdote in Da Shan's "Hai Wai Ji Shi" shows. In 1695 the *chúa*, Nguyễn Phúc Chu (1691-1725) thanked the visiting monk for his successful prayers for "favorable weather and a fruitful year" for Đàng Trong. However, the ruler's measure of the year's fruitfulness, Da Shan related, was calculated in terms of shipping: "whereas only six or seven junks and ships had been coming each year, about seventeen came [in 1695], bringing the state more than enough money for its use."[43]

But if overseas trade was a central concern of the state, to what extent did the ordinary people in Đàng Trong benefit from this market economy? Or, as Innes puts it, what happened to the profits—the surplus?[44] Certainly, there is no doubt that their own involvement in trade brought the Nguyễn rulers great benefits. But the situation here differed tremendously from that of Tongking. As silk was virtually the only product the Dutch bought from Tongking, it could be easily controlled and monopolized by the court, as was obvious when the VOC first began trading there in 1637. By contrast, no royal monopolies existed in Cochinchina at the time. Later, even after royal monopolies were applied to calambac and gold, bulk commodities like sugar, silk, and others were traded freely each day on the local markets, leaving much room for common producers to profit. It is evident that merchants and others in the Hội An area greatly prospered. Vũ Minh Giang has provided a piece of evidence that illuminates southern prosperity in his comparison of donations recorded at two Buddhist pagodas in the mid-seventeenth century, one in the Marble Mountains near Hội An and the other at Phố Hiến, the principal commercial center in Tongking. His calculations show that contributions to the southern pagoda were on average eight times larger than to the northern one, and that whereas northern donations were mainly offered in rice, southern donations were usually money.[45]

As for ordinary people, the evidence of their relative prosperity can be found in Hội An market itself, not simply because of the abundance of trade goods offered there, but even more, because so many of the various goods available in the market were purchased for daily consumption. For example, in the early seventeenth century, the Vietnamese-speaking Jesuit, Cristoforo Borri, had noticed a lively trade in items of personal adornment for women. "Combs, needles, bracelets, beads of glass to hang on their ears, and such other trifles and womanish curiosities"[46] sold

---

[42] Alexander Woodside, "Central Vietnam's Trading World in the Eighteenth Century as seen in Lê Quý Đôn's 'Frontier Chronicles,'" In K. W. Taylor and John Whitmore, *Essays into Vietnamese Pasts* (Ithaca: Cornell Southeast Asia Program, 1995), p. 163.

[43] Da Shan, "Hai Wai Ji Shi" (Overseas Journal) in *Shi qi shi ji Guang Nan Xin Shi Liao* (A new source about Quang Nam in the seventeenth century), ed. Chen Jingho, vol. 3 (Taipei: Committee of Series of Books on China, 1960), p. 24.

[44] Innes, "Trade with Japan," p. 8.

[45] Vũ Minh Giang, "Contributions to Identifying Phố Hiến Through Two Stele," in *Phố Hiến* (Hanoi: Thế Giới, 1994), p. 123.

[46] Borri, *Cochinchina*, p. 12.

quickly in Hội An. Given the central role of women in internal trade and commerce, the buoyancy of the local market in personal finery is a sure indicator of economic prosperity. But if luxuries formed a large part of overseas trade in seventeenth-century Cochinchina, with the arrival of increasing numbers of small Chinese traders in the eighteenth century, items of daily consumption of ordinary people bulked large among the goods imported. *Phủ Biên* listed fifty-one available in the 1770s: silk, cotton, herbal medicines, gold or silver paper, joss sticks, gold and silver thread, color dyes, clothes, footwear, glass, fans, writing brushes and ink, needles, all kind of chairs, leadware and copperware, porcelain, earthenware, tea, and a wide variety of dried foods and sweets.[47] A generation earlier, Poivre had noticed some of the same goods coming from Europe, goods such as hardware, glass, and brightly colored cottons.[48]

Other evidence for the high local standard of living can be found in reports from northern Vietnamese visitors. Lê Quý Đôn, a famous scholar and high-ranking official who accompanied the Trịnh army south in 1774, described the extravagant life style of Đàng Trong Vietnamese in a report that was certainly exaggerated, but telling. The point behind this caustic catalogue of southern excesses may have been, as Woodside has suggested, to prove that "regional economic psychologies, as well as degrees of wealth, had become uncomfortably discordant between north and south."[49] It may also have served to fix the defeated enemy as moral inferiors, corrupted by being "accustomed to fancy things." Whatever the case, the report implicitly registers the shock Trịnh forces must have experienced when confronted by the wealth of the south:

> The officials, no matter how high or low their position, all lived in ornamented buildings, with gauze and satin as curtains and mosquito nets. Their pots were made of copper, their furniture of precious wood. Cups and trays were made of china, and saddles of gold and silver. Dresses were made of brocade and colored silk, and mats of very good quality rattan. They showed off and competed with each other for richness and distinction. The common people also wore satin shirts with flowers and damask trousers as their daily wear. To be dressed in plain cotton was considered a disgrace. The soldiers all enjoyed sitting on mats, with incense burners in their hands, having good tea with silver or china cups. Everything came from China, from spittoons to chinaware, even the food. For every meal they had three big bowls of rice. Women all dressed in gauze, ramie and silk, with embroidered flowers around a round collar. People here looked upon gold and silver as sand, millet and rice as mud; their lives could not be more extravagant.[50]

It is useful to compare this report to another one describing the reaction of Đàng Trong Vietnamese to the invading Trịnh army in 1774, after a century's separation. Again, the author is Lê Quý Đôn:

---

[47] *Phủ Biên*, vol. 4, p. 35b.

[48] Poivre, "Memoires," p. 335.

[49] Woodside, "Lê Qúy Đôn's 'Frontier Chronicles,'" p. 166.

[50] *Phủ Biên*, vol. 6, p. 227b.

When the army of the north came [to Thuận Hóa], the people [there] thought they could not be regular Trịnh troops, since . . . the generals only dressed in black cotton gowns, and the soldiers were very shabbily clad. Because the people in the south were so accustomed in living in a lavish style, they judged their enemies by their clothes.[51]

If Lê Quý Đôn's moral disdain is more manifest here, so too is the tacit underlying comparison between the higher living standards and different values of Cochinchinese compared to the northern invaders.

Let us now finish discussing the import-export economy by considering, to the extent possible, the volume of trade involved.

## THE TONNAGE OF SHIPPING AND VOLUME OF TRADE

From the late sixteenth century to 1635, the main trade in Cochinchina was carried out between the Chinese and Japanese. Unfortunately, our figures are not precise for this trade and scholars disagree in their interpretations. Iwao Seiichi, for instance, estimates the average transport tonnage of Red Seal ships at 270 tons, and the value of each cargo at about fifty thousand silver *taels*.[52] With an average of two to three Red Seal ships[53] coming to Cochinchina per year, the volume of Red Seal trade would have averaged six hundred tons, with a minimum annual value of 250,000 *taels* of silver. Robert Innes, however, has argued that this estimate should be doubled, and then multiplied by the number of ships arriving each year.[54] There is some merit in this approach: a 1628 report claimed that at least one Japanese ship per year traded in Cochinchina without a Red Seal, while Dutch sources recounted that in 1633 two Red Seal ships brought the equivalent of three hundred thousand silver *taels* in venture capital.[55] However, our purpose here is better served by estimating the regular minimum volume and value rather than speculating about possible maximum amounts. As for the Chinese, the junk trade from Cochinchina was worth anything from four thousand to nineteen thousand *taels* per junk. In 1637, for example, four junks from Quinam arrived in Nagasaki with cargoes reportedly worth a total of seventy-five thousand *taels* (162,750 *florins*) or about 18,750 *taels* each.[56] If four Chinese junks came yearly, itself quite a conservative estimate, they

[51] *Phủ Biên*, vol. 1, p. 47b.

[52] Iwao Seiichi, *Shuin-sen Boeki-Shi no Kenku* (A study of the trade of Red Seal ships) (Tokyo: Ko Bun Do, 1958), pp. 120, 269 (hereafter *Shuin-sen*).

[53] See Chapter Three.

[54] R. Innes, "The Door Ajar: Japan's Foreign Trade in the Seventeenth Century," vol. 2 (PhD Dissertation, University of Michigan, 1980), p. 386. See Borri's account, which seems to confirm the latter: he said that the annual trade between Japanese and Chinese in Hội An valued "four or five millions in silver." See Borri, *Cochinchina*, p. I.

[55] Iwao Seiichi, *Shuin-sen*, p. 87, and Buch, *De Oost-Indische Compagnie en Quinam*, p. 24.

[56] Buch, *De Oost-Indische Compagnie en Quinam*, p. 67. An entry of *Dagh-Register des Comptoirs Nangasaque* in September 1645 says that one junk from Quang Nam arrived with a cargo worth nine chests of *gold coins*. If it means *real* gold coins, the value would be ninety thousand *taels* of silver. If it means "currency," and a chest of silver in the seventeenth century was one thousand *taels* silver, then it might have been nine thousand *taels* of silver. The latter seems more likely.

would have shipped at least 350 tons to a minimum value of seventy-five thousand *taels* per year.[57]

In addition to this trade, there must have been quite a number of vessels coming to Cochinchina originating from other Southeast Asian ports during this period. However, they are only documented in scattered references. For example, William Adams mentioned the arrival of three ships from Manila at Tourane in May 1617.[58] Yet we do know that throughout the seventeenth century an unknown, but possibly considerable, rice trade was carried out, flowing from Cambodia and Siam to Cochinchina, before Mekong delta production became high enough to feed the population in the Huế area. We can notionally estimate the rice trade would have added another thousand tons in volume and ten thousand *taels* in value to Đàng Trong's trade. If we calculate to include quite frequent visits of Portuguese and Dutch ships to Đàng Trong, the annual value of trade in Cochinchina before 1640 could reasonably be estimated at about six hundred thousand *taels* of silver.

Turning to the volume that records data for the Cochinchina import-export trade after the Japanese "closed door" policy came into effect, we find that *Daghregister des Comptoirs Nangasacque* noted twenty-two junks from Cochinchina between 1641 and 1648, with cargoes estimated from fifty to seventy-five tons.[59] This estimate is supported by the records of *To ban ka motsu cho*, which listed the cargoes of two junks which came to Japan from Cochinchina in 1712. The tonnage of each was about sixty tons.[60] From 1641 to 1680 an average of four junks came from Cochinchina to Japan per year. If we take sixty tons as their average, it gives a total of 240 tons of trade by volume and sixty thousand *taels* of silver in value for each Chinese merchant junk operating inside the China-Cochinchina-Japan trading triangle. In addition, a larger number of smaller-sized junks, perhaps ten annually,[61] plied the waters between China and Cochinchina, with a total cargo tonnage of 120 to two hundred tons, and a value of about one hundred thousand *taels* of silver.

As for other areas, Portuguese from Macao traded more frequently with Đàng Trong in the second half of the seventeenth century, when Cochinchina emerged as an alternative to the Japanese market which was closed to them in 1639. Manguin says four ships arrived in 1651 and more in 1650.[62] At least one or two ships came from Macao each year, with a carrying capacity under three hundred European nautical tons each,[63] to a value of one hundred thousand *taels*.[64] Vessels originating

---

[57] Using a different method, Innes estimated the annual average value of such cargoes to Japan as: 500-1500 *taels* per junk before 1620; six thousand *taels* per junk between 1623 and 1629 and three hundred thousand *taels* after 1629. Innes, "The Door Ajar," pp. 390–391.

[58] Adams, *The Log-Book*, p. 233.

[59] Or one hundred thousand to 150,000 *jin*. *Dagh-Register des Comptoirs Nangasacque*, Japanese translation by Murakami Masajiro (Tokyo: Iwanami Shoten, 1938).

[60] *To ban ka motsu cho*, vol. 2 (Tokyo: Nai kaku bun ko, 1970), pp. 944–949; pp. 1058–1068.

[61] Da Shan, "Hai Wai Ji Shi," vol. 1, p. 24.

[62] Pierre-Yves Manguin, *Les Portugais sur les côtes du Viet-Nam et du Campa* (Paris: Ecole Française d'Extrême-Orient), p. 201.

[63] According to Boxer, this was a "unit of capacity and not of weight . . . a shipping ton [was] a space available for cargo of about sixty cubic feet." C. R. Boxer, *The Great Ship from Amacon* (Lisbon: Centro de Estudos Historicos Ultramarinos, 1963), p. 13. He also says that an occasional vessel of four hundred to five hundred tons came from Indochina in 1637. It was most likely from Cochinchina, as it was under Portuguese command.

[64] Innes, "The Door Ajar," p. 383.

in Taiwan probably accounted for another seven hundred tons, estimating two to four junks annually between the 1660s and the 1680s. Each junk averaged 235 tons,[65] with cargoes worth ninety thousand silver *taels*.[66] Finally, a considerable amount of trade must have occurred between Cochinchina and other Southeast Asian countries, though most of it is unrecorded. At least two junks per year could have come from Siam, Manila, or Batavia.[67]

Thus from the 1640s to the end of the century, it seems reasonable to assume a minimum annual average trade of two thousand to 2,500 tons of cargo, with a total estimated value of 580,000 *taels*.

The picture for the eighteenth century is even less clear. Certainly, Japanese trade must have fallen sharply after 1715, when the Japanese government limited the total value of foreign trade to three hundred thousand *taels* of silver per annum. Of this amount, thirty thousand *taels* was assigned to Cochinchina. This means that, until 1715, the volume of trade between Japan and Cochinchina was certainly worth more than thirty thousand *taels* of silver, and the value probably reached much higher in the late seventeenth and early eighteenth centuries.

In the late seventeenth century, Taiwan stopped sending junks to Đàng Trong. However, the number of junks from China rose beginning in the early eighteenth century to compensate for the reductions in the Chinese import quota from 1715. By mid-century, the number of Chinese junks visiting Cochinchina reached sixty to eighty, while the tonnage of shipping might have increased to 420–500 tons. The Dutch also continued to send ships occasionally, while one regularly came from Macao each year.[68] In 1753, the French traveler Bennetat recorded four European ships trading in Đàng Trong (one Dutch, one French, and two from Macao).[69] From these sketchy references we can guess that the total annual tonnage of shipping in the first half of the eighteenth century might have fluctuated between 1,500 and three thousand tons, with a value of four hundred thousand to 450,000 *taels*, depending on whether Western ships came or not.

These estimates show how much the Nguyễn economy relied on overseas trade, but at the same time were vulnerable to any external changes. This vulnerability is most evident if one examines the problems associated with the Nguyễn money system.

---

[65] *Copie-daghregister des Casteels Zeelandia op Tayoan*, February 27 to November 9, 1655 says that four junks went to Quang Nam in March 1655. Quoted from Cao Yong He, *Taiwan Zao Qi Li Shi Yan Jiu* (A study of the early history of Taiwan) (Taipei: Lian jing chu ban shi ye gong si, 1981), p. 377. According to *Kai-hentai*, vol. 8, p. 392, three junks of Zheng went to Quang Nam in 1683. Calculating from the three junks which arrived in Nagasaki from June to July 1641, the volume of transport per junk of the Zheng was 235 tons. See *Dagh-Register des Comptoirs Nangasacque*, Japanese translation, vol. 1, pp. 3-5, 9-11, 16-17.

[66] For the value of Zheng's junk, see Lin Ren Chuan, *Ming Mo Qing Chu Si Ren Hai Shang Mao Yi* (Private trade in the period of the end of Ming and the beginning of the Qing dynasty) (Shanghai: Press of Normal University of Hua Dong, 1987), p. 267. Lin's calculation was based on Zheng's demanding restitution from the Dutch, which might have been higher than the junk's real value.

[67] See J. Bertin, S. Bonin, and P. Chaunu, *Les Philippines et le Pacifique des Iberiques* (Paris: Ecole Practique des Hautes Etudes), pp. 60-61; J. C. van Leur, *Indonesian Trade and Society*, 2nd. edition (The Hague: Nijhoff, 1967), p. 213.

[68] "Description of Cochinchina, 1749-50," in Li Tana and Anthony Reid, *Southern Vietnam under the Nguyễn*, p. 95.

[69] Launay, *Histoire de la mission de Cochinchine*, vol. 2, p. 354.

## COINS AND COPPER

Cochinchina's money supply basically derived from external sources. On any import list, coins featured among the most desirable items, and we know from Iwao Seiichi's work that coins were one of the main Japanese exports to Tongking and Cochinchina in the early seventeenth century.[70] This trade started after 1608, when the Japanese government began unifying its national currency by prohibiting Chinese Yung-lo (*Eiraku-tsuho*) or privately minted Chinese or Japanese coins (*bita-sen*). Many such coins existed in Japan since they had been regularly imported from the fifteenth century. Now as part of its attempt to standardize Japanese currency, the government prohibited the circulation of *Eiraku* coins.[71]

Banned and thus substantially devalued in Japan, these coins provided Red Seal merchants with the chance to make huge profits by exporting them to Cochinchina. Indeed, the remarkable increase in Red Seal ships to Cochinchina from 1610 hints at a close connection between these two facts. The peak period for this trade was probably between 1610 and 1630, when supplies could be had in Japan relatively cheaply: in 1633, twenty-five years after they had been prohibited, the VOC could still only buy *Eiraku* coins (which they called "Ierack" or "Erack") at 10 percent discount,[72] suggesting they would have been much cheaper for well-connected Japanese merchants. Certainly the Dutch believed that Red Seal merchants like Hirano Tojiro had made vast profits in the Cochinchinese coin trade before the mid-1630s.[73] It tempted their own participation, which is quantified by the number and types of coins imported by the VOC from Japan in Table Three. The coins were bought in strings (*quan*) of nominally one thousand pieces, though in reality less 4 percent, i.e. 960 pieces.

| Table 3: Types of Coins Brought into Cochinchina by the VOC (1633-1637)[74] | | | | | | | |
|---|---|---|---|---|---|---|---|
| Year | Iarack | Saccamotta | Mito | Nume | Tammary | Unspec. | Total |
| 1633 | 930 | 15,420 | - | - | - | - | 16,530 |
| 1634 | 360 | 9,724 | - | - | - | - | 10,084 |
| 1635 | - | 41,625 | | | | | 41,625 |
| 1636 | - | 5,385 | - | 5,250 | - | 2,865 | 13,500 |
| 1637 | - | - | 2,505 | - | 510 | 21,260 | 24,275 |
| Total | 1,290 | 72,154 | 2,505 | 5,250 | 510 | 24,125 | 105,834 |
| *taels*[75] | 968 | 60,005 | 2,380 | 4,988 | 485 | 24,125 | 92,951 |

[70] Iwao Seiichi, *Shuin-sen*, p. 241.

[71] T. Takizawa, "Early currency policies of the Tokugawa's, 1563-1608," *Acta Asiatica* 39 (1980): 22.

[72] A. van Aelst, "Japanese coins in southern Vietnam and the Dutch East India Company, 1633-1638," *Newsletter of the Oriental Numismatic Society* 109 (Nov-Dec. 1987): n.p.

[73] *General Missiven van Gouverneurs-General en Raden aan Heren XVII der Verenigde Oostindische Companie*, vol. 1, p. 513. Quote in Innes, "The Door Ajar," vol. 2, p. 586.

[74] A. van Aelst, "Japanese coins," (n.p.).

[75] This is my calculation, according to the following prices given by A. van Aelst, "Japanese Coins":

Although the VOC knew that "coins were badly needed in Quinam, [as] the king of Quinam asked [them] to buy all the old coins in Japan and bring them there for casting cannons,"[76] the company's original profit margin was very slight. In 1634, when they shipped nothing but coins to Đàng Trong, their margin barely exceeded fourteen *taels* of silver per fifteen thousand coins, just above the break-even point.[77] This poor showing may have been due to the fact that the Japanese brought large amounts of coins into the region before the Dutch arrived. In 1635–36, the VOC appears to have traded more keenly since the company was able to reap more than ten times their purchase price, with strings of coin worth one *tael* each in Japan reselling in 1636 in Cochinchina for up to 10.5 *taels*.[78] It is not surprising therefore, that the VOC soon deemed coins its "most profitable item" in Cochinchina.[79]

Chinese traders also exported large quantities of Japanese coins to Đàng Trong. In September 1637, for example, four Chinese junks imported two million Japanese coins in their cargoes.[80] We also know that precious metals (gold, silver and copper) and copper coins featured heavily among the main items taken from Japan to Cochinchina by junks of the Taiwanese ruler Zheng (Coxinga) and later by Chinese junks. Japanese coin exports were so profitable that from 1659 to 1684 the Tokugawa government even allowed the Nagasaki city elders to mint copies of old Chinese coins for the export market.[81] Surely many of these coins found their way to Cochinchina.

But once in Đàng Trong, what happened to the imported coins? Were they cast into cannons and bullets or used as currency? Both were possible, depending on circumstances and quality. Thus the *Daghregister* in 1636 noted that the *chúa* (Nguyễn Phúc Lan) bought thirty thousand *taels* of poor quality coins imported from Nagasaki

| | |
|---|---|
| "Ierack": | 0.75 *tael* per string; |
| "Saccamotta": | 0.80-0.85 *tael* per string; |
| "Mito": | 0.95 *tael* per string; |
| "Nume": | 0.95 *tael* per string; |
| "Tammary": | 0.95 *tael* per string; |
| Unspec: | 1 *tael* per string. |

Innes gives the amount of 42,000 *kan* brought by the VOC from 1633 to 1638. See Innes, "The Door Ajar," vol. 2, p. 586.

[76] When one of the VOC ships failed to buy goods in Cochinchina in June 1633, "the king [of Cochinchina] regretted that the Japanese had taken all the goods this time, but if the Dutch returned in November with copper coins, coarse pottery and iron pots, they could trade it for gold and raw silk." Here the king used *"zenes,"* the special term for Japanese coins, which proves that the Japanese had been transporting their coins to Cochinchina. This may have been the origin of the Dutch coin trade to Cochinchina. See Buch, *De Oost-Indische Compagnie en Quinam*, p. 25.

[77] *Dagh Register*, vol. 1, pp. 126, 128. Thành Thế Vỹ, *Ngoại thương Việt Nam hồi thế kỷ XVII, XVIII và đầu XIX* (Vietnamese foreign trade in the seventeenth, eighteenth, and early nineteenth centuries) (Hanoi: Sử Học, 1961), p. 152.

[78] *Dagh Register*, vol. 1, p. 173.

[79] Ibid., vol. 1, p. 197. The Dutch in 1636 even decided to cast coins in Japan amounting to about 323,000 *taels* for sale in Cochinchina; but no action seems to have been taken. See ibid., p. 181.

[80] Buch, *De Oost-Indische Compagnie en Quinam*, p. 67.

[81] Innes, "The Door Ajar," vol. 2, p. 587.

and had them cast into cannons.[82] This suggests that, except during wartime emergencies, good coins were used in circulation. There were certainly huge supplies of them: the VOC alone imported one hundred million *Khoan Vĩnh* Japanese coins between 1633 and 1638. As the numismatist Van Aelst put it, "these Japanese coins were no occasional guests, but an everyday part of life" in Cochinchina.[83] Imported coins made up for the absence of state coinage and the deficiency in the existing currency, and their circulation met, and then further stimulated, the trading economy in seventeenth-century Đàng Trong.[84] Indeed, as the English merchant Richard Cocks realized, the use of money was one of the advantages of trading in Cochinchina.[85] Coins in wide circulation made rapid economic transactions possible. That explains why in 1688, during a time when fewer and fewer Japanese coins were being brought to Cochinchina, Nguyễn Phúc Trăn (Chúa Nghĩa, r. 1687-1691) dispatched four letters, one to the king of Japan and the other three to officials in Nagasaki, plus gifts to the Tokugawa government asking that coins be cast on his behalf in Japan.[86]

Although in the early seventeenth century the Chinese had brought large amounts of silk to trade with the Japanese in Cochinchina, silk ceased to be a staple import item when direct Sino-Japanese trade resumed late in the century. Chinese coins then largely took first place, as Bowyear confirmed in 1695: "from Canton is brought cashes, of which they make a great profit."[87] This may have been particularly so from 1684, when the weight of the *Kang Xi* coin was reduced. If in China one *tael* of silver was worth 1,400 to 1,500 copper coins in 1688, by 1697 one *tael* of silver was worth the equivalent of 3,030 of the lighter coins.[88] Those 3,030 coins would then have been worth over five *quan* of coins in Cochinchina, where gold was worth about thirteen *quan* for a *tael* or even less.[89] Thus, when the proportional value of gold to silver in China was 1:10, exchanging Chinese coins for Cochinchinese gold could bring 288 percent profit.[90] However, when the silver price fell and the copper price rose in eighteenth-century China, shipping coins became unprofitable.

If we examine Cochinchina's trade in the seventeenth and eighteenth centuries, we find that not only were progressively fewer coins being imported, but copper was also becoming increasingly expensive. Thus, while the price of copper was twenty

---

[82] *Dagh Register*, vol. 1, p. 174.

[83] A. van Aelst, " Japanese coins," p. 2.

[84] Or in Japanese, *Kwan-Ei Tsu-Ho* coins, cast from 1626 to 1859. A. van Aelst and Neil Gordon Munro, *Coins of Japan* (Tokyo: Yokohama, 1904), pp. 111–112.

[85] F C. Danvers and William Foster, eds., *Letters Received by the East India Company from Its Servants in the East* (Amsterdam: N. Israel, 1968), vol. 4, p. 16.

[86] Hayashi Shunsai, comp., *Kai-hentai*, vol. 15, pp. 1036-1045.

[87] Lamb, *The Mandarin Road*, p. 52.

[88] Peng Xin Wei, *Zhong Guo Huo Bi Shi* (A history of Chinese coinage) (Shanghai: People's Press, 1958), p. 567.

[89] Poivre said that before 1750 gold was valued at 130 *quan* for ten *taels*, in an expensive year 150 *quan*. See "Journal d'un voyage du vaisseau de la compagnie le Machault à la Cochinchine depuis le 29 août 1749, jour de nôtre arrivée, au 11 fevrier 1750," reproduced by H. Cordier in *Revue de l'Extrême-Orient* 3, (1885): 430.

[90] Before 1710 the official proportion of gold and silver was 1:10, but in reality the English bought gold at 9.85 *tael* silver in 1700. See H. B. Morse, *The Chronicles of The East India Company Trading to China, 1635–1834*, vol. 1 (Oxford: Clarendon Press, 1926), p. 69.

*quan* per *picul* in 1695,[91] it had doubled by 1750,[92] and in the 1770s had reached forty-five *quan* per *picul*.[93] In 1750, the official price ratio between silver and copper in China was 1:57,[94] whereas in Cochinchina it was 1:50, and dropped to 1:44 in the 1770s.[95] This disparity meant that it remained profitable for Chinese to trade copper in Đàng Trong. But even so, most of the copper the Chinese brought might still have come from Japan. Until 1712, the official price ratios between silver and copper in Japan had been 1:99, but in the late seventeenth century it rose to 1:112.[96] This represented almost one-third of the price of copper in Cochinchina. Since copper was valued more highly than copper coins, it was natural for people to melt the coins down, as the *Phủ Biên* showed. But this only exacerbated the coin shortage and made copper even more expensive.

Not all Đàng Trong coinage was imported. Some locally made coins circulated, including coins stamped with the characters *Thái Bình* and *An Pháp*, which had been minted under the Mạc and presumably arrived early in the Nguyễn period. The *Phủ Biên*, too, said that, on acceding to the throne, each *chúa* cast some coins that imitated the Mạc *Thái Bình* (or "great peace") coins.[97] However, they were produced largely for ceremonial reasons and in amounts too small for economic purposes.[98] Basically, Japanese and Chinese coins circulated so widely in Đàng Trong up to the late seventeenth century that the Nguyễn had no interest in creating their own currency, even though East Asian rulers usually regarded casting coins as one attribute of kingship.

---

[91] Lamb, *The Mandarin Road*, p. 52. The text says "*tael*" which means *quan*. See ibid., p. 53: "Their *tael* is accounted by cashes . . . 600 the thousand or *tael.*"

[92] Poivre, "Memoires," p. 336.

[93] *Phủ Biên*, vol. 4, p. 21a.

[94] Peng Xin Wei, *Zhong Guo*, p. 571.

[95] According to Poivre, one *tael* of silver in Cochinchina in 1750 was worth two *quan*. Poivre, "Journal d'un voyage," p. 406.

[96] *Nihongo Nagasaki* (Tokyo: Yashikama Kobun Kan, 1964), pp. 216-218.

[97] Tạ Chí Đài Trường has suggested from his reading of the *Phủ Biên* that the *Thái Bình* coins were cast not by the Mạc in the north, but by Mạc Thiên Tứ in Hà Tiên. Tạ Chí Đài Trường, "Tiền đúc Đàng Trong: Phương diện loại hình và tương quan lịch sử" (Coins cast in Đàng Trong: the types and their relevance to history), in *Văn Học*, California, 32 (September 1988): 91. Yet the two Mạc are written differently in Chinese characters, and the Saigon edition of *Phủ Biên* clearly indicates these coins were from the northern Mạc, not those from Hà Tiên. See *Phủ Biên*, p. 21b.

On the other hand, the Nguyen did permit the Mạc in Hà Tiên to cast coins to facilitate trade. Thus, it may be that *Thái Bình* coins were cast both by the Mạc in the north and by Mạc Thiên Tứ who copied the earlier northern coins. There were also far more southern coins, as the northern Mạc only cast a small amount compared to the many *Thái Bình* coins found in the south. Indeed, as the scholar Ngô Thế Lân pointed out at the time, the zinc coins cast in the Mekong delta were the direct cause of the inflation in the Gia Định area. See *Phủ Biên*, vol. 5, p. 190.

[98] There are nine *Thái Bình* coins in Albert Schroeder's *Numismatique de l'Annam*, one of zinc and others of copper. Two *An Pháp* coins, both made of copper, are put into the category of "monaies incertaines" by the author. See Albert Schroeder, *Numismatique de l'Annam*, (Paris: reprinted by Trismegiste, 1983), pp. 493, 499. Also Đỗ Văn Ninh, *Tiền Cổ Việt Nam* (Ancient Vietnamese coinage) (Hanoi: Khoa Học Xã Hội, 1992), pp. 90–92.

### THE DEMAND FOR CURRENCY IN THE EIGHTEENTH CENTURY AND ITS CAUSES

This situation changed in the eighteenth century, prompting a Nguyễn ruler, Nguyễn Phúc Tru (r. 1725-1738), for the first time to try casting local coinage to meet the country's need for currency. The experiment proved so expensive, however, that he soon had to stop.[99] It was no accident that the Nguyễn needed to cast coins by 1725. A shortage of currency had been looming for some time, at least since 1688 when the Nguyễn ruler had unsuccessfully asked the Japanese to cast coins for them. At that time they had been saved by the fall in value of Chinese coins, which caused large numbers to be exported in the late seventeenth century. As part of a "dynamic South China Sea economy,"[100] Cochinchina's demand for coins had been met by the market itself and, as Bowyear's narrative shows, the imported Chinese coins did fill the gap to a certain degree.[101] But the situation deteriorated in the early eighteenth century. The price of copper, and therefore of coins, went up in China, and from the 1710s Japan started limiting copper exports, creating an urgent demand for coinage in Cochinchina.

Other important factors made the problem of currency more pressing. In the first place, Nguyễn Phúc Khoát (r. 1738-1765) was perhaps the most ambitious and extravagant of Nguyễn rulers. Conflicts between Cochinchina and the Khmer in the 1750s must have been costly, while his royal building program in Phú-Xuân, where palaces, temples, pleasure gardens, and other embellishments were constructed from 1754 onwards, must have consumed huge amounts of money and labor.[102]

Second, population growth played an important role, both directly and indirectly. As Thuận Hóa did not produce enough rice to feed the residents of the capital and members of the army stationed there, from the early eighteenth century a large amount had to be transported to Thuận Hóa from the south, from the Mekong delta particularly. Until 1714, the government required people who owned boats to transport rice to Thuận Hóa twice a year. They earned tax-exemptions for their trouble, as well as receiving some money for boat maintenance and to pay for the rite of praying for a good wind. But many people disliked these arrangements because, according to the *Tiền Biên*, "trade often [brought] much more profit, and therefore, although there were many boats, few were willing to transport rice to the capital."[103] When the capital area was under-populated, the situation was tolerable, but the insufficient supplies of rice presented a serious problem in the eighteenth century, when population increased, causing the Nguyễn to change the rules in 1714. To encourage transport, the government now offered to pay for rice in cash according to boat size and the distance covered.[104]

This event marked the start of a major transition in Đàng Trong in the 1710s. Previously the country had been under a military form of government, which now,

---

[99] *Phủ Biên*, vol. 4, p. 21b.

[100] Woodside, "Lê Qúy Đôn's 'Frontier Chronicles,'" p. 163.

[101] Lamb, *The Mandarin Road*, p. 52.

[102] "Description of Cochinchina, 1749-50," in Li Tana and Reid, *Southern Vietnam under the Nguyễn*, pp. 69–70. The extravagance did not end with him: Lê Quý Đôn said that from 1770 to 1771, more than 7000 kg of brass and 2300 kg of tin were used to decorate the Nguyen palace. *Phủ Biên*, vol. 4, p. 20b.

[103] *Tiền Biên*, vol. 8, p. 119.

[104] Ibid.

in the eighteenth century, the Nguyễn rulers found hard to maintain. The early labor force in Cochinchina had very likely worked for no pay at all. When the *Tiền Biên* described the huge project of building two great walls in Quảng Bình in 1630 and 1631, it used the word "levy" to describe how labor was recruited.[105] But from 1714 that clearly changed. In that year not only was transported rice paid for in cash, but the Nguyễn also had to pay the people who worked for the mail posts in the provinces.[106] In addition, many taxes were now levied in cash rather than in kind. Even buying a government post also now required a large cash bribe, contrasting with practices in the north, where rice was used to buy posts in 1739.[107] The cumulative effect of all these changes was to increase the demand for currency.

## ZINC COINS AND EIGHTEENTH CENTURY INFLATION

To meet the demand for currency, Nguyễn Phúc Khoát cast zinc coins[108] worth 72,396 *quan* from 1746 to 1748. This represented 70 percent less than the quantity brought in by the Dutch alone in the seventeenth century. But while the seventeenth-century imports had been absorbed into the economy with little difficulty, the eighteenth-century castings led to a disastrous inflation, not so much on account of the material used as on account of the weight and amount of the coins.

According to Poivre, one *picul* of zinc produced forty-eight to fifty *quan* in coins in Cochinchina.[109] This may well be the figure of the later period of casting. According to information given by Lê Quý Đôn, "the price [of zinc] was eight *quan* per *picul*, beside the costs for charcoal and craftsmen, there were still twenty *quan* left [as profit]."[110] He did not mention what charcoal and craftsmen cost in the 1740s, but did say casting in Huế in 1774 cost eight *quan* per *picul*. As it seems unlikely that costs in 1774 were higher than in the 1740s, I think that the figures given by Lê Quý Đôn came from the Nguyễn records of the 1740s. If so, the amount of *quan* cast from each *picul* of zinc should be thirty-six. That yields a profit 125 percent, and gives a real value for the coin of 44 percent of its face value. In this case the weight of each coin would be 2.3 grams. If what Poivre said was true, then the weight of one zinc coin was only about 1.7 grams. In either case, the zinc coins weighed only half, or one-third of the *Kang Xi* coins, which had been circulating for decades in

---

[105] Ibid., vol. 2, pp. 38, 40. Da Shan also said that "when the people did corvée, they brought their own food with them." See Da Shan, "Hai Wai Ji Shi," p. 3. Choisy said in 1695 that people in Cochinchina had to provide over half their labor when required. Abbé de Choisy, *Journal du voyage de Siam fait en 1685 et 1686*, ed. Maurice Garçon (Paris: Editions Duchartre et Van Buggenhoult, 1930), p. 254.

[106] *Tiền Biên*, vol. 8, p. 119.

[107] Phan Huy Chú, "Quan Chức Chí," *Lịch Triều Hiến Chương Loại Chí* (A reference book of the institutions of successive dynasties), translated into modern Vietnamese by Lương Thần and Cao Nãi Quang (Saigon: Nhà in Bao Vinh, 1957), p. 320.

[108] There has been considerable confusion about the term "tutenague" for several centuries. In Appendix Four I consider the problem in more detail. Here I refer to zinc coins, for "tutenague" was essentially that metal.

[109] Poivre, "Journal d'un voyage," p. 430.

[110] *Phủ Biên*, vol. 4, p. 21b. See also Nguyễn Thanh Nhã, *Tableau économique de Viet Nam aux XVII et XVIII siècles* (Paris: Editions Cujas, 1970), pp. 167–170.

Cochinchina and weighed from five grams to seven grams.[111] This difference in weight mattered more to people in Cochinchina than whether the coins were made of copper or zinc.

If Poivre was correct, and assuming the price of zinc and other costs remained the same in 1749, then the Nguyễn government would have made about 200 percent or more in profit by casting every *picul* of zinc into coins. If so, the face value of a zinc coin was more than twice its real value. This provided a great incentive for private casting. While it is hard to determine how many coins were cast privately in the late 1740s, we can make a guess about the numbers of foundries. According to *Phủ Biên*, the value of the coins cast by the government in the three years of 1746, 1747 and 1748 was 72,396 *quan*. Based on what we know from China, if one foundry cast 583,200 coins per year,[112] it would have required about twenty-five foundries to work three years to cast 72,396 *quan* in coins. Lê Quý Đôn says that "in a short time more than 100 private foundries were established."[113] This suggests that the coins cast privately might have doubled the number of those officially cast (presuming that private foundries would have been much smaller) and increased the specie circulating in society in the late 1740s to about two hundred thousand *quan*. Ironically, it was these private coins which made the face value of zinc coins close to their real value.

Zinc, cheap and abundant, may have seemed just what the Nguyễn needed in the early eighteenth century. Yet it was a mixed blessing. At the same time that zinc coinage insured enough currency for continued economic activity, it also provided the opportunity for others to exploit private casting. Realizing this, the Nguyễn government made some weak efforts to issue copper coins in order to stop the casting and circulation of counterfeits. But the effort proved very costly,[114] and the good money was quickly driven out by the bad.

Ultimately, the 1740s attempt by the government to cast coinage brought disastrous results and undermined the regime. Yet, given the needs of a growing economy for increased supplies of currency at a time when it was difficult even to maintain previous levels, the Nguyễn had little choice but to make their own. Thus, by influencing the trade in coins, Chinese and Japanese market forces contributed significantly to the disaster in Cochinchina. The problem was Nguyễn ignorance of the extent to which their new local coinage would be acceptable to society at large, and also their greed, which compounded their ignorance. By starting to cast thinner, lighter and therefore lower quality coins, the Nguyễn government itself made private

---

[111] Peng Xin Wei, *Zhong Guo Huo Bi Shi* (A history of Chinese coinage) (Shanghai: People's Press, 1958), p. 567.

[112] In late fourteenth-century China, the production of the foundries for casting coins in different areas were about the same, each producing 583,200 coins per year. Although this sounds like a bureaucratic standard, it does indicate the capacity of the casting at the time. The technique of casting did not improve much in China, and presumably in Cochinchina also, until the late Qing dynasty when a machine for casting was introduced to China from the West. See Peng Xin Wei, *Zhong Guo*, pp. 478-479.

[113] *Phủ Biên*, vol. 4, p. 22a.

[114] Lê Quý Đôn said that the price of copper was forty-five *quan* per *picul*. If the cost of casting was eight *quan* per *picul*, and forty *quan* of coins could be cast out of one *picul*, then it would cost one *quan* of money to cast 0.75 *quan* of coins, and the real value (if the face value did not increase) would be 130 percent of the face value.

casting possible, indeed almost inevitable. The result was an unprecedented inflation.

In 1749 Poivre commented: "Commerce in this country is becoming a real mess because they introduced a new sort of zinc coin. . . this situation cannot last long, but I do not know when it will end."[115] According to Lê Quý Đôn, because everyone wanted to keep the good money and spend the bad, even regions like Gia Định, where people had never bothered to store rice, now withheld their rice from the market. In the 1770s, he observed that even women and children buying trifles had to pay in silver,[116] a metal rarely used in Cochinchina previously. Under such circumstances, local trade could not avoid declining, nor could overseas trade escape the dire effects of the monetary crisis. Indeed, overseas trade was possibly the most severely affected sector. Robert Kirsop said in 1750 that after zinc coins were introduced, the price of gold in Hội An rose from 150-190 *quan* per bar to 200–225 *quan*, while rent in Hội An also increased remarkably.[117] The price of pepper leaped to fourteen *quan* per *picul* in 1750, and in 1749 it even reached fifteen to sixteen *quan* for a time, compared to the usual price of ten *quan*.[118] The price of zinc also increased. According to the same source, in the 1750s zinc cost thirteen to fourteen *quan* per *picul*, in contrast to eight *quan*, the going price immediately before the Nguyễn began casting in the 1740s.[119]

The currency-related inflation occurred in conjunction with the codification of the increased shipping duties as shown in Table Two. The two factors acting together undoubtedly played a major role in causing the sharp decline in the number of overseas junks in the next two decades. In the late 1740s, sixty to eighty junks came each year, according to the observations of Poivre and Koffler respectively, both of whom resided in Đàng Trong in 1749–50.[120] Calculated according to the customs regulations in Table Two, the average revenue from each junk was about two thousand *quan*. The annual taxes collected from seventy junks (at least 140,000 *quan*), which seems a reasonable estimate for the 1740s to early 1750s at least, represented from a third to a quarter of the state's revenue at least. By 1771, with only sixteen junks recorded, overseas trade contributed a mere 38,000 *quan* to state revenue, and this fell to 14,300 *quan* collected from only twelve junks in 1772.[121] If Lê Quý Đôn's information is correct, the sharpest drop probably occurred some time in the 1760s, as *Phủ Biên* said that arrival and departure taxes for ships were lowered to 2,100 *quan* in 1772 and 1773,[122] a substantial reduction for most large ships though perhaps less so for junks. But the reduction of customs duties failed to arrest the decline in shipping trade, and only eight junks arrived in 1773.[123] The outbreak of the Tây Sơn

---

[115] Taboulet, *La geste française en Indochine*, vol. 1, p. 124.

[116] *Phủ Biên*, vol. 4, pp. 22-23.

[117] Robert Kirsop, "Some accounts of Cochinchina," in A. Dalrymple, *Oriental Repertory*, vol. 1, p. 249.

[118] Poivre, "Journal d'un voyage," p. 418.

[119] *Phủ Biên*, p. 21b. The source of this information must have been Nguyễn records of the 1740s.

[120] Koffler lived there longer, from 1744 to 1753. See Koffler, "Description historique de la Cochinchine," *Revue Indochine* 16 (1911): 585.

[121] *Phủ Biên*, vol. 4, p. 32a.

[122] Ibid. He did not say what happened to junks that already paid less than 2,100 *quan*.

[123] *Phủ Biên*, vol. 4, p. 32a.

rebellion doomed this effort to restore Đàng Trong's merchant economy; compromise had come too late. Certainly when the Tây Sơn some years later tried to apply the mid-century Nguyễn customs regulations to Chapman, asking seven thousand *quan* for a large ship and four thousand for a smaller one, he complained that such charges "would deter any merchants from sending their vessels."[124]

The disintegration of overseas trade was a serious loss to the Nguyễn, who had long relied on it as a vital factor in state finances and the local economy. They responded by seeking to tighten their control over the trade of the mountain regions and uplanders within their reach, hoping to recoup in the west their losses from the east. As we will see later, whatever short term success they enjoyed came only at the ultimate cost of inciting the Tây Sơn rebellion, which brought Đàng Trong to ruin.

Maritime trade was no doubt a most important stimulus to Nguyễn state formation. It provided the Nguyễn with a major source of the cash income they needed for early political survival and for their military expeditions against enemies to the north and the south. Their decisive military advantage over the Trịnh—their advanced weaponry—was also ultimately dependent on the trade economy and its circulating cash. Yet this active, profitable trade economy involved certain grave dangers and threats to the established order. As the economy largely relied on maritime trade, particularly trade with markets in Japan and China, Đàng Trong became susceptible to economic, climactic, and political fluctuations in those countries, to forces beyond Nguyễn control. Cochinchina thus differed from Tongking and other mainland Southeast Asian states like Burma, which had retreated from international trade about a century earlier and were less vulnerable to changing external forces. Cochinchina's vulnerability was most evident in the crisis of money supply, a crisis that ultimately ruined Đàng Trong's international trade and shook its economy to the foundations. We can therefore identify market changes as one of the major historical factors that brought down the Nguyễn.

---

[124] Lamb, *The Mandarin Road*, p. 99.

# LIFE IN ĐÀNG TRONG:
# A NEW WAY OF BEING VIETNAMESE

## INTRODUCTION

In the seventeenth and eighteenth centuries, the land the Vietnamese occupied in their *nam tiến* was not empty. As they pushed south, Vietnamese in Đàng Trong came into close contact with local peoples of distinctive and different cultures, foremost among them the Cham. Although this process of Vietnamese expansion has often been portrayed as the simple replacement of one culture and civilization by another, in fact something quite different occurred. Vietnamese immigrants freely adopted and adapted many aspects of these other cultures in a long process that involved selective borrowing of the new and discarding of the old. It resulted in the localization of Vietnamese society and culture in Đàng Trong. This fruitful interaction ended by creating a new way of being Vietnamese, with a different sense of Vietnamese identity rooted in the social, cultural, and physical environment of the new southern state. In Đàng Trong, the hallmark of this period can be summed up by the Vietnamese term *địa phương hóa*—localization. *Việt hóa*, or the Vietnamization of the local people along more orthodox cultural lines, only really happened much later.

Official nineteenth-century court sources give us little sense of this significant process, however. To a considerable extent, this is because works like the *Đại Nam Thực Lục Tiền Biên* consciously tried to project a quite different impression, one picturing a continuity that stretched from the fifteenth-century foundations laid by Lê Thánh Tôn into the nineteenth century. This is largely because official nineteenth-century historiography of this era was implicitly organized on the principle of orthodox succession, designed to demonstrate that the Nguyễn forebears had not been rebels against the Lê, but in fact had been their legitimate imperial successors from the time of Nguyễn Hoàng onwards.[1] This claim is asserted quite bluntly in the 1844 Preface to the *Tiền Biên*, which was signed by two of the most influential and prestigious court officials of the time, Trương Đăng Quế and Vũ Xuân Cẩn. Speaking of "our government," they wrote that Nguyễn Hoàng (referred to as "Thái tổ Gia dự hoàng đế," that is, by his retrospective imperial title) had "laid its foundations in the South, it was improved and handed on [by] sacred kings, all bearing the mandate of Heaven [and] developing the country."[2] This single sentence was loaded with contemporary political significance. When the *Tiền Biên* stated categorically that Đàng Trong rulers from Nguyễn Hoàng onwards were kings who had borne the

---

[1] Philippe Langlet, *L'Ancien historiographie de l'état au Vietnam*, vol. 1 (Paris: Ecole Française d'Extrême-Orient, 1990). I would like to thank Nola Cooke for drawing this work to my attention.

[2] *Đại Nam Thực Lục Tiền Biên* (hereafter *Tiền Biên*) (Chronicle of Nguyen Dynasty, Premier Period) (Tokyo: Keio Institute of Linguistic Studies, 1961), p. 7.

Mandate of Heaven, a central emblem of royal legitimacy in classical Chinese political theory, this could only mean one thing: dynastic ideology ruled that Heaven had abandoned the Restored Lê in favor of the early Nguyễn, and consequently, based on the principle of orthodox succession, the Nguyễn's nineteenth-century descendants were part of a line of legitimate rulers stretching back for more than two hundred years.[3]

Such a transparently political attempt to rewrite recent history and reinvent the past was highly contentious, and the revised story was not willingly accepted by northern literati whose own loyal ancestors and forebears it denigrated. But if struggles over the content of official political histories ultimately failed to unsettle the ruling family and the highest echelons of the political elite, in large part men whose families derived from former Đàng Trong, they did forestall the appearance of an authorized Nguyễn history of Vietnam until late in the Tự Đức reign, after Lower Cochinchina had been seized by the French. Even the *Tiền Biên*, the first significant product of the Nguyễn Office of State Historiography established by Minh Mạng in 1820, took twenty-four years to compile.

For our purposes, however, what matters most is the extent to which nineteenth-century dynastic concerns shaped official accounts of the earlier period. Their shadowy presence helps explain why Đàng Trong was so often presented in the *Tiền Biên* as nothing new or unusual, as if no local or heterodox cultural or political elements had ever been absorbed by the Đàng Trong Vietnamese in these two hundred years. Compiling their materials so long after the event, having to cope with the destructive impact of a thirty year civil war on perishable sources and with an implicit political agenda that required the region appear orthodox, the nineteenth-century historians, many of whom were themselves degree-holding Confucian-educated literati, acted as one might expect: they glossed over or ignored evidence that did not conform to the carefully cultivated court perspective on the era and region. The post-1690s treatment of Panduranga, which portrayed the region as if it were merely another Vietnamese administrative region, "*trấn* Thuận Thành," is a prime example of the distortions imported into the historical record by this approach. However, the problem is much larger than the misrepresentation of Panduranga alone. Trying to impose a degree of Sino-Vietnamese political and cultural orthodoxy onto Đàng Trong's history and society has created a quite misleading image of the south. The localized Nguyễn state was no simple continuation or mere regional variant of northern Vietnam but, on the contrary, the product of numerous differing—and often quite heterodox—forces and influences.

The process of localization in the south, where Vietnamese found themselves seeking to survive and prosper in diverse environments, often in situations where native non-Vietnamese outnumbered them, tested their sense of identity. In some way, this had always been the case at the margins of Vietnamese settlement, along the Cham-Viet border. In the fourteenth century, the boundary of this cultural frontier was located at Nghệ An, and its men fought with both invaders and defenders during the 1380s Cham invasions that so strained the late Trần kingdom.[4]

---

[3] For a longer discussion of this point, see Nola Cooke, "The Myth of the Restoration: Dang-Trong Influences in the Spiritual Life of the Early Nguyen Dynasty (1802-47)," in *The Last Stand of Asian Autonomies: Responses to Modernity in the Diverse States of Southeast Asia and Korea, 1750-1900*, ed. Anthony Reid (Melbourne: Macmillan, 1997), pp. 269–95.

[4] John K. Whitmore, *Vietnam, Ho Quy Ly, and the Ming (1371-1421)* (Lac-Viet Series No. 2, Yale Center for International and Area Studies, 1985), pp. 18–19, 29–31.

In the fifteenth century, the region of ambivalent marginality had shifted, in the eyes of delta literati, to Thuận Hóa, which the scholars regarded as "contaminated by the old customs of the Chams."[5] In the seventeenth century, however, the emergence of a hostile power to the north complicated the situation at the southern cultural frontier. In the first place, it forced Đàng Trong Vietnamese to rely exclusively on their own resources, and it reduced the flow of new Vietnamese settlers from long established areas to a trickle. In these circumstances, ultimate success was no foregone conclusion. Secondly, it meant that rather than succumbing to the allure of the Sino-Vietnamese cultural heartland in the Red River plains, as elites at the margins had usually done in the past, the Nguyễn elite were required to differentiate themselves from their own ancestral people in the north in order to secure their own political survival. This desire for a separate identity showed through in virtually every element of the Nguyễn administration: in the different names they gave to essentially the same official posts, their different pay system, their different style of dress, and so on. Perhaps most significant of all, it culminated in 1744, when Nguyễn Phúc Khoat proclaimed himself king and proudly declared: "our country rose and developed from Ô Châu" (that is, from Thuận Hóa).[6] Instead of choosing Đại Việt, or even Thanh Hóa, where the Nguyễn themselves and most of their retainer elite originated, he chose to locate the kingdom's origins in the separate and distinctive local region of Ô Châu. Thereafter, this declaration of southern origin became a standard element in nineteenth-century official historiography.

The Nguyễn had a two-fold task if they were to survive in Đàng Trong: they had to build a separate and distinct polity; and they needed to encourage a more homogeneous society to develop and include the various peoples under their rule. For most of Đàng Trong's history, these two aims turned out in practice to be complementary, thanks to the increasing localization of the Vietnamese population. This chapter examines in detail some of the diverse elements involved in this localization process. Almost every facet of Vietnamese life in Đàng Trong was touched in some way by the different physical and cultural challenges posed in the south. Rather than catalogue a series of disparate examples, however, we focus mainly on two areas: the heterodox emphases that developed in Đàng Trong religious life and cultural values; and the changes to Vietnamese material life and culture here. This chapter concentrates mainly on the local peculiarities of Đàng Trong life that reflected Vietnamese cultural borrowing from the Chams, although some other sources are also considered. The next chapter explores cultural interactions with upland peoples.

## RELIGIOUS LIFE AND CULTURAL VALUES

It was during the seventeenth century that a clear sense of regional identity developed in Đàng Trong. Up until 1600, the first *chúa*, Nguyễn Hoàng, had been

---

[5] Marginal note by Lý Tử Tấn in Nguyen Trai's *Du Dia Chi* (Geography), quoted in Nola Cooke, "Nineteenth-Century Vietnamese Confucianization in Historical Perspective: Evidence from the Palace Examinations (1463-1883), *Journal of Southeast Asian Studies*, 25, 2 (1994): 282.

[6] *Tiền Biên*, vol. 10, p. 136.

content to see his domain as a frontier or border region.[7] For example, the *Tiền Biên* boasted that, in the late sixteenth century:

> at the time the Lê emperor had exhausted the resources of the country in the war [against the Mạc], [Nguyễn Hoàng] collected taxes from the Thuận Hóa region to support the court, so that the capital relied on [Thuận Hóa].[8]

But from the early seventeenth century we find developing a sense of separateness, and with it the beginnings of a sense of local identity. This feeling was particularly heightened at the end of the Trịnh-Nguyễn wars, when the victorious southern regime increasingly turned its back on the north and began to regard its own territories with new interest. Nguyễn rulers confidently looked towards a new era defined by consolidation within its own boundaries, expansion at the southern border, and reassessment in an international context, for the Nguyễn leaders hoped to gain international acceptance as a separate, powerful, and sovereign state from their neighbors in the South China Sea. Success in this endeavor required that the Nguyễn themselves become naturalized to the region so that they lost any lingering traces of foreignness in the eyes of local peoples. One of the principal means by which the Nguyễn successfully domesticated their regime was through an eclectic weaving of indigenous spirits and beliefs into a syncretic (Vietnamese) Buddhist framework, a hybrid religious system that bestowed moral legitimacy on Nguyễn authority in Đàng Trong. We will discuss Buddhism first, since it provided the overarching framework for Đàng Trong official religion.

Buddhism flourished in Đàng Trong under official patronage, offering moral support and spiritual comfort and protection to all immigrant Vietnamese, from the Nguyễn rulers down. There were two main reasons for Buddhism's great success here. The first involved the culture shock that accompanied first-hand Vietnamese encounters with Cham civilization; and the second reflected Nguyễn political needs. We will consider them in turn.

When Vietnamese moved down the coast to the region later known as Đàng Trong, they discovered for themselves the alien yet fascinating Cham culture that had always attracted their forebears in the past, despite the fact that it had been presented as the culture of the defeated. Cham music had been popular in the Lý dynasty in the eleventh century; Vietnamese women in the Cham-Viet border area loved Cham clothing as late as the fifteenth century.[9] Until the fifteenth century, Vietnamized Cham goddesses were worshipped in the capital itself, while pioneers in the south could only marvel at the magnificently ornate Cham towers which Vietnamese architecture could not equal. Vietnamese immigrants, far from their native places and often living in small groups on former Cham lands, must have found Cham culture both peculiarly beautiful and disturbingly exotic. In an insecure psychological borderland, Vietnamese were attracted to, and at the same time eager

---

[7] Thus Keith Taylor believes Nguyễn Hoàng stayed in the north from 1592 to 1600 because he "had ambitions of supplanting the Trịnh and uniting all the Vietnamese lands under his hand." See "Nguyen Hoang and the Beginning of Viet Nam's Southward Expansion," in *Southeast Asia in the Early Modern Era*, ed. Anthony Reid (Ithaca: Cornell University Press, 1993), p. 55.

[8] *Tiền Biên*, vol. 1, p. 24, entry of 1589.

[9] Dương Văn An, *Ô Châu Cận Lục* (A record on Ô Châu, present Quảng Bình and Quảng Trị provinces) (Saigon: Văn Hóa Á Châu, 1961), p. 46.

to escape from (or subdue), the foreign culture that had preceded, and often still surrounded, them.

In this new situation, the Nguyễn rulers needed to provide an alternative to Cham beliefs that would help sustain Vietnamese immigrants spiritually and psychologically. The symbols and trappings of Lê imperial Neo-Confucianism were hardly appropriate, even if they had been considered by early Nguyễn ruling circles. These men after all were no Confucianists: the Tống Sơn district, from which most of them came, never produced a single palace-level graduate in over three hundred years of Lê dynasty examinations (1463-1787), nor a single regional-level graduate later under the pre-colonial Nguyễn dynasty, while Thanh Hóa province itself, by the early sixteenth century, had accounted for only 4 percent (or forty) of early Lê palace graduates, fewer even than neighboring Nghệ An (which had forty-eight).[10] In the seventeenth-century wars, the Nguyễn had countered Trịnh denunciations portraying them as rebels by broadcasting propaganda identifying themselves as the only loyal subjects of the Lê emperors whose powers had been all but usurped by the Trịnh. However, the posture was largely a wartime device intended to divide northern sentiment, and thus it reappeared in a different form during the 1790s when Nguyễn Ánh allowed northerners to believe he intended to restore the Lê.[11] But it is clear that the basic premises of Chinese political theory and Neo-Confucian philosophy, if studied in any depth, would not serve Nguyễn needs. They would have potentially focused attention northward, to the captive Lê emperor, instead of inwards and southwards, onto the expanding separatist state itself, and the Nguyễn needed an inclusive ideology, not one that would highlight qualities distinguishing the Vietnamese from the other peoples of the region. Of necessity, therefore, Confucianism in Đàng Trong played a political and social role that was relatively minor compared to its role in the north, where the Chinese-style examination system ensured neo-Confucianism never lost its grip on the literati elite. Instead, to borrow Nola Cooke's words:

> uncoupled from this institutional nexus and thrust into a new environment whose political masters sponsored the most eclectic . . . syncretism, Confucianism in Đàng-trong became a matter of private choice and practice to an extent unknown in the north since the thirteenth century . . . [S]o modest was its niche in the southern ideological spectrum that no one even bothered to record when the first humble Confucian Temple of Literature was actually founded here.[12]

But the Nguyễn could not risk venturing too far afield by seeking a solution radically different from existing Vietnamese traditions. Mahayana Buddhism provided a compromise solution appropriate to Nguyễn needs. It shored up Vietnamese ethnic identity and calmed immigrants' anxieties while at the same time reinforcing the legitimacy of the Nguyễn rulers. Indeed, Mahayana Buddhism helped establish a clear contrast between Nguyễn rulers, who acted on Buddhist-

---

[10] Cooke, "Nineteenth-Century Vietnamese Confucianization," p. 282, fn. 71.

[11] Leopold Cadiere, "Documents relatifs a l'époque de Gia-Long," *Bulletin de l'Ecole française d'Extrême-Orient* XII (1912).

[12] Cooke, "Nineteenth-Century Vietnamese Confucianization," p. 284. The first mention is of moving the existing temple in 1697.

based authority, and the Lê/Trịnh of the north, who relied on a Confucianist authority base. The Japanese scholar Momoki Shiro has sensed exactly this distinction suggested in a phrase written by Nguyễn Phúc Chu in 1714 on a stele at Thiên Mụ: "The king of Đại Việt [meaning himself] lived in the Kun Ye garden inside the temple."[13] Nothing similar to this has been seen among northern temple inscriptions of the same period. In addition, Mahayana Buddhism's syncretic nature allowed room to incorporate local spirits and deities; indeed, its many gods and spirit entities already echoed the polytheism of the Cham. A deliberate Nguyễn association of Cham and Buddhist sites of worship appeared very early in Đàng Trong. The *Tiền Biên* repeatedly recorded how Buddhist pagodas were consciously raised on the ruins of Cham temples early in Nguyễn rule, although of course this may also have reflected a Vietnamese desire to exploit the magical power of existing religious sites to their own ends. But the *Tiền Biên* also recorded how old Cham temples were respected by Nguyễn rulers who wanted to replace them with Buddhist pagodas: instead of simply tearing them down, on these occasions the *chúa* would order the Cham temples to be dismantled and relocated elsewhere.[14] Building pagodas was one of the principal occupations of Nguyễn ruling circles and ordinary Vietnamese, especially in Thuận Hóa around the capital. Pierre Poivre reported that by 1750 there were about four hundred Buddhist temples in the Phú Xuân/Huế area alone, plus many more elsewhere.[15] The majority of them were later destroyed in the Tây Sơn rebellion, either because of their pro-Nguyễn associations or because the Tây Sơn had a policy allowing only one pagoda for each district.[16] It is for this reason that later European travelers like Barrow in 1792 only reported the existence of smaller Buddhist shrines. We note this observation at Đà Nẵng:

> On the skirts of every little grove of trees near Turon bay small boxes of wood or baskets of wicker work were either suspended from or fixed among the branches, some containing images made of various materials.[17]

That this southern Buddhism was highly syncretic gave it a more inclusive appeal. For instance, the most famous temple in Huế, the Thiên Mụ, illustrates how different religious currents combined here, and how, from Nguyễn Hoàng onwards, the new rulers were able to weave these various strands together into a local religious tapestry that domesticated and supported their own power. Thiên Mụ stood on a hill whose geomantic force was so powerful that, local legend held, it had forced a ninth-century Chinese governor to try to neutralize its dragon vein by

---

[13] Momoki Shiro, "The Nguyen Lords and 'Vietnam,'" in Momoki Shiro, ed., *Historical Environmental Situation of Hoi An, a Port of Central Vietnam in the South-China Sea Trade World*, Interim Report, The Japanese Ministry of Education and Culture, no. 02041055, (September 1995): 35.

[14] *Tiền Biên*, entries 1602, 1607, 1609, 1667, 1721.

[15] Pierre Poivre, "Journal d'un voyage du vaisseau de la compagnie le Machault à la Cochinchine depuis le 29 août 1749, jour de notre arrivée, au 11 fevrier 1750," reproduced by H. Cordier in *Revue de l'Extrême-Orient* III (1885): 381. Today Huế, has several hundred temples and is called the "capital of Buddhism." See Thanh Tùng, *Thăm Chùa Huế* (Huế: Hội Văn Nghệ Thành Phố Huế, 1989), p. 3.

[16] L. Cadiere, "Documents relatifs," pp. 8, 14.

[17] John Barrow, *A Voyage to Cochinchina* (Kuala Lumpur: Oxford University Press, 1975), p. 330.

digging a ditch across it. The site also housed an important Cham temple to the great earth goddess, Po Nagar. Vietnamese legend held that in 1600 the goddess miraculously appeared in the form of an old women, a "Heavenly Mother" whose description combined qualities of Po Nagar and the Taoist Queen of Heaven. She announced that the true lord of the land had arrived and would restore the dragon vein beneath the hill by building a pagoda to concentrate its spirit forces in his cause. Whether this prophecy was actually made before or after Nguyễn Hoàng answered it by constructing a pagoda in 1601 may never be known. What matters here is that when the first Nguyễn *chúa* consciously erected a Buddhist pagoda on this site traditionally identified as having great spirit potency, he was making a gesture of enormous political significance. If, as Nguyễn Thế Anh has recently reported, this was a symbolic construction at an existing temple whose spirit had not been officially recognized by the Lê court, the act would have been even more charged with local meaning.[18]

As for Po Nagar herself, this great Cham goddess was soon Vietnamized into Thiên-Y-A-Na, and the area around Huế abounded with her shrines. In the early twentieth century Leopold Cadiere listed so many of them still extant that Nguyễn Thế Anh has suggested "the Nguyễn center of power never ceased to be steeped in an atmosphere deeply influenced by the spiritual imprint of this deity."[19] Certainly in this area her worship remained unconstrained, and far closer to its Cham roots than in the north at the same time. Following the 1509 massacre of Chams living around Thăng Long, the Lê capital, the previously popular cult of Po Nagar there only survived, if at all, by a transmutation into the later holy mother cult of princess Liễu-Hạnh which emerged in late sixteenth-century Thanh Hóa. Legends surrounding this new female cult suggest that Confucian-trained officials opposed the spread of her cult during the seventeenth-century literati revival in Đàng Ngoài and vainly tried to expel her, but at last the court was forced to acknowledge her power by officially bestowing titles.[20] This Confucian effort to tame a goddess not only contrasts with the ready acceptance of Po Nagar/Thiên-Y-A-Na by both rulers and people further south, but also with the welcome the Nguyễn accorded all useful local spirits, whatever their background. In this context it is interesting to note that female spirits were readily honored and recognized by the Nguyễn right from the start. Perhaps Nguyễn Hoàng's 1572 dream encounter with the spirit of Ái Tử River set the tone, since it was her advice that enabled him to rout an invading enemy force; the ruler built her a temple in recognition of his gratitude.[21] Southern Vietnamese also honored the rock goddess discovered in the mid-sixteenth century by a fisherman near Huế, Thai Dương Phu Nhân. It was said that on two occasions, only she could bring about changes to the weather that the *chúa* had prayed for elsewhere in vain; her responsiveness was recognized officially and duly rewarded.

---

[18] Nguyễn Thế Anh, "The Vietnamization of the Cham Deity Po Nagar," in *Essays into Vietnamese Pasts*, ed. Keith Taylor and John Whitmore (Ithaca: Cornell Southeast Asia Program, 1995), p. 49. Also see A. Bonhomme, "La pagode Thien-Mau: Historique," *Bulletin des Amis du Vieux Hue* II, 2 (1915): 175–77.

[19] Nguyễn Thế Anh, "The Vietnamization of the Cham Deity Po Nagar," p. 49

[20] Đào Thái Hành, "La princesse Lieu-Hanh," *Bulletin des Amis du Vieux Hue*, I, 2 (1914): 180–81; Nguyễn Thế Anh "The Vietnamization of Po Nagar," p. 46–48.

[21] *Tiền Biên*, vol. 1 , pp. 22–23.

As with Thiên-Y-A-Na, veneration of this goddess also continued under the Nguyễn dynasty in the nineteenth century.[22]

The common people worshipped more eclectically. There were rites of worship for a piece of rock (*thờ đá*), for the crocodile (*thờ cá sấu*), or for the tiger (*thờ cọp*).[23] As one of Poivre's companions recalled:

> Mountains, forests, rivers, the memory of ancestors, respect for the dead and especially spirits are subjects of worships. . . . There is a god for each man's fancy. Some worship a tree, others a stone, etc.; it would thus be difficult to determine what sort of idol worship predominates in Cochinchina.[24]

There were other Cham influences that persisted among the people though they seem to have played little or no direct political role in upholding the Nguyễn regime. They included a local cult of the whale, the Fish of Benevolence in Phú Yên, or Cá Ông. The nineteenth-century provincial gazetteers for the south underlined the regional particularism inherent in this whale cult, remarking that the Great Fish "helps people in storms at sea . . . but is only effective in the south, from the Gianh River to Hà Tiên, and does not work in other parts of the sea."[25] The reason for the whale's lapse of power in the north, according to Lê Quang Nghiêm, was that northerners, following the Chinese Confucian practice, did not believe in the Cá Ông. The Cá Ông, therefore, was considered, in a popular saying in the south, as "*tại Bắc vị ngư, tại Nam vị thần*" (fish in the north, deity in the south).[26] Even today, cult ceremonies to welcome the Great Fish of the Southern Sea are still held annually in southern Vietnam.[27] Other rituals that indicate Cham origins or associations were recorded as late as the early twentieth century. Lê Quang Nghiêm, for example, has reported that certain Vietnamese fishing villages in Khánh Hòa province used to venerate two divinities they called Lổ Lường and Bộ Đồ, terms derived from the sacred Cham *yoni* and *linga*, Hindu concepts that celebrated male and female generative power.[28] In the twentieth century, Vietnamese in other former Đàng Trong provinces were also recorded as inviting Cham shamans to perform ceremonial offerings to a Cham spirit called *Dang* in Vietnamese. "Dang" is a Vietnamese corruption of the Cham word *yang*, cognates of which appear in Javanese

---

[22] Cooke, "Myth of the Restoration," pp. 279–80.

[23] Nguyễn Công Bình, Lê Xuân Điệm and Mạc Đường. *Văn Hóa và Cư Dân Đồng bằng Sông Cửu Long* (Culture and residents in the Mekong delta region) (Hô Chí Minh City: Khoa Học Xã Hội, 1990), pp. 376–377.

[24] "Description of Cochinchina, 1749-50," in Li Tana and Anthony Reid, eds., *Southern Vietnam under the Nguyễn, Documents on the Economic History of Cochinchina (Đàng Trong), 1602–1777* (Singapore: Institute of Southeast Asian Studies/ECHOSEA, Australian National University, 1993), p. 84.

[25] *Đại Nam Nhất Thống Chí, Lục Tỉnh Nam Việt* (Gazetteer of Dai Nam, the six southern provinces), vol. 1 (Saigon: Nha Văn Hóa, 1973), pp. 43–44.

[26] Lê Quang Nghiêm, *Tục thờ cúng của ngư phủ Khánh Hòa* (Rites in the fishing region of Khánh Hòa) (Los Alamitos: reprinted by Xuân Thu, n.d.), p. 36.

[27] Nguyễn Công Bình, Lê Xuân Điệm and Mạc Đường. *Văn Hóa và Cư Dân Đồng bằng Sông Cửu Long* , p. 385.

[28] Lê Quang Nghiêm, *Tục thờ cúng của ngư phủ Khánh Hòa*, p. 110.

and Malay languages with the meaning of "divinity."[29] In this Vietnamese ritual, the spirit in question was understood to be Cham, and its local origin was underlined by a rule that allowed only banana leaves to be used in the ceremony: cups, plates, chopsticks or spoons were all banned.

Lê Quang Nghiêm has aptly summarized the state of spiritual uncertainty that troubled ordinary Vietnamese newcomers as they pushed further south, uncertainty that encouraged their borrowing and adaptation of foreign cults:

> living on the former land of Champa, Vietnamese immigrants were under the [immediate] influence of Cham culture. In an environment which was full of effective magic power, poisons, and incantations, they made themselves adopt Cham customs and rites. [30]

From the standpoint of traditional Vietnamese peasants, the whole world was inhabited with spirit forces. Some were concentrated in natural features like rocks or trees or places of great geomantic power, but others, notably the spirits of the unsatisfied dead, could wander to prey on living men. Given such fundamental beliefs, it is hardly surprising that Vietnamese from the Nguyễn rulers down to their most humble subjects sought to recognize and appease the existing spirits of the land, and in so doing evolved a syncretic religion particularly suited to their new environment.

It might be argued that, in an era distinguished by the "three religions" (*tam giáo*) syncretism in northern Vietnam, what was occurring in Đàng Trong differed only in degree, not in kind, from the situation in the north. There is some merit in this argument when it is applied in the context of the common people, though it still seems unlikely that northern Vietnamese peasants would have adopted some of the more extreme elements included in the Đàng Trong ritual and religious spectrum, elements like human sacrifice, which we will discuss in the next chapter. Where Buddhism was concerned, the real qualitative difference between the two polities could be found at the court level, where the Nguyễn consistently championed syncretic Buddhism as the effective state religion of Đàng Trong. It is true that at times both Lê kings and Trịnh *chúa* patronized Buddhism, some enthusiastically. At the height of revived literati influence in the 1660s, and only a few years after scholarly officials had prepared a forty-seven article edict of moral education attacking superstitious practices and restricting the unlicensed building of Buddhist pagodas,[31] the Trịnh family itself had imported Chinese monks to renew local Buddhism in 1667. Trịnh princes frequented Buddhist sites and went on pilgrimages; one family member even founded a new sect. However, even at its height of influence, at no stage did Buddhism challenge the Chinese political concepts and official ideology that formed "the vital principle of the state."[32] Buddhism was

---

[29] See Gerald Hickey, *Sons of the Mountains* (New Haven and London: Yale University Press, 1982), p. 24.

[30] Lê Quang Nghiêm, *Tục thờ cúng của ngư phủ Khánh Hòa*, p. 110.

[31] *Tiền Biên*, vol. 19, p. 974; Lê Sĩ Giác, *Lê Triều Chiếu Lệnh Thiện Chính* (translated into modern Vietnamese) (Saigon: Bao Vinh, 1961), p. 311; K. W. Taylor, "The Literati Revival in Seventeenth-Century Vietnam," *Journal of Southeast Asian Studies*, 18, 1 (1987): 1-23.

[32] Philippe Langlet, *La Tradition vietnamienne: un état national au sein de la civilisation chinoise* (Saigon: BSEI, 1970), pp. 70–71, quote p. 71.

sanctioned very much as a vehicle of personal salvation which posed no threat to the established political order.[33] Had it appeared to threaten the status quo, even potentially, it would no doubt have been as tightly controlled as Catholic Christianity, whose foreign origins and European associations made it suspicious to the authorities in both the north and the south at the time.

In the later seventeenth and eighteenth centuries, by contrast with Tongking, greater openness to foreign trade in Cochinchina meant greater openness to outside influences. This was not simply a result of the fact that Japanese Christians, and then Christian missionaries, came to live there; it was also reflected in the number of Chinese Buddhist monks who either visited Đàng Trong (as Da Shan did in 1695) or came to establish monasteries there themselves. Several of these Buddhist monks, such as Tạ Nguyên Thiều and Giác Linh, attained such stature that they later received short official biographies in the nineteenth-century compilation, *Đại Nam Liệt Truyện Tiền Biên.*[34] That this steady influx of well-trained, literate monks from China did not purify local Buddhism or eradicate its heterodox elements surely supports the view that Nguyễn rulers exploited this very syncretism politically, as a means of incorporating local spirits or deities into an overarching framework of shared religious belief. But their politic handling of Buddhism did not mean that particular Nguyễn rulers were not themselves devout Buddhists. In this respect, the priest Da Shan's reported experience was interesting. In 1695, he claimed to have formally converted *chúa* Nguyễn Phúc Chu, together with his mother, his queen, and all the members of the royal family, on the Buddha's birthday. Three days later the high court officials were also converted. Such was the influence of the court's action that within a few days fourteen hundred converts followed the example set by the ruling elites; all of them received certificates stamped with the king's seal, according to Da Shan.[35] But as these people were all Buddhists to begin with, how should we understand Da Shan's anecdote? The key seems to lie in Nguyễn Phúc Chu's claim thereafter to be in the thirtieth generation of the Lâm Tế (*Lin ji* in Chinese) school of Buddhism; Da Shan stood in the twenty-ninth generation of the Lâm Tế school.[36] In other words, the mass conversion of the Đàng Trong court elite was an initiation into a particular Buddhist school. The royal family's conversion, which then instigated this wholesale enrollment of converts, recalls actions of those kings of the eleventh-century Lý dynasty who became the first, third, and fifth generations of the Thảo Đường (*cao tang* in Chinese) school, and of the Trần kings, Thái Tôn and Nhân Tôn, who were famous for their Trúc Lâm school. Yet the establishment of the Lê dynasty, with its foundations in classical Chinese political theories, had put an end to such practices in the north. From then on northerners held that the king was the pinnacle of society, society's direct link to heaven, and thus superior to all other beings. For a king to become simply one among the successive generations of any particular

---

[33] Insun Yu, *Law and Society in Seventeenth and Eighteenth Century Vietnam* (Seoul: Asiatic Research Center, Korea University, 1990), p. 29.

[34] *Đại Nam Liệt Truyện Tiền Biên* (hereafter *Liệt Truyện Tiền Biên*) (Collection of Biographies of Nguyen Dynasty, Premier Period) (Tokyo: Keio Institute of Linguistic Studies, 1961), vol. 6, pp. 264–266.

[35] Da Shan, "Hai Wai Ji Shi," in *Shi Qi Shi Ji Guang Nan zhi Xin Shi Liao*, ed. Chen Ching-ho (Taipei: Zhong Hua Cong Shu Bian Sheng Wei Yuan Hui, 1960), pp. 19–23.

[36] This claim appeared in his 1715 inscription on a Thiên Mụ stele. See "Ngự kiến Thiên Mụ từ chung" (The royal inscription on a bell in Thiên Mụ temple), Hán-Nôm Institute, Hanoi, shelf number 5683.

religious school would have been perceived there as degrading. Freed from such imperial constraints, however, the Nguyễn kings in Đàng Trong were free to practice their religion as they wished and as it had been done by earlier Vietnamese rulers.

But in the political realm, promoting local cults within a syncretic Buddhist framework was still not enough. The Nguyễn did not simply have to survive with this diversity; they also had to insure their dominant role in society. In this they were wise enough to give themselves and their regime a strong local color. As Oliver Wolters has argued, in early Southeast Asia "the king's status was unique only because it was a religious one."[37] The seventeenth century Nguyễn seem to have been aware of this, for they soon acted to provide a religious coloration to their position as rulers. According to the *Việt-Nam Khai Quốc Chí Truyện*, an early history of the Nguyễn period written in the style of a novel, Nguyễn Phúc Tần, Nguyễn Phúc Trăn and Nguyễn Phúc Khoát were all called *nam thiên vương* (southern king of heaven) by the Khmer, while Nguyễn Hoàng was called *thiên vương* (king of heaven).[38] It is worth noting that despite the apparently sinicizing reforms to royal titles and terminology involved in formally establishing the kingdom in 1744, Nguyễn Phúc Khoát took care to stipulate that in regard to their Southeast Asian neighbors Đàng Trong rulers would still use the style *thiên vương*.[39]

Perhaps because his initiation into the thirtieth generation of the Lâm Tế school made it appropriate, Nguyễn Phúc Chu preferred to be called *chúa Sãi* (Buddhist Priest Lord). Da Shan observed Nguyễn Phúc Chu's palace was decorated with Buddhist flags, hangings, wooden fish, and inverted bells, just like a Buddhist temple.[40] With these signs, the Nguyễn symbolically announced that they combined the powers of religious and political authorities in Đàng Trong. They not only located Vietnamese national and cultural identity in the ruling family, but also showed the local peoples that they embodied the highest authority in the region. In the process, they drew a sharp line between themselves and the Trịnh of the north, who continued to accept the Confucian concept that the emperor could only be the son of heaven, not heaven itself.[41] Whether knowingly or not, the Nguyễn's acceptance of the local trappings of divine rulership recalled what neighboring kings in Champa and Cambodia had been doing for centuries. Interestingly, too, they faintly echoed the practice of some early Vietnamese kings; one thinks of Lý Cao Tôn (1175-1210), who identified himself with the Buddha in imitation of his Ankor contemporary, Jayavarman VII.[42]

Overall, it was a successful experiment. This more identifiably Southeast Asian (or perhaps simply pre-Lê) pattern worked so well in Đàng Trong that it helped create a new social space—an intersection between the styles of their neighbors and themselves—in which southern Vietnamese could develop in ways different from

---

[37] O. W. Wolters, *History, Culture, and Region in Southeast Asian Perspectives* (Singapore: Institute of Southeast Asian Studies, 1982), p. 19.

[38] *Việt-Nam Khai Quốc Chí Truyện*, Collection Romans & Contes du Vietnam écrits en Han, vol. 4 (Paris and Taipei: Ecole Française d'Extrême-Orient and Student Book Co. Ltd, 1986), p. 300.

[39] *Tiền Biên*, vol. 10, p. 137.

[40] Da Shan, "Hai wai ji shi," p. 15.

[41] Tạ Chí Đài Trường, *Thần, Người, và Đất Việt* (Deities, people and the land of Viet) (California: Văn Nghệ Press, 1989), pp. 220–223.

[42] Nguyễn Thế Anh, "Buddhism and Vietnamese Society throughout History," *South East Asia Research*, 1 (March 1993): 98–114.

their northern contemporaries. It proved that Vietnamese society, even as late as the seventeenth and eighteenth centuries, could live, and indeed flourish, outside the Sino-Vietnamese framework that had organized northern politics and culture for centuries. Just how far from northern tradition Đàng Trong had moved is illustrated by an anecdote concerning a Tây Sơn general in Nghệ An, who laughed at *xã tắc* (*she ji* in Chinese), the god of land and crops and thus an important Confucian deity, exclaiming: "A dog is more useful than *xã tắc*."[43] The southern general was not being consciously iconoclastic: he was simply ignorant. *Xã tắc* was basically unknown in Đàng Trong under the Nguyễn. According to Tạ Chí Đài Trường, *xã tắc* temples did not appear here until the middle of the Minh Mạng reign, when the court tried to unify and centralize Vietnamese religious expression from about 1830.[44]

This incident typifies the differences in beliefs and values that evolved between Đàng Trong and Đàng Ngoài in two centuries of separation. Values brought from the north lost their meaning, while things unknown or heretical in Đàng Ngoài could become important to people in Đàng Trong. In particular, Buddhism, which Confucian scholars from the late Trần to the Lê dynasties had criticized for centuries, developed here into the dominant religion, both in terms of official policy and popular belief.

Other changes in values also occurred, particularly in regard to the role of the village. The village had been crucially important in traditional Vietnamese society. It combined social, economic, and religious functions, and reflected the way Vietnamese peasantry had related to their land and each other for centuries. However, only in the land-scarce Red River delta and the Thanh Hóa-Nghệ An region did Vietnamese villages fully approach what has often been described as their ideal type, inward-looking corporate entities deeply concerned with the control of communal resources, especially land, and the corresponding need for its periodic redistribution. Furthermore, in these long settled and relatively immobile villages, as Đào Duy Anh noted, social positions tended to be quite fixed, with the only form of social mobility commonly available dependent on winning an academic degree in the Sinic examinations.[45] While a degree of physical mobility always existed, peasants who did quit their own villages usually ended up in a worse situation socially if they sought to settle in another established village. As newcomers, they had to exchange their previous full rights as village members for a lesser status as transient residents, a status their descendants might be forced to maintain for several generations. In Đàng Trong, however, the situation in newly opened areas was quite different, particularly from Quảng Nam south. With abundant land and an expanding frontier, moving was quite a common experience for Vietnamese here, whether as individuals or as family groups, and sometimes even whole villages. Such a degree of mobility meant that relationships to a particular village or area of land could be far less close and far more mutable than in the majority of northern villages.

---

[43] *Việt Điện U Linh Tập* (Anthology of the spirits of the departed of the Vietnamese domain), "comments about 'xã tắc'" by Cao Huy Diệu in the early nineteenth century. Translated into Vietnamese by Lê Hữu Mục (Saigon: Khai Trí, 1961), p. 218.

[44] Tạ Chí Đài Trường, *Thần, Người, và Đất Việt*, p. 235.

[45] Đào Duy Anh, *Việt Nam Văn Hóa Sử Cương* (Outline of Vietnamese history of culture) (Saigon: Bốn Phương, 1961), pp. 125–26.

This sort of easy mobility clashed directly with the primacy of the collectivity, a basic Confucian tenet that emphasized the value of the social group—the family, the village—above the needs or desires of its constituent members. Individuals who belonged to such a group had no worth or purpose in isolation but only mattered in terms of how they discharged a number of fixed relationships within the community. In other words, anyone who lacked standing in a social group, like the family or the village, was less than a full person and could hope for no better future in traditional village society. Such people seem to have formed one of the main currents in the stream of Vietnamese immigrants to the far south. As one Vietnamese scholar, Huỳnh Lứa, has described it, the south was a land for "those who did not have the right to live on the older opened land."[46] Hickey, too, has underlined that same point:

> With the new village [of the south] therefore being established by lower status people rather than the patricians of the traditional society, a certain amount of esoteric knowledge concerning the old ways was inevitably lost. . . . By the same token, however, the pioneers were less bound by the highly restrictive social ranking and the behavior expectations of the older society, so they were free to innovate, an essential feature of their successful adjustment (and survival) as they moved continually southward.[47]

Such circumstances prompted people to be more open and spontaneous, to be risk-takers like Nguyễn Hoàng, whom Keith Taylor perceptively described as one who dared "to risk being pronounced a rebel, because he had found a place where this no longer mattered."[48] It was a larger world and gave people a greater sense of freedom—freedom to choose the place they preferred or the way they wanted to live, including the social freedom to marry non-Vietnamese, including Japanese and Chinese merchants and adventurers who came to live and trade in the new land. This immigrants' way of thinking also showed through in other aspects, including the one with which we conclude: their remarkable generosity towards others, foreigners and strangers included. Cristoforo Borri, an early Vietnamese-speaking Jesuit priest, noted how easily people in 1620s Đàng Trong were "touched with compassion," if someone cried *đói* (I am hungry) at their doors. This liberality may have formed one half of a protective frontier ethic of generosity whose other side was the right to ask anything one needed from a stranger and expect the same prompt response as when the situation was reversed. As Borri recalled:

> A Portuguese merchant, nothing liking this strange custom, seeing himself every day importuned to give whatsoever good thing he had, was one day disposed to carry himself in like manner toward them, and so coming to a poor fisherman's boat, and laying hands on a great pannier full of fish, he says unto him in the

[46] Huỳnh Lứa, "Quá trình khai phá vùng Đồng Nai-Cửu Long và hình thành một số tính cách, nếp sống và tập quán của người nông dân Nam Bộ" (Process of opening the Mekong delta and of forming some characteristics and customs of southern peasants), in *Mấy đặc điểm Đồng bằng Sông Cửu Long* (Some characteristics of the Mekong Delta) (Hanoi: Viện Văn Hóa, 1984), p. 121.

[47] Gerald Hickey, "The Vietnamese Village Though Time and War," *The Vietnam Forum*, Yale Southeast Asia Studies, 10 (1987): 18.

[48] Keith Taylor,"Nguyen Hoang," p. 64.

language of that country, *sin mocay* [*xin một cây? xin một cái?*], give me this. The good man without further discourse gave him the pannier as it was, to carry away, which the Portuguese carried to his house accordingly, wondering at the liberality of the poor man.[49]

## MATERIAL CULTURE

Some of this liberality, of course, may have reflected the comparative wealth of early Đàng Trong. The scattered population was not dense, while food and resources were abundant and easily accessible. It made possible a way of life that more closely resembled the habits of their Southeast Asian neighbors than their Vietnamese compatriots in the north, and encouraged them to experiment with useful aspects of the material culture of other peoples in the region. Examples are numerous. For instance, until the late eighteenth century the houses of most common people in Cochinchina stood on poles, just as in other Southeast Asian countries. As Alexander de Rhodes described them, they were "so constructed that they can be opened up below to let the water pass through, and for this reason they are always perched on huge stilts."[50] Perhaps more importantly, as Anthony Reid has remarked, this style of construction helped "to ensure that the house could be bodily moved if required."[51] The small box shrines on trees which we mentioned above seemed to follow the same principle.

Moving from houses to ships, we find a Malay type of boat, *ghe bầu*, which was widely used between the sixteenth and nineteenth centuries in Đàng Trong. It was almost certainly borrowed from the Chams, who had long traded with the Malays, for the region where it was used basically extended from Hội An south to Thuận Hải, the area where the Cham had lived. Some Vietnamese scholars suggest that not only the techniques involved but also the words *ghe* and *bầu* were borrowed from the Malays. They point to the similarity of the Vietnamese word *ghe* and the Malay word *gai* (meaning a rope or stay to hold a mast), and suggest that *bầu* was a corrupt pronunciation of the Malay *prahu*.[52] Certainly Barrow's observation of the vessels in the Tourane region would support this. He noted they were "of various descriptions: many of them, like the Chinese *sampans*, covered with sheds of matting, . . . and others resembling the common *proas* of the Malays, both as to their hulls and rigging."[53]

---

[49] Christoforo Borri, *Cochinchina* (London: 1633. New York: Da Capo Press, facsimile republished, 1970), p. E6.

[50] Alexandre de Rhodes, *Rhodes of Viet Nam: The Travels and Missions of Father Alexandre de Rhodes in China and Other Kingdoms of the Orient*, trans. S. Hertz (Maryland: Newman Press, 1966), p. 44. Da Shan, "Hai Wai Ji Shi," vol. 2, p. 4; John Barrow, *A Voyage to Cochinchina in the years 1792 and 1793* (Kuala Lumpur: Oxford University Press, reprint, 1975), p. 301.

[51] Anthony Reid, *Southeast Asia in the Age of Commerce, 1450-1680*, vol. 1 (New Haven and London: Yale University Press, 1993), p. 62.

[52] Nguyễn Bội Liên, Trần Văn An, and Nguyễn Văn Phi, "Ghe bầu Hội An - Xứ Quảng" (Ghe bau junks in the Hội An-Quảng Nam area), in *Ancient Town of Hội An*, ed. National Committee for the International Symposium on the Ancient Town of Hội An (Hanoi: Foreign Languages Publishing House, 1991, pp. 86–87.

[53] Barrow, *A Voyage*, p. 319.

Turning to farming tools, some Vietnamese historians have noticed clear Cham influences, especially in regard to the local Vietnamese plow. The plow used by Vietnamese further north, in the Red River and the Mã River deltas, is not strong at its sole, possesses a small tongue, and is light enough for one draft animal to pull. This kind of plow suits earth which is not compacted and where the grass is not thick. It was matched to the characteristics of the land in the north—cultivated for thousands of years by a comparatively dense population—and can only be seen north of the Gianh River, the border between Đàng Ngoài and Đàng Trong. When Vietnamese came down from the north, the land they discovered was thick with grass and hard to farm with this plow. It was for this reason that they adapted the Cham plow and then improved it for their own use. The plow used by the Cham farmers was strong, especially at its sole. Vietnamese added a *nang* (follicle) to adjust the angle, in the process making it into a new style of plow. Strikingly, all the names for parts derived from the Cham plow retained Cham names, such as *poh lingal* for the colter, *iku* for the handle, and *thru* for the tongue; while the parts associated with the *nang* have purely Vietnamese names, like *to nang* or *tế nang*. This kind of plow traveled south to the Mekong delta with immigrant Vietnamese peasants where it was further strengthened to make it suitable for marshland.[54]

Apart from these examples, the influence of Cham culture was so ubiquitous that it has often survived in the customs of central Vietnam right up to the present. Cham influence can be detected through a range of disparate customs like eating raw food (*ăn gỏi*), to the style of wrapping one's hair into a piece of cloth (*đội khăn*),[55] right up to burial in Cham-style graves,[56] although of course modern Vietnamese may not realize the non-Vietnamese origin of these local peculiarities. Amazingly, even *mắm nem*, the well-known fish sauce that is considered to be so typically Vietnamese, may actually have a Cham origin, according to some Vietnamese scholars. One Vietnamese scholar of southern customs has even pointed to the great similarity between the so-called "traditional" Vietnamese women's dress, the *áo dài*, which every Vietnamese woman wears for special occasions today, and the dress of Cham women (*tah* in Cham), with only the addition of a collar differentiating the *áo dài*. This style is very different indeed from the *áo tứ thân*, the long, open, and sleeveless garment that was the formal northern Vietnamese women's outfit before this century.[57]

Many of the borrowed Cham customs which have disappeared today concerned the use of elephants. Following the Cham example, Đàng Trong Vietnamese used

---

[54] Ngô Đức Thịnh and Nguyễn Việt, "Các loại hình cày hiện đại của dân tộc ở Đông Nam Á" (Types of ploughs in Southeast Asia), *Khảo Cổ Học* (Journal of Archaeology), 4 (1981): 55–56. For the Khmer plow, see Đặng Văn Thắng, "Nông cụ truyền thống ở Cần Đước" (The traditional tools of agriculture in *Cần Đước*), in *Cần Đước, Đất và Người* (Land and people in *Cần Đước*) (Long An: Sở Văn hóa—Thông tin Long An 1988), pp. 135–136.

[55] This Cham way of decorating one's hair is recorded in *Xing Jue Sheng Lan*, written in the fifteenth century by Fei Xin. See *Xing Jue Sheng Lan* (Beijing: reprinted by Zhong Hua Shu Ju, 1954), p. 3.

[56] The graves around the Huế area are quite different from those of both north and south Vietnam. I am grateful to Prof. Đỗ Văn Ninh, who kindly pointed out to me that they are exactly in the old Cham style.

[57] Phan Thi Yến Tuyết. *Nhà ở, trang phục, ăn uống của các dân tộc vùng Đồng bằng sông Cửu Long* (Housing, clothes and food of the peoples in the Mekong delta region) (Hanoi: Khoa Học Xã Hội, 1993), pp. 92, 290. The *áo dài* has not been recorded for the *chúa* Nguyễn period, so the similarity may be accidental.

elephants in many more ways than people did in the north. One of them was as a form of entertainment. Although the Vietnamese army certainly had elephant troops in earlier times, and elephants were used in royal ceremonies, elephant catching and fighting did not seem to be staged for entertainment in Đại Việt as they were for Cham kings. The Cham way of catching elephants was described by a Spaniard in 1595:

> The fifth [festival] is when the king goes hunting elephants, taking with him nobility and chief men of his kingdom, and they take along their female elephants, together with five hundred or six hundred Indians with their fiber nets, which are cords of rattan, and they surround the hill where the elephants are, which follow after the former into a little space which they have very strongly stockaded for this purpose, and there they keep them for some days until they are tamed.[58]

Da Shan described exactly the same technique used by Đàng Trong people in 1695; no doubt the technique was adopted from the Cham. The Cham royal festival of hunting elephants was further developed by the Nguyễn rulers to amuse foreigners. Barrow related that the kings usually entertained foreign ambassadors with an excursion into the forests to hunt elephants, "on which occasion they usually celebrate the royal feast of elephants,"[59] by which he meant they ate elephant meat as well. Elephant and tiger fights, also borrowed from Cham practices, were a favorite amusement. Poivre described in 1750 how the king, his high officials, and ordinary people were entertained by watching twelve tigers killed by forty elephants in a single day.[60] Crawfurd and Finlayson observed the same sort of fight in 1822. A similar practice occurred among the Siamese and the Malay,[61] but would have seemed strange and barbarous to the king and mandarins in the Lê/Trịnh north.

The Nguyễn also adopted the Cham method of executing criminals by using elephants, as recorded in Chinese sources since the sixth century. As Borri graphically described it:

> first he [the elephant] shall seize on him [the criminal], take him and strain him with his trunk, and holding him so cast him up with violence, and receive him again on the point of his teeth, that by the heavy fall of his weight he may gage himself thereon, and that then he dash him against the ground, and that in the end he tread him under his feet.[62]

Elephants continued to be used for public executions into the early nineteenth century, when captured Tây Sơn leaders were torn to death by them. According to John White, too, elephants were even employed in Saigon to make fire breaks within the town:

---

[58] C. R. Boxer, "A Spanish description of the Chams in 1595," *Readings on Asian Topics* (Scandinavian Institute of Asian studies, 1969), pp. 41–42.

[59] Barrow, *A Voyage*, p. 290. Poivre confirmed that people in Đàng Trong ate elephants. See Poivre, "Journal d'un voyage," p. 472.

[60] Poivre, "Journal d'un voyage," pp. 471–472.

[61] Reid, *Southeast Asia in the Age of Commerce*, vol. 1, pp. 184–185.

[62] Borri, *Cochinchina*, p. H1.

To prevent the fire from spreading, the adjacent houses are prostrated by means of the elephants, one of these powerful animals being sufficient to level with the ground any common building in the country; sometimes, however, two are required. The mode of effecting this is by pushing with their heads against the object to which they are directed by their drivers, by which its total demolition is speedily effected. His excellency [i.e. Lê Văn Duyệt] was in great humor, and laughed heartily while he directed the attention of our party to the summary operations of his elephants, who were throwing down several houses.[63]

Finally, it is worth noting that the non-Sinic elements in Nguyễn official practices may also have reflected influences from the wider Southeast Asian region, although this is not always well documented. One of the more intriguing examples is that Phú Xuân, the capital which later became Huế, had no walls. Here is Da Shan's description from 1695: "There was no city wall, not even for the court, but many bamboos had been planted to serve as walls."[64] While this openness to the outside world recalls Archipelagic Southeast Asian cities such as Melaka and Aceh,[65] it differs totally from any of the Vietnamese capitals in the north. Citadel building was an integral part of Vietnamese royal tradition, no doubt reflecting a constant awareness of their massive neighbor to the north. It began as early as the third century BC when King An Dương built Cổ Loa, with nine circuits of walls reminiscent of a snail shell,[66] and continued under every independent dynasty, even the short-lived Hồ dynasty (1400–07). In the south, however, the only fortifications erected by the Nguyễn were the long defensive walls in Quảng Bình. The Nguyễn capital itself was not given man-made defenses[67] until the Gia Long era, when the experience of thirty years of civil war no doubt prompted him to build citadels throughout the country, not only at Huế.

Another area in which local influence may be detected was in the way the Nguyễn administration operated, especially in its salary arrangements. As we noted previously, officials collected their salaries directly from a certain number of taxpayers allocated for the purpose. This was a Cham practice, also found in Laos at the time, as the *Nam Chưởng Ký Lược* (Records on Lan Chang) confirmed: "The officials have no salaries. They live on their taxpayers who were given them according to their ranks by the king."[68] The practice was common in other mainland Southeast Asian kingdoms. In Cambodia, for example, a common term for "to govern" also meant "to consume" while the term for "command" equally meant "to

---

[63] John White, *A Voyage to Cochin China* (London: Longman, 1824. Reprinted Kuala Lumpur: Oxford University Press, 1972), p. 320.

[64] Li Tana and Anthony Reid, eds., *Southern Vietnam under the Nguyễn*, p. 55.

[65] Anthony Reid, *Southeast Asia in the Age of Commerce, 1450-1680*, vol. 2, pp. 87–88.

[66] Keith Taylor, *The Birth of Vietnam* (Berkeley: University of California Press, 1983), p. 21.

[67] Huế "is situated on a fine plain surrounded by mountains and cut across by a large river . . ." according to the "Description of Cochinchina, 1749-50" in Li Tana and Anthony Reid, eds., *Southern Vietnam under the Nguyễn*, p. 77.

[68] *Nam Chưởng Ký Lược*, microfilm, Ecole Française d'Extrême-Orient, Paris.

use."[69] In Burma officials were granted territories "to eat,"[70] a striking but most accurate way of describing the pay system in most of mainland Southeast Asia at the time. Though rather less graphic than these Cambodian or Burman words, "fertile men," the Nguyễn term for the human appanages given in place of payment to their officials, was equally telling. In northern Vietnam, by contrast, the Trần dynasty had started to pay official salaries as early as 1236 AD, and where appanages were granted they were in land, not men. We thus can see an interesting antithesis: if an official in seventeenth and eighteenth century Đàng Ngoài took any of the taxes he collected for his own use it was a criminal act, whereas for his counterpart in Đàng Trong, it constituted the legitimate way he made his living. In this as in may other things, the Nguyễn must have found that taking on local customs was not only convenient but usually also worked to their own advantage.

The four highest officers of the early Nguyễn government were called "*tứ trụ đại thần*," literally meaning "four-pillar high officers."[71] They were in turn called inner left, outer left, inner right, and outer right, which made both name and arrangement of the Nguyễn officers strikingly similar to the Malay "pillars of the state," which are characterized by two left and two right positions.[72] This structure of power could be found in all Indianized Southeast Asia,[73] but is tremendously different from that of the northern Vietnamese bureaucratic system, which followed the Chinese model with six Boards.

---

[69] David Chandler, "Cambodia: The Roots of Conflict," in Damien Kingsbury and Greg Barton, *Difference and Tolerance* (Geelong: Deakin University Press, 1994), p. 102.

[70] Victor Lieberman, *Burmese Administrative Cycles: Anarchy and Conquest, c. 1580-1760*, (Princeton: Princeton Unversity Press, 1984), chapter two; Michael Aung-Thwin, *Pagan: The Origins of Modern Burma* (Honolulu: University of Hawaii Press, 1985), p. 105.

[71] *Tiền Biên*, vol. 3, p. 46.

[72] David Steinberg, ed., *In Search of Southeast Asia*, revised edition (Sydney: Allen & Unwin, 1987), pp. 78, 86. Also see Barbara W. Andaya and Leonard Y. Andaya, *A History of Malaysia* (London: MacMillan, 1982), pp. 46-47 on the four ministers in Melaka.

[73] Steinberg, ed., *In Search of Southeast Asia*, p. 86.

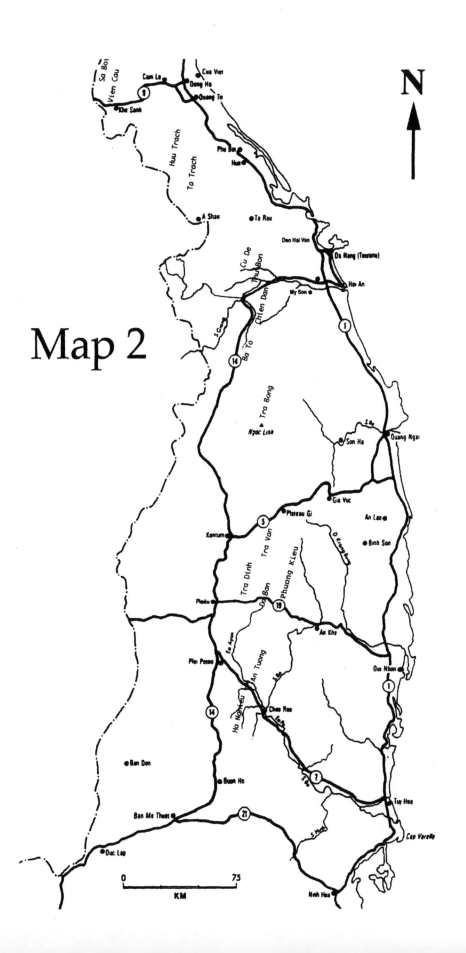

# VIETNAMESE AND UPLANDERS

## INTRODUCTION

In the Red River heartland of traditional Vietnamese culture, agriculture was honored as "*gốc*," the root or foundation of a benevolent society. Most Vietnamese dynasties took as their guiding principle the policy of preventing any unsettling changes or developments, especially trade, that might threaten the stable agricultural base that provided their taxes and manpower levies. From the earliest independent dynasties, like the Early Lê and the Lý, we see kings carrying out the important ritual of royal plowing, like Lê Hoàn in 987 or Lý Thái Tôn in 1038. In two centuries of Đàng Trong history, however, no such ritual enactment was ever recorded. The *chúa* Nguyễn were far more likely to see the prosperity of their state in terms of the numbers of ships or junks that arrived each year rather than in terms of agricultural production, since rice could always be imported. But while overseas trade became the central pillar of the Nguyễn economy, most of the precious local items exported came not from lowland Vietnamese villages but from the western mountains of the Central Highlands. In the Đàng Trong economy, in sharp contrast to the north, the two rather alien fronts of mountain and sea dominated over agriculture. We find this unique arrangement reflected in two key rituals, the *mở núi* (opening the mountain) and the *cầu gió* (praying for a good sea wind). Some version of the first probably existed in the region for centuries, while the second was common Chinese practice in coastal areas. The Vietnamese adopted both, as well as sensibly maintaining in their ritual armory a prayer for good harvests (*kỳ hoa*) which, however, never predominated over the other two.[1]

In keeping with this orientation, the nineteenth-century Nguyễn dynasty concerns about *sơn phòng* (defense against the mountains) and *hải phòng* (defense against the sea) do not appear in the sources for seventeenth- and eighteenth-century Đàng Trong. Rather, the sea to the east and the mountains to the west presented opportunities and advantages, not problems. Nguyễn Hoàng himself apparently recognized this strategic truth in his dying words:

> While to the north Hoành Sơn mountain and the Gianh river are hard to cross, and in the south Hải Vân Pass and Thạch Bi[2] mountain are equally good for

---

[1] Vũ Minh Giang says that in the An Khê region in Quy Nhơn *cầu huê* (or *kỳ hoa*) is still held on the tenth of the second lunar month every year. It usually involved both Vietnamese and the minority peoples from the mountains, who would take it as an important chance for trade. See Vũ Minh Giang, "Tây Sơn Thượng đạo, căn cứ đầu tiên của cuộc khởi nghĩa" (The Tây Sơn upper trail, the first base for the uprising), in *Tây Sơn Nguyễn Huệ* (Nghĩa Bình: Ty Văn Hóa và Thông Tin Nghĩa Bình, 1978), p. 132.

[2] In Phú Yên, close to Cape Varella. This mountain was the southern border of Đại Việt in the early seventeenth century.

defense, the gold and iron produced from the mountains, and fish and salt from the sea, make this region exactly what a hero needs to display his talents.[3]

In other words, for the Nguyễn the resources of the west and the east could be managed to deal with the problems of the north and the south.

This chapter examines some of the ways in which Đàng Trong Vietnamese later put these words into effect in regard to the west. Their relations with the upland peoples of the mountainous west added an extra dimension to Vietnamese localization here; these interactions were more visible at the level of popular culture than some of the influences discussed in the previous chapter. The political strategy that sustained these relations for nearly two hundred years after the arrival of Nguyễn Hoàng was quite different from that applied to the Chams and to other lowland people. Rather than seek to settle or make vassals in the mountains, the Nguyễn essentially sought to insure friendly, non-threatening relations with these important suppliers of precious commodities. Central to this effort was the important consideration that, in the early period especially, the Vietnamese were but one of the local peoples and lived on land that had formerly belonged to others. Facing the hostile Trịnh in the north, and Cham to the south, the Nguyễn could not afford to make enemies on their flank as well. This strategic assessment underlay their policies towards the highlands.

Rather than try defending themselves against the sea or the mountains, the hard-pressed early Nguyễn sought alliances there instead. We see this in marriages in 1619 between a daughter of Nguyễn Phúc Nguyên and Araki Sotaao, the Japanese merchant, and in 1620 between his second daughter and King Chetta II of Cambodia.[4] Hickey adds that a little later another Nguyễn court lady was wed to Po Rome,[5] the most powerful king of seventeenth-century *nagara* Campa (1627-51) and himself a Curu, descended from a refugee Cham group that had intermarried among the Roglai in the Phan Rang area. Those who arranged this marriage probably sought to neutralize Cham hostility during the war with the Trịnh; but it is impossible to tell, since none of the marriages were recorded in the nineteenth-century chronicle. However, one *Tiền Biên* entry of 1621 does confirm the basic policy towards upland peoples:

> rulers of Ai Lao [Laos] and Lục Hoàn [Savannakhet region] let their soldiers cross Hiếu Giang river to rob our people . . . [Nguyễn Phúc Nguyên] ordered Tôn Thất Hòa to pacify them. Hòa laid an ambush on the main routes and asked the traders to do business there to lure [the Lao]. The barbarians came . . . and were all caught by our soldiers. His Highness wanted to make a show of conciliation with favors and trust towards the remote peoples, so he ordered them untied and gave them food and clothes, and so tried to make them see

---

[3] *Đại Nam Thực Lục Tiền Biên* (hereafter *Tiền Biên*) (Chronicle of Greater Vietnam, Premier Period of the Nguyễn) (Tokyo: Keio Institute of Linguistic Studies, Mita, Siba, Minato-ku, 1961), vol. 1, p. 29.

[4] Although this woman later brought a large piece of Khmer land to the Vietnamese, initially the marriage was perhaps more a defensive strategy.

[5] Gerald Hickey, *Sons of the Mountains* (New Haven & London: Yale University Press, 1982), p. 89.

reason. The barbarians were all abashed and convinced. They have never rebelled since.[6]

This incident set the tone for relations between the Nguyễn court and uplanders until the late 1740s. In the seventeenth and early eighteenth centuries, uplanders participated in only five anti-Nguyễn rebellions, a tribute to a policy of conciliation rather than of control. Until the 1750s, the Nguyễn preferred to push to the south, while keeping peace with the west. There was a distinct difference between the way they dealt with the Khmer to the far south-west and the Lao to the west. If in late 1714 the Nguyễn court sent two generals to intervene in a Khmer civil war, instructing them to be "determined to gain victory and pacify the remote peoples," their response to a civil war in Laos several months later was far more muted. The court decided only to send an "envoy to show friendship and watch the situation there."[7] It was not until the Nguyễn Phúc Khoát era in the mid-eighteenth century that this posture of benevolent neutrality towards the Central Highlands was replaced by a desire to push Vietnamese authority further into the area. This would be one of the most fateful decisions in Đàng Trong's history, for twenty years later uplander anger against Vietnamese control helped trigger the revolt that became the Tây Sơn rebellion.

Until the mid-eighteenth century, however, the strategy of cordial relations insured easy access to upland trade, and fostered cultural interaction. The next sections examine these various aspects of Vietnamese-uplander relations before considering the changes of the 1750s and their consequences.

## TRADING ROUTES AND ITEMS

Trade constituted the most ancient relationship between lowlanders and uplanders in this region, as active trading had gone on long before the Vietnamese arrived from the north. When the Vietnamese population grew and overseas trade expanded, highland-lowland trade was equally stimulated. New trading locations sprang up for exchanges which became increasingly more regular. Map 2 gives a rough idea of how Vietnamese in Đàng Trong related to uplanders, Lao, and Khmer in the Nguyễn period. This interaction between Vietnamese and uplanders in Đàng Trong was far more important economically than the similar small-scale trading activities that always occurred under other Vietnamese dynasties. Although its organization was different, at least from Quảng Ngãi south, its scale and significance resembled what we know of economic relations between uplanders and Chams within *nagara* Campa in previous centuries and in the trans-Mekong basin.

The most important trading route in early Đàng Trong ran through the upper reaches of the Ai Lao Pass, enabling goods to pass from the Mekong river to the coast near Quảng Trị. Focused on the town of Cam Lộ, the route went down to Cửa Việt port, and up to Lao Bảo. It was the busiest trading route in the Thuận Hóa area and seems to have been unrestricted by the sort of government organization common further south. *Phủ Biên* described trade as it moved west: from Lao Bảo it took two

---

[6] *Tiền Biên*, vol. 2, p. 33.

[7] Both quotes, *Tiền Biên*, vol. 8, pp. 120-121.

days to reach Tchepone, and then another three days to Muong Vinh.[8] Thereafter the Bang Hieng (or Bang Hian) rapids were navigable by small boats for part of the year, depending on the rainfall levels,[9] after which it was easy to reach the central Mekong basin and arrive either at Savannakhet to the west, Khemarat to the southwest, or across the Mekong River to Mukdahan in modern Thailand. It was via this route, secured by Ai Lao camp since the 1620s, that Vientiane sent its "tribute" to the Nguyễn, and their influence advanced back into the mountains in the mid-eighteenth century. In the nineteenth century, Cam Lộ continued to be a linchpin of Vietnamese trade and diplomacy with the Lao. [10]

The trade itself was lively. As *Phủ Biên* recounted, Vietnamese traders here brought:

> salt, fish sauce, dried fish, iron wares, copper pots, silver hairpins and bracelets with them up along this route to the uplanders and inhabitants of Lao settlements, to trade for rice, chicken, oxen, hemp, wax, rattan and cotton cloth woven by uplanders. When the trading was done, the traders hired elephants to carry the goods back to Cam Lộ. The uplanders and Lao also brought goods to sell in Cam Lộ . . . It is said that sometimes they drove as many as three hundred oxen to trade at one fair [so that] the price of an ox was only ten *quan* [222 grams of silver in the 1770s] at the most, while an elephant was worth two *thoi* [756 grams] of silver.[11]

From Ai Lao Pass south to Kontum the terrain becomes more rugged and difficult, so that trade here was restricted to exchanges between lowlanders and nearby uplanders. Uplanders here traded precious woods, rattan, wax, honey, oxen, cinnamon (from western Quảng Nam), areca, and gold for the same sorts of goods offered at Cam Lộ. Lowland merchants of course were not always Vietnamese. Resident Chinese, like Châu Tiên Lợi's family from mid-eighteenth century Hội An, might also be licensed to trade in the area; this particular family bought wood from the uplanders to resell on the coast.[12]

Perhaps only the An Khê area, from where the Tây Sơn rose, could be compared favorably with Cam Lộ in terms of its important trading position, with its linkages to Bahnar, Jarai, Choreo, and other peoples in the Quy Nhơn, Quảng Ngãi, and Phú Yên regions. Hickey suggests that the Ba river valley was a likely route of entry into

---

[8] Lê Quý Đôn, *Phủ Biên Tạp Lục* (hereafter *Phủ Biên*), vol. 2 (Hanoi: Khoa Học Xã Hội, 1977), p. 69a. Muong Vinh was either Muong Phine, in the Bang Hieng river basin, or the Bang Hieng river basin in general.

[9] Kennon Breazeale and Snit Smukarn, *A Culture in Search of Survival, The Phuan of Thailand and Laos*, Monograph Series 31 (New Haven: Yale University Southeast Asia Studies, 1988), p. 2.

[10] This is undoubtedly not how it was seen by the Lao ruler of Lan Sang (Laos), which flourished at the same time as the Nguyễn, especially under Souligna-Vongsa (r. 1637–1694). For Laos it was important to maintain balanced relations with Siam, Cambodia, and the two Vietnams.

[11] *Phủ Biên*, vol. 4, pp. 4b-5a. Silk had also been sold in Laos early in the previous century, according to Borri. See Christoforo Borri, *Cochinchina* (London: 1633. New York: Da Capo Press, facsimile republished, 1970), p. D.

[12] From a MS family history now kept by Châu's descendants, Châu Quang Chương and Châu Diệu Cư, in Hội An. My gratitude to Mr. Châu and his family for kindly allowing me to read this valuable source when I visited Hội An in July 1990.

the mountains.[13] This observation is confirmed by the name "Đèo Mang" for An Khê, for in the Bahnar language the phrase means "passing door," that is, a gateway between the plain and the mountains.[14] It is indeed a pass for the route between Quy Nhơn port to the east and Strung Treng on the Cambodian side of the Mekong to the west, passing via Pleiku and the land of the Jarai and Bahnar, among others. Early French missionaries from the 1840s described the part of this route controlled by the Vietnamese as "terminat[ing] at the An Sơn [An Khê] market, the gathering-place of customs officials and Annamese hangers-on."[15] As late as 1884, An Khê still remained the last Vietnamese post. Beyond it lay only uplanders' country.[16]

An Khê was, therefore, the gate between the commercial center of Quy Nhơn and the trans-Mekong basin. Beside calambac, ivory, and other luxuries, many everyday items of Vietnamese consumption, like betel nut, came from here. Nguyễn Nhạc, one of the Tây Sơn leaders, was a betel nut trader dealing with local uplanders long before he and his brothers raised the revolt which involved so many of the surrounding people. An Khê was also an important center for cross-regional trade among various upland peoples themselves, according to Dourisboure, one of the earliest French missionaries who reached the highlands in 1851. He recorded that almost all the other mountain peoples came here to obtain their iron tools and weapons from the Sedang, who had access to iron deposits and learned the technique from the Laos, while the Rengao and western Bahnar wove cotton for cloth, and the Bahnar Alakong to the east traded salt which they had purchased from the Vietnamese, as salt was the most essential trade item the Vietnamese brought to the mountains.[17] As a Vietnamese folk song from the Quy Nhơn area neatly expressed it:

*Ai về nhắn với nậu nguồn,*
*Măng lê gửi xuống, cá chuồn gửi lên.*
(Whoever goes to see the uplanders please remind them,
[if] forest products are brought down, sea products are carried up.)[18]

The commercially strategic location of An Khê perhaps accounts for why Kiom, a Bahnar leader from this area,[19] was designated "chief of the Mois" by Huế in the 1840s.

Vietnamese and other newcomers never entirely displaced the Cham in uplander trade in the seventeenth and eighteenth centuries. Given the close and long-standing

---

[13] Hickey, *Sons of the Mountains*, p. 116.

[14] *Tây Sơn Nguyễn Huệ*, p. 48. This could be compared to a Rhade name Tvea Phreah Nakor (meaning "The Gate of the Capital"), which marked the frontier between the Cambodian kingdom and the highlands. See Hickey, *Sons of the Mountains*, p. 141.

[15] Pierre Dourisboure and Christian Simmonet, *Vietnam: Mission on the Grand Plateaus*, trans. Albert J. LaMothe, Jr., (New York: Maryknoll Publications, 1967), p. 13.

[16] E. Navelle, "De Thi-Nai au Bla," cited in Gerald Hickey, *Kingdom in the Morning Mist* (Philadelphia: University of Pennsylvania Press, 1988), pp. 67–68.

[17] Dourisboure and Simmonet, *Vietnam: Mission on the Grand Plateaus*, p. 67.

[18] Phan Đai Doãn, "Ap Tay Son Nhi," in Trên Đất Nghĩa Bình (On the land of Nghĩa Bình), ed. Phan Huy Lê et al. (Qui Nhơn: Sở văn hóa thông tin Nghĩa Bình, 1988), p. 27.

[19] Or Kiem in other sources. Raymond Le Jarriel, "Comment la mission catholique a servi la France en pays Moi," *Bulletin des Amis du Vieux Hue* 1 (1942): 41.

interconnections between Cham and uplander groups in the hinterland of Phú Yên, Bình Thuận, Khánh Hòa, and Phan Rang especially, this is not surprising. It is still not clear how calambac and other luxury goods actually reached overseas ships or junks in Đàng Trong at the time, but it seems most likely that the trade involved Cham middlemen. It may even be that ready Cham access to calambac explains why Cham trade still continued for some time after Hội An established its dominant position in overseas trade in the early seventeenth century. By all accounts, the best calambac came from Khánh Hòa, which was close to Phan Rang, the last remaining trading port of Panduranga. Cornelis van Neyenroode, head of the Dutch factory in Firando (Japan), recorded in 1623 that a Red Seal ship was sent "to Champa, which carried the king's investment to buy calambac there."[20] The *Kai-hentai* records also repeatedly mentioned junks going to Champa to load calambac. As late as the nineteenth century, Aymonier described Roglai who were associated with Cham in procuring calambac for transport to the lowlands, perhaps the last vestiges of a relationship established centuries before. An important Cham dignitary in the Phan Rang valley called *po-gahlao* (lord of eaglewood) organized the search for calambac during the dry season.[21] After special prayers and offerings to the Cham kings, regarded as the "protectors of eaglewood," the Cham went to Roglai villages where village heads would assemble bands of men to help them search for the precious wood,[22] a degree of cooperation that Vietnamese traders seem not to have established.

Where non-Chams were concerned, it appears likely that at least one or two secondary traders acted as links between mountain collectors and coastal exporters. Periodic markets might also have been another important source. The nineteenth-century provincial gazetteer, *Đại Nam Nhất Thống Chí*, certainly indicated that some intermediary points in Khánh Hòa and Quy Nhơn served this purpose, noting that uplanders used elephants and horses to bring commodities there to trade with Vietnamese.[23]

Trading between Vietnamese and upland peoples in seventeenth- and eighteenth-century Đàng Trong was much more important than would be imagined today. So important were mountain products in Đàng Trong's economy that Vietnamese ritualized the process of trade in a ceremony called "*đi nguồn*," literally meaning "to go to the source or spring" but better understood as "going to collect precious things in the mountains."[24] Perhaps because of the hardship and mystery involved in finding these precious commodities, especially perfumed woods, and the enormous profits to be reaped from them, the Vietnamese quickly learned to imitate Cham and uplander rituals involved in the process. They adopted the existing belief

---

[20] Originele Missive van Cornelis van Niewroode uyt Firando in dato 20 December 1623 [Kol. Archief 995], quoted from Iwao Seiichi, "The capital and trading port of Champa in its last period," *Toyo gaku* 39, 2 (1956): 128.

[21] Yet Gabrielle Bertrand in the early twentieth century said "lord of eaglewood" referred to a man who resold eaglewood, whereas *thuoc lai* applied to those who were in charge of collecting. See Gabrielle Bertrand, *The Jungle People*, trans. Eleanor Brockett (London: Robert Hale, 1959), p. 46.

[22] Etienne Aymonier, *Les Tchames et leur religion* (Paris: Leroux, 1891), pp. 72–77, cited in Hickey, *Sons of the Mountains*, p. 117.

[23] *Đại Nam Nhất Thống Chí* (Gazetteer of Greater Vietnam) vol. 11 (Tokyo: Society of Indo-China Studies, 1941), p. 1264.

[24] Tạ Chí Đài Trường, *Thần, Người, và Đất Việt* (California: Văn Nghệ, 1989), p. 257.

that the great Cham goddess Po Nagar, or Thiên-Y-A-Na in her Vietnamized form, was the guardian of these perfumed woods[25] at the same time that they borrowed Cham and uplander techniques for finding them. Nguyễn Khải records that as late as the 1980s Vietnamese eaglewood collectors made offerings to the *Bà* ("The Lady") before they started their journeys, and when they reached the foot of the mountains they held a ceremonial opening of the mountain (*khai sơn*),[26] more or less as their forebears had done in the seventeenth and eighteenth centuries. In the early 1940s, Rolf Stein also observed that along with statues of local divinities in a Huế temple there stood a goddess called *Cô Bảy*, with the dark, naked breasts of a highland woman. She had a tree branch in her right hand and a small bottle in her left, which, according to the temple shaman, was for "holding perfume."[27] Stein also recorded that in this temple Vietnamese worshipped local gods and goddesses called *"Thượng ngàn chư ông,"* which he translated as Masters of the Upper [River] Bank (Messieurs de la Rive supérieure). All those "Masters" thus designated were considered to be of indigenous, non-Vietnamese origin.[28]

These examples indicate that, just as the Vietnamese borrowed aspects of economic life from uplanders, they equally absorbed or adapted some of the latter's religious beliefs. This pluralism of belief became a key feature of southern culture. It survived the centralizing and regimenting impulses of the Minh Mạng era, to emerge later as a significant underlying factor in the politics of nineteenth- and twentieth-century Vietnam. One other important element of Vietnamese-uplander relations in Đàng Trong did not survive the nineteenth century, however. This was the slave trade.

## THE SLAVE TRADE

Cham and uplanders were engaged in a slave trade long before the establishment of Đàng Trong,[29] and Vietnamese had joined them by at least the eighteenth century, as several sources indicate. Here is Poivre's account:

> I asked the king to give me at least several savages or slaves to be craftsmen (because the slaves in this region are only those barbarians who were caught by Cochinchinese from the mountains). The king answered that it was not difficult, but he suggested I wait until the next year, and he promised me that he would supply me with as many slaves as I wanted by then. He added that this year I would only be able to buy two kinds of slaves: one kind was uncivilized, since they had only been recently caught and were not well trained and could therefore do nothing useful, the other kind included ones who had become

---

[25] Rolf Stein, "Jardins en miniature d'Extrême-Orient," *Bulletin de L'Ecole Française d'Extrême-Orient* (hereafter *BEFEO*) XLII (1942): 74-75.

[26] Nguyễn Khải. *Một Cõi Nhân Gian Bé Tí* (A tiny small world) (Ho Chi Minh City: Văn Nghệ, 1989), pp. 26–27.

[27] Stein, "Jardins," p. 71.

[28] Ibid., p. 69.

[29] Champa was widely known as a major source of slaves who were traded from its ports to the Asian world. See Kenneth Hall, *Maritime Trade and State Development in Early Southeast Asia*, (Honolulu: University of Hawaii Press, 1985), p. 192.

familiar with the area and trained in certain techniques. But soon after I bought them they would escape, because they desperately wanted to go back to their wives and children.[30]

It is clear from this that the *chúa* himself was quite familiar with slavery and the slave trade, and was even able to offer advice on its finer points to the visiting Frenchman. Certainly, Poivre observed slaves at the *chúa*'s court, remarking that a princess usually had among her attendants some "small savage slaves."[31] He also often mentioned how influential at court was a slave or ex-slave, a "favorite black subject of the king, who was a Cambodian, or rather, a Laotian."[32] All this indicates that slavery was an accepted institution in Cochinchina at the time, a conclusion also supported by scattered seventeenth- and eighteenth-century Vietnamese sources.

Our first example comes from the inscription on a tablet set up in 1697 by a Nguyễn official, Nguyễn Đức Hòa, in modern Phú Hòa village, Tam Kỳ prefecture, Quảng Nam. It concerned the 43.69 *mẫu* of land he had set aside to fund the burning of joss sticks and candles in his family temple. The tablet listed the restrictions governing the allotment and the slaves (*hương hỏa nô*[33]) who were designated to cultivate it. The rules dictated that the slaves were to live in separate quarters, segregated by sex, with the most intelligent male and female selected to be their leaders; that any who tried to escape and were recaptured could be sold elsewhere by the family; and that if any future family members tried to seize the slaves for their private purposes, they should be expelled from the family.[34] This inscription also revealed that, apart from these slaves in charge of joss sticks, the *hương hỏa nô*, ordinary slaves of both sexes, also existed in seventeenth-century Cochinchina. Indeed, so common was the enslavement of uplanders in Đàng Trong that it led to the coining of a word that still exists. In Vietnamese, compounds with "*tôi*" generally denote some sort of servant, as *tôi con*, *tôi đòi*, *tôi tớ*, but only *tôi mọi* means "slave or bondman."[35] Since the northern Vietnamese term for uplanders was *Man* rather than *Mọi*, the word *tôi mọi* might be a linguistic vestige of uplander slavery in Đàng Trong.

Vietnamese sources generally indicate that slaves were used mainly in agriculture, to supplement manpower shortages in under-populated Đàng Trong, especially in the Mekong delta. Particular families might own quite large numbers of slaves. Nguyễn Đức Nghinh has suggested, for instance, that forty or fifty slaves were needed to cultivate forty-five *mẫu* (one *mẫu* in central Vietnam = five thousand square meters, thus twenty-two hectare). Lê Quý Đôn recorded their use in his *Phủ Biên*:

---

[30] Pierre Poivre, "Journal d'un voyage du vaisseau de la compagnie le Machault à la Cochinchine depuis le 29 août 1749, jour de notre arrivée, au 11 fevrier 1750," reproduced by H. Cordier in *Revue de l'Extrême-Orient* III (1885): 439.

[31] Poivre, "Journal d'un voyage," p. 429.

[32] Ibid., pp. 466, 474.

[33] Meaning slaves in charge of keeping joss sticks.

[34] A MS in the Han-Nom Institute, Hanoi, shelf number 20922-20923. For analysis of the inscription, see Nguyễn Đức Nghinh, "Những nô tì phục vụ cho việc thờ cúng" (Slaves used in the making of offerings), *Nghiên cứu lịch sử* (Journal of historical studies) 2 (1981): 80–83.

[35] Bùi Phụng, *Từ Điển Việt-Anh* (A Vietnamese English dictionary) (Hanoi: Trường Đại Học Tổng Hợp Hà Nội, 1978), pp. 1135-1136.

The Nguyễn ruler also let those people gather up *mọi* from the highlands and sell them as slaves to the rich. These slaves married each other and produced more children to work and grow more rice. There may have been forty to fifty rich families in these places [and] . . . some owned fifty to sixty slaves and three hundred to four hundred oxen per family.[36]

The *Phủ Biên* also suggested that the opening of fertile lands in Bình Sơn and Chương Nghĩa counties may have owed something to uplander slavery. It said that the Nguyễn initially established seventy-two settlements there managed by farmers "recruited from the mountains." In this context, however, that recruitment should be understood in its widest sense to include people bought or captured and enslaved.[37]

So routine was the trade in uplanders, according to the *Phủ Biên*, that the court taxed it at the same rate as the elephant trade. Given this, it seems reasonable to assume that the two—elephants and slaves—fetched roughly comparable prices. If so, a slave, like an elephant, would have cost two bars of silver, or about forty *quan* in the 1770s,[38] less than one *picul* of copper at the time. The *Phủ Biên* claims that slaves in the Mekong delta were much cheaper than in Thuận Hóa, around the capital. A dark-skinned, curly-headed slave cost only twenty *quan* here, or half the likely price in the Thuận Hóa area. Fairer slaves cost even less again, only ten *quan*.[39]

Two reasons may account for the differing prices. First, the price might vary depending on a slave's distance from home. As elsewhere in the world, to borrow Philip Curtin's words, "once enslaved, a captive near home was less valuable than one far from home, simply because he or she might escape."[40] If that were the case in eighteenth-century Đàng Trong, dark-skinned slaves might have originated from remote mountain areas, while the fairer ones might have come from areas closer to the coast, where intermarriage had occurred between Vietnamese and upland peoples. Alternatively, the difference in price might have reflected varying degrees of Vietnamization. This is suggested in a monograph on Thủ Dầu Một published in 1910, which describes the Stieng people as divided into two main groups, one living around the modern An Lộc region, and the other in Bù Đốp, both situated north of modern Sông Bé province. The first group, although dark skinned like negritoes, was more Vietnamized; the second, paler skinned like Malays or Chams, nonetheless

---

[36] *Phủ Biên*, vol. 6, p. 243.

[37] *Phủ Biên*, vol. 2, p. 82b.

[38] *Phủ Biên*, vol. 4, pp. 5a-5b. This is the highest price we have for the price of a slave in the eighteenth century. Yet it is lower than the price given by *Zhu Fan Zhi*, a Chinese book on twelfth- and thirteenth-century Southeast Asian countries. According to this source, a male slave was worth three *taels* of gold. In the 1770s this amount of gold would be equal to about fifty-four to sixty *quan* of copper coins.

[39] *Phủ Biên*, Hanoi edition, p. 345. The Saigon edition does not have the price. A MS kept in the Institute of History, Hanoi, gives different prices: "The one who is dark with curly hair [which] means [this slave] being one of the *Mọi* race, costs twenty *quan*; if the one is fair and fat, he is a *Kinh* (Vietnamese), he then would cost fifty to sixty *quan*. For one hundred to ten (110?) slaves the cost would be more than one thousand *quan*."

[40] Philip D. Curtin, "Migration in the Tropical World," in *Immigration Reconsidered*, ed. Virginia Yans-Laughlin (Oxford: Oxford University Press, 1990), p. 26.

appeared less "civilized" in Vietnamese eyes.[41] Of course, both factors may have operated together.

Whatever the reason, the low price of slaves explains why a family might own fifty or sixty in the Mekong delta in the eighteenth century. Certainly slave labor seems to have been an important factor in the development of large-scale rice production in the far south during the early years of its settlement by Vietnamese. It continued to exist right up to the nineteenth century, with Silvestre reporting the presence of slavery in the region to the north and northeast of Saigon in particular.[42] Trương Vĩnh Ký even identified a slave market, called "Cây đa thằng Mọi," close to Thuận Kiều Street in northeast Saigon.[43]

French missionaries who visited the central highlands in the nineteenth century seldom failed to record the slave trade in this region. Some pointed out that "the slave trade consisted primarily of lowlanders hunting down the 'savage' populations of the interior, selling them into slavery."[44] Yet uplanders also participated as slave hunters: Kon Trang, a Sedang village in the Bla river area, was said to function as a center for the Sedang, Rengao, and Lao slave traders, who often traveled up the tributaries of the Mekong river to purchase slaves.[45] The trade was not exclusively one-way: Vietnamese were also captured by uplanders and enslaved. Hickey notes that Kiom, the Bahnar leader mentioned above, also "reputedly was involved in the slave trade," capturing uplanders and Vietnamese and taking them to the Mekong River valley to sell in the Lao markets.[46] Sometimes Vietnamese slaves were sold directly to the Haland and Jarai by Sedang bandits.[47] This phenomenon was said to have existed further north in the Cam Lộ area in the nineteenth century as well. French archives mention Vietnamese being kidnapped and sold as slaves in the Lao region between Attapu and Nakhon Phanom.[48] This kind of trade must have been carried on in Cochinchina and along its western border before and after the appearance of Vietnamese in the region.

It is not surprising that slavery was contrived in a frontier region where the institution was common among the local people and manpower was desperately lacking among the Vietnamese.[49] The ethnic mix itself may also have encouraged it; slavery enables a stronger group to absorb a weaker one. It is interesting, however, that while seventeenth- and eighteenth-century Vietnamese sources recorded the

---

[41] See "Monographie de la province de Thudaumot," *Bulletin de la Société des Etudes Indochinoise* 58 (1910): 28.

[42] P. Silvestre, "Rapport sur l'esclave," quoted in Hickey, *Sons of the Mountains*, p. 211.

[43] Trương Vĩnh Ký, "Souvenirs historiques sur Saigon et ses environs," *Excursions et Reconnaissances* 23 (1885): 24-25. He said that this market was part of the Dieu Khien market.

[44] Hickey, *Sons of the Mountains*, p. 210. He mentions too that in the 1880s "Vietnamese and Chinese merchants trading with villagers in the mountainous zone from Quang Nam to Binh Thuan also purchased slaves which were then sold in Annam."

[45] Hickey, *Kingdom in the Morning Mist*, p. 65.

[46] Ibid., p. 64.

[47] Hickey, *Sons of the Mountains*, pp. 279–280.

[48] Breazeale and Smukarn, *A Culture in Search of Survival*, p. 86.

[49] Slavery had disappeared in the Red River delta since the Trần dynasty, but it may well have continued along the shifting Viet-Cham border, as the sixteenth-century source, *Ô Châu Cận Lục*, mentions some Vietnamese villages in Hai Lang county (Quảng Trị) still engaged in the slave trade. See Dương Văn An, *Ô Châu Cận Lục* (Saigon: Văn Hóa Á Châu, 1961), p. 46.

slave trade prices and taxes openly, slavery was treated as non-existent in nineteenth-century sources like the *Tiền Biên*. This reflects a deeply changed idea about the ideal model of society.

## SIDE BY SIDE

In the eighteenth century, the Vietnamese lived much closer to other ethnic groups than they do today. The word *nguyên* deserves attention here. The inhabitants of these *nguyên* (same derivation as *nguồn*) need not always be understood as "uplanders," or as "montagnardes," the common French designation. The word *"nguyên"* means "origin,"[50] referring to places where rivers originate. While *nguyên* might in many cases refer to the mountains where rivers arise, in other instances mentioned in *Đại Nam Nhất Thống Chí*, minority peoples did not always live in the mountains. Rather, they lived along river banks or in valleys, as noted by Ngô Đức Thịnh for Quảng Bình.[51] These were the people first in contact with the Vietnamese, who subsequently came to know and record facts about them. The word *nguyên* therefore might have referred to areas upriver in general, while in practice the *nguyên* residents acted as intermediaries between Vietnamese and more remote highlanders.[52]

When Vietnamese immigrants came they always occupied land along the river first. Villages therefore usually followed the rivers in shape, being long and narrow.[53] Hence, it seems likely that, in early Đàng Trong at least, Vietnamese settlers might have lived physically quite close to other peoples, despite the different agricultural systems whereby one planted dry rice, the other wet. Map 2 indicates this intermingling quite clearly, as does the location of the various *nguyên* (see discussion below).[54] Viên Cầu *nguồn*, for instance, lay only thirty-one kilometers from modern Vĩnh Linh county, while Thu Bồn *nguồn*, the site of seventeenth- and eighteenth-century gold mining, was less than thirty kilometers from Quế Sơn,

---

[50] Chinese derivation.

[51] Ngô Đức Thịnh, "Vài nét về sự phân bố và tên gọi hành chính của các làng xã ở Quảng Bình trước Cách mạng Tháng Tám" (Some notes on the distribution of villages and the village administrative names in Quang Binh before the August Revolution), in *Nông Thôn Việt Nam trong Lịch Sử* (The Vietnamese countryside in history), vol. 1 (Hanoi: Khoa Học Xã Hội, 1977), p. 402.

[52] In this context, it is interesting to note that south Vietnamese coined the term *người Thượng* or *người Thượng Du* in the 1960s, which can be translated accurately as "peoples who live upriver," although *Thượng/Hạ* does not always refer to upriver/down river. This term seems to be a direct continuation of the idea captured in the word *nguyên*.

[53] By contrast, villages in the north are relatively round or square, surrounded with bamboo and usually possessing a small main entrance. As Vietnamese scholars put it, a village in the north is an almost closed community, while in the south it is an open one. See Ngô Đức Thịnh, "Vài nét về sự phân bố và tên gọi hành chính của các làng xã ở Quảng Bình," pp. 401–403; Nguyễn Công Bình, Lê Xuân Điệm and Mạc Đường. *Văn Hóa và Cư Dân Đồng bằng Sông Cửu Long* (Culture and residents in the Mekong River delta) (Hồ Chí Minh City: Khoa Học Xã Hội, 1990); and *Mấy đặc điểm Đồng bằng Sông Cửu Long* (Some characteristics of the culture of the Mekong Delta) (Hanoi: Viện Văn Hóa, 1984).

[54] Although the territory of Đàng Trong forms one of the most ethnolinguistically complex areas of the world, for our purpose here we consider the non-Vietnamese peoples as a single undifferentiated group.

Quảng Nam. Other *nguồn* were even closer, like Nha Trang in Diên Khánh, which was located only fourteen kilometers from Phước Điền county, or Cư Đê, located a mere five kilometers from Hòa Vang county in Quảng Nam.[55]

Vietnamese and minority communities were more likely to be physically located in close conjunction in seventeenth- and eighteenth-century Đàng Trong and were also more likely to share the more accessible lowlands nearer the coast. Not all minority groups in the region who are uplanders today lived in the mountains in the early days of Nguyễn Cochinchina. For example, the Chứt people from Quảng Bình say that their ancestors used to live on the coast of present-day Bố Trạch and Quảng Trạch counties, but piracy forced them to move to the mountainous region in the west. Similarly, the Vietnamese ethnologist Đặng Nghiêm Vạn believes the Bahnar people from the hill region of the Quảng Ngãi-Phú Yên hinterland may be the Mada people who are mentioned in Cham inscriptions and who earlier lived in coastal Quảng Ngãi.[56] We find the same idea in a local term from the Quảng Bình area, "*mọi biển*," which referred to indigenous people who lived by fishing at sea.[57] The use of *Mọi* here surely indicates that this group, whether Chams or some minority fishing people, remained in the region for some time after the arrival of Vietnamese newcomers. Seventeenth century social composition is illuminated in a comment in the Chinese source *Xiamen Zhi* (Local Records of Xiamen): "Local people [Vietnamese] here are mixed with barbarians."[58] Indeed, this intermingling of discrete ethnic groups was one of the most distinctive social characteristics of Đàng Trong.

The upland villages marked in Map 2 all paid taxes to the Nguyễn in the eighteenth century. It is likely, therefore, that these peoples corresponded to those called "*Mọi thuộc*" (dependent *mọi*), in contrast to the "*Mọi hoang*" (wild *mọi*). How did they come under the control of the Nguyễn? Surely geography was one reason, but their need for trade with the coast, occupied by the Vietnamese, might have been another. Interestingly, we find another word "*Mọi buôn*" (trading *Mọi*), which referred to uplanders who had commercial relations with the Vietnamese, presumably including uplanders who paid taxes to the Nguyễn. The peoples who carried on such contacts with Vietnamese probably lived mainly in the lower hill regions, in contrast to the *Mọi cao* (high *Mọi*). Even so, some minority peoples seem to have escaped Vietnamese penetration and control successfully, despite living in very close proximity to Vietnamese settlements. Thus, Christian Simonnet reports two tribes, the Die and the Khatu, that remained untouched until the 1950s, even though their territories lay no more than eighteen miles due west of the city of Đà Nẵng. The Khatu's reputation of being "the blood hunters" suggests that they were too ferocious for the Vietnamese to have wanted anything to do with them.[59]

---

[55] *Đại Nam Nhất Thống Chí*, pp. 879, 686, 687, 1265.

[56] See *Sổ Tay về các Dân Tộc ở Việt Nam* (A handbook on peoples in Vietnam) (Hanoi: Khoa Học Xã Hội, 1983), pp. 31, 40.

[57] See Ngô Đức Thịnh, "Vài nét về sự phân bố và tên gọi hành chính của các làng xã ở Quảng Bình," p. 403.

[58] *Xiamen Zhi* (Local Records of Xiamen), *Zhong guo fang zhi cung shu* (serials of Chinese local records), no. 80, first printed in 1839, reprinted in 1967 (Taipei: Cheng Wen Press), p. 151.

[59] Dourisboure and Simmonet, *Vietnam, Mission on the Grand Plateaus*, p. 245. Khatu here might be Katu. This tribe thus might be the Low Katu living in the lower areas near the coastal plain. See Hickey, *Sons of the Mountains*, pp. 11–12.

As the Vietnamese population grew, the preferred land along the rivers and coast was quickly exhausted, despite the still relatively sparse population in the seventeenth and eighteenth centuries. The lands next occupied were valleys, and then the lands along major roads, whose existence suggests that population density had risen in the region.

The general process of Vietnamese occupation seems to have occurred peacefully, in large part no doubt because minority peoples who wanted to avoid Vietnamese political authority retreated deeper into the mountains. Nevertheless, the Vietnamese always took care to make symbolic reparation to the spirits of the new land. Tạ Chí Đài Trường notes a practice called *"Lễ cung chủ đất cũ"* (making an offering to the former lord of the land) was quite common among the Vietnamese, even into the late nineteenth century. One such ceremony held in 1879 in Chợ Lớn, for example, was said to have lasted for seven days and seven nights.[60] While it was in progress, people would "rent land" from the former lord, understood to be a spirit, by paying 1500 *quan* in gold or silver colored paper money and promising to offer him a pig every three years. Hopefully this would satisfy the "former lord," who would allow the Vietnamese to expand their settlements further.

Sometimes, as another ritual suggests, the process may not have been quite so easy. A darker version of the same ceremony has also been recorded in which the *Chúa Ngu* (local spirit lord), with face blackened to resemble a *"Mọi,"* would cry out asking for the land to be returned (*"la hết đòi đất"*). A Vietnamese shaman then appeared and, alternately by intimidation or bribery, persuaded the *Chúa Ngu* to give up the land. In this ritualized bargain the Vietnamese always ended up paying some money for the land they relinquished.[61] Tạ Chí Đài Trường reports that, as late as the 1920s, a large ceremony of *Tả Thổ* (buying or renting land) was held each year in Quy Nhơn.[62] Indeed, something akin to this is still carried out in Tiền Giang, Long An, and Bến Tre provinces, the areas of the Mekong delta earliest settled by Vietnamese. Here the *Tả Thổ* ceremony seems to have merged somewhat with the ceremony of *Lễ cung chủ đất cũ*. It is held in lunar March, significantly not in a temple but in the open air, with three bowls of offerings set out: one for Bà Chúa Sứ (the female master of the region), another for a couple Chúa Ngung Mang Nương, and the third for the goddess Uma. All three deities are of local origin.[63]

It is striking that similar ceremonies concerning land ownership were reported in almost all the former territory of Đàng Trong, always with Vietnamese on one side and the *"Mọi"* on the other. No one knows when the practice began in Cochinchina, but it clearly reflected the anxiety felt by the immigrant Vietnamese who wanted to insure that their settlement did not offend the spirits of the new land and to guard against any retaliation mounted by the "former lord" of the land. The same idea seems to lie behind Minh Mạng's construction of a temple for the kings of Champa in 1833, exactly at the time when, by his own order, Vietnamese officials and soldiers were ruthlessly seeking to crush all vestiges of Cham ethnic and cultural identity in a

---

[60] Tạ Chí Đài Trường, *Thần, Người, và Đất Việt* (Deities, people, and the land of Viet) (California: Văn Nghệ, 1989), p. 281.

[61] Ibid., pp. 280-284.

[62] Ibid., p. 287.

[63] Phan Thi Yến Tuyết *Nhà ở, trang phục, ăn uống của các dân tộc vùng Đồng bằng sông Cửu Long* ([Customs of] Housing, clothes and food of the peoples in the Mekong delta region) (Hanoi: Khoa Học Xã Hội, 1993), pp. 87–88.

Panduranga brought for the first time under direct Vietnamese rule.[64] The temple was built on an old Cham ruin, and offerings were made twice yearly by civil officers of high rank in the Nguyễn court. This obviously has the same nature as the ceremony of *lễ cung chủ đất cũ* discussed above.[65]

If some lands were "bought" with ceremonial money, others were definitely paid for in blood, especially the blood of uplander children. Unknown numbers of them were offered as sacrifices in the seventeenth and eighteenth centuries. Lê Quang Nghiêm cited one example. Some Vietnamese immigrants came to fish on a small island called Hòn Do in Khánh Hòa, but they felt so threatened by local devils in their first four months that they moved away. Still the good fishing attracted others who believed (perhaps at the suggestion of local people[66]) that performing a ritual human sacrifice each year would enable them to stay and exploit the area peacefully. So in lunar March of every year a child of five to seven years of age would be bought from the mountains and burned alive, and the corpse thrown into the sea afterwards. This custom persisted until the late nineteenth century, when a pig replaced the child.[67] A similar practice was said to have occurred in Hòn Một and Hòn Nhàn regions in Khánh Hòa as well, where Vietnamese ritually sacrificed an uplander child to *Nhang Dang*, a Cham-derived expression for devil or spirit.[68]

A ceremony in Hàm Hòa village, Quảng Ninh county, Quảng Bình province shows that human sacrifice was not only used directly to propitiate local spirits. Here it was used to demarcate the village. Some elderly people from this village recounted stories they had heard from their fathers or grandfathers explaining an old way of delimiting the area belonging to the village. It happened as a grand ceremony in which a virgin girl (origin unstated) was cut into two pieces and then her corpse was carried swiftly around the outskirts of the village by one of its young men. The traces of the girl's blood marked and established the sacred border of the village. This association between human sacrifice and local habitation suggests a connection with local uplander minority customs. [69]

Despite the various contacts between Vietnamese and minority peoples in the region, the two usually remained quite distinct. (Intermarriages between Vietnamese and Cham descendants should be noted as an exception here; these might have occurred quite commonly, especially in Bình Thuận.) But if we except the An Khê

---

[64] Late Cham chronicles translated by Po Dharma relate this sombre story in Po Dharma, trans., *Le Panduranga (Campa) 1802–1835. Ses rapports avec le Vietnam*, vol. II (Paris: EFEO, 1987).

[65] *Đại Nam Nhất Thống Chí*, vol. 1, p. 80.

[66] Several occasions in the highlands required human sacrifice, including the construction of a new house. Dourisboure and Simmonet, *Mission on the Grand Plateaus*, p. 243.

[67] Lê Quang Nghiêm, *Tục thờ cúng của ngư phủ Khánh Hòa* (Rites in the fishing region of Khanh Hoa) (Los Alamitos: reprinted by Xuân Thu, n.d.), pp. 115–122. The notion of human sacrifice seems to have remained powerful in the far south for even longer. In 1940, a human sacrifice was carried out by the Thinkers Sect in Tân Châu district on the Viet-Khmer border area, while a second occurred in a Cần Thơ village in 1941. Hue Tam Ho Tai, *Millennarianism and Peasant Politics in Vietnam* (Cambridge: Harvard University Press, 1983), pp. 120–123.

[68] Lê Quang Nghiêm, *Tục thờ cúng của ngư phủ Khánh Hòa*, pp. 128–131. The fact that uplander children were used as sacrifices strongly suggests the connection with uplander customs since other tribal children, usually captured by raiding parties, were common sacrifical victims in uplander rituals. Hickey, *Sons of the Mountains*, p. 27

[69] Ngô Đức Thịnh, "Các quan hệ sở hữu," in *Nông Thôn Việt Nam trong Lịch Sử* (Hanoi: Khoa Học Xã Hội, 1977), pp. 388–389.

area, where some intermarriage apparently took place, we find that very few marriages were ever recorded between Vietnamese and uplanders. The absence of intermarriage no doubt reflected Vietnamese cultural prejudices about the uncivilized nature of tribal minority peoples, as well as the Vietnamese settlers' long-standing fear of the mountains and deep forests, which they perceived as deadly regions of malarial infestation—understood in terms of an unhealthy miasma (*chương khí*) and powerful evil spirits. Certainly this latter conviction helped channel Vietnamese expansion mainly to the south, though frontier settlements in the form of military colonies (*đồn điền*) always existed to insure the peace. It seems, too, that most minority peoples in the hinterland, especially those in the mountains, also preferred to limit their contacts to trade and otherwise keep their social distance from the newcomers. This meant that most Đàng Trong Vietnamese basically remained outsiders to the Central Highlands, strangers to the western quarter of their new land.

## TAXES COLLECTED FROM UPLANDERS

Judging from Lê Quý Đôn's account, it appears that by the eighteenth century, in parts of the Thuận Hóa hinterland, minority residents of *nguồn* communities had been brought closer to the Vietnamese norm of a registered taxpaying population, albeit sometimes in a locally distinctive way. The crucial factor here was Nguyễn control of Cam Lộ and of the Ai Lao Pass, where a large military camp and outlying posts had existed since the 1620s. The local terrain allowed comparatively easy communication from this axial point and enabled the Vietnamese to extend their administrative sway over surrounding settlements. The process was well underway before the end of the seventeenth century, since the *Tiền Biên* recorded that in 1697 "taxpaying barbarians" (*thuế man*) from Phú Vang county (modern Thừa Thiên) were pillaged by "cruel barbarians" (*ác man*),[70] undoubtedly non-taxpaying "high *mọi* " (*mọi cao*) from deeper in the mountains.

So well established was this tax administration that by the 1770s merchants in the hinterland of modern Quảng Trị and Thừa Thiên provinces were confronted with a battery of taxes on trade goods, including rice, buffalo, and pigs as well as more exotic items like elephants and elephant tusks, beeswax, rhinoceros horn, gold, and silver. These taxes, usually levied as a proportion of the quantity or value of the goods involved, were paid either to the official supervising the *nguồn*, or at inspection posts. In the various *nguồn* of this area, several uplander villages had been drawn into the Nguyễn tax system to differing degrees. The three villages of *nguồn* Hưng Bình, in Phú Vang county, for instance, paid head tax on a graded system similar to that operating in the plains, although they acquitted it in kind, not cash.[71] Elsewhere, as in the *nguồn* Sơn Bồ, in Quảng Điền county, the seventeen uplander villages were assessed as having thirty-six taxpaying males, each one of whom had to provide one thousand pieces of rattan and were liable for conscription into the local militia.[72] However here, as in some other places, the government reciprocated a

---

[70] *Tiền Biên*, vol. 7, p. 102.

[71] *Phủ Biên*, vol. 4, p. 10b. My thanks to Nola Cooke for drawing my attention to these three *nguon*.

[72] Ibid., p. 9b.

little with an annual distribution of salt and rice by the *nguồn* official, along with some trade on the side. Other local peculiarities existed. The three *nguồn* in Khang Lộc county (modern Quảng Trị province), for instance, seem to have had separate systems, the most unusual being that of Yên Đãi. Here the eleven *đinh* (registered taxpayers) were all recorded by name, and their head tax, divided into three categories, was levied in money on both themselves and their wives.[73] Overall, it seems that uplanders in Thuận Hóa were more heavily taxed than lowland Vietnamese peasants, although it is difficult to generalize as our only detailed information comes from the late 1760s and early 1770s, a time which was far from typical. Even so, the most lucrative element of the fiscal system remained taxes on trade. So profitable were such taxes in the two *nguồn* around Cam Lộ (Sãi and Cam Lộ) that lesser officials actively lobbied to be appointed tax collectors there. Lê Quý Đôn characterized their exactions as "rapacious," and it appears that his description was accurate, for the Trịnh administration of the late 1770s and early 1780s reduced the sums collected by one-third in the hope of stimulating trade and bringing down prices.[74]

Given how long the Nguyễn controlled the Cam Lộ-Ai Lao area, it is not surprising that their authority and prestige extended westwards along this route towards the Lao principalities. This apparently culminated in 1761, when *Tiền Biên* recorded that the principality of Van Tượng (formerly Ai Lao in Vietnamese texts) first sent "tribute" (*cống*) to Phú Xuân. Whether this represented any real political change is uncertain, however. *Tiền Biên* made no such claim and described the delivery and arrival of this "tribute" as a natural outgrowth stemming from long established and amicable trading arrangements with uplanders in the Cam Lộ area.[75] This suggests we must take care not to read too much into the term "tribute" here, as it may indicate nothing more than a Nguyễn decision to identify an old practice with a new, symbolically charged name that suggests regal domination of one country by another. The Nguyễn's newly asserted royal status made it appropriate to characterize the time-honored exchange of "gifts" between Phú Xuân and the Lao ruler of Vientiane as "tribute" from a vassal king, without implying any substantial alteration in the relationship. When the Lê dynastic rebel, Lê Duy Mật, wrote from his mountainous base in Trấn Ninh (Thanh Hóa) to the post commander at Ai Lao seeking Nguyễn Phúc Khoát's help in his revolt against the Trịnh, the request was rejected. As late as 1764, the *chúa* upheld conventional Nguyễn thinking and "did not want to provoke enmity on the borders."[76]

In Quảng Nam Protectorate, however, things were different. Sometime during Nguyễn Phúc Khoát's reign, the strategy of peaceful co-existence with the minority peoples of the Central Highlands began to break down. For reasons which are unclear, but may have involved a combination of factors—population growth, bad harvest years, and harassment by outsiders[77]—from the late 1740s on, the Đá Vách in Quảng Ngãi returned to raiding the lowlands after two centuries of peace. Nguyễn Phúc Khoát appointed the famous civil official Nguyễn Cư Trinh as governor of

---

[73] Ibid., 8a–9a.

[74] Ibid., 6a–6b.

[75] *Tiền Biên*, vol. 10, p. 149.

[76] *Tiền Biên*, vol. 10, p. 150.

[77] Cửu Long Giang and Toan Ánh, *Cao Nguyên Miền Thượng* (The uplanders in the Central Highlands), vol. I (Saigon: n.p., 1974), pp. 92–93.

Quảng Ngãi in 1750 to find a solution to the problem. He divided the border area into sections, established a military command to patrol them, and laid out military colonies to secure the frontier before inquiring into the causes of the revolt. His 1751 report advocated a number of changes, including, significantly, forbidding outsiders who went hunting in the mountains from stirring up or interfering with the local people and requiring their papers be checked by local authorities empowered to arrest them if they caused trouble. However, his report was not passed to the *chúa*, according to his official biography.[78] The court continued to tolerate licensed merchants abusing their stranglehold over trade with the *nguồn* and outsiders fomenting discord, while beginning itself to seek increased tax revenue in the west to help fund Nguyễn Phúc Khoát's extravagant royal building program and to compensate for declining overseas trade revenues. By 1761, the situation had deteriorated to the point of open warfare in the Central Highlands hinterland of Quảng Ngãi. Raiding parties attacked all along the border from modern Quảng Nam to Bình Định and forced the evacuation of Vietnamese settlements. It was not until 1770 that the tribesmen were pushed back into the mountains.[79]

We do not know why the report of Nguyễn Cư Trinh was not passed to Nguyễn Phúc Khoát in 1751, but fiscal information in *Phủ Biên* hints that the *nguồn* residents here, and perhaps also the people deeper in the interior, were more directly exploited by the court than was true of residents in Thuận Hóa, as they were charged to pay the salaries of designated high officials. In Thuận Hóa, only three *nguồn*, all in Khang Lộc county, were involved in the official salary system; monies collected from those three were granted as remuneration (*ngụ lộc*) to the governor of Quảng Trị. In Quảng Nam, by contrast, eight of the twenty-two *nguồn* were distributed to officials as sources of revenue to pay their salaries, several of them to the highest ranking officials at court. By the 1770s, each *nguồn* in Quảng Nam paid more *ngụ lộc* to the high officials involved than any *nguồn* in Thuận Hóa paid as taxes. The amounts could be extremely large: the usurping Regent Trương Phúc Loan, for example, reportedly collected each year 2,500 *quan* from two such *nguồn* in Qui Nhơn, and more than 220 ounces of good silver from another in Bình Khang. Three of the four most prestigious Nguyễn officials (known as "the Four Pillars") each collected over two hundred ounces of silver every year from *nguồn* granted to them as communities that could be charged to pay their salaries. Only the Cham *nguồn* of Nha Trang contributed more: according to Lê Quý Đôn, they paid a staggering ten thousand *quan* per year in 1774.[80] It may be that the court officials who were granted uplander districts to exploit for *ngụ lộc* came to regard them as more or less their own domains and acted accordingly, not only in Quảng Nam but deeper in the mountains as well. There seems a hint of this in Nguyễn Cư Trinh's 1751 report, where criticism of men "going to hunt in the mountains" may have obliquely referred to influential figures close to the ruler who ventured into the uplands to exploit the people for their own benefit, and not, as Nguyễn Cư Trinh pointedly reminded the *chúa*, "according to the

---

[78] *Đại Nam Liệt Truyện Tiền Biên* (hereafter *Liệt Truyện Tiền Biên*) (Collection of Biographies of Nguyen Dynasty, Premier Period), vol. 5 (Tokyo: Keio Institute of Linguistic Studies, 1961), p. 254.

[79] Bernard Bourotte, "Essai d'histoire des populations montagnardes du sud-indochinois jusqu'à 1945," Bulletin de la Société des Etudes Indochinoises (NS), XXX (1955): 46-47.

[80] *Phủ Biên* (Hanoi edition), vol. 4, pp. 213-215. My gratitude to Nola Cooke for drawing my attention to the whole issue of *ngụ lộc*.

good intentions of the court."[81] Certainly, if such men were involved, it would help explain why Nguyễn Cư Trinh's critical report was prevented from reaching the *chúa*.

Our difficulty here is, again, that almost all detailed information about the fiscal position of uplanders comes from the period of Trương Phúc Loan's dominance, that is, from the mid-1760s to the early 1770s. We do not even know, for instance, whether granting *nguồn* taxes as *ngụ lộc* to the highest court officers was a normal practice or an innovation designed to buy official support for the usurping (and increasingly unpopular) Regent. Whatever the case, it does seem that trade with the *nguồn*, and by extension with uplanders deeper in the mountains, was increasingly exploited during this period as foreign trade, the more usual source of revenue, began to dry up. Its fiscal significance rose both proportionally and absolutely. The change was evident in taxation details for 1774 preserved in *Phủ Biên*, details which showed uplander contributions comprised almost half the secondary taxes collected that year at a time when many minority areas were already in Tây Sơn hands. With international trade a mere 4 percent of secondary revenue, taxes collected from uplanders now constituted an important source of revenue in the Nguyễn fiscal system, as the following composite table shows.

| Table 1: Receipts from Secondary Taxes Around the 1770s | | |
|---|---|---|
| | (in *quan*) | % |
| •gold (1769) | 15,190 | 18.58% |
| •fishing (1768) | 11,403 | 13.94% |
| •ferries (1768) and port transit | 10,658 | 13.04% |
| •overseas trade (1773) | 3,200 | 3.91% |
| •domestic junks (1768) | 2,639 | 3.23% |
| •markets (1768) | 2,601 | 3.18% |
| •edible birds' nests(1768) | 773 | 0.95% |
| •salt producing land in Thuận Hóa | 221 | 0.27% |
| •uplanders (1768) | 38,728 | 48.67% |
| Total Secondary Taxes | 81,748 *quan*[82] | |

That tax demands were unusually high in this period is demonstrated by a comparison between the taxes extracted from the trade of the original four *nguồn* in Quảng Ngãi in 1774 and at the start of the nineteenth century, in the early years of the Gia Long reign. In 1774, as reported by Lê Quý Đôn, the nineteenth-century historian of the Quảng Ngãi uplands, taxes on these four *nguồn* alone totaled 6,903.43 *quan* in money, with *nguồn* Cù Ba also required to give 180 ounces of silver, eaglewood, and rattan. Under Gia Long, however, the same four *nguồn* were assessed at 1,470 *quan* in all.[83] Lê Quý Đôn added that, later, under the Tây Sơn, the tax on merchants trading with *nguồn* Da Bong was so high (1,200 *quan*, or twice that of the Gia Long era) that it had driven them to tax evasion; if so, what must their

---

[81] *Liệt Truyện Tiền Biên*, vol. 5, p. 254.

[82] Of this total, 76,467 *quan* was in money, plus fourteen bars and eight *lang* in gold (worth 2,816 *quan*) and 145 silver bars (worth 3,625 *quan*) using Lê Quý Đôn's value for silver bars as one silver bar = seventeen *quan* (1728) rising to twenty-five *quan* in 1766. *Phủ Biên*, vol. 3, pp. 98 b, 125a-125b.

[83] *Phủ Biên*, vol. 4, p. 13a. My thanks to Nola Cooke for this information.

reaction have been to the 1,910 *quan* recorded for 1774? Some scant evidence also shows tax rates rose steeply at the time. According to Lê Quý Đôn's information, the tax revenue from the three uplander districts in Khang Lộc county jumped from 1768 to 1774 in the following way:[84]

| District | 1768 | 1774 | Increase % |
|----------|------|------|-----------|
|          | (*quan*) | (*quan*) |       |
| Yên Đãi  | 230.2 | 434.33 | 88% |
| Yên Nẻo  | 280.9 | 395.9 | 41% |
| Cẩm Lý   | 68.9 | 102.4 | 49% |

From these scattered references, it seems possible to conclude that when overseas trade was still flourishing, before the 1750s, Nguyễn tax collectors did not pay special attention to the mountains. Of the two main taxes levied there, the one on trade between licensed merchants and uplanders was no doubt the most important; this was certainly true in Quảng Nam, as taxes there could be easily collected at military posts or at strategic locations near the mountain trade routes. Head taxes in cash or kind only seem to have applied to a relatively small number of uplanders, all from Thuận Hóa. But by the late 1760s, as inflation and dwindling overseas trading created a fiscal crisis for the government, even these people found themselves squeezed by increasing taxation demands. The eleven *đinh* of *nguồn* Yên Đãi are the most obvious examples: in 1774 they were collectively responsible for paying an exorbitant 434.3 *quan*, an amount they must have had to raise from their own communities if they were to acquit it. This incredible imposition could only be a short-term, desperate measure: no one could seriously hope to extract this amount of tax for very long. But not only the enormous levies are significant here. The people might well have felt exploited by taxes that brought in relatively small amounts of money to the government. For instance, Lê Quý Đôn noted the tax on rattan collected in *nguồn* Tả Trách (Hương Trà county). Before 1769, the Nguyễn had collected ten *quan*'s worth of rattan in taxes each year. In 1769, however, the amount raised increased almost five-fold to forty-seven *quan* and 197 *dong*, thanks to the increased efforts of a new tax collector.[85]

Although the evidence is scattered, it all points toward the growth of an unendurable tax burden on uplander peoples in the later 1760s and early 1770s. It is hardly surprising that the Tây Sơn reportedly claimed, early in the revolt, to be legitimist rebels opposed to Trương Phúc Loan's usurpation of power. There may have been little or no residual loyalty to the Nguyễn among upland peoples by the 1770s, but a different Nguyễn candidate on the throne meant the end of Trương Phúc Loan and his hated taxes. As noted in Chapter Two, the idea of establishing tighter control over taxes did not originate with the usurping Regent: as early as 1741, Nguyễn Phúc Khoát had listed all the taxes collected between 1738 and 1740 and identified those levied but not paid. A similar exercise in 1765 showed many taxes still remained unpaid, but by then the economic situation had become far more serious. In the midst of a worsening crisis in money supply and with state revenues from overseas trade dwindling, the government decided to shore up its revenue base. Four years later it issued a revised taxation rule, to make "the numbers detailed

---

[84] For the first group, see *Phủ Biên*, vol. 4, pp. 8b–9a; for the second group, pp. 11b–12a.

[85] *Phủ Biên*, vol. 4, pp. 10a–10b.

and clear."[86] The 1769 tax system initiated a critical era for the Nguyễn regime, pushing the state's interests into conflict with those of its officials and of its subjects. Squeezing uplanders for an increasingly disproportionate share of the tax burden may have seemed a way of lessening some of the tensions provoked by growing government demands within Vietnamese communities. It was no surprise, therefore, that a few short years later the taxation system triggered the Tây Sơn uprising. We note that one of the rebels' first acts in 1773 was the murder of a tax official and all his family.[87]

But the Tây Sơn rebellion was not simply a consequence of Nguyễn government miscalculation; it was also a product of Vietnamese localization in Đàng Trong. Its outbreak and early development can only be understood within its southern context, as the next chapter will contend.

---

[86] *Phủ Biên*, vol. 4, pp. 40a–40b. Unfortunately, hardly any information about taxes after 1769 collected from Quảng Nam south appears in *Phủ Biên*.

[87] *Đại Nam Chính Biên Liệt Truyện Sơ Tập* (First collection of the primary compilation of biographies of Imperial Vietnam), vol. 30 (Tokyo: Keio Institute of Linguistic Studies, Mita Siba, Minato-Ku, reprint, 1962), pp. 319-320.

# THE TÂY SƠN

T
he Tây Sơn rebellion was the most successful and spectacular revolt in pre-
colonial Vietnamese history. It brought about the collapse of Đàng Trong
and paved the way for the creation of a single Vietnamese state in 1802
under the Nguyễn dynasty. The Tây Sơn rebellion and the thirty year
civil war it initiated form a major subject in itself, although one unfortunately not yet
seriously analyzed in English-language historiography. A study such as this on
Nguyễn Cochinchina cannot presume to do it justice. Nevertheless, an examination
of the outbreak of the Tây Sơn revolt and its early years certainly belongs here. The
Tây Sơn rebellion is conventionally described as a peasant revolt, and its brilliant
leader said to have harnessed this eruption of popular energy to overthrow both
existing regimes in late eighteenth-century Vietnam. But this chapter argues, on the
contrary, that closer examination shows the rebellion was essentially a Đàng Trong
phenomenon, a movement stirred up by changing local conditions and responding
primarily to local factors. Before we consider the evidence, and by way of
introduction, let us survey a cross-section of other opinions.

## SHORTCOMINGS OF CURRENT EXPLANATIONS OF THE TÂY SƠN

Thousands of books and articles have been published on the Tây Sơn in Vietnam
since the beginning of this century.[1] Most of them have focused on its outstanding
leader, Nguyễn Huệ, the later Quang Trung emperor (1789-92), praising him as the
most brilliant figure in Vietnamese history. As leader of a peasant revolt, he has been
deemed superior to Hong Xiu Quan, leader of the Tai Ping Heavenly Kingdom
movement that convulsed China in the 1850s. As a general victorious over foreign
invaders, he has been judged greater than Lý Thường Kiệt and Trần Quốc Tuấn in
the Lý and Trần dynasties. As a king who promoted demotic Vietnamese (nôm) in
literature and administration, he may well have been more culturally progressive
than Hồ Quý Ly in the early fifteenth century. As an ethnic Vietnamese, he is said to
have exemplified the strategy of rallying minority peoples against feudalist rulers.
As a consummate, dominant representative of the Tây Sơn, Quang Trung has
fulfilled the requirements of both nationalist and Marxist historiography by
embodying all the qualities appealing to advocates of the twentieth-century
Vietnamese revolution.

Certainly the Tây Sơn appealed to modern nationalists for numerous reasons.
Since the 1860s Vietnam had been forced to face the question of whether it could
exist as an independent country, and it needed all the heroes it could muster to
inspire its national forces to meet the situation. As a result, the Tây Sơn, and Nguyễn

---

[1] There are so many books, papers and articles written on the subject that in 1988 Nghĩa Bình
province published a book called *Thủ Mục về Tây Sơn Nguyễn Huệ* (A catalogue on the works
on the Tây Sơn and Nguyễn Huệ), ed. Nguyễn Trí Sơn (Nghĩa Bình, Ủy ban khoa học kỹ
thuật, 1988). 461 pp., with 1,623 entries, most of them written by modern Vietnamese scholars.

Huệ in particular, became mythologized and transformed into symbols of Vietnamese characteristics now defined as essential. Here for instance is Jean Chesneaux's 1960s view, heavily influenced by the wartime apotheosis of the peasantry as the progressive driving force of Vietnamese national history:

> The rise of . . . the Tây Sơn once more confirms the fact that peasant insurrection was the driving force in the political development of feudal Vietnam. It was peasant insurrection which succeeded in maintaining Vietnamese independence by repulsing the Manchus under the banners of the Tây Sơn . . . Peasant insurrections had constantly strengthened the tendencies making for the unity of Vietnam.[2]

Such political myths and symbols tell us more about the needs of the people who developed them than they do about the historical figures they praise: the Tây Sơn cannot be understood historically in this way. While scholars have devoted almost all their pages to extolling the Tây Sơn rebellion, they have paid very little attention to the rebels' earliest and most persistent adversaries, the Nguyễn. As a consequence, the more brilliantly the Tây Sơn's accomplishments and heroism shine, the darker and more mysterious their dramatic fall must then appear. Scholarship of this sort fails to realize that the Tây Sơn's strength grew out of, and reacted to, two hundred years of Nguyễn rule. In these two centuries, southern Vietnamese history took such a different course from northern Vietnamese history that to try to understand the Tây Sơn according to outside models assures failure, or worse. A sampling of current explanations of the causes of the Tây Sơn will illustrate the problem.

Nguyễn Hồng Phong and Văn Tân, along with other Marxist historians in the north, have claimed the revolt broke out because of the landholding system, since the Tây Sơn aimed, in Nguyễn Hồng Phong's words, to "share the land equally among the people."[3] This factor might explain other peasant rebellions, but unfortunately it does not suffice to explain the Tây Sơn. According to *Phủ Biên*, in 1769 the arable land of Quy Nhơn averaged four *mẫu* per taxpayer, whereas in the Thuận Hóa region it averaged only one *mẫu* per taxpayer.[4] Yet the rebellion erupted in Quy Nhơn, not Thuận Hóa. Indeed, with an agricultural economy basically characterized by abundant land, but relatively scarce manpower, land ownership was not a major problem and could hardly be the cause of such a big rebellion. Perhaps for that reason the Tây Sơn themselves when in power did little or nothing about the landholding system, much to the regret of some Hanoi historians who have asserted this was the basic reason the Tây Sơn fell.[5]

Others have claimed it was famine that caused the Tây Sơn rebellion. Basically this accepts the conventional explanation of mid-nineteenth century court historians

---

[2] Jean Chesneaux, *The Vietnamese Nation*, trans. Malcolm Salmon (Sydney: Current Book Distributors, 1966), p. 44.

[3] Nguyễn Hồng Phong, "Vấn đề ruộng đất trong lịch sử chế độ phong kiến Việt Nam" (The land question in the history of Vietnam's feudal system), *Nghiên cứu lịch sử* (Journal of historical studies) 1 (1959): 54. Văn Tân, Nguyễn Huệ, *Con người và sự nghiệp* (Nguyễn Huệ, his personality and the course) (Hanoi: Khoa Học, 1967).

[4] Lê Quý Đôn, *Phủ Biên Tạp Lục* (hereafter *Phủ Biên*), vol. 3 (Hanoi: Khoa Học Xã Hội, 1977), p. 105b.

[5] For example, Nguyễn Lương Bích, "Nguyên nhân thành bại của cách mạng Tây Sơn" (The reasons for the success and the fall for the Tây Sơn revolution), *Văn Sử Địa*, 14 (1956): 45–50.

who wrote that "it was during a bad harvest year that the [Tây Sơn] bandits rose."[6] Yet *Tiền Biên*, complied only a few years earlier from essentially the same sources, recorded no natural disasters or harvest losses for 1770–71.[7] Indeed, when the Trịnh army invaded Đàng Trong, they removed seven hundred kiloliters of rice from the first granary they encountered.[8] In the main Nguyễn storehouse, in 1774, they also found three hundred thousand *quan* in excellent coins, or about 176,471 *taels* of silver.[9] In fact, the worst famine in Cochinchina's history, which Nguyễn Lương Bích presented as a convenient explanation for the Tây Sơn,[10] actually happened some years after the rebellion broke out, in October 1774, when Tây Sơn success in Quy Nhơn cut the transport route between Gia Định and Huế. In other words, the famine was a result rather than a cause of the Tây Sơn upheaval.

So, if there are serious objections to the standard Vietnamese explanations of the outbreak of the Tây Sơn movement, how should it be explained? I believe we need to reorient our perspective. We must interpret the rebellion as a product of Đàng Trong society, and hence as a special case rather than as the most successful example of an international phenomenon: the peasant rebellion. Placing the movement in its proper local and historical context, as the following overview seeks to do, readily reveals it to have been the direct but unexpected result of Đàng Trong's own spectacular growth and an example of successful Vietnamese localization in the new southern land.

## ADMINISTRATIVE OVER-EXTENSION AND THE CONTENTIOUS MEKONG DELTA

By the mid-eighteenth century, the Nguyễn state system was becoming a victim of its own success. To begin with, its principal administrative divisions badly needed adjustment. In the eighteenth century, Đàng Trong still remained divided administratively into the two protectorates that had existed under Nguyễn Hoàng and derived from the Hồng Đức period of Lê Thánh Tôn's reign a century before that. They were Thuận Hóa, which reached from Quảng Bình, its northern border, to Huế; and Quảng Nam, which by the mid-eighteenth century had grown to comprise all the territory from the Huế area as far south as the Mekong delta. This administrative division had worked reasonably well until the later seventeenth century when, from the 1680s, the Mekong delta had been increasingly drawn into the orbit of the Quảng Nam protectorate. From then on it began to develop rapidly as a rice producing area. In reality, the Nguyễn kingdom now comprised at least three distinctive regions: land taken from Champa in the late fifteenth century (Thuận Hóa to Quy Nhơn); land taken from the Cham from the mid-seventeenth century (Phú Yên to Bình Khang); and Đồng Nai (the Mekong region), which only came under

---

[6] See *Đại Nam Chính Biên Liệt Truyện Sơ Tập* (First collection of the primary compilation of biographies of Imperial Vietnam), vol. 30, biographies of the Tây Sơn (1831. Tokyo: Keio Institute of Linguistic Studies, Mita Siba, Minato-ku, reprint, 1962), p. 1,331.

[7] *Đại Nam Thực Lục Tiền Biên* (Chronicle of Greater Vietnam, Premier Period of the Nguyen), vol. 2 (Tokyo: Keio Institute of Linguistic Studies, Mita, Siba, Minato-ku, 1961), pp. 155-158 (hereafter *Tiền Biên*).

[8] *Phủ Biên*, vol. 1, p. 46b.

[9] *Phủ Biên*, vol. 4, p. 21a.

[10] Nguyễn Lương Bích, *Quang Trung Nguyễn Huệ*.(Hanoi: Quân Doi Nhân Dân, 1989), p. 10.

Nguyễn rule from the late seventeenth century. Yet the huge and expanding area south of Thuận Hóa all fell under the administrative authority of Quảng Nam. This impractical system created institutional and administrative difficulties for the distant Nguyễn court in Huế.

It also reflects the inadequate administrative control wielded by the Nguyễn in eighteenth-century Đàng Trong as a consequence of its own rapid southward expansion. Not only was Đàng Trong long and narrow, with its capital far to the north, but also a small Cham state (Panduranga) still existed between it and the Mekong delta. Thus, if the Mekong delta brought treasure to the Nguyễn, it also presented itself as an increasingly serious challenge to the Cochinchinese state in the eighteenth century. In the seventeenth century, the elementary machinery of government of the time had proved sufficient to administer successfully the relatively compact territory of older Đàng Trong. Expansion into the Mekong delta, however, generated new stresses and tensions for which the existing administrative regime was poorly adapted. The far south was a different world. It was charged with more complex and competing forces than the Nguyễn system had previously experienced, as the pitfalls associated with extending Nguyễn power to the semi-independent Mạc Cửu fiefdom in the Hà Tiên region made manifest.

The port of Hà Tiên[11] on the modern Viet-Khmer border probably first became prosperous at the turn of the eighteenth century, following the efforts of a group of Chinese settlers led by Mạc Cửu. It soon attracted the unwelcome attention of the Siamese state, itself vigorously seeking to expand eastward. Recognizing that Hà Tiên could hope for no real help from the weak Cambodian court, in 1708 Mạc Cửu solicited the Nguyễn as protectors.[12] Cambodia felt the first repercussions from this move. If the Vietnamese advance into the Mekong delta had cut off the most important outlet of Khmer foreign trade, then Hà Tiên's falling under Nguyễn's control must have effectively sealed off Cambodia's maritime access to the outside world, as David Chandler has noted.[13] This in turn could only increase Cambodia's vulnerability to Vietnamese and Thai encroachments. But even for the Nguyễn, Hà Tiên was something of a mixed blessing. From a strategic point of view, Hà Tiên's submission to the Nguyễn was far more significant than merely adding another tract of formerly Cambodian land to their territory. At the time, Vietnamese expansion to, and Nguyễn political authority over, the Mekong delta extended only as far as the Tiền Giang river region,[14] which meant that half the delta still lay beyond Nguyễn control. As in a game of *go* chess, Hà Tiên could be deployed as a Nguyễn game token placed in the opponent's territory, a token which then transformed its surroundings into Nguyễn land. With Gia Định in the north already under Vietnamese administrative control and now Hà Tiên in the west submitting to the Nguyễn's political suzerainty, it was inevitable that a powerless Cambodia would ultimately lose its remaining half of the Mekong delta; this occurred in 1756 and

---

[11] Hà Tiên was variously known as Cancar or Cancao in Chinese, as Ponthiamas or Ponteamas among Europeans, and Peam in Khmer.

[12] Chen Chingho, "He xian zhen ye zhen mo shi jia pu zhu shi" (Notes on the genealogy of the Mac family in Hatien), *Quo li taiwan da xue wen shi zhe xue bao* (Bulletin of the College of Arts of Taiwan National University) 7 (1956): 89–90.

[13] David Chandler, *A History of Cambodia*, 2nd. edition (Sydney:Allen & Unwin, 1993), p. 95.

[14] Đào Duy Anh, *Đạt nước Việt Nam qua các đời* (Vietnamese territories in the different periods) (Hanoi: Khoa Học 1964), pp. 159-160.

1757.[15] Economically, too, Hà Tiên was a bonus. With its convenient location and the energetic leadership of the Mạc, it soon replaced Phnom Penh as the region's chief international port, as evidenced by an account of junks trading in Canton in 1767 which listed nine from Cochinchina, seven from Kang-kow (a Chinese name for Hà Tiên) and only two from Cambodia.[16] This evidence suggests that Hà Tiên was becoming, or perhaps had already become, the most important port in far southern Vietnam and the coastal area of Cambodia, a position it probably maintained until the rise of Saigon as a major port. Nguyễn control over Hà Tiên turned Khmer Panday Mas, meaning "inland" or "rear area,"[17] into a Vietnamese frontier.

And at this frontier the Nguyễn encountered the strongest rival imaginable in this part of mainland Southeast Asia—Siam. If Hà Tiên was an important salient in the Vietnamese encirclement of the Mekong delta, it was just as important a strategic location for the Siamese in their drive to control the Cambodian court, for it was the most convenient point from which to deploy troops to march on the Khmer capital at Udong.[18] Vietnamese suzerainty over Hà Tiên thus guaranteed a Siamese-Vietnamese rivalry throughout the eighteenth century and beyond.

Such a rich and politically complex area was likely to invite suspicion, envy, and interference from even more sides, from the Khmer, the Teochiu Chinese, and even certain Nguyễn generals posted to Gia Định, far from the court in distant Thuận Hóa.[19] That Nguyễn generals could play a semi-autonomous hand in Hà Tiên's affairs derived from the decisive weakness on the Nguyễn side in their eighteenth-century duel with Siam. Đàng Trong's political center was far away to the north, and that government could not provide the same prompt and effective leadership as the nearer Siamese court could. The chain of command was one thousand kilometers long: news from Hà Tiên had first to be reported to the generals in the Gia Định area before then being relayed to Huế, and then Huế's orders had to be carried back south, where they might be delivered many days or even weeks later, depending on sailing conditions. The execution of these orders then depended on generals far from Huế's active supervision, generals who may have been less determined than their distant Nguyễn king, and liable to be swayed by local considerations unknown or only poorly understood in Huế. Historically, such "considerations" included bribes from Khmer kings to do whatever they could to slow down the pace of the Nguyễn's southern expansion. At times the bribes were successful. In 1689 and 1690, for instance, two chief commanders in succession agreed to ignore orders to attack the

---

[15] The areas concerned were modern Trà Vinh, the Hậu Giang river region, and Châu Đốc. See *Tiền Biên*, vol. 10, pp. 147-148.

[16] Alexander Dalrymple, *Oriental Reportory* (London: East-India Company, 1808), p. 282. The others were nine from Surubaya, four from Palambang, and one from Batavia. Surabaya in the document was Pa-chuck, which seems like a corrupt pronuciation for Pachekan, in the south of Surubaya. See Chen Jia Rong, Xie Fang, and Lu Jun Ling, *Gu dai nan hai di ming* (Ancient place names in South China Sea region) (Beijing: Zhonghua Press, 1986), p. 1009.

[17] Chen Chingho, "He Xian zhen Ye zhen Mo shi jia pu zhu shi" (Notes on the geoealogy of the Mac family from Ha Tien), *Quo li Taiwan da xue Wen shi zhe xue bao* (Bulletin of the College of Arts of Taiwan National University) 7 (1956): p. 84.

[18] Puangthong Rungswasdisab, "War and Trade: Siamese Intervention in Cambodia, 1767–1851" (PhD dissertation, University of Wollongong, 1995), p. 46.

[19] For the last two groups see *Tiền Biên*, vol. 11, pp. 156–158.

Khmer, and thus delayed fuller Nguyễn penetration of the area for another decade.[20] Relations between the Nguyễn generals and the Mạc in Hà Tiên had the potential to generate even further complications.[21]

It is not surprising, therefore, that the Nguyễn chronicles often betray a tone of anxiety, and sometimes even helplessness, when discussing issues in the Mekong delta from the 1720s onward. Culturally, the far south was almost another universe from the regions of Thuận Hóa and Quảng Nam, where the Vietnamese had been settled much longer. Politically, it could not be successfully governed for long as a simple extension of the older Nguyễn territory. It needed active and energetic leadership on the spot if the Vietnamese administration was to respond effectively to complex local circumstances. In fact, the Đàng Trong administrative system needed to be reorganized and at least a third of the protectorate brought under stricter administrative control if the Nguyễn regime was to deal successfully with the challenges of incorporating the Mekong delta. But instead, when pushed too hard, the whole system was thrown out of its normal orbit into unprecedented instability.

In the eighteenth century the far south formed an extremely fluid picture, with an intricate and delicate power balance that was constantly liable to change as circumstances shifted. At no time was this more apparent than in the 1780s, when the collapse of Nguyễn power and the failure of the Tây Sơn to replace it threw the area wide open to the play of forces and interests that had been restrained, at least in part, by the previous regime. The 1786 assessment of the local situation by Nguyễn Nhạc, one of the principal Tây Sơn leaders, summarized it succinctly: "There are six [political] forces competing with each other in Đồng Nai [Mekong delta]: the Khmer, Siam, Hà Tiên, the female [Cham] leader [Thị Hỏa], and the Chinese Li [Tài]."[22] Here, the sixth force probably represents Nguyễn Nhạc' himself, since the Tây Sơn's great future rival, Nguyễn Phúc Ánh, was at the time languishing in Siamese exile. Ironically, the ultimate winner in the heterogeneous competition for power would be that same Nguyễn Phúc Ánh, the future Gia Long emperor, who returned from Siam later that decade to establish a resistance base in the Gia Định region. One of the foundations of his later success, and one of the principal attractions of the Mekong delta to his pre-Tây Sơn forebears, was the region's rice trade. But if control over the rice trade ultimately helped Nguyễn Ánh to a throne, it proved rather more of a mixed blessing to earlier Nguyễn kings.

## QUY NHƠN AND THE MEKONG DELTA RICE TRADE

Rice growing in the Mekong delta was originally a by-product of the Vietnamese southward expansion, but as a result of expanding rice production, the center of gravity for Đàng Trong's agricultural economy eventually shifted southward. In response, from the 1720s, the Nguyễn court stepped up its efforts to integrate the Mekong Delta and the export rice trade into its own political and economic system.

---

[20] See *Tiền Biên*, vol. 6, pp. 91–95. Corruption by chief commanders was also reported in 1711 and 1732.

[21] Two Nguyen generals refused to help save Hà Tiên when it was taken by the Siamese in 1771.

[22] Lê Đản, *Nam Hà Tiệp Lục*, manuscript kept in École Française d'Extrême-Orient, Paris, shelf number I481, vol. 3, p. 48.

But the methods the Nguyễn government employed to achieve these aims, and the consequences of their actions, would later form important factors facilitating the outbreak of the Tây Sơn rebellion.

Although Vietnamese grew rice in virtually every area they settled, it had never been produced as a large-scale trade commodity before they began to colonize the Mekong delta and take advantage of the flourishing rice trade established there by Chinese settlers. The agricultural pattern in the Mekong Delta represented an historic departure from the more-or-less subsistence norms of the traditional Vietnamese agricultural economy. Considered in this light, commercial production of Mekong rice was undoubtedly one of the most significant developments in eighteenth-century Cochinchina and a major event in Vietnamese economic history. It generated serious social and political repercussions at the time, most of which arose because people living in the longer settled central areas of Thuận Hóa and Quảng Nam became increasingly reliant on inexpensive and plentiful rice from the Mekong Delta. As we noted previously, Lê Quý Đôn reported that before the Tây Sơn rebellion Mekong delta rice was so cheap that 180 *dong* would buy enough to feed a person for one month at Thuận Hóa market. The result was that: "People in Thuận Hóa thus did not work hard on their own land."[23]

The dependence of approximately one-third of the Đàng Trong population, including the people around the capital, on imported rice was a matter of great political significance. It increased the importance of the transport route between the Thuận Hóa-upper Quảng Nam market and the source of rice in the far south; organizing and controlling traffic on the route became a vital, though difficult, matter. According to the account of one trader from the Thuận Hóa region, it took ten days for a single journey to Gia Định,[24] and a very large number of junks had to be involved to maintain the flow. The Nguyễn government was thus constantly apprehensive about the extensive transport links between the capital region and the Mekong Delta. Until 1714, boat owners were required to transport rice to Thuận Hóa twice a year; in exchange for carrying out this duty, they were granted tax-exemption and a small sum to maintain their boats. These arrangements were unpopular, however; trade often realized much more profit, with the result that although there were many boats, few willingly shipped rice to the capital under these conditions.[25] So potentially serious was the problem that in 1714 the Nguyễn compromised and changed the rules, shifting from compulsion to financial encouragement by offering to pay for rice cargoes in cash, according to amount and distance covered.[26] Significantly, with declining government revenues in the 1760s, the system reverted to the earlier, less successful compulsory model. In 1768, *Phủ Biên* recorded the government had levied 341 boats to bring rice from the Mekong Delta to Thuận Hóa.[27]

---

[23] Li Tana and Anthony Reid, eds., *Southern Vietnam under the Nguyễn: Documents on the Economic History of Cochinchina (Đàng Trong), 1602-1777* (Singapore: Institute of Southeast Asian Studies/ECHOSEA, Australian National University, 1993), p. 105.

[24] Li and Reid, *Southern Vietnam under the Nguyễn*, p. 101.

[25] *Tiền Biên*, vol. 8, p. 119.

[26] *Tiền Biên*, vol. 8, p. 119.

[27] *Phủ Biên*, vol. 4, p. 41. This trend developed further during the early nineteenth century, when two thousand junks were engaged in transportation between Saigon and Huế Consequently, as observed by Crawfurd, rice became the "source of the most extensive branch" of Vietnam's internal trade. John Crawfurd, *Journal of An Embassy from the Governor-*

To serve the vital rice trade, as its numerous small craft plied the thousand kilometer trip from Saigon to the capital, required a number of staging points. The most important was the Quy Nhơn-Bình Thuận region, ideally located between the capital and the Mekong delta so that it acted as a kind of fulcrum for the rice trade. By the mid-eighteenth century, as the Nguyễn were drawn more into the contentious southern frontier, this area came to bear a disproportionately heavy share of government demands. In the 1760s and the early 1770s in particular, its manpower and wealth were repeatedly called on by the court. Taxation rules here were tightened, and special arrangements made to collect taxes from Phú Yên in 1758 and later from Quy Nhơn in 1772.[28] Manpower was conscripted too. Thus when the feared Đá Vách tribes attacked Quảng Ngãi peasants in 1770, Huế requisitioned soldiers from Quy Nhơn and Phú Yên to repel the raiders. Even more striking, in 1772, a full year after the Tây Sơn had risen in the Quy Nhơn hinterland, the Nguyễn still removed ten thousand soldiers and thirty galleys from neighboring Bình Khang and Bình Thuận to fight the Siamese in Hà Tiên.[29]

Pressure on Quy Nhơn also came from its north. Population growth in Thuận Hóa, and perhaps also in the area around Quảng Nam proper in the eighteenth century, required that more and more rice be transported from the far south.[30] This demand weighed heavily on Quy Nhơn. According to the *Phủ Biên*, in 1768 Quy Nhơn supplied nearly 30 percent of the 341 boats officially requisitioned to bring Mekong rice to Thuận Hóa. The boats levied per region were:[31]

| Place | Number of Boats |
|---|---|
| Triệu Phong | 40 |
| Quảng Bình | 10 |
| Nam Bố Chính | 10 |
| Quảng Nam | 60 |
| Quy Nhơn | 93 |
| Phú Yên | 44 |
| Diên Khánh | 32 |
| Bình Thuận | 45 |
| Gia Định | 7 |

While the major rice producing area, Gia Định, contributed only seven boats to this task, neighboring Quy Nhơn, Phú Yên, Diên Khánh, and Bình Thuận were burdened with 214, or 60 percent of the whole contingent. The Gia Định figure surely reflected the limited administrative control of manpower and resources in the far south at the time, and the consequent need to squeeze better controlled nearby regions like Quy Nhơn. It all implies that, as an intermediate region of little influence on, or apparent concern for, the distant government, Quy Nhơn had to bear increasing demands on its manpower and wealth, from both northern and southern Đàng Trong, as a consequence of Vietnamese southward expansion. In this sense, the

---

*General of India to the Courts of Siam and Cochi China* (Kuala Lumpur: Oxford University Press, reprint, 1987), p. 511.

[28] *Tiền Biên*, vol. 11, pp. 148, 158.

[29] Ibid., vol. 11, p. 158.

[30] See discussion on currency demand in Chapter Four.

[31] *Phủ Biên*, vol. 4, p. 41.

fact that the Tây Sơn rose in this region and the fact that Quy Nhơn became one of its main strongholds suggest the rebel movement is better understood as a provincial rebellion, as a conflict between a center and an expanding periphery, rather than as a peasant revolt.[32] Indeed, the revolt itself began at the periphery among disgruntled uplanders in the Quy Nhơn hinterland and not among Vietnamese peasants.

The Nguyễn accelerated their expansion into the Mekong delta at a time when overseas trade was beginning to decline in the 1750s. Needing resources for this ambitious new undertaking, as well as Nguyễn Phúc Khoát's grandiose royal building program, the court began to pressure mountain peoples to become registered taxpayers; it also allowed a freer hand to local officials and their emissaries in their dealings with minority peoples. Certainly the latter was one of the main points in the rejected 1751 petition that led to the resignation of its author, the Quảng Ngãi governor, Nguyễn Cư Trinh. Despite the rebellion of the Đá Vách peoples in the Quảng Ngãi hinterland from 1761, in this decade uplanders (apart from the Đá Vách peoples) had to shoulder an increasing tax burden to help make up the revenue shortfall that resulted from dwindling overseas trade. East and west had served the Nguyễn well in the past, allowing the Nguyễn to focus their attentions, first, on the threat from the north, and then on expansion to the south. These relatively peaceful relations for two centuries had encouraged the Nguyễn to take the west for granted. As a result, they pushed its peoples to the limit.

New taxation demands and the harassment associated with these demands were undoubtedly the main causes of popular participation in the revolt by people from the Quy Nhơn area. First came the additional Quảng Nam land taxes imposed in the later 1760s, followed in 1769 by an even steeper increase for the area between Quảng Nam and Diên Khánh. This rise lifted taxes in rice by 55 percent and in cash by 75 percent.[33] The nineteenth-century official dynastic biography of the Tây Sơn leaders, Nguyễn Nhạc and Nguyễn Huệ, attributed the revolt essentially to the imperious and despotic activities of the usurping Regent, Trương Phúc Loan.[34] This might seem a transparent and later attempt to exonerate the Nguyễn royal family, except that Lê Quý Đôn, a reporter who stood much closer to the events, also reported a connection between Loan's palace coup in 1765 and the initiation of the miscellaneous levies collected from the Quảng Nam region.[35] Yet, regardless of who controlled the state at the time, in the 1760s and early 1770s the worsening decline of overseas trade, one of the government's main revenue sources for so long, would have undoubtedly triggered similar urgent measures to repair the shortfall by collecting increased revenues through a different fiscal channel. But this maneuver only exacerbated the problem inherent in the organization of government finances. If allowing officials to recoup their salaries, expenses, and perquisites directly from their subordinates and ultimately from the taxpaying population had been

---

[32] For instance, when the Tây Sơn movement erupted, Nguyễn Khắc Tuyên, the provincial governor in Quy Nhơn, as well as Đằng and Lượng, two tax collectors (*đồ trưng*) sent by the central government, were said to have escaped. Interestingly, Nguyễn Khắc Tuyên escaped easily, but Nguyễn Nhạc continued to chase Đằng and Lượng, "killed Lượng, and exterminated the entire family of Đằng." See *Đại Nam Chính Biên Liệt Truyện Sơ Tập* (First collection of the primary compilation of biographies of Greater Vietnam), vol. 30 (Tokyo: Keio Institute of Linguistic Studies, Mita, Siba, Minato-ku, 1962), p. 1332.

[33] See Table 7 in Chapter Five.

[34] *Đại Nam Chính Biên Liệt Truyện Sơ Tập*, vol. 30, p. 1331.

[35] *Phủ Biên*, vol. 4, p. 2a.

convenient and relatively effective in good times, it harbored long-term dangers. For if circumstances changed, these tax-collecting policies would generate potentially catastrophic conflicts-of-interest between the state and the people and the state and its own officials, since it basically pitted the personal interests of officials against those of government and tax-payers alike. In the 1770s both potential confrontations were realized. Nguyễn officials competed with the state to maintain their own salaries at a time of rising government demands, but the more they looked to satisfy their own needs, the worse the situation became for the government; both revenues and the peace and security of the state were negatively affected. It is perhaps for this reason, because officials chose to avoid exacerbating existent tensions in the lowland Vietnamese communities, that uplanders came to be seen as an important source of additional revenue in the early 1770s. Certainly, as we have seen, the new tax regulations were particularly harsh on them.

By the mid-eighteenth century, then, the Nguyễn regime had entered a new stage of development at a time when its traditional fiscal base was suffering erosion. It needed to adjust to the unprecedented conditions created by its own success; its territorial over-expansion, the growth of commercial agriculture in the far south, and the rise of factionalism and serious political divisions within the ruling group at court all figured as new circumstances challenging the Nguyễn state. Dealing with these stresses and changes required innovative responses, which the Nguyễn government essentially failed to provide. Whether they might have been able to adapt and meet these challenges eventually cannot be known since the Tây Sơn rose up in rebellion at precisely this juncture.

## THE TÂY SƠN AS A PRODUCT OF ĐÀNG TRONG LOCALIZATION

Occasional other revolts had occurred in Đàng Trong without seriously threatening the government. What made the Tây Sơn movement different? Where did it find the energy, the drive, and the determination that helped push it to a previously unimagined level of success? First and foremost, and especially in its early years, the movement benefited from its close involvement with uplanders. While the Nguyễn themselves had earlier been rewarded by their contacts with the local peoples and from utilizing elements of their cultures, this same process ironically helped create the enemy that destroyed their state.

The Tây Sơn movement was a direct product both of Vietnamese southern expansion and of Vietnamese localization in Đàng Trong. The Tây Sơn first arose in an area of intermixed cultures and, judging from a contemporary description of Nguyễn Huệ, may themselves have been ethnically mixed.[36] Certainly, Nhạc was credited with a second wife, a Bahnar who was good at taming elephants.[37] Significantly, in this part of Đàng Trong alone, the usual Vietnamese marriage

---

[36] *Minh Đô Sử*, vol. 12, a manuscript kept in the Institute of History, Committee of Social Sciences, Hanoi, shelf number HV.285, gives a description of Nguyễn Huệ that hints at a mixed background: "Nguyễn Huệ is tall, with curly hair and a pockmarked face. He is dark and thin, with . . . a full beard around his face."

[37] Vũ Minh Giang, "Tây Sơn Thượng đạo, căn cứ đầu tiên của cuộc khởi nghĩa" (The upper trail of Tây Sơn mountain region, the first base for the uprising), in Tây Sơn *Nguyễn Huệ* (Nghĩa Bình: Ty Văn hóa và Thông tin, 1978), pp. 134–135.

pattern was matrilocal, similar to that of Thailand, Burma, and Malaya.[38] According to a note in the nineteenth-century official gazetteer: "it is most common that [in Quy Nhơn] a son-in law resides in the home of his wife's parents."[39] The gazetteer noted that the custom existed only in this region, where Cham and uplander cultural influences persisted most strongly. Even directly to the north of Quy Nhơn, in Quảng Nam and Quảng Ngãi, this practice was unknown. The An Khê plateau, the site of Tây Sơn village, was the principal channel between the plain and the mountains, that is between east and west, for this section of south-central Đàng Trong. The distinctive local marriage custom here suggests that cultural traffic between the Vietnamese and various minority peoples flowed in many directions, and that the intermingling of Cham, uplander, and Vietnamese influences spawned a considerable degree of local particularism. This localism may have had a potentially subversive character. In the Cham and uplander revolt during the reign of Lê Uy Mục (1504-09), this area had been one of the most strongly contested; and the Quảng Ngãi Bahnar were most likely involved in the mid-eighteenth century resurgence of Đá Vách raids on lowland settlements.[40] It may be, too, that, as certain archeological and anthropological evidence suggests, the Bahnar around An Khê had formed part of the *nagara* Campa principality of Vijaya, whose defeat by Lê Thánh Tôn the Nguyễn had later rendered total.[41] It was surely no accident that the oldest Tây Sơn brother, Nguyễn Nhạc, proclaimed himself king in the ruins of Vijaya, a spiritually potent location situated on a small inland plain almost visible from Tây Sơn village, a mere twenty kilometers away in the hills. This act reflected the fusion of Vietnamese and local forces which had originally made the Nguyễn so powerful and now made their opponents unbeatable. This dynamism gave the Tây Sơn a tremendous energy which, under Nguyễn Huệ's leadership, none could resist—not the Nguyễn, the Trịnh, the Siamese, nor the Chinese.[42]

The Tây Sơn movement began as a southern phenomenon. To a very considerable extent, it should be understood in the 1770s as little more than a local attempt to displace the equally southern Nguyễn regime and to rule Đàng Trong in its stead. The movement's local characteristics played an important part in attracting and keeping the Tây Sơn's core followers, many of them uplanders. We will conclude by surveying some of these features, beginning with the significant role of local legends and myths in generating support for the Tây Sơn. One of the most

---

[38] Anthony Reid, *Southeast Asia in the Age of Commerce: 1450-1680*, vol. 1 (New Haven and London: Yale University Press, 1993), p. 147.

[39] *Đại Nam Nhất Thống Chí* (Gazetteer of Greater Vietnam), vol. 9 (Tokyo: Society of Indo-China Studies, 1941), p. 1085.

[40] Bernard Bourotte, "Essai d'histoire des populations montagnardes du sud-indochinois jusqu'à 1945," *Bulletin de la Société des Etudes indochinoises* (ns) XXX, 1955: 41, 46-47.

[41] Gerald Hickey, *Sons of the Mountains* (New Haven and London: Yale University Press, 1982), pp. 93, 95–96, 102–04, 118-19.

[42] Interestingly, there is a parallel between the environment of Tây Sơn and that of Lam Sơn, the place from which Lê Lợi rose to fight the Ming and found the Lê dynasty. According to Gaspardone, Lam Sơn was very much a frontier region in the fifteenth century, "situated in between plain and mountain in the Annamite-Muong area," where Vietnamese and Tai mixed with a predominantly Muong population. In the context of the times, it was of course also "southern." From these two examples we might speculate that the mixture of cultures provided a degree of flexibility and unpredictability that favoured rebel movements. Quoted from John Whitmore, "The Development of Le Government in Fifteenth-Century Vietnam," (PhD dissertation, Ann Arbor: Michigan University Microfilms, Inc., 1970), p. 4.

important of these concerned the existence of a sacred sword that conferred invulnerability on its owner. Similar legends about such a sword existed among the Jarai, Bahnar, and other upland peoples as well as the Khmer. Indeed, the ownership of such a sacred sword by the Jarai shaman known as the "Water Master" prompted the Khmer king to exchange gifts with him every three year.[43] So powerful was the sword that it guaranteed its owner supernatural success in battle. It was, not surprisingly, a potent symbol of sovereignty, closely associated with both Cham and Khmer political interconnections in the region before the Vietnamese arrival. The French scholar Leclere, for instance, cited the Cambodian chronicles' description of how, in 1613, the Khmer ruler Soryopor, "took the sacred sword and sat under [a] sacred parasol" in the ceremony of royal oath-taking.[44] Gerald Hickey has discussed how Cham rulers gave vassal chiefs "a Cham saber and seal" when they took the Cham title of *botao* or *potao*, meaning "lord" or "master." In some contexts *potao* also signified "king."[45]

It is therefore easy to see why Nguyễn Nhạc claimed to possess a "sacred sword" at the start of the rebellion, although important scholarly works on the Tây Sơn which present it overwhelmingly from a political perspective have failed to mention this sword.[46] Indeed, local cultural and religious aspects of the movement have been largely overlooked, even though evidence of their significance exists. According to the nineteenth-century compilation of dynastic biographies, which includes accounts of the Tây Sơn brothers in the volume devoted to the Nguyễn Ánh-Gia Long era (1770-1820), Nguyễn Nhạc:

> obtained a sword one day when he was passing An Dương Sơn mountain. He claimed that it was sacred and deluded people with the sword. Many people believed in him.[47]

An Dương Sơn mountain is in the south of Tuy Viễn county. Sedang and Bahnar peoples here were reputedly fine sword-makers, so it would have been easy to obtain a special sword from such a region.[48]

The extent of Tây Sơn localization appears more clearly if we place this avowed sacred sword in conjunction with the title Nguyễn Nhạc is said to have given himself, that of "king of heaven."[49] It is possible that the local word signified by the two Chinese characters used for this term was *potao*, the Cham word for "lord," or sometimes "king." But "King of Heaven," it should be recalled, was the same title the

---

[43] Hickey has discussed these legends in detail in *Sons of the Mountains*, pp. 126–136.

[44] A. Leclere, *Histoire du Cambodge* (Paris: P. Guethner, reprint, 1975), p. 337.

[45] Hickey, *Sons of the Mountains*, p. 117.

[46] For a cross-section, see Hoa Bằng, *Quang Trung Nguyễn Huệ*, 4th. edition (Saigon: Xuất Bản Bốn Phương, 1958); Tạ Chí Đài Trường, *Lịch Sử Nội Chiến ở Việt Nam, từ 1771 đến 1802* (A history of civil war in Vietnam, 1771-1802) (Saigon: Văn Sử Học, 1973); or Nguyễn Lương Bích, *Quang Trung Nguyễn Huệ* (Hanoi: Nhà Xuất Bản Quân Đội Nhân Dân 1989).

[47] *Đại Nam Chính Biên Liệt Truyện Sơ Tập*, vol. 30, p. 1331.

[48] *Đại Nam Nhất Thống Chí* read as Dương An Sơn, or Phúc An Sơn. See *Đại Nam Nhất Thống Chí*, vol. 9, p. 1092. For local sword-making skills, see Cửu Long Giang and Toan Ánh, *Cao Nguyên Miền Thượng*, vol. 2 (Saigon: 1974), pp. 284 and 309.

[49] *Hoàng Lê Nhất Thống Chí*, Collection Romans et Contes du Vietnam écrits en Han (Paris-Taipei: École Française d'Extrême-Orient & Student Book Co. Ltd, 1986), p. 62.

Nguyễn used when they were dealing with indigenous peoples to the south, as was specifically stipulated in Nguyễn Phúc Khoát's 1744 reforms. In other words, Nhạc had claimed for himself the local title attributed to the Nguyễn by non-Vietnamese but was using it to refer to his own subjects in the new kingdom he established in central-southern Vietnam. Not only did he style himself in this way, but he established his capital in Vijaya, where he was surrounded by "old Cham temples, stone elephants, and lions."[50] Nothing could have more eloquently or more effectively encapsulated the Tây Sơn's local characteristics than all of these symbolic actions, which the constant focus on Nguyễn Huệ's exploits has tended to obscure.

The Cham featured early among the supporters of the Tây Sơn as well, though not in such numbers as the Bahnar and other upland groups. They included a group of Cham from Phú Yên, isolated from the Cham vassal king in Panduranga and led by a female chief called Thị Hỏa. (In the 1780s they would break with the Tây Sơn in an attempt to carve out their own territory in the far south.) According to *Phương Đình Địa Dư Chí*, a geography book written in 1855, when the Tây Sơn began their revolt, the Cham king of Panduranga also presented them with "objects of national vitality (*quốc khí*) that had been handed down over generations."[51] Undoubtedly this refers to his sacred royal regalia. If done voluntarily, the act was charged with meaning. In *nagara* Campa, all royal objects were believed to be infused with divine potency, and none more so than these treasures whose remnants even today are only ever touched by their uplander guardians with solemn ceremony on ritually appointed days.[52] Such a transfer of the royal regalia therefore implies that the Cham king at the time perceived the Tây Sơn as more or less legitimate successors.

Another tantalizing scrap of information that hints at Cham connections comes from the Vietnamese scholar Hồ Hữu Tường, one of the rare authors to interest himself in the religious elements of the uprising. He wrote that the Tây Sơn worshipped a God of Fire, and that there was a Vietnamese phrase which described the three brothers as: "*ông Hai trầu, chú Ba thơm, thầy Tư Lữ.*" He translated this as "the second brother [Nhạc] has the areca, the third [Huế] has the eaglewood, and the fourth is a priest of Mani, that is, of Islam."[53] The eaglewood trade in this area was closely associated with the Chams, and no other source has suggested Nguyễn Huệ's involvement in it. However, collecting eaglewood was not simply an economic activity for the Chams but, reflecting its ritual significance, a religiously prescribed occupation open only to select men initiated into the ritual prescribed for the search.[54] If the saying reflects a historical reality, it hints that Nguyễn Huệ may have been known in certain Cham circles, or perhaps in uplander communities well beyond Tây Sơn village, before the revolt broke out. Long before then, too, as is well known, a large proportion of lowland Chams had embraced a syncretic variant of

---

[50] *Minh Đô Sử*, vol. 14. Phan Huy Lê has also decribed it in "Di tích thành Hoàng đế (The ruins of the Imperial City)," in *Tây Sơn Nguyễn Huệ* (Nghĩa Bình: Ty Văn hóa và Thông tin, 1978), p. 150.

[51] Nguyễn Văn Siêu, *Phương Đình Địa Dư Chí*, trans. Ngô Mạnh Nghinh (Saigon: XB Tự Do, 1960), p. 185

[52] Po Dharma, *Le Panduranga (Campa) 1802-1835. Ses rapports avec le Vietnam*, vol. 2 (Paris: l'Ecole Française d'Extrême-Orient, 1987), p. 80, fn. 154.

[53] Hồ Hữu Tường, "Một vài phương thuật để nghiên cứu Tây Sơn" (Some ways of understanding the Tây Sơn), *Tập San Sử Địa*, 9 & 10 (1968): 188.

[54] Po Dharma, *Le Panduranga*, pp. 63–64, fn. 98.

Islam. If the other Tây Sơn brother, who always seems such a shadowy figure in traditional accounts of the movement, actually was a Muslim priest, it may imply that he acted as a religious facilitator helping to bind the various insurgent elements together. Whatever the case, these fascinating glimpses remind us that there are still important elements in the early Tây Sơn period which remain poorly understood, and which all point to a close and multivalent relationship between the Tây Sơn leaders and indigenous peoples.

Another indicator of this relationship was the Tây Sơn use of a locally significant color, red, on their banners. This matter was badly misconstrued by traditional scholars who applied a classical Sino-Vietnamese interpretation to it. Nineteenth-century literati explained the Tây Sơn's use of red by reference to the *Yi Jing* (The Book of Changes), according to which red was the color of the south. Tạ Chí Đài Trường has corrected this Sinic interpretation. He argues that the color had nothing to do with the *Yi Jing*, or with a classical Chinese frame of reference. On the contrary, he believes the Tây Sơn had a strong sense of being western, as shown in their prophecy "*Tây khởi nghĩa, Bắc thu công*" (rebel from the west, succeed in the north). For them, red was the "colour of the western deity, a colour of mountains, and of the hidden supernatural."[55] It was also the color of Nguyễn Nhạc's royal robes. The English merchant Chapman reported that Nhạc's clothing was "distinguished by being red, which colour no subject is allowed to use in dress or equipage."[56] This observation underlines the extent of local divergence involved here from the traditional imperial yellow reserved for Lê emperors (and the nineteenth-century Nguyễn) which derived from Chinese practice. As Tạ Chí Đài Trường concludes: "It is clear that the influence of the mountain region, and the religions of the minority peoples, penetrated and became the dominant ideology of the Tây Sơn in its early period."[57] Ritual cannibalism was even said to have occurred during the Tây Sơn uprising.[58]

Indeed, "western" was how people at the time referred to the Tây Sơn, whether in Đàng Trong or Đàng Ngoài. The most common Nguyễn term for the Tây Sơn was "western bandits" (*Tây tặc*), while in the north the words used were "western people" (*Tây nhân*), or western dynasty" (*Tây triều*). The word *Tây* underlines this most distinctive characteristic of the Tây Sơn. Differing from the Nguyễn, whose attention had mainly focused on the north and the south, the Tây Sơn manifested a particular interest in the west. In 1791,[59] for example, when the Tây Sơn general Trần

---

[55] Tạ Chí Đài Trường, *Thần, Người, và Đất Việt* (California: Văn Nghệ, 1980), p. 234.

[56] Chapman's narrative, in Alastair Lamb, *The Mandarin Road to Old Hue* (Toronto: Clarke, Irwin and Co. Ltd., 1970), p. 101.

[57] Tạ Chí Đài Trường, *Thần, Người, và Đất Việt*, p. 234.

[58] See Hue Tam Ho Tai, *Millennium and Peasant Politics in Vietnam* (Cambridge: Harvard University Press, 1983), p. 123.

[59] Sources disagree about the date of this attack. Hoa Bằng says it was in 1791. See Hoa Bằng, *Quang Trung Nguyễn Huệ, Anh Hùng Dân Tộc* (Nguyễn Huệ, national hero) (Saigon: Bốn Phương, 1958), p. 262. But in Maha Sila Viravong, *History of Laos* (New York: Paragon Books Reprint Corp., 1964), pp. 109–110, it is given as 1788. Viện Sử Học, *Biên Niên Lịch Sử Cổ Trung đại Việt Nam* (A chronological table of Vietnam) (Hanoi: Khoa Học Xã Hội 1987), says it happened from lunar June to October 1790, and Siamese chronicles agree with this date. See *The Dynastic Chronicle, Bangkok Era, the First Reign*, translated and edited by Thadeus and Chadin Flood, vol. 1 (Tokyo: The Center for East Asian Studies, 1978), pp. 170-171. However, other Vietnamese documents contain several letters between the Lao and the Tây Sơn which indicate an attack between 1792 and 1793. From this it seems likely that the Tây Sơn mounted

Quang Diệu attacked Vientiane, it was something new in over two hundred years of Nguyễn history. We also detect a "western" or uplander connection in the construction of the strategic trail through the Quảng Ngãi hinterland which helped the Tây Sơn successfully attack Phú Xuân in 1785 and then Thăng Long in 1786.[60] *Đại Nam Nhất Thống Chí* recorded that "local people here said that this trail was opened by Trần Quang Diệu, the Tây Sơn general"[61] and mainly constructed by minority peoples from the area. Although the Tây Sơn had an auxiliary naval force, its leaders preferred to launch these decisive attacks from friendly mountain territory rather than risk their forces to the sea. Tây Sơn identification with the west prompted supercilious northern scholars to call Nguyễn Nhạc "barbarian chief" (*man tù*), and the Tây Sơn army "barbarian soldiers" (*man binh*) or "barbarian bandits" (*man khấu*).[62] Similar connotations may explain why they referred to Nguyễn Huệ as Chế Bồng Nga, after he attacked Thăng Long in the late eighteenth century just as Chế Bồng Nga, the greatest Cham king, had done in the fourteenth century. While identification with the west may have seemed strange and barbarian to northern scholars at the time, in Đàng Trong on the contrary it served to strengthen the Tây Sơn's position.

As Hickey has pointed out, when the Vietnamese occupied growing areas of Khmer territory in the mid-eighteenth century, the "advance southwards" effectively became an "advance westward," causing the central highlands to assume a most significant place in the overall Nguyễn strategy.[63] The Tây Sơn were thus a product of Vietnamese expansion to the south (*nam tiến*) and to the west (*tây tiến*). Historically, the Vietnamese advance in both directions brought them tremendous success in terms of territorial expansion and other rewards; but this advance on two fronts also entailed enormous short-term difficulties and stirred up tensions that the Nguyễn could not resolve adequately and which ultimately destroyed them.

The final collapse of the Nguyễn regime in Đàng Trong, therefore, seems to have had everything to do with its expansion in the southern and western directions. In merely two hundred years, this regime had acquired three-fifths of Vietnam's contemporary territory, a spectacular achievement indeed. Yet, as James Lowell mused in his "New England Two Centuries Ago," "truly there is a tide in the affairs of men, but there is no gulf-stream setting forever in one direction."[64] While the Nguyễn concentrated all its attention on its competition with Siam in the Mekong delta, fire (in the literal sense, as the Tây Sơn worshipped fire) broke out in their own backyard. Even then, events might have turned out differently if the Nguyễn had not had to contend with their old enemy, the Trịnh, who grasped this opportunity to invade their beleaguered foe. For a while the tide seemed to run strongly in another

---

two attacks on Vientiane. Trần Văn Quý, "Tư liệu lịch sử về quan hệ Việt-Lào phát hiện ở Quy Hợp-Hương Khê Nghệ Tỉnh" (On Vietnamese-Lao relations according to documents discovered in Quy Hợp-Hương Khê region, Nghệ Tỉnh province), mimeograph, June 1989, pp. 9–12.

[60] Lê Trọng Khánh, "Về những con đường hành quân của Nguyễn Huệ" (On the march routes of Nguyễn Huệ), *Tây Sơn Nguyễn Huệ*, p. 335.

[61] *Đại Nam Nhất Thống Chí*, vol. 2, p. 784. It said that the trail runs from Bình Định (Quy Nhơn) to as far north as Nghệ An.

[62] *Hoàng Lê Nhất Thống Chí*, pp. 101, 120.

[63] Hickey, *Sons of the Mountains*, p. 167.

[64] James Lowell, "New England Two Centuries Ago," in *A Collection of American Essays*, translated into Chinese by Xia Ji An (Hong Kong: Ji ri shi jie Press, n.d.), p. 100.

direction as the Tây Sơn conquered the north, and to a lesser degree the west, thus establishing itself as the dominant political force in Vietnam. Yet the real story was happening in the Mekong delta. It is illuminating, from this point of view, to note that the Nguyễn regime's loose control over the Mekong delta for most of the eighteenth century was only consolidated when Nguyễn Ánh located his political base there from the late 1780s. From there the restored Nguyễn went on in the nineteenth century to incorporate the semi-autonomous vassal states of Panduranga and Hà Tiên into Vietnam. Ironically, it was not until the Nguyễn were driven out of their long-settled Thuận Hóa-Quảng Nam base region and forced to seek their survival in the Mekong delta that the tensions of the *nam tiến* were finally and effectively settled, and Vietnamese possession of the whole region become irreversible.

# CONCLUSION:
# THE END OF ĐÀNG TRONG AND
# OF AN OLD ORDER?

Seventeenth- and eighteenth-century Đàng Trong has a unique place in Vietnamese history. It successfully acted as the engine of change in Vietnam for well over two centuries, pulling the national center of gravity, whether cultural, economic, or political, to the south. It was vital to the success of the southern movement (*nam tiến*). Without the establishment of the Nguyễn state here, it is impossible to say how far south the Vietnamese would have ultimately been able to extend their power. But after the creation of a new southern state, we find an end to the seesawing battles between Vietnamese and Chams that had marked the previous centuries. We can only speculate whether this would have been possible without the Nguyễn state, or whether Champa as a kingdom would have disappeared as completely as it did. Nguyễn Cochinchina was not only central to the process of southern expansion, it was also its most spectacular product.

Đàng Trong was a migrant country stretched on a long and narrow piece of land between the mountain and the sea, whose southern border always beckoned to individuals, clans, and whole villages willing to venture into a new region. The mountains to the west and the sea to the east also attracted Vietnamese to try their luck as merchants and traders. Nothing could have been more different from the pattern of life in the north, which was characterized mainly by cultivation in a region situated between these largely alien and dangerous fronts.

Đàng Trong's economic base clearly differentiated itself from most of pre-colonial Vietnamese states, characterized as they were by an almost purely agricultural economy. Administratively, too, Nguyễn Cochinchina differed from most other Vietnamese kingdoms by remaining for most of its existence a military regime whose officials were paid according to Southeast Asian practices, not Chinese precepts. Being themselves in the rebel or "illegal" position gave the Nguyễn a sense of freedom and the courage necessary to choose to try anything workable, irrespective of whether it matched or flouted standards of Confucian propriety or orthodoxy. The need to legitimize their authority locally also led the Nguyễn far from Confucianism and prompted them to encourage Mahayana Buddhism as an official religion and present themselves as "kings of heaven" more akin to their neighboring rulers than to the Lê emperor in the north. Đàng Trong Vietnamese went much further still, embracing a degree of syncretism and adopting whatever local customs and beliefs might help them survive and prosper among the new spirits of the south. Cham and uplander rituals and customs flourished as late as the twentieth century among Vietnamese in this area.

Encouraged by the Nguyễn rulers, local Vietnamese adopted and adapted whatever aspects of indigenous (or foreign) cultures and traditions they believed useful. Almost as important, they showed themselves willing to discard or downgrade aspects of those older Vietnamese customs and traditions, still significant in the north but no longer so relevant in the new southern land. Overall, the dynamic and flexible Nguyễn rulers in this period met the requirements of developing Đàng Trong society by being more open to external opportunities and more extrovert in character than their Trịnh counterparts in the north.

The south meant a diversity of options. It provided space to maneuver and enabled the growth of new economic, social, and cultural elements far from the narrow Confucian expectations of the north. Their willingness to conceive of themselves as part of the larger world of Southeast Asia enabled Vietnamese immigrants to borrow, blend, and absorb extensively from the cultures of the Cham and other peoples in the region. As a result, Vietnamese themselves became localized. This is not to say that Vietnamese in Đàng Trong became "non-Vietnamese" or lost their identity. Rather, they created here another way of being Vietnamese, one which grew from their willingness to experiment, to adopt and naturalize whatever was useful in their new environment, regardless of its origin. The southern region posed its own challenges, and their solution led the immigrant Vietnamese here far from their immediate past in the Lê Confucian state, back much closer to their Southeast Asian roots. Many characteristic traits of southerners, such as their curiosity and tolerance towards new things and new ideas, their more open and spontaneous character, their unwillingness to be fettered by history and tradition, can all be traced back to the influence of these two centuries.

One of the most notable examples of this process was the way the Nguyễn took over, and built on, the overseas trade that Champa had carried out for centuries before. The weak agricultural base in seventeenth-century Đàng Trong could hardly sustain a desperate struggle with the superior forces of the Trịnh north, and this disadvantage compelled the early Nguyễn to flout the usual practice of Vietnamese states (that traditionally maintained tight control of trade) and instead allow fairly free trade, an adaptation that soon worked to their advantage. They lost no time in seizing the chance to make Cochinchina the crucial link between Chinese and Japanese trade, with the result that seventeenth-century Cochinchina become Japan's number one trading partner and a major player in wider Asian commercial relations. Cochinchina's independent existence, and the Nguyễn's own power and wealth, rested largely on this overseas trade. Cochinchina thus found the resources and the vitality to undergo a great period of expansion in population, wealth, and land, despite having to fight a fifty years war with the north. This was an extraordinary achievement, both in itself and by comparison with historical Vietnamese achievements in general.

Historians have asked why, despite the tremendous impact of foreign trade and increasing supply of and reliance on money in Vietnam during the seventeenth and eighteenth centuries, the traditional Vietnamese socio-economic framework remained relatively unbroken. In answer to this question, Nguyên Thanh Nhã suggests that the fundamental factor impeding change and helping conserve the old framework was the ongoing expense incurred by the armies. He argues that states in both Đàng Ngoài and Đàng Trong blocked real economic progress because the taxes required by their military obsession with each other absorbed the new trade surpluses.[1]

---

[1] Nguyên Thanh Nhã, *Tableau economique du Vietnam aux XVIIe et XVIIIe siecles* (Paris: Editions Cujas, 1970), p. 227.

Thành Thế Vỹ, on the other hand, suggests that although the Nguyễn management of foreign trade tended to be monopolistic, their political control of trade was not comprehensive enough to block economic development, and that the tension between the Trịnh and the Nguyễn was not the main reason for the "stagnation" of the Vietnamese trade in the eighteenth century. Instead, he believes that the relatively limited economic efflorescence of Vietnam must be explained in extra-national terms: foreign trade indeed created a remarkable prosperity in these two centuries, but its creative force was not powerful enough to change Vietnam's economic basis. Foreign merchants in the 1700s valued the Vietnamese market less than others—such as Guangdong—because of its weaker consumer demand. Relatively weak consumer demand could be explained by various factors: relative poverty, communal village lands which helped keep peasants on the land and slowed down urbanization.[2]

Both scholars shed light on the questions concerning the impact of the economy on the formation of the state, and both views are valid in different aspects. There is no doubt that the military obsessions preoccupying both states consumed a large part of the wealth generated by trade. Thành Thế Vỹ's interpretation of the ways in which international trade influenced the Vietnamese economy is illuminating. These views, however, share two weaknesses which, in my view, are related to each other. The first one is that both scholars speak about "Vietnam" as a whole: Nguyên Thanh Nhã blames the wars between the Trịnh and the Nguyễn, while Thành Thế Vỹ cites the Dutch decision to close its factory in Phố Hiến in 1700 as evidence that foreign merchants considered the Vietnamese market to be a weak one. But as we have discussed in the previous chapters, if one recognizes that two separate Vietnamese states and two distinctive Vietnamese economic systems existed in these two centuries, then talking about a vague "Vietnam" with generalized characteristics can only obscure our understanding of the country during this period.

Secondly, both Nhã and Vỹ built their arguments on a basic assumption that the economy of Đàng Trong, like the economy of Đàng Ngoài, was marked by stagnation or decline at the end of the seventeenth century. This is not accurate for Đàng Trong. As we have shown in Chapters Three and Four above, foreign trade in Đàng Trong increased rather than decreased before the late 1740s, and rice production in the Mekong delta was rapidly multiplying at the time. On top of this, active trade was also carried out in Hatien in the Bay of Siam-Khmer-Malay peninsular region. Clear evidence of vigorous growth and development flourishing within the Đàng Trong socio-economic framework is available.

It was the very expansion of Đàng Trong that brought it problems, particularly problems that grew out of its own efforts—some of them failed—to accomplish political and economic integration, as discussed in Chapter Seven. In other words, Đàng Trong was the victim of its own success, rather than a victim of a declining economy.

And what made Đàng Trong strong also made it vulnerable. As discussed earlier, Đàng Trong's economy largely relied on maritime trade, particularly on Japanese and Chinese markets. Naturally it had to pay, and it did, for such

---

[2] Thành Thế Vỹ, *Ngoài thương Việt Nam hồi thế kỷ XVII, XVIII và đầu XIX* (Foreign trade in Vietnam in the seventeenth, eighteenth, and nineteenth centuries) (Hanoi: Sử Học, 1961), pp. 200–202. I am grateful to Alexander Woodside for his analysis on the views held by the two scholars.

connections and the changes that went with it. Hội An, Cochinchina's most important port, can be taken as a marker indicating the dramatic ups and downs of the Nguyễn economy. Almost coincident with the decline of its international trade in the mid-eighteenth century, it also suffered an environmental crisis; sandy mud began to form sand bars in the Thu Bồn estuary, the lifeline of Hội An, and these sand bars divided and ruined the channel.[3] After having been the busiest and biggest port in the South China Sea outside China,[4] Hội An was reduced to a small town standing quietly on the Thu Bồn river bank, a remnant of its glorious past incarnation. When the currency crisis set in motion by changes in the Japanese and Chinese markets reached Đàng Trong, its trade too was left stranded, its once proud order slowly eroded by forces it could not control.

But the story did not end there. A fresh and vigorous round of development had already begun in the Mekong delta and the Hà Tiên region. Although rice had always been produced in virtually every region where Vietnamese resided, before the Vietnamese claimed the Mekong Delta, it had never been produced on a large scale as a trade commodity. From the early eighteenth century, however, large amounts of rice began to be produced in the Mekong delta, and rice soon became the staple commodity of the region. To produce rice for commercial purposes was undoubtedly one of the most momentous episodes in eighteenth-century Cochinchina and a significant event in Vietnamese history. This transformation of the agricultural pattern in the Mekong Delta figured as a tremendous variation from the traditional Vietnamese economic order. It became the impetus for further Vietnamese southward expansion and stimulated the southward shift in the economic center of gravity. All this provided enough reason for the Nguyễn regime to accelerate its efforts to integrate the Mekong Delta into its own political and economic system. But unavoidably, this brought confrontation with Siam, a country that had been accelerating its territorial expansion to the east. It is in this context that the most celebrated rebellion in Vietnamese history—the Tây Sơn rebellion—broke out, and that Saigon was founded.

It was the Mekong Delta that ultimately saved the Nguyễn, however. To Nguyễn Ánh it became another horizon, a resourceful base from which he could stage a comeback. It was the resources of the Mekong Delta, particularly its rice, that enabled Nguyễn Ánh to defeat the Tây Sơn thirty years later and found the Nguyễn dynasty and a new united state. Đàng Trong, born in civil war, died in civil war, but it reshaped Vietnam in every possible way.

---

[3] Vu Van Phai and Dang Van Bao, "Geomophological Features of Hoi An and Its Neighbourhood," in *Ancient Town of Hoi An*, ed. National Committee for the International Symposium on the Ancient Town of Hoi An (Hanoi: Foreign Languages Publishing House, 1991), pp. 62–63.

[4] Alexander Woodside, "Central Viet Nam's Trading World in the Eighteenth Century as Seen in Lê Quý Đôn's 'Frontier Chronicles,'" in *Essays into Vietnamese Pasts*, ed. K. W. Taylor and John Whitmore (Ithaca: Cornell Southeast Asia Program, 1995), p. 162.

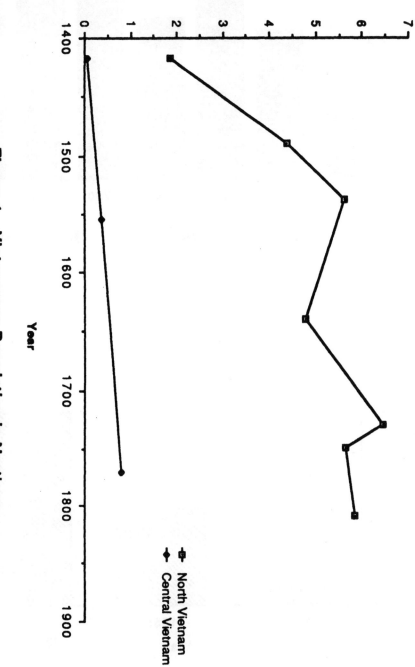

**Figure 1. Vietnamese Population in Northern and Central Vietnam during the 15th to 18th Centuries**

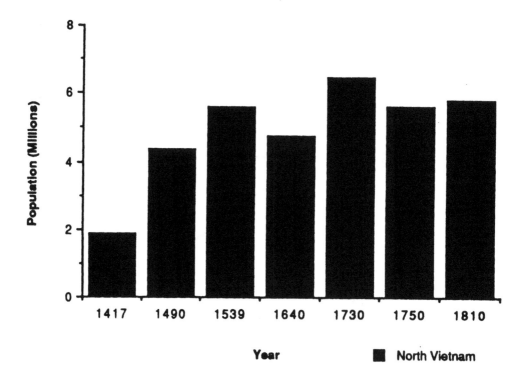

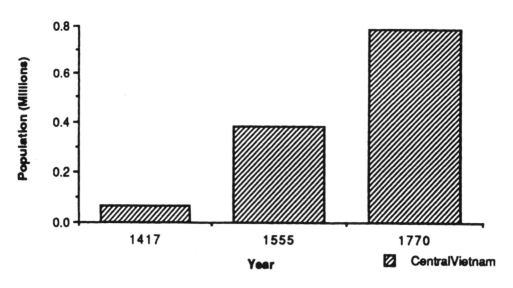

Figure 2.  Growth of Vietnamese Population in Northern Vietnam (top) and Central Vietnam (bottom) during the 15th to 18th Centuries

# APPENDIX 1
# POPULATION CHANGE IN VIETNAM FROM THE SIXTEENTH TO EIGHTEENTH CENTURIES

When discussing the population of Tongking, Gourou asked:

Does distant emigration assure an outlet to this swarming peasantry? The question is important and merits close examination, but in this realm again the scarcity of statistics prevents giving precise answers.[1]

Although scholars are agreed that the Vietnamese moved southward "vigorously" or "exclusively," they seem to hesitate judging how significant immigration was as a factor in the overall growth rate of the southern population. When discussing the growth rate of the population of Cochinchina from 1901 to 1936, Smolski claimed that immigration accounted for only 1.2 percent of the total growth of the population.[2] Gourou said that in the 1920s there was

an overall population reduction [from the Red River delta moving to the south] of fifteen thousand persons per year, when the excess of births over deaths is at least sixty-five thousand and very probably holds at a figure approximating one hundred thousand.[3]

Even so, if one-fifth to one-ninth of the north's excess population immigrated to another place, that would make quite a difference, both for the old, densely populated Tongking and also for the newly opened, thinly populated Cochinchina. In 1417 the population in the Thuận Hóa area was recorded as only 2.3 percent of the total population of Đại Việt. According to the *Ngan Nam Tche Yuan* (Records on Annam), there were only 3,602 families and 10,400 Vietnamese living in the Thuận Hóa area in that year. Yet in 1847 the *đinh bộ* gave a total of 1,024,388 taxpayers in the country. When these figures are divided into two groups according to former Đàng Trong and former Đàng Ngoài, they are:

---

[1] Pierre Gourou, *The Peasants of the Tonkin Delta, A Study of Human Geography*, trans. R. R. Miller, vol. 1 (New Haven: Human Relations Area Files, 1955), p. 256.

[2] See Ng Shui Meng, *The Population of Indochina* (Singapore: Institute of Southeast Asian Studies, Field Report Series No. 7, 1974), p. 30.

[3] Gourou, *The Peasants*, vol. 1, p. 265.

Đàng Trong (Quảng Bình to its south)    444,992
Đàng Ngoài (Hà Tĩnh to its north)    579,396 [4]

This shows that by the first half of the nineteenth century, about 55 percent of the total population lived in the older Vietnamese land, and 45 percent lived in the newly occupied land. We can see how close these two figures are to each other. In a few hundred years, the Vietnamese had produced another Vietnam, both in terms of territory and manpower.

Probably because the demographic sources of this period are so few and unreliable, no one has attempted a detailed study. I, too, would prefer not to take the risk. However, available sources suggest that, although hard figures are few, there are numerous statements that provide a basis for comparison with the few figures that I believe to be reliable. Because the issue is so historically significant, I will hazard a longer examination.

One common explanation for Vietnamese expansion southward is population pressure on limited agriculture land. But the immediate causes which drove large numbers of people to the south were famine and war. Ironically, big waves of emigration only happened when the population was decreasing, or in danger of decreasing.

Two disastrous periods between the sixteenth and eighteenth centuries were mainly responsible for the increase in the number of refugees. The first happened in the second half of the sixteenth century. In the *Đại Việt Sử Ký Toàn Thư* (hereafter referred to as *Toàn Thư*) annals dealing with the years from 1559 on, refugees are often mentioned, most strikingly in sections describing the years 1561, 1570, 1571, 1572, 1586, 1588, 1589, 1592, 1594, 1595, 1596, 1597, and 1608. Here is one example from 1572:

> Nghệ An harvested nothing this year, what is more, pestilence broke out. Half of the people died. People fled either to the south, or to the northeast.[5]

This from 1594:

> The harvest in several counties around Hải Dương area is very poor, people are so hungry that they eat others. A third of the population has died of starvation.[6]

This was perhaps the longest period of disaster in Vietnamese history, with civil war raging for several decades and widespread agricultural failures marking fourteen years out of forty-nine. Never before in Vietnamese history had there been so many refugees mentioned repeatedly in such a short time. In fact, before this period a phrase like *"phiêu tán"* (drift, wander), describing the refugees, had rarely

---

[4] Nguyễn Thế Anh, "Quelques aspects economiques et sociaux du probleme du riz au Viet Nam dans la première moitié du XIXe siecle," *Bulletin de la Société des Études Indochinoises*, XLII, 1 and 2 (1967): 16.

[5] *Đại Việt Sử Ký Toàn Thư* (hereafter *Toàn Thư*), ed. Chen Chingho (Tokyo: Institute of Linguistic Studies, Keio University, 1984), vol. 3, p. 867.

[6] *Toàn Thư*, vol. 3, p. 902.

been seen in the *Toàn Thư* annals, but after 1559 the phrase recurs with some frequency.

The Vietnamese population at this time must have been at a low point. In addition to those who died from starvation and pestilence, the war between the Lê and the Mạc took a heavy toll. There were more than forty major battles between 1539 and 1600, with the area from Thăng Long to Thanh Hóa often the scene of these confrontations. A Vietnamese scholar estimates that "several hundred thousand young men died" in the period.[7] Some extracts from the *Toàn Thư* give evidence to support his statement:

> [in 1555] The bodies of the soldiers of the Mạc stuffed the Đai Lài river [in Thanh Hóa], so the water turned red. The Mạc sent several tens of thousands of soldiers to this battle and almost all of them died.

> [in 1581] The heads of more than six hundred Mạc soldiers were chopped off in this battle.

> [in 1589] The heads of more than one thousand Mạc soldiers were chopped off.

> [at the end of 1591, in the battle where the Lê recaptured Thăng Long] The heads of more than ten thousand Mạc soldiers were chopped off. Residents rushed out of the city, because all strove to be the first to get on board junks [to cross the river], so that many junks sank, and about one thousand people drowned.

> [in the beginning of 1592, still in the battle of recapturing Thăng Long] The heads of several thousands Mạc soldiers were chopped off.
> (in February 1593) decapitated several thousand.
> (in May 1593) decapitated ten thousand.
> (in 1595) decapitated six hundred.
> (in 1596) decapitated 2,298.

Even allowing for some exaggeration on the part of the victors, it seems likely that the Vietnamese population decreased during this period, when numerous natural disasters coincided with deadly, persistent wars.

In contrast to the miserable situation in the north, the Thuận Hóa area was relatively peaceful. This naturally encouraged a north-south migration in the following two centuries, as discussed in Chapter One.

The 1730s and 1740s marked the second wave of migration. The *Khâm Định Việt Sử Thông Giám Cương Mục* (hereafter *Cương Mục*) reports that in 1730 the inhabitants of 527 villages in the north fled their homes to live in an unspecified new location. However, the trend had appeared long before this. There was a big famine in 1681,[8] and three years of bad harvests in Thanh Hóa in the first five years of the eighteenth

---

[7] Trương Hữu Quýnh, *Chế độ Ruộng đất ở Việt Nam* (The land system in Vietnam), vol. 2 (Hanoi: Khoa Học Xã Hội, 1983), p. 16.

[8] See Japanese source, *Kai-hentai*, for some accounts on this famine. Hayashi Shunsai, comp., *Kai-hentai*, (Tokyo: Toyo Bunko, 1958-59), pp. 342–344, 417–418.

century. Famines followed in 1712, 1713, 1721 in other regions of the north. In 1726 and 1728, the Trịnh state had to take two hundred thousand *quan* from the treasury to relieve the misery of people in Thanh Hóa and Nghệ An. Matters were further complicated by another flood in the Red River delta in 1729 and widespread pestilence in 1736.

The 1740s brought even worse conditions. In a report to the government in the mid-eighteenth century, Ngô Thì Sĩ, a famous scholar, said that

> there used to be 9,668 villages in the Red river delta, among them 1,070 villages were gone, which was about the number of villages in one *trấn* [*trấn* designates an area of land; there were four *trấn* in the Red River delta at the time]. In Thanh Hóa there used to be 1,392 villages, but 297 of them were gone. In Nghệ An there used to be 706 villages, but 115 of them were gone.[9]

It seems likely that at least 15 percent of the villages disappeared. The main reason why people fled in this case was to escape anti-Trịnh rebellions. The *Cương Mục* says that the situation was better in Vũ Tiên, Thư Trì, Kiến Xương, and Chân Định counties (in today's Thái Bình province). Yet, according to the history of a Lê family branch, because of the fighting, even in so-called "better places" like the above-mentioned counties, "hundreds of families fled, one *đấu* (twenty-eight liters) of rice cost several hundred *đồng* (cash), there were only six to seven people left in one village, [and] some villages had only four to five people left."[10]

Dire situations involving Vietnamese refugees were also mentioned several times between 1738 and 1743 in the *Qing Shi Lu* (Annals of the Qing Dynasty). This source first mentions that the Chinese bought Vietnamese (as slaves?) in the year 1738. After records for this year, descriptions of the movements of Vietnamese refugees recur frequently in the annals. The chronicle describes the problems confronted by Vietnamese refugees who crossed the Sino-Vietnamese border to China in June and August 1742, then February and April 1743 and reports that Chinese bought Vietnamese youths. One report even claimed that "since the war [the rebellions in the north], nine out of ten houses are empty in Annam."[11]

A report of a canton called Võ Liệt Xã, in Nghệ An province, written in 1780, gives a detailed description of one local exodus. It says that attempts of the Lê government to register taxpayers in 1722 were so exacting that people in the canton, both rich and poor, fled away. As a result, the old and weak people who remained in the canton had to be added to the list; the number of the soldiers that the canton had to provide remained the same, which imposed a heavier burden on the canton and caused more residents to flee. In 1740, the canton was ordered to provide fifty-three soldiers, of whom thirty-six had to be dismissed because they were not up to standard. Families were detained and beaten by the officers so that the father would come back and the son could be drafted; if the elder brother was returned, the younger one went in his stead. Yet the village still could not meet the demands of the

---

[9] *Ngô Gia Văn Phái*, a MS kept in the Han-Nom Institute, Hanoi, vol. 5.

[10] Quoted from Trương Hữu Quýnh, *Chế độ Ruộng đất ở Việt Nam*, vol. 2, p. 129. On the capacity of *dau*, I am grateful to Prof. Nguyen Duc Nghinh for providing the information.

[11] Momoki Shiro, ed., *Dai shin Jitsuraku chutonana kiji* (*Ta Qing Shi Lu zhong Dong Nan Ya Guan Xi Ji Shi*) (Sources of Southeast Asia in the Qing Annals), vol. 1 (Tokyo: Tonan ajia shigaku-kai kansai reikai, 1984), p. 63.

government. Many who were drafted into the army escaped as soon as they were registered. In one case more than twenty clans in the canton fled. In 1774, when the northern army traveled south, another twenty men from the canton had to go with it. Those twenty did not come back when the army returned to the north. Between 1776 and 1779 every harvest failed, while another pestilence broke out as well, allegedly leaving less than half of the people in the canton alive.[12]

Let us turn now to the size of a typical Vietnamese village. In 1931 Gourou considered Tongking villages typically ranging from five hundred to 2,100. The most densely populated ninety-seven villages in Hà Đông and Hà Nam Ninh held from four thousand to over five thousand inhabitants in each village.[13] Villages in Thanh Hóa and Nghệ An were not as large as the latter, so I have assumed their size to be between five hundred to two thousand inhabitants. The report of Võ Liệt village, discussed above, attests to this calculation, stating that the village was supposed to provide eighty-seven men to the army. According to the rule of the Lê, in the Thanh Hóa and Nghệ An areas one out of every five đinh (registered taxpayers) had to go into the army. We should also remember that in a traditional Vietnamese village, the former heads of the village, former mandarins and people who had passed the civil exams were exempt from military service. There were forty-four people in these categories in Võ Liệt village. A village which sent eighty-seven men, then, probably had about 440 đinh or more. For a village which had about five hundred men in it, the total inhabitants would number around two thousand, or more, if we remember that the number of men in a village were usually more than the registered number, and women and children were not counted.

It is striking to learn that 15 percent of such villages were abandoned between the 1730s and 1750s. The *Cương Mục* reports:

> From the years of Vĩnh Hựu (1735-1739), the whole area was in chaos, especially in Hải Dương, where people planted nothing and all the stored rice had been eaten. Conditions in the Sơn Nam area were slightly better, and thus the roads were congested with starving people trying to go there. The price of rice was so high that one hundred cash was not enough to buy one meal. People had to eat wild herbs, snakes, or even rats. The land was strewn with bodies of those who had starved to death. Only one out of ten people survived this famine. Although Hải Dương used to be the most densely populated area, now in some villages only three to five families were left.[14]

The *Toàn Thư* entry for 1754 said that the government had to waive all taxes between 1742 and 1754[15] because a large number of people had either died or fled. The government could not collect taxes from anywhere, even if it wanted to do so. Besides proving how bad the situation was during those thirteen years, the declaration shows the intention of the government to collect taxes from 1754 on. I

---

[12] A MS in the Han-Nom Institute, with a title *"Thân Bạ,"* shelf number VHv 2493, Hanoi.

[13] Gourou, *The Peasants*, vol. 1, p. 162.

[14] *Khâm Định Việt Sử Thông Giám Cương Mục* (Text and explanation forming the complete mirror of the history of Vietnam), vol. 7 (Taipei: reprint, The National Library of Taiwan, 1969), p. 3523.

[15] *Toàn Thư*, vol. 3, p. 1140; see also *Cương Mục*, vol. 8, p. 3675.

doubt that this effort was successful, because, according to the *Cương Mục*, in the same year a famine occurred in the Cao Bằng area that was so devastating the government had to provide money for relief. Then there was a big drought in the Red River delta in 1756. And according to the *Toàn Thư*, in 1757 another big famine and epidemic swept through eleven counties of Sơn Tây, when "the people who survived numbered only one or two out of ten."[16]

The records discussed above provide some basis for a discussion of population change in Vietnam from the sixteenth century.

## A HYPOTHESIS

| Table 1: Vietnamese Population Figures in the North (from 757 AD) | | |
|---|---|---|
| Year | Taxpayers | Sources |
| 807 | 40,586 (households) | *Tong Dian* |
| Lê (10th c.) | 5,006,500 (taxpayers) | *Địa Dư Chí* |
| Ly | 3,300,100 | *Địa Dư Chí* |
| Tran | 7,004,300 | *Địa Dư Chí* |
| Ho (1408) | 5,200,000 | *Ming Shi Lu* |
| Ming (1417) | 450,288 | *Ngan-nan tche yuan* |
| 1430 | 700,940 | *Địa Dư Chí* |
| 1539 | 1,750,000 | *Ming Shi Lu* |
| 1713 | 206,315 | *Cương Mục* |
| 1733 | 311,670 | *Địa Dư Chí* |

What can we say about those tremendously vacillating figures? The fact that they stand alone, without any other sources to compare them to, already creates a problem almost impossible to solve, even without anomalies like the entry showing there were five million taxpayers in the tenth century. If we multiply that by five, a common size for a family, we get a ridiculous twenty-five million, even more than the census of 1972 for North Vietnam. It is not surprising, therefore, that after researching the Vietnamese population in the Red River delta extensively, Gourou said sadly in the 1930s: "It would be better to entitle this chapter, 'On the impossibility at present of writing the history of the settlement of the Tongking Delta.'" When struggling to compute an accurate calculation of the Vietnamese population in past centuries, I found that I had to fight against my own inclination, six decades later, to adopt Gourou's title and surrender too.

Yet, is there another source, besides the so-called "census," that would enable us to establish a relatively firm basis from which to estimate the Vietnamese population in the past? By going over the sources, I found one characteristic of Vietnamese historical geography that might help. This is the importance of the village. Unlike China, in which the *hu* (household) and *kou* (register) were always emphasized, in Vietnam the *xã* (village) was the important unit, probably reflecting the importance of the *xã* in Vietnamese heritage.[17] Is it merely a coincidence that we now have

---

[16] *Toàn Thư*, vol. 3, p. 1145.

[17] A fight almost always occurred between the government and the *xã* whenever a census was taken by the government. See the description by the Vũ Liệt canton discussed above, and the

nothing but a few absurd figures about the population provided by Nguyễn Trãi in his *Địa Dư Chí*, while almost every historical geography book gives the numbers of the villages in different periods?

I have therefore attempted to review all the records which give numbers of villages that might be relevant to population changes.

First I found that the villages in early fifteenth-century Vietnam were quite small. According to the *Toàn Thư*, in 1433

> the large *xã* with more than one hundred residents had three chiefs; in the medium-sized *xã*, with more than fifty residents, there were two chiefs; and in the small *xã* with more than ten residents, one chief.

"Resident" here signifies only men recorded on the government-controlled registers, men who could probably be more accurately identified as the *đinh* of each household. It suggests that biggest villages at that time were about one hundred households, or perhaps five hundred people.

The *Thiên Nam Dư Hà Tập*, dated 1483, suggests a rapid population increase in villages during the previous five decades:

> The office of *xã* chief shall be established according to the number of households in the *xã*. It is decreed that in a *xã* of more than five hundred households there shall be five chiefs; those with more than three hundred shall have four chiefs; those with more than one hundred shall have five chiefs, and those not exceeding sixty families shall have one chief.[18]

The strengthening of government control over registration procedures may account for some of this growth; but, at the same time, the substantial population increase cannot be discounted as the mere result of better reporting. The biggest village then had five hundred households, or about 2,500 people. The size of the smallest village also saw a five-fold increase, or more.

The numbers of villages also increased rapidly. In 1490, when the *Toàn Thư* reported that there were 7,950 villages in the whole country, it also made the following statement about the division of villages into smaller units:

---

*Toàn Thư*. Two officials tried to be tough on the issue in different periods: one was Nguyễn Công Kháng, who tried to issue a restrictive registration rule in 1722, only to be attacked by officials in the government; the rule caused many people to flee from their villages. He was ordered to kill himself in 1733. The other was Lê Quý Đôn in 1770, who again made "people gnash their teeth in hatred," as described in the *Toàn Thư*. His enemies urged the government to sack him. So a compromise was worked out and the census that year was "slightly less than that of the years of the Bảo Thái (1720-1728 )." This again proved that the so-called "census" in the eighteenth century was actually the product of many compromises between the Vietnamese villages and the government. It is interesting to see that whenever the government tried to tighten its control, people fled. Villages fought constantly to reduce their register numbers on the government list, which reminded me of the well-known Vietnamese proverb: "*Phép vua thua lệ làng*" (the law of the king loses out to village custom). Perhaps census procedure lost out because officials at the time knew they were far from the truth anyway, whereas the figures of villages were relatively accurate?

[18] Quoted from Sakurai Yumio, "The change in the name and number of villages in Medieval Vietnam," *Vietnam Social Sciences*, 1 and 2 (1986): 131.

If a *xã* has more than five hundred households, and that excess number of households reaches one hundred, than these one hundred households can separate from the village to form a small *xã*. When they apply to do so, the officials should give them permission, to make our map look better.[19]

This quote indicates that the population increased quickly enough in the villages for separation to become a general issue in the country; but the Lê government took the division of villages seriously and would not let a village be formed with less than one hundred households. The quote tends to confirm Gourou's 1930s observation that a village with five hundred to two thousand residents was the most common one in the north, not only at that time, but stretching back four centuries.[20] The rule of the Lê might have established the basis for the size of Vietnamese villages in later centuries.[21]

My next step was to list the total numbers of villages from the fifteenth century to the early nineteenth century, to see if the number increased or decreased. Here is the result:[22]

---

[19] *Toàn Thư*, vol. 2, p. 736.

[20] It is more than likely that this rule referred mainly to the Red River delta, the area where the population increased most quickly. The interesting point is that the most densely populous area today probably was not fully opened until the Lê dynasty. Lê Thánh Tôn started to carry out the Đồn Điền policy (having garrison troops or peasants open up wasteland to grow grain) and set up forty-two units of *đồn điền* in 1481. Although it is still not clear where the units were established, historians tend to think that it was in the Thái Bình area, one of the most densely populated areas today. Gourou says that many villages listed in Thái Bình records were established in the fifteenth century. The *Lịch Sử Việt Nam* states that the history of many villages in the seaside districts indicates they were established from the fifteenth century. Several land records of the Thái Bình area indicate that the private land there in the eighteenth century was only 23 percent of the total land. According to Nhan Van Dinh, Quan Phuong village in Nam Định province was opened from 1512. See *Nam Phong*, April (1931): 385-398. The fast growing population in the fifteenth century might very much be due to population growth in those areas.

[21] This size was certainly influenced by a number of factors, such as distance from the fields, etc.

[22] Sakurai suggests that village numbers decreased rather than increased in the fifteenth century. See Sakurai Yumio, *Betonamu Sonraku no keisei* (The forming of Vietnamese villages) (Tokyo: Soubunsha, 1987), pp. 144–166. His idea is as follows: while Nguyễn Trãi's *Địa Dư Chí* gives 9,728 villages in 1435, there were only 7,090 villages in 1490. After a textual study on *Địa Dư Chí*, I tend to think that although Nguyễn Trãi did write a work called *Địa Dư Chí* in 1435, the evidence indicates that both *Địa Dư Chí* and *Địa Dư Chí Cẩn Án* (the commentary of the *Địa Dư Ch*) were altered by several authors throughout the fifteenth, sixteenth, seventeenth, eighteenth, and nineteenth centuries. To begin with, the main administrative divisions *Địa Dư Chí* employs, such as "Sơn Nam," "Kinh Bắc," "Sơn Tây," "Hải Dương," "Cao Bằng," and "Hưng Hóa," did not appear before 1469, twenty-seven years after Nguyễn Trãi's death. Most of the county names listed in *Địa Dư Chí* were newly changed in the seventeenth century. This book, in my opinion, is a work heavily modified between the mid-seventeenth century and early eighteenth century. As a result, the work that Nguyễn Trãi had done was only left as an outer form. I intend to discuss this source in a separate article. See Nguyễn Trãi, *Ức Trai Tập* (A collection of Ức Trai Nguyễn Trãi's works) (Saigon: Phư quốc vụ khanh đặc trách văn hóa, 1972).

Table 2: Numbers of Vietnamese Villages,
Fifteenth through Nineteenth Centuries

| Year | Number of Villages | Sources |
|---|---|---|
| 1417 | 3,385 | *Ngan-nan tche yuan*[23] |
| 1490 | 7,950 | *Toàn Thư*[24] |
| 1539 | 10,228 | *Yue Qiao Shu*[25] |
| 1634–43 | 8,671 | *Địa Dư Chí*[26] |
| 1730s (?) | 11,766 | *Ngô Gia Văn Phái*[27] |
| 1750s (?) | 10,284 | *Ngô Gia Văn Phái*[28] |
| 1810 | 10,635 | *CTTXDBL*[29] |

Can we relate the growing village numbers with a growth of population? At first I thought it was impossible, because there is no way to tell how many big villages of five hundred households existed, nor how many small ones with one hundred or even sixty households numbered in the calculations. Then I found this quotation in the *Toàn Thư*, dated 1419: "Setting up the *lý* system. Every 110 households are to be formed as one *lý*. In every year a chief of the *lý*, together with ten taxpayers within the *lý* are to do the corvée."[30] This means that 10 percent of all taxpayers performed the corvée each year, under the assumption that each household had one taxpayer.

If we examine the administrative system in operation from the Tang dynasty onward, considering only that part of the system below the county level, we will find that the *lý* system was actually a continuation of a taxation system from ancient times. The *Ngan-nan tche yuan* says that Qiu He, the governor in 618 AD, set up units under the county as big and small villages and big and small *xiang* (townships): ten to thirty households represented a small village, forty to sixty a big one; seventy to 150 households formed a small township, and 160 to 540 constituted a big one. Probably because of an increase in population, Zhao Chang, the Tang governor in the late eighth century, omitted differentiating between the big and small townships by giving the general designation as *xiang* (township). It is said that between 864 and 866 AD there were 159 townships in northern Vietnam. In 907, Khúc Thừa Hạo, the Vietnamese governor, changed the *xiang* into *giáp*, and added 155 onto the former

[23] *Ngan-nan tche yuan* (Hanoi: Imprimerie d'Extrême-Orient, 1932), p. 60. A Chinese scholar, Zhang Xu Min, suggests that the book was actually *Jiao zhi zong zhi* (A general gazette of Jiao Zhi), officially compiled by Huang Fu and other Chinese high officials in the early fifteenth century. Because it was bound together with Gao Xong Zheng's *An nan zhi*, the French scholars Aurouseau and Gaspardone mistakenly put it under Gao's name and his book's title. See Zhang Xu Min, *Zhong yue guan xi shi lun wen ji* (A collection of papers on history of Sino-Vietnamese relations) (Taipei: Wen shi zhe, 1992), pp. 139–144.

[24] *Toàn Thư*, vol. 2, p. 736.

[25] Li Wen-feng, *Yue Qiao Shu*, first published in 1540 (mimeographed ed., n.p. ca. 1950), vol. 14, p. 8.

[26] Nguyễn Trãi, *Ức Trai Tập*, vol. 2, p. 735.

[27] *Ngô Gia Văn Phái*, a MS kept in the Hán-Nôm Institute, Hanoi, vol. 5.

[28] Ibid.

[29] *Tên Làng Xã Việt Nam đầu thế kỷ 19* (Names of Vietnamese villages in early nineteenth century) (Hanoi: Khoa Học Xã hội, 1981), pp. 25–121.

[30] *Toàn Thư*, vol. 2, p. 517.

159, making 314 *giáp* altogether in early tenth-century Vietnam.[31] All of these reorganizations and computations shared one main aim: collecting taxes.

According to Nguyễn Thế Anh, Vietnamese society was built up on the basis of the organization of *xã*. He says that

> the government did not deal directly with the people in the villages, rather they looked upon people as a part of the community of the *xã*. The government did not expect people to pay taxes or corvée directly to it, rather, they put the village in that position; the government itself did not need to know how the taxes and the corvée were divided among the people in the villages.[32]

For those interested in the history of the Vietnamese population, the number of taxpaying units may be even more meaningful than the figures registering numbers of *đinh*: individuals listed on government registers. The *đinh*, as Alexander Woodside explains, identified only "the numbers of adult males between eighteen and fifty-nine years of age who were unfortunate enough to be known to the tax collectors."[33] Whenever the numbers of *đinh* were given, they were often either unbelievably high or unquestionably low, as the table above shows. On the other hand, the numbers of villages remained relatively consistent throughout the centuries, therefore providing a more reliable basis for the study of the Vietnamese population history.

But how do we estimate the average size of the Vietnamese village? To calculate the population from the number of villages, a magic figure is needed. I have chosen to use the term *lý* (meaning 110 households) for the following reasons. First, the statement of the *Toàn Thư* about the size of the village in 1490, as cited above, suggests that an average of 110 households per village would be a reasonable guess. Second, the observations of Gourou in 1931 suggest that this estimation is reasonable; in the 6,639 villages he listed, there were 2,100 villages with approximately five hundred to 2,100 inhabitants. Despite the fact that the mean population of the villages was 910 inhabitants, as a result of population increase from the late nineteenth century, they still showed traces of their former village size.

To check how accurate (in rough terms) my estimation of this size might be, I also tried a calculation working from data provided by another nineteenth-century source. According to the *Tên Làng Xã Việt Nam đầu thế kỷ 19* (Name of villages in the nineteenth century), a book which lists the villages of the north down to Nghệ An in 1809, eleven villages were depopulated in Nam Xương county of Sơn Nam. These villages formerly had 1,123 taxpayers, or an average of 102 in each village.[34]

By comparing the figures recording the numbers of *đinh* in the early Lê dynasty and the numbers of villages in each province recorded in the *Hồng Đức Bản Đồ*, we can be fairly sure that the numbers of villages corresponded to the population, as Table Three indicates:

---

[31] See *Ngan-nan tche yuan*, p. 60; *Xin Tang Shu*, vol. 90; *Jiu Tang Shu*, vol. 183.

[32] Nguyễn Thế Anh, *Kinh Tế và Xã Hội Việt Nam dưới Các Vua Triều Nguyễn* (Saigon: Trình Bày, 1968), p. 21.

[33] Alexander Woodside, *Vietnam and the Chinese Model* (Cambridge, MA: Harvard University Press, 1971), p. 158.

[34] *Tên Làng Xã*, p. 57.

| Table Three: Number of Villages in Each Province in the Fifteenth Century | | | |
|---|---|---|---|
| Province | Number of *xã* | Total Taxpayers | Taxpayers per *xã* |
| Hải Dương | 1,316 | 110,000 | 84 |
| Sơn Nam | 1,951 | 140,000 | 71 |
| Sơn Tây | 1,453 | 100,000 | 68 |
| Kinh Bắc | 1,070 | 100,000 | 93 |
| Thái Nguyên | 653 | 20,000 | 30 |
| Tuyên Quang | 282 | 18,000 | 63 |
| Hưng Hóa | 257 | 18,000 | 67 |
| Thanh Hóa | 1,091 | 100,000 | 91 |
| Nghệ An | 876 | 50,000 | 57 |
| Lạng Sơn | 223 | 11,200 | 50 |
| Cao Bằng | 273 | 11,200 | 41 |
| Total | 9,445 | 578,400 | |
| Average per *xã* | | | 61 |

There was an average of sixty-five taxpayers in each village, according to the table above. The *Địa Dư Chí* said that there were 311,670 registered in 1733, but 32,676 of them were free from tax and corvée, i.e. about 10 percent of those registered. It is reasonable to assume that 20 to 30 percent of the people in the village escaped being registered successfully. All these bits of information support the hypothesis that we can estimate population by positing that there were approximately 110 households in each village, on average.

CONCLUSION

The hypothesis that pre-colonial villages in northern Vietnam averaged 110 households, with five persons included per household, gives the following results:

| Table 4: Estimated Population in North Vietnam from the Fifteenth to Nineteenth Centuries | | | | |
|---|---|---|---|---|
| Year | Number of *xã* | Households | Population | Annual Growth Rate |
| 1417 | 3,385 | 372,350 | 1,861,750 | |
| 1490 | 7,950 | 874,500 | 4,372,500 | 0.50% |
| 1539 | 10,228 | 1,125,080 | 5,625,400 | 0.22% |
| 1634–43 | 8,671 | 953,810 | 4,769,050 | -0.07% |
| 1730s | 11766 | 1,294,260 | 6,471,300 | 0.13% |
| 1750s? | 10,284 | 1,131,240 | 5,656,200 | -0.29% |
| 1810 | 10,635 | 1,169,850 | 5,849,250 | 0.16% |

The accuracy of those figures clearly leaves much to be desired. Yet this table roughly reflects the fall and rise of Vietnamese population between the fifteenth and nineteenth centuries, a fluctuation that corresponds with the existing accounts. For instance, when giving the figure for 1638, one author said that because of the separation of Đàng Trong, the villages in Đàng Ngoài between 1634 and 1643 numbered only 8,671.[35] But if we subtract the number of the villages in Thuận Hóa and Thăng Hoa (755) from 10,228 villages in 1539, there are still 803 villages missing, not to mention the additional villages that would have been created during the one hundred years. This fall indicates a 441,650 loss of population in the late sixteenth century, while the figure for the 1760s probably incorporates losses in the early eighteenth century.

It is a pity that we do not have any figures for the late seventeenth century. Yet after evaluating data from the early seventeenth and early eighteenth centuries, we see that there was an increase in numbers. This suggests a rise of population in the seventeenth century. The *Lê Triều Chiếu Lệnh Thiên Chính* (a collection of instructions instituted by the Lê government) recorded that the government forbade people from engaging in cock fighting, chess playing and gambling in the years 1649, 1662, 1663, 1664, and 1698. These entertainments may have been a sign of a peaceful, and thus growing, society, since we find no such record throughout the disastrous sixteenth century. Also, according to Trương Hữu Quỳnh, a Vietnamese historian who specializes in the land regulation, the most detailed land tax system in Vietnam from the sixteenth to the eighteenth centuries was published in 1625 and 1664.[36] It seems unlikely that any detailed tax regulation would be established in years of turmoil or famine.

Unless new sources appear, I will therefore maintain my conclusion that the curve of a chart tracing Vietnamese population growth in the north from the sixteenth to eighteenth centuries has two rises and two falls. This contrasts with the table that McEvedy and Jones provide for Vietnamese population in the *Atlas of World Population History*, which suggests a steady growth from two million in 1500, to three million in 1700, and four million in 1800. I conclude that the population rose rapidly to four to five million in the late fifteenth to early sixteenth centuries, but then lost about ten to fifteen percent in the late sixteenth century. There may have been a steady recovery in the seventeenth century, but another fall in the first half of the eighteenth century. All of this insured that the long-term population growth in the north showed only a small increase. In other words, population fluctuated around five to six million from the fifteenth to eighteenth centuries.

---

[35] *Địa Dư Chí*, p. 735.

[36] Trương Hữu Quỳnh, *Chế độ Ruộng đất ở Việt Nam*, vol. 2, p. 118.

# APPENDIX TWO
# ON THE "KING" OF COCHINCHINA, THE NAMES "QUINAM" AND "GUANG NAN GUO"

From the earlier accounts Westerners have given about Cochinchina, the "king" appears to have been a mysterious figure. According to the *Tiền Biên*, until 1626 the Nguyễn capital was in Dang Xuong county (in today's Quảng Trị province), more than 150 kilometers away from Hội An (Faifo). This would have taken about five days' return journey at the time.[1] When Bowyear paid a visit from Faifo to Sinoa[2] in 1695, it took him five days for a one-way trip. But in a letter written by Jeronimus Wonderaer, a Dutch merchant who visited Cochinchina in 1602, we find the following: "After midday, I learned that I was summoned by the king at about three or four o'clock in the afternoon."[3] William Adams came to Faifo on April 22, 1617, but on April 24 he had already been visited by the Japanese interpreter for the king, who "bade me very welcome and told me that the king was very glad that there were English come again."[4]

Actually the letter written by the Dutch merchant noted above itself suggests where this "king" was. It was written in Tachem, which might refer either to *Đại Chiêm*, the seaport which Hội An (Faifo) faces; or *Thanh Chiêm*, the residence of the governor of Quảng Nam, who was a Nguyễn prince. The latter seems more possible, judging from the statement. Also, when talking about the death of Peacock, Richard Cocks wrote that "it was done by the young king and the old king knowth nothing of it." The "young king" was therefore more than likely the prince who often resided in Quảng Nam. The confusion about the "king" among the foreigners seems to have continued until quite late. We find, for instance, that a Dutch story from 1652

---

[1] A report by Johan van Linga in 1642 about Quinam says that it took one day and one night sailing from Thoron (Tourane) to Senua (two kilometers southeast of today's Huế), the capital. The distance is only half of that from Hội An to Dang Xuong.

[2] Sinoa, or Senoa, should refer to Shunhua, a Chinese pronunciation for Thuận Hóa. It might have been taken by Westerners from the Chinese traders in Đàng Trong. Maybon referred to it wrongly as Thanh Hóa. See Charles Maybon, *Histoire moderne du pays d'Annam, 1592-1820* (Paris: Librairie Plon, 1920, reprinted by Gregg International Publisher Ltd., Westmead, England, 1972), p. 60 n.

[3] "The trials of a foreign merchant. Jeronimus Wonderaer's letter from Vietnam, 1602," translated by Ruurdje Laarhoven, in Li Tana and Anthony Reid, *Southern Vietnam under the Nguyen, Documents on the Economic History of Cochinchina (Dang Trong), 1602-1777*, (Singapore: Institute of Southeast Asian Studies, Singapore/ECHOSEA, The Australian National University, 1993), p. 8.

[4] William Adams, *The Log-Book of William Adams, 1614-19*, ed. C. J. Purnell, ed. (London: Easten Press, 1916), p. 290.

recounted how, having arrested and humiliated the five Dutchmen remaining in Cochinchina,

> the king took for himself the *lakens* and *perpetuanen* . . . evaluating and paying for them according to his pleasure, without listening to any arguments against this . . . Despite all this the king has sent with our people at their departure another five hundred *tael* of silver to buy him here in Batavia some *lakens*, *perpetuanen* and other things which are acceptable to him.[5]

The "king" here was either a son of *chúa* Hiền or perhaps the top mandarin in Hội An.

The reason that the "young king" or high mandarin was so powerful was because he issued the Cochinchinese "Red Seal" to ships from overseas. We find this reference explicitly in the journals of Ed. Saris, who traveled to Cochinchina along with Adams in 1617: "I should have his [the king's] *goshuin* or his Chope which is his seal to come with shipping yearly or to settle a factree in any part in his dominions and that he would protect me."[6] The existence of *goshuin* is supported by the *Dong Xi Yang Kao* (A study of Southeast Asian countries) written in seventeenth-century China. It says:

> The governor of Quảng Nam is above all the small countries in the area, even stronger than Tongking. Xin-chou (Qui Nhơn) and Ti-yi (Đề Di seaport, in Phú Yên province) all pay tributes to Quảng Nam. The ships which come to Xin-chou and Ti-yi to trade have to spend several days to go to Quảng Nam to pay tribute there. The governor of Quảng Nam also gives wooden plates to the traders. When passing the wooden plate, people always salute [the plates] first, then go, no one dares to make a noise. The fame of Quảng Nam is really impressive.[7]

Judging from the accounts above, the main difference between the *goshuin* of Japan and of Cochinchina was that the Japanese *goshuin* was given to the ships which left to sail overseas, while the wooden plates in Cochinchina were given to the ships that came from overseas.[8]

We know that Nguyễn Hoàng came to be the garrison commander of Thuận Hóa in 1558, but that Quảng Nam did not come under his power until 1570. Since until 1600 Nguyễn Hoàng never gave up hope of gaining power in the Lê court in the north, it seems that he did not pay much attention to Quảng Nam until 1602 (judging from the *Tiền Biên* report). When he visited Hai Van pass in that year he realized it was like the throat of Thuận Hóa and Quảng Nam, and quickly sent his sixth son to

---

[5] "The end of Dutch relations with Cochinchina, 1651-2," translated by Anthony Reid, in Li and Reid, *Southern Vietnam under the Nguyễn*, p. 37.

[6] Adams, *The Log-Book of William Adams*, p. 104.

[7] Zhang Xie, *Dong Xi Yang Kao* (Beijing: reprinted by Zhong Hua Shu Ju, 1981), p. 20.

[8] According to the *Phủ Biên Tạp Lục*, people in Cochinchina had to have a certain certificate too if they wanted to go the Mekong delta to trade. But they got that certificate in Thuận Hóa See Lê Quý Đôn, *Phủ Biên Tạp Lục* (hereafter *Phủ Biên*), vol. 2 (Hanoi: Khoa Học Xã Hội, 1977), p. 90a.

govern Quảng Nam.[9] Nguyễn Phúc Nguyên, the first *chúa*'s son, who governed Quảng Nam, became ruler after his father. But the position enjoyed quite independent power, and the garrison could easily dream of independence. Thus Anh, the sixth son of Nguyễn Phúc Nguyên, and the garrison commander of Quảng Nam plotted rebellion in 1633, with help from several Japanese living in Hội An. When they were discovered by Nguyễn Phúc Nguyên, the city was drowned in blood, with one thousand people executed by the Nguyễn government.[10]

Quảng Nam, and its special political and economic position in the early seventeenth century, might be why Cochinchina was called *Guang Nan Guo* (the kingdom of Quảng Nam) by the Chinese, and *Quinam* by the Dutch. A map drawn in 1655 by Martino Martini called the whole area of Cochinchina "Gan Nan," and put "Quinam" in the place of Hội An.[11] The Dutch name of the country—*Quinam*—most probably derived from the city of Qui Nam. The overseas trade of Quảng Nam was so well known that other parts of the country were neglected by the foreigners; while the governor in Quảng Nam was so powerful and independent that this "young king" was almost regarded as a king in his own right.

---

[9] *Đại Nam Thực Lục Tiền Biên* (Chronicle of Greater Vietnam, Premier Period of the Nguyen) (Tokyo: Keio Institute of Linguistic Studies, Mita, Siba, Minato-ku, 1961), vol. 1, p. 21.

[10] Phan Khoang, *Việt Sử Xứ Đàng Trong* (Saigon: Khai Trí, 1969), p. 191.

[11] Egon Klemp, *Asia in Maps, from Ancient Times to the Mid-Nineteenth Century* (Weinheim: Acta Humaniora, Edition Leipzig, 1989), p. 61.

# APPENDIX THREE
# CONFLICTS BETWEEN THE DUTCH AND
# THE NGUYỄN

Although the Netherlands was the only Western country to fight the Vietnamese before the nineteenth century, actual military encounters between the Trịnh, the Nguyễn, and the Dutch East India Company (the *Verenigde Oostindische Compagnie*, here afterwards the VOC) in the 1630s and 1640s remain vague. Different stories crop up about almost every aspect. The following is an attempt, made with the generous help of Professor Anthony Reid, to survey the situation.

We begin with a letter sent in 1637 by the Trịnh to the Governor General of the VOC (the letter, translated by the Japanese, called him *Sessche Quan Kichio*) in Batavia which seems not to have been given enough attention by scholars. This is the main part of the letter:

> [. . .] Some beasts in human shape [meaning the Nguyễn] have set up a separatist regime on our southern border and are relying on their tenable defensive position to resist the court [of the Lê in Thăng Long]. We have not yet done anything about them because we are afraid that something unforeseen may happen at sea. Since you intend to be friendly with us, could you give us either two or three ships, or two hundred soldiers who are good at shooting, as proof of your kindness. These soldiers can help us with the cannons. In addition, please send fifty galleys with picked soldiers and powerful guns to us, and we will send some of our trusted soldiers to lead your galleys to Quảng Nam, as our reinforcements. At the same time our army will attack Thuận Hóa. [. . .] After the victory we will give your soldiers twenty thousand to thirty thousand *taels* of silver as a gift. As for Your Excellency, we will give you Quảng Nam to govern. You can select some soldiers to build and guard the city, and we will order the people there to do corvée for you. You collect the products of the area and give a part of it to our court, so both sides will benefit from it. God will punish us if the foregoing is not honest.[1]

This letter is quite striking. The Trịnh would not have made such an offer had they had not recognized that it would be hard to defeat the Nguyễn on their own in the late 1630s, ten years after war had broken out between the two.[2]

---

[1] As it was written in Chinese, which no Dutch understood at the time, this letter was sent to Japan for Meison, a Japanese interpreter in Nagasaki to translate into Dutch. Giving the translated letter to the VOC, Meison kept the original letter for himself. See Iwao Seiichi "Annan koku no uran koku suigun kyuen tosho ni tsuite" (About the letter asking help from the Dutch navy, sent by Annam to Wulan [Netherlands], *Toyo-gaku*, no. 23 (1962): 109-118.

[2] On the other hand, it also suggests the way Vietnamese rulers in the north, up to the Tây Sơn period, were willing to sacrifice the south—a land formerly belonging to others, which was

The letter seems to have convinced the Dutch, who were angry with the Nguyễn because they had plundered two Dutch ships wrecked near the coast of Cochinchina. One of the ships, the *Grootenbroeck*, was said to carry a cargo worth 23,580 *reals*, all of which had been seized by the Nguyễn.[3] After repeated negotiations between 1637 and 1638 concerning the formation of a military alliance between the Dutch and the Trịnh, in 1639 the Dutch decided they would send four ships the next year to help attack Cochinchina in return for trade concessions from Tongking. The Trịnh in 1639 sent another letter in response to the Dutch Governor-General, insisting that the Dutch send five ships and six hundred well-armed men.

After another two years of negotiations, impeded by Trịnh hesitation, an agreement finally seems to have been struck. On May 14, 1641, the Dutch Governor-General in Batavia wrote to Trịnh Tráng to say they were ready to send ships to mount a combined action against Quinam (Cochinchina).

In November 1641, another event hardened Dutch attitudes towards Quinam, confirming their desire to have Quinam punished and Dutch honor restored. Two additional Dutch ships, the *Eulden Buis* and the *Maria de Medicis*, were wrecked on the Cochinchinese coast near Champelo island on November 26, 1641. All survivors—eighty-two Dutchmen—were taken prisoner and transported to Hội An, and the ships were confiscated by Cochinchina.

Fortunately for the Dutch, Jacob van Liesvelt had 120 Cochinchinese in his hands who had been captured in early 1642 at Tourane at the request of an ambassador of the Trịnh who was traveling with the Dutch to Batavia.[4] Later, when he learned of the imprisonment of Dutchmen at Hội An, these prisoners were offered in exchange for the Dutch prisoners held by the Nguyễn. But after the Dutch released the Cochinchinese, the *chúa* Thượng (Nguyễn Phúc Lan, r. 1635–1648) refused to release the Dutch unless van Liesvelt also surrendered the ambassador of the Trịnh to him.

Negotiations broke down, despite threats from both sides. Van Liesvelt not only refused to surrender the Tongking envoy, but also made captives of the Quinam mandarin and the Japanese translator, Francisco, who had been sent to negotiate. He then sailed off to Batavia.[5]

---

not under their own power at the time—to meet their own more urgent needs. Interestingly enough, about 150 years later, Nguyen Anh did almost exactly the same thing when he asked the Portuguese to help him against the Tay Son in 1786. See Pierre-Yves Manguin, *Les Nguyen, Macau et le Portugal* (Paris: Ecole Française d'Extrême-Orient, 1984), PI. 1. The only difference was that he said he would give the Portuguese the small town and anchorage of Vũng Tàu to govern.

[3] J. M. Dixon, trans., "Voyage of the Dutch ship 'Grol' from Hirado to Tongking," *Transactions of the Asiatic Society of Japan* (Tokyo: reprint, Yushodo Booksellers Ltd. 1964), pp. 192, 212.

[4] W. J. M. Buch, *De Oost-Indische Compagne en Quinam* (Amsterdam: H. J. Paris, 1929), p. 80.

[5] The *chúa* Thượng must have taken the threat from the Dutch seriously. As a gesture of good-will, he released fifty Dutchmen in March 1642, possibly soon after van Liesvelt left. But the Dutch did not know this until 1643. These ill-fated men met another misfortune on their return to Batavia. On April 15, they were attacked by a junk manned by Portuguese and some Chinese (Vietnamese sources say it was a Spanish ship which did this), their ship burned and many were killed. Eighteen managed to swim away and regain the hulk of their boat after the Portuguese had gone. When they took it to the Champa coast, and four more had died, the king of Champa seized the remainder and divided them as slaves among his men. One of them, Juriaan de Rode, was sent to the king of Cambodia, who let him get back to Batavia, where he arrived on January 5, 1643, and told his remarkable story. See Buch, *De Oost-Indische Compagne* , pp. 82–83.

In May 1642 the Dutch sent a fleet of five ships with 125 sailors and seventy soldiers aboard. Its commander, Jan van Linga, was instructed by Batavia to seize many "Quinammers" along the coast, then send an ultimatum to the king threatening to kill half of them if Dutch demands were not met within forty-eight hours, with the other half to be taken to Tongking. Then they were ordered to sail north to the Tongking border to await the arrival of the Trịnh forces (though few believed they would actually come).

On May 31, 1642, the Dutch entered the Bay of Cambir (Qui Nhơn), burned four to five hundred houses together with rice stores, and took thirty-eight people prisoner. Probably at this point they decided to attempt to release the Dutch captives in Hội An by force, without waiting for the Governor-General's permission. They continued to take captives along the coast, but the number did not seem to increase rapidly, as only another eleven were added within ten days. To take more captives, Jacob van Liesvelt suggested they go to Champelo Island in apparent friendship and lure the Cochinchinese, whom he had met before, into one of the ships in order to seize them.

Either because people in Quy Nhơn had reported the Dutch actions or because the scouts of Cochinchina got the news beforehand, when the Dutch arrived they found that "the Quinam government had already put the coastal regions in a defensive position."[6] When van Liesvelt went ashore with 150 men, he was attacked and killed, together with ten of his men.

Curiously, the *Đại Nam Thực Lục Tiền Biên* does not mention this story at all. The Nguyễn, who definitely were seeking to prevent the Dutch from joining Tongking against them, showed van Linga their disappointment about the Dutch attack on them, but were slow to respond to the demand for release of Dutch captives. On June 16 the Dutch killed twenty Cochinchinese hostages in Tourane, then left for Tongking. When the Dutch commander asked the Trịnh for forces to attack Cochinchina, Trịnh Tráng said that he had already sent them, only to have them return because the Dutch had not appeared. But this seems like a diplomatic falsehood offered to conceal Trịnh unwillingness to join forces; the *Đại Việt Sử Ký Toàn Thư* does not mention the Trịnh taking any military action in 1642, nor does the *Tiền Biên* report anything in the south.

In January 1643, the Dutch sent a new fleet of five ships to Tongking, led by Johannes Lamotius, for a joint attack on Cochinchina, only to find that the army of Tongking was not ready. In June 1643 the patient Dutch sent yet another fleet of three ships, led by Pieter Baeck. Once more he was instructed to capture as many Cochinchinese as possible when sailing along the coast. Five miles south of the Gianh River,[7] however, they were surprised to see fifty galleys of the Nguyễn coming towards them. According to Lê Thanh Khôi: "The battle was a total disaster. The *de Wijdenes* [the flag ship] was destroyed, Baeck was killed, another two ships took great pains to escape."[8] Buch gives a more detailed report, saying that the *de Wijdenes*

---

[6] Buch, *De Oost-Indische Compagne* , p. 86.

[7] The *Tiền Biên* said that it happened in Eo seaport. According to the *Đại Nam Nhất Thống Chí*, the Eo seaport was also called the Noan seaport; both refer to Thuận An in the Huế area. See *Đại Nam Nhất Thống Chí* (Tokyo: reprinted by the Society of Indo-China Studies, 1941), vol. 1, p. 256.

[8] Lê Thanh Khôi *Histoire du Vietnam des origines à 1858* (Paris: Sudestasie, 1981), p. 248. This disaster even influenced the attitude of Japanese towards the VOC: "Having been told by the Chinese and local people who trade to Japan that the de Wijdenes was destroyed and other

caught fire and was blown up by its own stock of gunpowder, killing all on board, including Baeck. A Vietnamese version has it that the Dutch were so dispirited that they destroyed *de Wijdenes* themselves.[9] During this battle seven Quinam galleys were destroyed and seven to eight hundred Quinam men killed, according to Dutch claims, but the *Tiền Biên* makes no mention of Quinam losses at all.

The Dutch post-mortem heavily criticized the Dutch commanders for being unprepared for enemy attack. In both battles Nguyễn surprise attacks had put the Dutch into a defensive posture from the first minute. According to the *Tiền Biên*, the Nguyễn were well prepared because they received reports from a special team called the *tuần hải* (sea patrol).[10] In addition, they had lookout towers along the coast.[11]

The contacts between the Trịnh and the Dutch suggest that the Trịnh already recognized in 1637 that it would be too hard to fight against the Nguyễn on their own. The Dutch believed in 1643 that the Trịnh had only a very slight advantage over the southern enemy and concluded at the end of 1644 that "the king of Tongking had had enough of war [against Cochinchina]." The period of the 1640s, therefore, may have represented a turning point in Nguyễn military power, and perhaps in economic power as well.

---

ships damaged by the Quinamers, the Japanese started to think that we have nothing to be afraid of and so started looking down on us, and our company's credit has been lost a great deal [among Japanese]." See *Dagh Register gehouden int Casteel Batavia Vant*, Chinese trans. by Guo Hui and Cheng da Xue, vol. 2 (Taipei: Taiwan sheng Wen xian wei yuan hui, 1989), p. 398.

[9] *Quảng Nam qua các Thời đài* (Quảng Nam through the centuries), vol. 1 (Đà Nẵng: Cổ học Tùng Thư, 1974), p. 144.

[10] *Tiền Biên*, vol. 3, p. 48.

[11] For details see Chapter Two.

# APPENDIX FOUR
## ON TUTENAGUE AND SILVER USED IN ĐÀNG TRONG

### TUTENAGUE

In 1746, Nguyễn Phúc Khoát was persuaded by a Chinese named Huang to begin casting coins. Vietnamese sources say that the coins were made from "white lead," brought from Macao by the Portuguese.[1] Western sources, however, all maintain that the material used was tutenague.[2]

We know that lead was brought by Western merchants in large amounts and that it was "as good as money" in the seventeenth and eighteenth centuries. Yet it is also true that tutenague was produced in large quantities in China from the seventeenth century.[3] What is more, many scholars confused tutenague with white copper,[4] another metal produced in China which became well-known in Europe in the eighteenth century.[5] How do we know which of the three metals mentioned above was the so-called "white lead" used by the Nguyễn for casting coins in the eighteenth century ?

Although tutenague was confused by eighteenth-century Europeans with two other metals, Asian designations were more precise. In Chinese sources *bai tong* (*paktong*, white copper) meant nickel-brass, while *ya qian* (inferior lead) meant zinc. The *Phủ Biên* employed the latter when discussing the material used for casting coins in the 1740s.[6]

---

[1] Lê Quý Đôn, *Phủ Biên Tạp Lục* (hereafter *Phủ Biên*), vol. 4 (Hanoi: Khoa Học Xã Hội 1977), pp. 21b, 22b; *Liệt Truyện Tiền Biên* (Collection of Biographies of Nguyễn Dynasty, Premier Period), vol. 10 (Tokyo: Keio Institute of Linguistic Studies, 1961), p. 140.

[2] Pierre Poivre, *Journal de voyage du vaisseau de la companie le Machault à la Cochinchine*, reproduced by H. Cordier in *Revue de l'Extrême-Orient* 3 (1885): 430; Robert Kirsop, "Some Accounts of Cochinchina," in A. Dalrymple, *Oriental Repertory*, vol. 1 (London: 1808), p. 245.

[3] A. Schroeder, *Annam études numismatiques* (Paris: Imprimerie Nationale, 1905, reprinted by Trismegiste, Paris, 1983), p. 493. Needham: "Under the name of tutenag (derived from *tutiya*, but spelled in a hundred curious ways) zinc metal had been an important article of export commerce from China to Europe since about 1605." See Joseph Needham, *Science and Civilization in China*, vol. 5, Part II (Cambridge: Cambridge University Press, 1971), p. 212.

[4] Joseph Needham: "There was great confusion for three centuries in Europe in the naming of the two great metal exports from China, tutenag (hence 'tooth-and-egg metal') being properly zinc, and *paktong* (white copper) properly cupro-nikel." Ibid., p. 212.

[5] Needham says that the maximum intensity of the importation of "white copper" was between 1750 and 1800. Ibid., p. 228.

[6] *Phủ Biên*, vol. 4, p. 22b.

Was this *ya qian* the same thing referred to by Westerners as tutenague? According to the Japanese book *Wakan Sanzai Zue*, published in the eighteenth century, *ya qian* was "also called *totamu*."[7] This *totamu* is obviously a corrupt word for tutenague. Thus the word *ya qian* used in eighteenth-century China, Japan, and Cochinchina, and the word "tutenague" used by the Westerners both referred to zinc, the metal most probably imported into Vietnam both by the Chinese and the Portuguese from China, either directly or indirectly. In the numismatic catalogue of Albert Schroeder, eight out of nine coins stamped with the characters *Thái Bình*[8] are made of brass, while the other *Thái Bình* coin, and one other coin imprinted with the characters *Thiên Minh*, are made of zinc.[9]

Zinc production in Yunnan was well developed, and it became a staple export item to European countries from the late seventeenth century. Although Poivre claims that zinc ("tutenague") was first brought to Cochinchina by the Chinese in 1745, it might well have come earlier.[10] Certainly it rapidly became the most important import item. Again, according to Poivre, zinc "today [the 1740s] makes up the bulk of their [Chinese] trade. The huge profit they make on this substance has led them to suspend [trade in] all other articles."[11]

## SILVER

Due to the strong trade connection between Japan and Cochinchina, through Japanese merchants in the early period, and through Chinese merchants later, Japanese coins and silver played perhaps the most important role in the exchange system of Cochinchina. Although Đàng Trong did not produce silver, its taxes paid to the Nguyễn were three thousand *lạng* in silver yearly, at least in the 1770s, according to Lê Quý Đôn.[12] Bowyear said in 1695 that silver was one of the main cargoes sent from Batavia and Manila to Cochinchina, which indicates a source from another direction. But as we will see, Japanese silver was still the most important one in Cochinchina.

As he was preoccupied with Chinese culture, Lê Quý Đôn might have sometimes mistaken Japanese coins for Chinese. For instance, he said that in 1774 the Trịnh army found more than three hundred thousand *quan* of the best copper coins in the Nguyễn treasury in Huế. According to him, most of them were Chinese coins of the

---

[7] *Wakan Sanzai Zue* (A large Japanese-Chinese dictionary), vol. 2 (1713. Tokyo: reprint, Nihon zuihitsu taisei kanko kai, 1929), p. 645. Boxer says that the word *totunaga* is from the Tamil *tattanagam*, meaning "zinc." See C. R. Boxer, *Seventeenth Century Macau* (Hong Kong: Heinemann Educational Books, Ltd., 1984), p. 198.

[8] *Thái Bình* coins were first cast by the Mạc in the late sixteenth century. The Nguyễn also cast *Thái Bình* coins, as discussed in Chapter Five.

[9] A. Schroeder, *Annam études numismatiques*, p. 493.

[10] In 1739 the Harrington, an English ship, alone took 1697 *piculs* from Canton to Bombay. See H. B. Morse, *The Chronicles of the East India Company Trading to China, 1635-1834* (Oxford: Clarendon Press, 1926), p. 271.

[11] "Description of Cochinchina, 1749-50," translated by Kristine Alilunas-Rodgers, in Li Tana and Anthony Reid, *Southern Vietnam under the Nguyễn, Documents on the Economic History of Central (Nguyễn) Vietnam, 1558-1777* (Singapore: Institute of Southeast Asian Studies, Singapore/ECHOSEA, The Australian National University, 1993), p. 85.

[12] *Phủ Biên*, vol. 4, p. 37a.

Song dynasty (960–1279 AD), and when the Nguyễn cast their zinc coins in the 1740s, they copied the design of Chinese *Xiang Fu* coins (1008–1016 AD). Yet, if we compare the zinc coin which has the characters *"Xiang Fu yuan bao"* imprinted on it,[13] the one most likely cast by the Nguyễn during the 1740s, we will find that it was different from the Chinese *Xiang Fu* coin of the Song dynasty. Rather, it copied the Japanese *Shofu gempo* coin, one of the most common Japanese imitations of Chinese Song and Ming coins. It was cast in Nagasaki between 1659 and 1684 and has the same Chinese characters, but a different design.[14] Most likely, therefore, the three hundred thousand *quan* of fine copper coins found in the Nguyễn treasury in 1774 included a large percentage of Japanese coins.

This discussion sheds light on some other questions in regard to silver. The *Phủ Biên* lists three kinds of silver: first-class silver (*giáp ngân*), *dung ngân*, and *kê ngân*.[15] When translating the *Phủ Biên* into modern Vietnamese, both the scholars in Saigon and those in Hanoi give vague explanations about these terms. *Dung ngân* is identified as "silver in the shape of a banyan leaf," while *kê ngân* is "silver in the shape of a chicken."[16] All this sounds strange. I tend to think that there is a connection between Japanese silver *cho-gin* and the name *dung ngan*, which in Chinese reads as *rung yin*. *Cho-gin* was an alloy containing 80 percent silver, placed in circulation as legal tender in 1699 by the Tokugawa government. Furthermore, I suspect that the first-class silver (*giáp ngân* in Vietnamese, *jia yin* in Chinese) was a corrupt pronunciation for the Japanese *jo-gin*, a refined crude ore of silver used before 1699.[17] The third kind of silver, *kê ngân*, is hard to identify. It might refer to a type of silver coin cast in Cambodia around 1600, decorated with "a cock, a serpent or a heart." [18] It is certainly possible that this kind of coin circulated in Cochinchina, particularly in the Mekong delta region, in the eighteenth century. The phrase might, however, refer to all kinds of European coins.

---

[13] Albert Schroeder, *Annam études numistiques*, p. 495, coin no. 509.

[14] This study was done by Francois Thierry. See his *Catalogue des monnaies vietnamiennes* (Paris: Bibliotheque Nationale, 1987), p. 75.

[15] *Phủ Biên*, vol. 4, p. 37a.

[16] *Phủ Biên*, see Saigon edition, vol. 4, p. 76; Hanoi edition, vol. 4, p. 236.

[17] See Kobata Atsushi, "Coinage from the Kamakura period through the Edo period," *Acta Asiatica* .21, pp. 98–108.

[18] See Anthony Reid, *Southeast Asia in the Age of Commerce, 1450-1680*, vol. 2 (New Haven and London: Yale University Press, 1993), pp. 101–102.

# CHRONOLOGICAL LIST OF NGUYỄN RULERS

| Ruler's Name | Popular Title | Reign |
|---|---|---|
| 1. Nguyễn Hoàng | Chúa Tiên | 1558-1613 |
| 2. Nguyễn Phúc Nguyên | Chúa Sãi | 1613-1635 |
| 3. Nguyễn Phúc Lan | Chúa Thượng | 1635-1648 |
| 4. Nguyễn Phúc Tần | Chúa Hiền | 1648-1687 |
| 5. Nguyễn Phúc Trăn | Chúa Nghĩa | 1687-1691 |
| 6. Nguyễn Phúc Chu | Minh Vương | 1691-1725 |
| 7. Nguyễn Phúc Tru | Ninh Vương | 1725-1738 |
| 8. Nguyễn Phúc Khoát | Vo Vương | 1738-1765 |
| 9. Nguyễn Phúc Thuần | Định Vương | 1765-1777 |

# BIBLIOGRAPHY

A. van Aelst. "Japanese coins in southern Vietnam and the Dutch East India Company, 1633-1638." *Newsletter*, The Oriental Numismatic Society, 109, Nov.-Dec. (1987), (n.p.).

Adams, William. *The Log-Book of William Adams*, edited by C. J. Purnell. London: Eastern Press, 1916.

Aurousseau, L. "Sur le nom de 'Cochinchine.'" *Bulletin de l'Ecole Française d'Extrême-Orient* 24, (1924): 563-579.

Barrow, John. *A Voyage to Cochinchina, in the years 1792 and 1793*, reprint. Kuala Lumpur: Oxford University Press, 1975.

Benda, Harry. "The Structure of Southeast Asian History." *Journal of Southeast Asian History* 3, 1, (1962): 106-138.

Bertin, J., S. Bonin, and P. Chaunu. *Les Philippines et le Pacifique des Ibſeriques*. Paris: Ecole Pratique des Hautes Etudes, 1966.

Bertrand, Gabrielle. *The Jungle People*, translated by Eleanor Brockett. London: Robert Hale Ltd., 1959.

Birdwood, George. *Report on the Old Records of the India Office*. London: W. H. Allen & Co., Ltd., 1891.

Bonhomme, A. "La pagode Thien-Mau: Historique." *Bulletin des Amis du Vieux Hue* II, 2 (1915): 175-77.

Borri, Christoforo. *Cochinchina*. London, 1633. New York: Da Capo Press, facsimile republished, 1970.

Bourotte, Bernard. "Essai d'histoire des populations montagnardes du sud-indochinois jusqu'à 1945." *Bulletin de la Société des Etudes indochinoises* (ns), XXX, 1955.

Bowyear, Thomas. "Bowyear's Narrative," in *The Mandarin Road to Old Hue*, edited by Alastair Lamb. Toronto: Clarke, Irwin & Co. Ltd., 1970.

Boxer, C. R., *Portuguese Conquest and Commerce in Southern Asia 1500-1750*. London:Variorum Reprints, 1985.

— *Portuguese India in the Mid-Seventeenth Century*. Delhi: Oxford University Press, 1980.

— *Seventeenth Century Macau*. Hong Kong: Heinemann Educational Books, Ltd., 1984.

— *The Great Ship from Amacon*. Lisbon: Centro de Estudos Historicos Ultramarinos, 1963.

— "A Spanish description of the Chams in 1595." *Readings on Asian Topics*. Scandinavian Institute of Asian Studies Monograph Series, 1969.

Breazeale, K. and Snit Smukarn. *A Culture in Search of Survival, The Phuan of Thailand and Laos*. Monogragh Series 31. New Haven: Yale University Southeast Asia Studies, 1988.

Brocheux, Pierre. *The Mekong Delta: Ecology, Economy, and Revolution, 1860-1960*. Madison: Center for Southeast Asia Studies, University of Wisconsin-Madison, 1995.

Buch, W. J. M. *De Oost-Indische Compagnie en Quinam*. Amsterdam: H. J. Paris, 1929.

— "La Compagnie des Indes Neerlandaises et l'Indochine." *Bulletin de l'Ecole Française d'Extrême-Orient* XXXVI (1936): 97-196; XXXVII (1937): 121-237.

Bùi Phụng. *Từ Điển Việt-Anh* (A Vietnamese English dictionary). Hanoi: Trường Đại Học Tổng Hợp Hà Nội, 1978.

Bulbeck, David and Li Tana. "Maps of Southern Vietnam, c. 1690." In *Southern Vietnam under the Nguyen,* edited by Li Tana and Anthony Reid. Singapore: Institute of Southeast Asian Studies of Singapore/ECHOSEA, Australian National University, 1993.

Cadiere, L. "Geographie historique du Quang-Binh d'après les annales imperiales." *Bulletin de l'Ecole Française d'Extrême-Orient* II (1902): 55-73.

— "Le mur de Dong-hoi." *Bulletin de l'Ecole Française d'Extrême-Orient* VI (1906): 87-254.

Cao Yong He. *Taiwan Zao Qi Li Shi Yan Jiu* (A study of the early history of Taiwan). Taipei: n.p., 1979.

Chaigneau, J. B. "Notice sur la Cochinchine." *BAVH* (avril–juin 1923): 252-283.

Chandler, David. *A History of Cambodia.* Second edition. Sydney: Allen & Unwin, 1993.

— "Cambodia: The Roots of Conflict." In Damien Kingsbury and Greg Barton, *Difference and Tolerance.* Geelong: Deakin University Press, 1994.

Chen Chingho, "Shi qi ba shi ji Hui An zhi tang ren jie ji qi shang ye (The Chinese town of Hoi An and its trade during the seventeenth and eighteenth centuries). *Xin Ya Xue Bao* (New Asia Journal) 3, 1 (Hong Kong, 1960): 273-332.

— "He Xian zhen Ye zhen Mo shi jia pu zhu shi" (Notes on the genealogy of the Mac family from Ha Tien." *Quo li Taiwan da xue Wen shi zhe xue bao* (Bulletin of the College of Arts of Taiwan National University) 7, (1956): 77-140.

— *Historical Notes on Hoi-An.* Carbondale: Center for Vietnamese Studies, Southern Illinois University. Monograph Series IV. 1973.

Chen Jia Rong, Xie Fang, and Lu Jun Ling, *Gu dai nan hai di ming* (Ancient place names in the South China Sea region). Beijing: Zhonghua Press, 1986.

Chen Lun Jong, *Hai Guo Wen Jian Lu* (A record of things heard and seen among the maritime states). Zhengzhou: Zhong Zhou Gu Jí Press, 1984.

Chesneaux, Jean. *Tradition et revolution au Vietnam.* Paris: Editions Anthropos, 1971.

— *The Vietnamese Nation,* translated by Malcolm Salmon. Sydney: Current Book Distributors Pty. Ltd., 1966.

Choisy, Abbé de. *Journal du voyage de Siam fait en 1685 et 1686,* edited by Maurice Garçon. Paris: Editions Duchartre et Van Buggenhoult, 1930.

Cocks, Richard. *Diary of Richard Cocks, 1615-1622.* 2 vols. London: Hakluyt Society, 1883.

Coedes, G. *The Indianized States of Southeast Asia,* edited by Walter F. Vella, translated by Susan Brown Cowing. Honolulu: East-West Center, 1968.

Cooke, Nola. "Colonial Political Myth and the Problem of the Other: French and Vietnamese in the Protectorate of Annam." PhD thesis, The Australian National University, 1991.

— "Nineteenth-Century Vietnamese Confucianization in Historical Perspective: Evidence from the Palace Examinations (1463-1883)." *Journal of SE Asian Studies* 25, 2 (1994): 270-312.

— "The Myth of the Restoration: Dang-Trong Influences in the Spiritual Life of the Early Nguyen Dynasty (1802-47)." In *The L:ast Stand of Asian Autonomies: Responses to Modernity in the Diverse States of Southeast Asia and Korea, 1750-1900,* edited by Anthony Reid. Melbourne: Macmillan, 1997.

Crawfurd, John. *Journal of an Embassy from the Governor-General of India to the Courts of Siam and Cochin China.* Reprint. Kuala Lumpur: Oxford University Press, 1967.

Curtin, Philip D. "Migration in the Tropical World." In *Immigration Reconsidered,* edited by Virginia Yans-Laughlin. Oxford University Press, 1990.

Cửu Long Giang and Toan Ánh. *Cao Nguyên Miền Thượng* (The uplanders in the Central Highlands). Saigon: n.p., 1974.

Da Shan. "Hai Wai Ji Shi" (Overseas Journal). In *Shi qi shi ji Guang Nan Xin Shi Liao* (A new source on Quang Nam in the seventeenth century), edited by Chen Jingho. Taipei: Committee of Series of Books on China, 1960.

*Dagh Register des Comptois Nangasaque.* Japanese translation with title *Nagasaki Oranda shokan no nikki* (Dutch Company's Journal of Nagasaki), edited and translated by Murakami Masajiro. Tokyo: Iwanami Shoten, 1938.

*Dagh Register gehouden int Casteel Batavia Vant*, Chinese translation by Guo Hui and Cheng Da Xue. 3 vols. Second edition. Taipei: Taiwan Sheng Wen Xian Wei Yuan Hui, 1989.

*Đại Nam Chính Biên Liệt Truyện Sơ Tập* (First collection of the primary compilation of biographies of Greater Vietnam). Tokyo: Keio Institute of Linguistic Studies, Mita, Siba, Minato-ku, 1962.

*Đại Nam Nhất Thống Chí* (Gazetteer of Greater Vietnam). Tokyo: Society of Indo-China Studies, 1941.

*Đại Nam Nhất Thống Chí, Lục Tỉnh Nam Việt* (Gazetteer of Greater Vietnam, the six southern provinces). 3 vols. Saigon: Nha Văn Hóa, Phủ Quốc Vụ Khanh Đặc Trách Văn Hóa, 1973.

*Đại Nam Thức Lục Chính Biên Đệ Nhất Kỳ* (Chronicle of Greater Vietnam, Period of Gia Long, Part 1). Tokyo: The Oriental Institute, Keio University, Mita, Siba, Minato-ku, 1968.

*Đại Nam Thực Lục Tiền Biên* (Chronicle of Greater Vietnam, Premier Period of the Nguyen). Tokyo: Keio Institute of Linguistic Studies, Mita, Siba, Minato-ku, 1961.

*Đại Việt Sử Ký Toàn Thư*, ed. Chen Chingho. Tokyo: Institute of Linguistic Studies, Keio University, 1984.

Dalrymple, Alexander. *Oriental Reportory*. London: East-India Company, 1808.

Đặng Văn Thắng, "Nông cụ truyền thống ở Cần Đước" (The traditional tools of agriculture in Can Duoc). In *Cần Đước, Đất và Người* (Land and people in Can Duoc). Long An: Sở Văn hóa—Thông tin Long An, 1988.

*Danh Nhân Bình Trị Thiên* (Famous individuals of Binh Tri Thien Province). Vol. 1. Huế: Nhà Xuất Bân Thuận Hóa, 1986.

Danvers, F. C. and William Foster, editors. *Letters Received by the East India Company from Its Servants in the East.* 6 vols. Amsterdam: N. Israel, 1968.

Đào Duy Anh. *Việt Nam Văn Hóa Sử Cương* (An outline history of Vietnamese culture). Saigon: Bốn Phương, 1961.

—— *Đat nước Việt Nam qua các đời* (Vietnamese territories in the different periods). Hanoi: Khoa Học, 1964.

Dixon, J. M., translator. "Voyage of the Dutch ship 'Grol' from Hirado to Tongking." In *Transactions of the Asiatic Society of Japan.* Vol. XI. Reprint. Tokyo: Yushodo Booksellers Ltd. Tokyo, 1964.

Đỗ Văn Ninh. *Tiền Cổ Việt Nam* (Ancient Vietnamese coinage). Hanoi: Khoa Học Xã Hội, 1992.

Dourisboure, P. and C. Simmonet. *Vietnam: Mission on the Grand Plateaus*, translated by Albert J. LaMothe, Jr. New York: Maryknoll Publications, 1967.

Dương Văn An, *Ô Châu Cần Lục* (A record on Ô Châu, present Quảng Bình and Quảng Trị provinces). Saigon: Văn Hóa Á Châu, 1961.

Fei Xin. *Xing Jue Sheng Lan* (Records on Southeast Asian countries). First published in 1436. Reprint. Beijing: Zhong Hua, 1954.

Flood, Thadeus and Chadin, translators and editors. *The Dynastic Chronicle, Bangkok Era, the First Reign.* Tokyo: The Center for East Asian Studies, 1978.

Gaelen, Jan Dircsz. "Journael ofte voornaemste geschiedenisse in Cambodia." In Hendrik Muller, *De Oost-Indische Compagnie in Cambodia en Laos: Verzameling van bescheiden van 1636 tot 1670*. Nijhoff: The Hague, 1917.

Gao Xiong Zheng. *Ngan-nan tche yuan* (Records on Annam). Hanoi: Imprimerie d'Extreme-Orient, 1932.

Gay, Bernard. "Une nouvelle sur le composition ethnique du Campa." In*Actes du Seminaire sur le Campa organise a l'Universitaire de Copewlaque, le 23 mai 1987*. Paris: Travaux du Centre d'Histoire et Civilisations de la Penisule indochine, 1988.

Goscha, Christopher, E. "La presence vietnamienne au royaume du Siam du XVIIe au XIXe siecle: Vers une perspective peninsulaire." Paper presented at the Seminar "La conduite des relations entre sociétés et Etats: Guerre et paix en Asie du Sud-Est," Paris, November 1996.

Gourou, Pierre. *The Peasants of the Tonkin Delta, A Study of Human Geography*. Translated by R. R. Miller. 2 vols. New Haven: Human Relations Area Files, 1955.

Hall, D. G. E. *A History of South-East Asia*. Third edition. London: Macmillan & Co Ltd., 1968.

Hall, Kenneth. *Maritime Trade and State Development in Early Southeast Asia*. Honolulu: University of Hawaii Press, 1985.

Hamilton, A. "A new account of the East Indies." In *A General Collection of the Best and Most Interesting Voyages and travels in All Parts of the World*, edited by John Pinkerton. Vol. 8. London, 1811.

Hayashi Akira et al., compilers. *Tsuko ichiran* (A collection of letters exchanged between the Japanese government and foreign countries in the seventeenth and eighteenth centuries). 8 vols. Tokyo: Kokusho Kankokai, 1912-13.

Hayashi Shunsai, compiler. *Kai-hentai*, 3 vols. Tokyo: Toyo Bunko, 1958-1959.

Hickey, Gerald, C. *Sons of the Mountains*. New Haven and London: Yale University, 1982.

— *Kingdom in the Morning Mist*, Philadelphia: University of Pennsylvania Press, 1988.

— "The Vietnamese village though time and war." *The Vietnam Forum*. Yale Southeast Asia Studies, 10 (1987): 1–25.

Hoa Bằng. *Quang Trung Nguyễn Huệ, Anh Hùng Dân Tộc* (Nguyen Hue, national hero). Saigon: Bốn Phương, 1958.

*Hua Qiao Zhi, Yue Nan* (The overseas Chinese, volume on Vietnam. Taipei: Committee of Overseas Chinese Affairs, 1958.

Huỳnh Công Bá. "Công cuộc khai khẩn và phát triển làng xã ở bắc Quảng Nam từ giữa thế kỷ XV đến giữa thế kỷ XVIII" (The opening and development of the villages in the northern Quang Nam region, from mid-fifteenth to mid-eighteenth centuries). Abstract of PhD dissertation, Hanoi Normal University, 1996.

Huỳnh Lứa. "Quá trình khai phá vùng Đồng Nai-Cửu Long và hình thành một số tính cách, nếp sống và tập quán của người nông dân Nam Bộ" (Process of the opening of the Mekong Delta and the making of some characteristics and customs of the peasants in the south). In *Mấy đặc điểm Đồng bằng Sông Cửu Long* (Some special characteristics of the Mekong Delta). Hanoi: Viện Văn Hóa, 1984, pp. 117-128.

Innes, R. "The Door Ajar: Japan's Foreign Trade in the Seventeenth Century." 2 vols. PhD dissertation, University of Michigan, 1980.

— "Trade between Japan and Central Vietnam in the Seventeenth Century: The Domestic Market," unpublished paper, n.p.

Iwao Seiichi, *Nanyo Nihon-machi no kenkyu* (A study of Japanese Streets in Southeast Asia). Tokyo: Minami Ajia bunka kenkyu-jo, 1940.

— *Shuin-sen Boeki-Shi no Kenkyu* (A study of the trade of Red Seal ships). Tokyo: Ko Bun Do, 1958.

— "Annan koku no uran koku suigun kyuen tosho ni tsuite" (About the letter asking for help from the Dutch navy, sent by Annam to Wulan [Netherlands]). *Toyo gaku* 23 (1962): 109–118.

— *Shuin-sen to Nihon-machi* (Red Seal Ships and the Japanese Street). Tokyo: Kei Bun Do, 1966.

— "Senjokoku makki no kokuto to boekiko ni tsuite" (The capital and trading port of Champa in its last period). *Toyo gaku* 2, 39 (1956): 117–138.

Jarriel, R. "Comment la mission catholique a servi la France en pays Moi." *Bulletin des Amis du Vieux Hue* 1, (1942): 37–53.

Kamashima Mocojiao. *Tokugawa shaki no kaigai boekika*(Merchants in the Tokugawa period). Tokyo: Jinjusha, 1916.

— *Shuin-sen Boeki-shi* (A history of trade carried on by the Red-Seal ships). Tokyo: Kojin Sha, 1942.

— Kirsop, R. "Some account of Cochinchina." In *Oriental Repertory*, edited by A. Dalrymple. 2 vols. London: East India Company, 1808.

*Khâm Ðịnh Việt Sử Thông Giám Cương Mục* (Text and explanation forming the complete mirror of the history of Vietnam). 8 vols. Reprint. Taipei: The National Library of Taiwan, 1969.

Klein, P. W. "De Tonkinees-Japanse zijdehandel van de Verenigde Oost-indische Conpagnie en het inter-Aziatische verkeer in de 17e eeuw." In*Bewogen en bewegen: de historicus in het spanningsveld tussen economie en cultuur*, edited by W. Frijhoff and M. Hiemstra. Tilburg: Gianotten, 1986.

Klemp, Egon. *Asia in Maps, from Ancient Times to the mid-nineteenth Century*. Weinheim: Acta Humaniora, Edition Leipzig, 1989.

Koffler, Jean. "Description historique de la Cochinchine." *Revue Indochinoise* 15 (1911): 448-462, 566-575; *Revue Indochinoise* 16: 273–285, 583–598.

Kobata, Atsushi and M. Matsuda. *Ryukyuan Relations with Korea and South Sea Countries*. Kyoto: Atsushi Kobata, 1969.

Joken, Nishikawa. *Zoho ka-i tsushoko*. Kyoto: Rakuyo Shorin, 1708.

Lafont, Pierre-Bernard. "Les grandes dates de l'histoire du Campa." In *Le Campa et la Monde Malais*. Paris: Centre d'Histoire et Civilisations de la Peninsule indochinoise, 1991.

Lam Giang. *Hùng Khí Tây Sơn* (The vigor of the Tây Sơn). Saigon: Sơn Quang), 1968.

Lamb, Alastair. *The Mandarin Road to Old Hue* (Toronto: Clarke, Irwin & Co. Ltd, 1970.

Langlet, Philippe. *L'Ancien historiographie de l'état au Vietnam*. Vol. 1. Paris: L'Ecole Française d'Extrême-Orient, 1990.

Launay, Adrien. *Histoire de la mission de Cochinchine 1658-1823, Documents historiques*. 3 vols. Paris: Archives des Missions Étrangères, 1923-1925.

Lê Quang Nghiêm. *Tục thờ cúng của ngu phủ Khánh Hòa* (Rites in the fishing region of Khánh Hòa province). Reprint. Los Alamitos: Xuân Thu, n.d.

Lê Quý Ðôn. *Phủ Biên Tạp Lục* (A compilation of the miscellaneous records when the southern border was pacified). 2 vols., with Chinese version (Saigon: Phủ Quốc-Vụ-Khanh Ðặc-Trách Văn-Hóa), 1973.

— *Lê Quý Ðôn Toàn Tập* (Complete works of Lê Quý Ðôn). Vol. 1. *Phủ Biên Tạp Lục*. Hanoi: Khoa Học Xã Hội, 1977.

Lê Thanh Khôi. *Le Viet Nam*. Paris: Les Editions de Minuit, 1955.

— *Histoire du Vietnam des origines à 1858*. Paris: Sudestasie, 1981.

Lê Trọng Khánh. "Về những con đường hành quân cua Nguyễn Huệ" (On the routes of march of Nguyễn Huệ). In *Tây Sơn Nguyễn Huệ*. Nghĩa Bình: Sơ Văn hóa và thông tin, 1978.

Leclere, A. *Histoire du Cambodge*. Reprintg. Paris: P. Geuthner, 1975.

Leur, J. C. van, *Indonesian Trade and Society*. Second edition. The Hague: Nijhoff, 1967.

Li Tana and Anthony Reid, editors. *Southern Vietnam under the Nguyen, Documents on the Economic History of Cochinchina (Dang Trong), 1602-1777*. Singapore: Institute of Southeast Asian Studies, Singapore/ECHOSEA, Australian National University, 1993.

Li Wen-feng. *Yue Qiao Shu*, first published in 1540. Mimeographed edition, n.p.ca., 1950.

Lieberman, Victor. "Local Integration and Eurasian Analogies: Structuring Southeast Asian History, c. 1350-1830." *Modern Asian Studies* 27, 3, (1993): 475-72.

— *Burmese Administrative Cycles: Anarchy and Conquest, c. 1580-1800*. Princeton: Princeton University Press, 1984.

Lín Ren Chuan. *Míng Mo Qing Chu Si Ren Hai Shang Mao Yi* (Private trade in the period of the end of the Ming and the beginning of the Qing dynasty). Shanghai: Normal University of Hua Dong Press, 1987.

Liu Xu. *Zhong Guo Gu Dai Huo Pao Shi* (A history of cannon in ancient China). Shanghai: Shanghai Ren Mín, 1989.

Maha Sila Viravong. *History of Laos*. New York: Paragon Book Reprint Corp., 1964.

Majumdar, R. C. *Champa*. Rerpint. Delhi: Goyal Offset Printers for Gian Publishing House, 1985.

Manguin, Pierre-Yves. *Les Portugais sur les côtes du Viᵉet-Nam et du Campa*. Paris: Ecole Française d'Extrême-Orient, 1972.

— *Les Nguyen, Macau et le Portugal*. Paris: Ecole Française d'Extrême-Orient, 1984.

Marr, David. *Vietnamese Anticolonialism, 1885-1925*. Berkeley: University of California, 1971.

Maybon, Charles, B. *Histoire moderne du pays d'Annam, 1592-1820*. Paris: Librairie Plon, 1920.

*Míng Jing Shi Wen Bian* (A collection of the reports to the emperors in Ming Dynasty). Hong Kong: Zhu Li Press, nd.

*Míng Shi* (History of the Ming dynasty). Reprint. Beijing: Zhong Hua Shu Ju, 1974.

*Minority Groups in the Republic of Vietnam*. Ethnographic Study Series, Department of the Army Pamphlet No. 550-105. Washington: Department of the Army, 1966.

Momoki Shiro, editor. *Ta Qing Shi Lu zhong Dong Nan Ya Guan Xi Ji Shi* (Records concerning Southeast Asian countries in the Annals of the Qing dynasty). Tokyo: Tonan Ajia Shigaku-kai kan sai, Yei Kai, 1984.

Momoki Shiro. "Historical Environmental Situation of Hoi An, a Port of Central Vietnam in the South-China Sea Trade World." Interim Report, The Japanese Ministry of Education and Culture, no. 02041055. (September 1995).

"Monographie de la province de Thudaumot." *Bulletin de la Société des Etudes Indochinoises* 58, (1910): 15–39.

Morse, H. B. *The Chronicles of the East India Company Trading to China, 1635-1834*. Oxford: Clarendon Press, 1926.

Munro, N. G., *Coins of Japan*, Tokyo: Yokohama, 1904.

*Nagasaki Shi* (Records on Nagasaki). Tokyo: Nagasaki Bunko Kanko Kai, 1928.

Navarrete, Domingo. *The Travels and Controversies of Friar Domingo Navarrete, 1618-1686*. Vol. 2. London: Cambridge Unversity Press, 1960.

Needham, Joseph. *Science and Civilization in China*, Vol. 5, Part II. Cambridge: Cambridge University Press, 1971.

Ng Shui Meng. *The Population of Indochina*. Singapore: Institute of Southeast Asian Studies. Field Report Series No. 7, 1974.

*Ngan-nan tche yuan*. Hanoi: Imprimerie d'Extrême-Orient, 1932.

Ngô Đúc Thịnh. "Vài nét về sự phân bố và tên gọi hành chính của các làng xã ở Quảng Bình trước Cách mạng Tháng Tám" (Some notes on the distribution of villages and the village administrative names in Quang Binh before the August Revolution). In *Nông Thôn Việt Nam trong Lịch Sử* (The Vietnamese countryside in history), 2 vols. Hanoi: Khoa Học Xã Hội, 1977.

Ngô Đúc Thịnh and Nguyễn Việt. "Các loại hình cày hiện đại của dân tộc ở Đông Nam Á" (Types of modern ploughs of peoples in Southeast Asia), *Khảo Cổ Học* (Journal of Archaeology) 4 (1981): 50-64.

Ngô Thời Chí, *Hoàng Lê Nhất Thống Chí* (A history of the unification of Royal Le). Collection Romans & Contes du Vietnam écrits en Han Paris-Taipei: Ecole Française d'Extrême-Orient & Student Book Co. Ltd.), 1986.

Nguyễn Bội Liên, Trần Văn An, and Nguyễn Văn Phi. "Ghe bầu Hội An - Xứ Quảng" (Ghe bau junks in the Hội An-Quảng Nam area). Paper given at the International Symposium on the Ancient Town of Hoi An, March 1990.

Nguyễn Công Bình, Lê Xuân Điệm and Mạc Đường. *Văn Hóa và Cư Dân Đồng bằng Sông Cửu Long* (Culture and settlement in the Mekong River delta). Hô Chí Minh City: Khoa Học Xã Hội, 1990.

Nguyễn Đức Nghinh, "Những nô tì phục vụ cho việc thờ cúng" (Slaves used in making offerings). *Nghiên cứu lịch sử* (Journal of historical studies) 2 (1981): 80-83.

— "Từ mấy văn bản thuế dưới Triều Quang Trung và Cảnh Thịnh" (On some tax records of the Quang Trung and Cảnh Thịnh periods). *Nghiên cứu lich sử* (Journal of historical studies) 5 (1982): 36–42.

Nguyễn Huyền Anh. *Việt Nam Danh Nhân Từ Điển* (A dictionary of famous Vietnamese). Saigon: Khai Trí, 1967.

Nguyễn Khải. *Một Cõi Nhân Gian Bé Tí* (A small world). Ho Chi Minh City: Văn Nghệ, 1989.

Nguyễn Lương Bích. *Quang Trung Nguyễn Huệ*. Hanoi: Quân Doi Nhân Dân, 1989.

Nguyễn Thanh Nhã. *Tableau economique du Viet Nam*. Paris: Editions Cujas, 1970.

Nguyễn Thế Anh. *Kinh Tế và Xã Hội Việt Nam dưới Các Vua Triều Nguyễn* (Economy and society of Vietnam during the Nguyen dynasty). Saigon: Trình Bày, 1968.

— "Quelques aspects économiques et sociaux du probleme du riz." *Bulletin de la Société des Etudes Indochinoises* 1 and 2, XLII (1967): 7-22.

— "Buddhism and Vietnamese Society throughout History." *South East Asia Research* 1 (March 1993): 98–114.

— "The Vietnamization of the Cham deity Po Nagar." In *Essays into Vietnamese Pasts*, edited by Keith Taylor and John Whitmore. Ithaca: Cornell Southeast Asian Program, 1995, pp. 42-50.

Nguyễn Trãi, *Ức Trai Tập* (A collection of Ức Trai Nguyễn Trãi's works). Saigon: Phủ quốc vụ khanh đặc trách văn hóa, 1972.

Nguyễn Trí Sơn, ed. *Thư Mục về Tây Sơn Nguyễn Huệ* (A catalogue on the works on the Tây Sơn and Nguyễn Huệ). Nghĩa Bình: Ủy ban khoa học kỹ thuật, 1988.

Nguyễn Việt, Vũ Minh Giang, and Nguyễn Mạnh Hụng. *Quân Thủy trong Lịch Sử Chống Ngoại Xâm* (The navy in the history of opposing foreign invaders). Hanoi: Quân Đội Nhân Dân, 1983.

*Nông Thôn và Nông Dân Việt Nam Thời Cần Đại* (Countryside and Peasants of Vietnam in the Modern Period). Hanoi: Khoa Học Xã Hội, 1990.

Odoric, of Pordenone. *Cathay and the Way Thither*. Reprint. Nendeln: Kraus Reprint Ltd., 1967.

Oishi Shinjahuro, *Edo to chiho bunka* (Local culture in the Edo period). Tokyo: Bunchi Sogo, 1977.

Osamu Osa, editor. *Tosen Shinko Kaitoroku Toijin Fusetu Gaki Wappu Tomecho* (Material for a Study of Chinese Merchants Sailing to and from Japan in the Edo Period). Kyoto: The Institute of Oriental and Occidental Studies, Kansai University, 1974.

Parker, Geoffrey. *The Military Revolution: Military Innovation and the Rise of the West, 1500-1800.* Cambridge: Cambridge University Press, 1988.

Peng Xin Wei. *Zhong Guo Huo Bi Shi* (A history of Chinese coinage). Shanghai: People's Press, 1958.

Phạm Đình Khiêm. "Đi tim địa điểm và di tích hai thành cổ Quảng Nam và Phú Yên đầu thế kỷ 17" (In search of the two old cities of Quang Nam and Phu Yên of the early seventeenth century). *Việt Nam Khảo Cổ Tập San* (Journal of Vietnamese Archaeology) 1 (1960): 71–96.

Phan Du. *Quảng Nam qua các Thời đài* (Quang Nam through the centuries). Nha Trang: Cổ học Tùng Thư, 1974.

Phan Huy Chú. *Lịch Triều Hiến Chương Loại Chí* (A reference book of the institutions of successive dynasties), translated into modern Vietnamese by Lưỡng Thần and Cao Nãi Quang. Saigon: Nhà in Bao Vinh, 1957.

Phan Huy Lê. "Di tích thành Hoàng đế" (The ruins of the Emperor's City). In *Tây Sơn Nguyễn Huệ*. Nghĩa Bình: Ty Văn hóa và Thông tin, 1978.

Phan Khoang. *Việt Sử Xứ Đàng Trong* (A Vietnamese history of Đàng Trong), (Saigon: Khai Trí), 1969.

Phan Phát Huồn. *Việt Nam Giáo Sử* (A history of Catholicism in Vietnam). Saigon: Khai Trí, 1965.

Phan Thị Yến Tuyết. *Nhà ở, trang phục, ăn uống của các dân tộc vùng Đồng bằng sông Cửu Long* (Housing, clothes and food of the peoples in the Mekong delta region). Hanoi: Khoa Học Xã Hội, 1993.

Pires, Tome. *The Suma Oriental of Tome Pires*, translated by A. Cortesão, 2 vols. London: The Hakluyt Society, 1944.

Po Dharma. *Le Panduranga (Campa) 1802-1835. Ses rapports avec le Vietnam* . 2 vols. Paris: Ecole Française d'Extrême-Orient, 1987.

— "Etat des derniers recherches sur la date de l'absorption du campa par le Vietnam." In*Actes du Seminaire sur le Campa organisé à l'Universitaire de Copenhague, le 23 Mai 1987*. Paris: Travaux du Centre d'Histoire et Civilisations de la Peninsule indochinoise, 1988, pp. 59–70.

Poivre, Pierre. "Memoires sur la Cochinchine, 1744." *Revue de l'Extrême Orient* 2 (1884): 324–37.

— "Journal de voyage du vaisseau de la compagnie le Machault à la Cochinchine depuis le 29 août 1749, jour de nôtre arrivée, au 11 fevrier 1750," reproduced by H. Cordier in *Revue de l'Extrême Orient* III (1885): 364–510.

Puangthong Rungswasdisab. "War and Trade: Siamese Intervention in Cambodia, 1767-1851." PhD dissertation, University of Wollongong, 1995.

Qi Jia Lín. *Tai Wan Shi* (History of Taiwan). Taipei: Zili Wanbao Press, 1985.

Ravenswaay, L. F. van. Translation of Jeremias Van Vliet's "Description of the Kingdom of Siam." *The Journal of the Siam Society* VII, 1, (1910): 92–93.

Reid, Anthony. "Europe and Southeast Asia: The military balance." Occasional Paper No. 16. Queensland: James Cook University of North Queensland, 1982.

— *Southeast Asia in the Age of Commerce, 1450-1680. The Lands below the Winds.* Vol. 1. New Haven and London: Yale University Press, 1988; *Expansion and Crisis.* Vol. 2. New Haven & London: Yale University Press, 1993.

— *Southeast Asia in the Early Modern Era: Trade, Power, and Belief.* Ithaca: Cornell University Press, 1993.

— *Sojourners and Settlers: Histories of Southeast Asia and the Chinese.* Sydney: Allen & Unwin, 1996.

Rhodes, Alexandre de. *Dictionarivm Annamiticvm, Lvsitanvm, et Latinvmope.* Rome: Typis & Sumptibus eiusdem Sacr. Congreg., 1651.

— *Rhodes of Vietnam, The Travels and Missions of Father Alexander de Rhodes in China and other Kingdoms of the Orient,* translated by Solange Hertz. Westminster: Newman Press, 1966.

— *Histoire du royaume de Tunquin.* Vietnamese edition. Hochiminh City: Uy ban Doan ket Cong Giao, 1994.

Sakurai, Yumio. "The change in the name and number of villages in medieval Vietnam." *Vietnam Social Science* 1 and 2 (1986): 124-145.

— *Betonamu Sonraku no keisei* (The forming of Vietnamese villages). Tokyo: Soubunsha, 1987.

Schroeder, A. *Annam Etudes numistiques.* Paris: Imprimerie Nationale, 1983.

Skinner, William. "Creolized Chinese Societies in Southeast Asia." In *Sojourners and Settlers: Histories of Southeast Asia and the Chinese* , edited by Anthony Reid. Sydney: Allen & Unwin, 1996.

Stein, R. "Jardins en miniature d'Extrême-Orient." *Bulletin de l'Ecole Française d'Extrême-Orient* XLII (1942): 1-104.

*Sổ Tay về các Dân Tộc ở Việt Nam* (A handbook on the peoples of Vietnam). Hanoi: Khoa Học Xã Hội, 1983.

Tạ Chí Đài Trường, *Lịch Sử Nội Chiến ở Việt Nam, từ 1771 đến 1802* (A history of civil war in Vietnam, 1771-1802). Saigon: Văn Sử Học, 1973.

— *Thần, Người, và Đất Việt* (Deities, people and the land of Viet. California: Văn Nghệ, 1989.

— *"Tiền đúc Đàng Trong: Phương diện loại hình và tương quan lịch sử"* (Coins cast in Dang Trong: the types and their relevance to history). *Văn Học* 32 (September 1988).

Taboulet, Georges. *La geste française en Indochine, Histoire par les textes de la France en Indochine des origines à 1914.* 2 vols. Paris: Maisonneuve, 1955.

Tai, Hue Tam Ho. *Millennium and Peasant Politics in Vietnam.* Cambridge: Harvard University Press, 1983.

Takizawa, Takeo. "Early currency policies of the Tokugawa, 1563-1608." *Acta Asiatica,* 39 (1980): 21–41.

*Tây Sơn Thuật Lược* (A brief history of Tây Sơn). Saigon: Phu Quoc-vu-khanh Dac trach Van Hoa, 1971.

Taylor, Keith. "Nguyen Hoang and the beginning of Viet Nam's southward expansion." In *Southeast Asia in the Early Modern Era,* edited by Anthony Reid. Ithaca, Cornell Unversity Press, 1993.

— "The literati revival in seventeenth-century Vietnam," *Journal of Southeast Asian Studies* 1, XVIII (1987): 1-23.

— *The Birth of Vietnam.* Berkeley: University of California Press, 1983.

*Tên Làng Xã Việt Nam đầu thế kỷ 19* (Names of early nineteenth century Vietnamese villages). Hanoi: Khoa Học Xã hội, 1981.

Thành Thế Vý, *Ngoài thương Việt Nam hồi thế kỷ XVII, XVIII và đầu XIX* (Foreign trade in Vietnam in the seventeenth, eighteenth, and nineteenth centuries). Hanoi: Sử Học, 1961.

Thierry, F. *Catalogue des monnaies vietnamiennes*. Paris: Bibliotheque Nationale, 1987.

*To ban ka motsu cho* (A collection of cargo-lists of overseas ships or junks to Japan). Vol. 2. Tokyo: Nai kaku bun ko, 1970.

Trần Văn Giàu et al. *Địa chí văn hóa Thành phố Hồ Chí Minh* (A cultural gazette of Ho chi Minh City). 2 vols. Ho Chi Minh City: Ho Chi Minh City Press. Vol. 1, 1987, vol. 2, 1988.

Trương Bá Phát, "Lịch sử cuộc Nam tiến của dân tộc Việt Nam" (The history of southward expansion of the Vietnamese people) in *Sử Địa* (History and Geography) 19 & 20 (1970).

Trương Hữu Quýnh. *Chế độ Ruộng đất ở Việt Nam* (The land system in Vietnam). 2 vols. Hanoi: Khoa Học Xã Hội, 1983.

Viện Sử Học. *Biên Niên Lịch Sử Cổ Trung đại Việt Nam* (Historical Chronology of Vietnam, from the Ancient times to Middle Ages). Hanoi: Khoa Học Xã Hội, 1987.

Viện Văn Hóa, *Mấy đặc điểm Văn Hóa Đồng Bằng Sông Cửu Long* (Some special characteristics of Mekong Delta culture). Hanoi: Viện Văn Hóa, 1984.

*Việt Điện U Linh Tập* (Anthology of the spirits of the departed of the Vietnamese domain), translated into Vietnamese by Lê Hữu Mục. Saigon: Khai Trí, 1961.

*Việt-Nam Khai Quốc Chí Truyện* (A story of the establishment of Vietnam). Collection Romans & Contes du Vietnam écrits en Han. Vol. 4. Paris-Taipei: Ecole Française d'Extrême-Orient and Student Book Co. Ltd., 1986.

Viravong, Maha Sila. *History of Laos*, New York: Paragon Book Reprint Corp., 1964.

Vũ Minh Giang. "Contributions to Identifying Phố Hiến Through Two Stele." In *Phố Hiến* Hanoi: Thế Giới, 1994.

Vũ Tự Lập. *Vietnam—Geographical Data*. Hanoi: Foreign Languages Publishing House, 1979.

*Wakan Sanzai Zue* (A large Japanese-Chinese dictionary). 2 vols. First published in 1713. Reprint. Tokyo: Nihon zuihitsu taisei kanko kai, 1929.

Whitmore, John, K. "The Development of Le Government in Fifteenth Century Vietnam." PhD dissertation, University Microfilms, Michigan, 1970.

— *Vietnam, Hồ Qúy Ly, and the Ming (1371-1421)*. New Havan and London: Yale Center for International and Area Studies, 1985.

White, J. *A Voyage to Cochin China*. London: Longman, 1824. Reprint. Kuala Lumpur: Oxford University Press, 1972.

Woodside, A. B. *Vietnam and the Chinese Model, A Comparative Study of Vietnamese and Chinese Government in the First Half of the Nineteenth Century,*. Massachusetts: Harvard University Press, 1971.

— "Central Viet Nam's Trading World in the Eighteenth Cemtury as Seen in Le Quy Don's 'Frontier Chronicles.'" in *Essays into Vietnamese Pasts*, edited by Keith Taylor and John Whitmore. Ithaca: Southeast Asia Program, Cornell University, 1995.

*Xia men Zhi* (Local Records of Xiamen)/ *Zhong guo fang zhi cong shu* (Serials of Chinese local records). No. 80. First printed in 1839. Reprint. Taipei: Cheng Wen Press, 1967.

Zhang Xie. *Tong Xi Yang Kao* (A study of overseas countries). First published in 1617. Edited by Xie Fang. Beijing: Zhong Hua Press, 1981.

Zhang Xu Min *Zhong yue guan xi shi lun wen ji* (A collection of papers on history of Sino-Vietnamese relations). Taipei: Wen shi zhe, 1992.

Zhao Ru Shi. *Zhu Fan Zhi* (Records on barbarian countries). First published in 1225. Edited by Feng Cheng Jun. Beijing: Zhong Hua Press, 1956.

*Zhong Guo Hai Yang Fa Zhan Shi Lun Wen Jí* (Essays on the history of China's maritime development). Taipei: Research Institute on Three Principles, Central Research Institute, 1986.

### UNPUBLISHED SOURCES:

*Bạ Phú Ngộ*, 1741, MS, kept in The Hoi An Relics Management Board, Hoi An.

"Bia Trại Liên Tri" (Inscription in Trai Liên Tri), MS in the Hán-Nôm Institute, Hanoi, shelf number 20922-20923.

*Châu Tiền Lời Gia Phả* (A genealogy of the Châu family), a MS kept by Châu's descendants, Châu Quang Chuong and Châu Dieu Cu, in Hội An.

Dã Lan (Nguyễn Đức Dụ), "Family history of the scholar Lê Ngọc Trụ (1909-1979)," typescript in possession of author.

*Gia Long Minh Mạng Tô Lệ* (The rules of the Gia Long and Minh Mạng reigns), a MS in the Hán-Nôm Institute, Hanoi, shelf number A.571.

Lê Đản, *Nam Hà Tiệp Lục*, manuscript kept in École Française d'Extrême-Orient, Paris, shelf number I481.

*Minh Đô Sử*, MS kept in the Institute of History, Hanoi, shelf number Hv.285.

*Nam Chưởng Kỷ Lược* kept in Ecole Française d'Extrême-Orient, in microfilm, shelf number I 127.

*Nam Hà Kỷ Văn* kept in the Hán-Nôm Institute of Hanoi, shelf number VHv. 2663.

*Nam Hanh Ký Đắc Tập* vol. 1. MS kept in the Hán-Nôm Institute of Hanoi, shelf number A.2939.

*Ngô Gia Văn Phái*, MS kept in the Hán-Nôm institute, Hanoi, shelf number A.117.

"Ngự kiến Thiên Mụ từ chung" (A royal made inscription on the bell in Thiên Mụ temple), kept in Hán-Nôm Institute, Hanoi, shelf number 5683. The 1729 inscription's shelf number is 5703, kept in the same institute.

Nguyễn Chí Trung, "Bước đầu tìm hiểu về quá trình hình thành khối cộng đồng cư dân Hội An" (The first step in understanding the process of the establishment of the residential community of Hoi An), roneo, 1988, in possession of author.

"Tiểu truyển Khổng Thiên Như" (A short biography of Khổng Thiên Như), a MS kept in the Hội An Relics Board, Hội An, Vietnam.

Trần Văn Quý, "Tư liệu lịch sử về quan hệ Việt-Lào phát hiện ở Quy Hợp-Hương Khê Nghệ Tĩnh" (On Vietnamese-Lao relations according to documents discovered in Quy Hợp-Hương Khê region, Nghe Tinh province), unpublished mimeograph, 1989, in possession of author.

*Vũ Liệt Xã Thân Bạ* (A collection of records made by Vũ Liệt village), a MS kept in the Institute of Hán-Nôm Institute, Hanoi, shelf number VHv. 2493.

### Abbreviations

| | |
|---|---|
| BAVH | *Bulletin des Amis du Vieux Hue* |
| BEFEO | *Bulletin de l'Ecole Française d'Extrême-Orient* |
| BSEI | *Bulletin de la Société des Etudes Indochinoises* |
| NCLS | *Nghiên cứu lịch sử* (Journal of historical studies) |

## SOUTHEAST ASIA PROGRAM PUBLICATIONS
Cornell University

### Studies on Southeast Asia

Number 32 *Fear and Sanctuary: Burmese Refugees in Thailand*, Hazel J. Lang. 2002. 204 pp. ISBN 0-87727-731-1.

Number 31 *Modern Dreams: An Inquiry into Power, Cultural Production, and the Cityscape in Contemporary Urban Penang, Malaysia*, Beng-Lan Goh. 2002. 225 pp. ISBN 0-87727-730-3.

Number 30 *Violence and the State in Suharto's Indonesia*, ed. Benedict R. O'G. Anderson. 2001. Second printing, 2002. 247 pp. ISBN 0-87727-729-X.

Number 29 *Studies in Southeast Asian Art: Essays in Honor of Stanley J. O'Connor*, ed. Nora A. Taylor. 2000. 243 pp. Illustrations. ISBN 0-87727-728-1.

Number 28 *The Hadrami Awakening: Community and Identity in the Netherlands East Indies, 1900-1942*, Natalie Mobini-Kesheh. 1999. 174 pp. ISBN 0-87727-727-3.

Number 27 *Tales from Djakarta: Caricatures of Circumstances and their Human Beings*, Pramoedya Ananta Toer. 1999. 145 pp. ISBN 0-87727-726-5.

Number 26 *History, Culture, and Region in Southeast Asian Perspectives*, rev. ed., O. W. Wolters. 1999. 275 pp. ISBN 0-87727-725-7.

Number 25 *Figures of Criminality in Indonesia, the Philippines, and Colonial Vietnam*, ed. Vicente L. Rafael. 1999. 259 pp. ISBN 0-87727-724-9.

Number 24 *Paths to Conflagration: Fifty Years of Diplomacy and Warfare in Laos, Thailand, and Vietnam, 1778-1828*, Mayoury Ngaosyvathn and Pheuiphanh Ngaosyvathn. 1998. 268 pp. ISBN 0-87727-723-0.

Number 23 *Nguyễn Cochinchina: Southern Vietnam in the Seventeenth and Eighteenth Centuries*, Li Tana. 1998. Second printing, 2002. 194 pp. ISBN 0-87727-722-2.

Number 22 *Young Heroes: The Indonesian Family in Politics*, Saya S. Shiraishi. 1997. 183 pp. ISBN 0-87727-721-4.

Number 21 *Interpreting Development: Capitalism, Democracy, and the Middle Class in Thailand*, John Girling. 1996. 95 pp. ISBN 0-87727-720-6.

Number 20 *Making Indonesia*, ed. Daniel S. Lev, Ruth McVey. 1996. 201 pp. ISBN 0-87727-719-2.

Number 19 *Essays into Vietnamese Pasts*, ed. K. W. Taylor, John K. Whitmore. 1995. 288 pp. ISBN 0-87727-718-4.

Number 18 *In the Land of Lady White Blood: Southern Thailand and the Meaning of History*, Lorraine M. Gesick. 1995. 106 pp. ISBN 0-87727-717-6.

Number 17 *The Vernacular Press and the Emergence of Modern Indonesian Consciousness*, Ahmat Adam. 1995. 220 pp. ISBN 0-87727-716-8.

Number 16 *The Nan Chronicle*, trans., ed. David K. Wyatt. 1994. 158 pp. ISBN 0-87727-715-X.

Number 15 *Selective Judicial Competence: The Cirebon-Priangan Legal Administration, 1680–1792*, Mason C. Hoadley. 1994. 185 pp. ISBN 0-87727-714-1.

Number 14 *Sjahrir: Politics and Exile in Indonesia*, Rudolf Mrázek. 1994. 536 pp. ISBN 0-87727-713-3.

Number 13    *Fair Land Sarawak: Some Recollections of an Expatriate Officer*, Alastair Morrison. 1993. 196 pp. ISBN 0-87727-712-5.

Number 12    *Fields from the Sea: Chinese Junk Trade with Siam during the Late Eighteenth and Early Nineteenth Centuries*, Jennifer Cushman. 1993. 206 pp. ISBN 0-87727-711-7.

Number 11    *Money, Markets, and Trade in Early Southeast Asia: The Development of Indigenous Monetary Systems to AD 1400*, Robert S. Wicks. 1992. 2nd printing 1996. 354 pp., 78 tables, illus., maps. ISBN 0-87727-710-9.

Number 10    *Tai Ahoms and the Stars: Three Ritual Texts to Ward Off Danger*, trans., ed. B. J. Terwiel, Ranoo Wichasin. 1992. 170 pp. ISBN 0-87727-709-5.

Number 9    *Southeast Asian Capitalists*, ed. Ruth McVey. 1992. 2nd printing 1993. 220 pp. ISBN 0-87727-708-7.

Number 8    *The Politics of Colonial Exploitation: Java, the Dutch, and the Cultivation System*, Cornelis Fasseur, ed. R. E. Elson, trans. R. E. Elson, Ary Kraal. 1992. 2nd printing 1994. 266 pp. ISBN 0-87727-707-9.

Number 7    *A Malay Frontier: Unity and Duality in a Sumatran Kingdom*, Jane Drakard. 1990. 215 pp. ISBN 0-87727-706-0.

Number 6    *Trends in Khmer Art*, Jean Boisselier, ed. Natasha Eilenberg, trans. Natasha Eilenberg, Melvin Elliott. 1989. 124 pp., 24 plates. ISBN 0-87727-705-2.

Number 5    *Southeast Asian Ephemeris: Solar and Planetary Positions, A.D. 638–2000*, J. C. Eade. 1989. 175 pp. ISBN 0-87727-704-4.

Number 3    *Thai Radical Discourse: The Real Face of Thai Feudalism Today*, Craig J. Reynolds. 1987. 2nd printing 1994. 186 pp. ISBN 0-87727-702-8.

Number 1    *The Symbolism of the Stupa*, Adrian Snodgrass. 1985. Revised with index, 1988. 3rd printing 1998. 469 pp. ISBN 0-87727-700-1.

## SEAP Series

Number 19    *Gender, Household, State: Đổi Mới in Việt Nam*, ed. Jayne Werner and Danièle Bélanger. 2002. 151 pp. ISBN 0-87727-137-2.

Number 18    *Culture and Power in Traditional Siamese Government*, Neil A. Englehart. 2001. 130 pp. ISBN 0-87727-135-6.

Number 17    *Gangsters, Democracy, and the State*, ed. Carl A. Trocki. 1998. Second printing, 2002. 94 pp. ISBN 0-87727-134-8.

Number 16    *Cutting across the Lands: An Annotated Bibliography on Natural Resource Management and Community Development in Indonesia, the Philippines, and Malaysia*, ed. Eveline Ferretti. 1997. 329 pp. ISBN 0-87727-133-X.

Number 15    *The Revolution Falters: The Left in Philippine Politics after 1986*, ed. Patricio N. Abinales. 1996. Second printing, 2002. 182 pp. ISBN 0-87727-132-1.

Number 14    *Being Kammu: My Village, My Life*, Damrong Tayanin. 1994. 138 pp., 22 tables, illus., maps. ISBN 0-87727-130-5.

Number 13    *The American War in Vietnam*, ed. Jayne Werner, David Hunt. 1993. 132 pp. ISBN 0-87727-131-3.

Number 12    *The Political Legacy of Aung San*, ed. Josef Silverstein. Revised edition 1993. 169 pp. ISBN 0-87727-128-3.

Number 10    *Studies on Vietnamese Language and Literature: A Preliminary Bibliography*,
             Nguyen Dinh Tham. 1992. 227 pp. ISBN 0-87727-127-5.

Number 9     *A Secret Past*, Dokmaisot, trans. Ted Strehlow. 1992. 2nd printing 1997.
             72 pp. ISBN 0-87727-126-7.

Number 8     *From PKI to the Comintern, 1924–1941: The Apprenticeship of the Malayan
             Communist Party*, Cheah Boon Kheng. 1992. 147 pp. ISBN 0-87727-125-9.

Number 7     *Intellectual Property and US Relations with Indonesia, Malaysia, Singapore,
             and Thailand*, Elisabeth Uphoff. 1991. 67 pp. ISBN 0-87727-124-0.

Number 6     *The Rise and Fall of the Communist Party of Burma (CPB)*, Bertil Lintner.
             1990. 124 pp. 26 illus., 14 maps. ISBN 0-87727-123-2.

Number 5     *Japanese Relations with Vietnam: 1951–1987*, Masaya Shiraishi. 1990.
             174 pp. ISBN 0-87727-122-4.

Number 3     *Postwar Vietnam: Dilemmas in Socialist Development*, ed. Christine White,
             David Marr. 1988. 2nd printing 1993. 260 pp. ISBN 0-87727-120-8.

Number 2     *The Dobama Movement in Burma (1930–1938)*, Khin Yi. 1988. 160 pp.
             ISBN 0-87727-118-6.


                              **Translation Series**

Volume 4     *Approaching Suharto's Indonesia from the Margins*, ed. Takashi Shiraishi.
             1994. 153 pp. ISBN 0-87727-403-7.

Volume 3     *The Japanese in Colonial Southeast Asia*, ed. Saya Shiraishi, Takashi
             Shiraishi. 1993. 172 pp. ISBN 0-87727-402-9.

Volume 2     *Indochina in the 1940s and 1950s*, ed. Takashi Shiraishi, Motoo Furuta.
             1992. 196 pp. ISBN 0-87727-401-0.

Volume 1     *Reading Southeast Asia*, ed. Takashi Shiraishi. 1990. 188 pp.
             ISBN 0-87727-400-2.


               CORNELL MODERN INDONESIA PROJECT PUBLICATIONS
                              Cornell University

Number 75    *A Tour of Duty: Changing Patterns of Military Politics in Indonesia in the
             1990s*. Douglas Kammen and Siddharth Chandra. 1999. 99 pp.
             ISBN 0-87763-049-6.

Number 74    *The Roots of Acehnese Rebellion 1989–1992*, Tim Kell. 1995. 103 pp.
             ISBN 0-87763-040-2.

Number 73    *"White Book" on the 1992 General Election in Indonesia*, trans. Dwight
             King. 1994. 72 pp. ISBN 0-87763-039-9.

Number 72    *Popular Indonesian Literature of the Qur'an*, Howard M. Federspiel. 1994.
             170 pp. ISBN 0-87763-038-0.

Number 71    *A Javanese Memoir of Sumatra, 1945–1946: Love and Hatred in the
             Liberation War*, Takao Fusayama. 1993. 150 pp. ISBN 0-87763-037-2.

Number 70    *East Kalimantan: The Decline of a Commercial Aristocracy*, Burhan
             Magenda. 1991. 120 pp. ISBN 0-87763-036-4.

Number 69    *The Road to Madiun: The Indonesian Communist Uprising of 1948*, Elizabeth Ann Swift. 1989. 120 pp. ISBN 0-87763-035-6.

Number 68    *Intellectuals and Nationalism in Indonesia: A Study of the Following Recruited by Sutan Sjahrir in Occupation Jakarta*, J. D. Legge. 1988. 159 pp. ISBN 0-87763-034-8.

Number 67    *Indonesia Free: A Biography of Mohammad Hatta*, Mavis Rose. 1987. 252 pp. ISBN 0-87763-033-X.

Number 66    *Prisoners at Kota Cane*, Leon Salim, trans. Audrey Kahin. 1986. 112 pp. ISBN 0-87763-032-1.

Number 65    *The Kenpeitai in Java and Sumatra*, trans. Barbara G. Shimer, Guy Hobbs, intro. Theodore Friend. 1986. 80 pp. ISBN 0-87763-031-3.

Number 64    *Suharto and His Generals: Indonesia's Military Politics, 1975–1983*, David Jenkins. 1984. 4th printing 1997. 300 pp. ISBN 0-87763-030-5.

Number 62    *Interpreting Indonesian Politics: Thirteen Contributions to the Debate, 1964–1981*, ed. Benedict Anderson, Audrey Kahin, intro. Daniel S. Lev. 1982. 3rd printing 1991. 172 pp. ISBN 0-87763-028-3.

Number 60    *The Minangkabau Response to Dutch Colonial Rule in the Nineteenth Century*, Elizabeth E. Graves. 1981. 157 pp. ISBN 0-87763-000-3.

Number 59    *Breaking the Chains of Oppression of the Indonesian People: Defense Statement at His Trial on Charges of Insulting the Head of State, Bandung, June 7–10, 1979*, Heri Akhmadi. 1981. 201 pp. ISBN 0-87763-001-1.

Number 57    *Permesta: Half a Rebellion*, Barbara S. Harvey. 1977. 174 pp. ISBN 0-87763-003-8.

Number 55    *Report from Banaran: The Story of the Experiences of a Soldier during the War of Independence*, Maj. Gen. T. B. Simatupang. 1972. 186 pp. ISBN 0-87763-005-4.

Number 52    *A Preliminary Analysis of the October 1 1965, Coup in Indonesia (Prepared in January 1966)*, Benedict R. Anderson, Ruth T. McVey, assist. Frederick P. Bunnell. 1971. 3rd printing 1990. 174 pp. ISBN 0-87763-008-9.

Number 51    *The Putera Reports: Problems in Indonesian-Japanese War-Time Cooperation*, Mohammad Hatta, trans., intro. William H. Frederick. 1971. 114 pp. ISBN 0-87763-009-7.

Number 50    *Schools and Politics: The Kaum Muda Movement in West Sumatra (1927–1933)*, Taufik Abdullah. 1971. 257 pp. ISBN 0-87763-010-0.

Number 49    *The Foundation of the Partai Muslimin Indonesia*, K. E. Ward. 1970. 75 pp. ISBN 0-87763-011-9.

Number 48    *Nationalism, Islam and Marxism*, Soekarno, intro. Ruth T. McVey. 1970. 2nd printing 1984. 62 pp. ISBN 0-87763-012-7.

Number 43    *State and Statecraft in Old Java: A Study of the Later Mataram Period, 16th to 19th Century*, Soemarsaid Moertono. Revised edition 1981. 180 pp. ISBN 0-87763-017-8.

Number 39    Preliminary Checklist of Indonesian Imprints (1945-1949), John M. Echols. 186 pp. ISBN 0-87763-025-9.

Number 37    *Mythology and the Tolerance of the Javanese*, Benedict R. O'G. Anderson. 2nd edition 1997. 104 pp., 65 illus. ISBN 0-87763-041-0.

Number 25    *The Communist Uprisings of 1926–1927 in Indonesia: Key Documents*, ed.,
             intro. Harry J. Benda, Ruth T. McVey. 1960. 2nd printing 1969. 177 pp.
             ISBN 0-87763-024-0.

Number 7     *The Soviet View of the Indonesian Revolution*, Ruth T. McVey. 1957. 3rd
             printing 1969. 90 pp. ISBN 0-87763-018-6.

Number 6     *The Indonesian Elections of 1955*, Herbert Feith. 1957. 2nd printing 1971.
             91 pp. ISBN 0-87763-020-8.

## LANGUAGE TEXTS

### INDONESIAN

*Beginning Indonesian through Self-Instruction*, John U. Wolff, Dédé Oetomo, Daniel
    Fietkiewicz. 3rd revised edition 1992. Vol. 1. 115 pp. ISBN 0-87727-529-7. Vol.
    2. 434 pp. ISBN 0-87727-530-0. Vol. 3. 473 pp. ISBN 0-87727-531-9.

*Indonesian Readings*, John U. Wolff. 1978. 4th printing 1992. 480 pp.
    ISBN 0-87727-517-3

*Indonesian Conversations*, John U. Wolff. 1978. 3rd printing 1991. 297 pp.
    ISBN 0-87727-516-5

*Formal Indonesian*, John U. Wolff. 2nd revised edition 1986. 446 pp.
    ISBN 0-87727-515-7

### TAGALOG

*Pilipino through Self-Instruction*, John U. Wolff, Maria Theresa C. Centeno, Der-Hwa
    V. Rau. 1991. Vol. 1. 342 pp. ISBN 0-87727—525-4. Vol. 2. 378 pp. ISBN 0-87727-
    526-2. Vol 3. 431 pp. ISBN 0-87727-527-0. Vol. 4. 306 pp. ISBN 0-87727-528-9.

### THAI

*A. U. A. Language Center Thai Course*, J. Marvin Brown. Originally published by the
    American University Alumni Association Language Center, 1974. Reissued by
    Cornell Southeast Asia Program, 1991, 1992. Book 1. 267 pp. ISBN 0-87727-506-
    8. Book 2. 288 pp. ISBN 0-87727-507-6. Book 3. 247 pp. ISBN 0-87727-508-4.

*A. U. A. Language Center Thai Course, Reading and Writing Text (mostly reading)*, 1979.
    Reissued 1997. 164 pp. ISBN 0-87727-511-4.

*A. U. A. Language Center Thai Course, Reading and Writing Workbook (mostly writing)*,
    1979. Reissued 1997. 99 pp. ISBN 0-87727-512-2.

### KHMER

*Cambodian System of Writing and Beginning Reader*, Franklin E. Huffman. Originally
    published by Yale University Press, 1970. Reissued by Cornell Southeast Asia
    Program, 4th printing 2002. 365 pp. ISBN 0-300-01314-0.

*Modern Spoken Cambodian*, Franklin E. Huffman, assist. Charan Promchan, Chhom-
    Rak Thong Lambert. Originally published by Yale University Press, 1970.
    Reissued by Cornell Southeast Asia Program, 3rd printing 1991. 451 pp. ISBN
    0-300-01316-7.

*Intermediate Cambodian Reader*, ed. Franklin E. Huffman, assist. Im Proum. Originally
    published by Yale University Press, 1972. Reissued by Cornell Southeast Asia
    Program, 1988. 499 pp. ISBN 0-300-01552-6.

*Cambodian Literary Reader and Glossary*, Franklin E. Huffman, Im Proum. Originally
    published by Yale University Press, 1977. Reissued by Cornell Southeast Asia
    Program, 1988. 494 pp. ISBN 0-300-02069-4.

HMONG

*White Hmong-English Dictionary*, Ernest E. Heimbach. 1969. 8th printing, 2002. 523 pp. ISBN 0-87727-075-9.

VIETNAMESE

*Intermediate Spoken Vietnamese*, Franklin E. Huffman, Tran Trong Hai. 1980. 3rd printing 1994. ISBN 0-87727-500-9.

\* \* \*

*Southeast Asian Studies: Reorientations.* Craig J. Reynolds and Ruth McVey. Frank H. Golay Lectures 2 & 3. 70 pp. ISBN 0-87727-301-4.

*Javanese Literature in Surakarta Manuscripts*, Nancy K. Florida. Vol. 1, *Introduction and Manuscripts of the Karaton Surakarta*. 1993. 410 pp. Frontispiece, illustrations. Hard cover, ISBN 0-87727-602-1, Paperback, ISBN 0-87727-603-X. Vol. 2, *Manuscripts of the Mangkunagaran Palace*. 2000. 576 pp. Frontispiece, illustrations. Paperback, ISBN 0-87727-604-8.

*Sbek Thom: Khmer Shadow Theater.* Pech Tum Kravel, trans. Sos Kem, ed. Thavro Phim, Sos Kem, Martin Hatch. 1996. 363 pp., 153 photographs. ISBN 0-87727-620-X.

*In the Mirror: Literature and Politics in Siam in the American Era*, ed. Benedict R. O'G. Anderson, trans. Benedict R. O'G. Anderson, Ruchira Mendiones. 1985. 2nd printing 1991. 303 pp. Paperback. ISBN 974-210-380-1.